The Big Book of
ADVENTURE TRAVEL

Third Edition

ABOUT THE AUTHOR

James C. Simmons is the author of eight books, more than 500 magazine articles, and hundreds of newspaper articles on travel, history, and wildlife. Raised in Cincinnati, he received his bachelor's degree from Miami University, Ohio, and a doctorate in 19th-century British literature from the University of California at Berkeley. Before becoming a freelance writer, he taught courses on British and American literature at Boston University and San Diego State University. His sixth book, *Americans: The View from Abroad*, won first prize as Best Travel Book of 1990 in the Lowell Thomas Competition of Travel Journalism. Simmons has been a member of the Society of American Travel Writers since 1983. His travels over the past three decades have taken him to more than 100 countries. He lives in San Diego.

Also by James C. Simmons

The Novelist as Historian: Essays on the Victorian Historical Novel

Truman Capote: The Story of His Bizarre and Exotic Boyhood (with Marie Rudisill)

The Secrets Men Keep (with Ken Druck)

Passionate Pilgrims: English Travelers to the World of the Desert Arabs

Americans: The View from Abroad

Castaway in Paradise: The Incredible Adventures of True-Life Robinson Crusoes

The Big Book of
ADVENTURE TRAVEL

Third Edition

James C. Simmons

JOHN MUIR PUBLICATIONS
SANTA FE, NEW MEXICO

The author would like to acknowledge the excellent services of Nancy Gillan, the Michelangelo of copy editors.

John Muir Publications, P.O. Box 613, Santa Fe, NM 87504

Third edition. Seventh printing September 1999.

Library of Congress Cataloging-in-Publication Data
Simmons, James C.
The big book of adventure travel / by James C. Simmons—3rd ed.
 p.   cm.
 Includes index.
 ISBN 1-56261-342-1
1. Outdoor recreation—Directories. 2. Safaris—Directories.
I. Title
GV191.35.S56   1997   96–39555
796.5'025—dc21   CIP

Editors: Kristin Shahane, Dianna Delling, Nancy Gillan
Production: Janine Lehmann, Nikki Rooker
Graphics Coordination: Jane MacCarter
Cover and Interior Design: Janine Lehmann
Illustrations: Diane Rigoli
Typesetting: Diane Rigoli
Printer: Publishers Press
Cover Photo: Ernst Hohne/Tony Stone Images
Back Cover Photos (top to bottom): Marine Expeditions;
Brent Olson/Inner Asia; John Mireles/Southern Yosemite
Mountain Guides

Distributed to the book trade by
Publishers Group West
Berkeley, California

For David Clippinger

CONTENTS

INTRODUCTION TO ADVENTURE TRAVEL

THE ADVENTURE APPEAL

More and more Americans are agreeing with Helen Keller that "Life is either a daring adventure or nothing at all," and seeking something different from the traditional margarita-by-the-poolside vacation. There has been, in short, a profound revolution in the travel habits of many Americans. People are now more interested in participatory vacation experiences. They want to get involved, not just go along with a group and tour director. They seek change, an alien environment, and, most of all, challenge.

"The urge for adventure is becoming recognized as a drive equal to hunger and sex," Arthur Koestler once perceptively observed. New scientific studies suggest that some people are biologically keyed toward sensation-seeking. They cannot help their desire to take physical and even death-defying risks. In 1986 the President's Commission on Americans Outdoors determined that more Americans than ever before are taking up "risk-adventure" activities—from skydiving to white-water kayaking. It counted 16 percent of U.S. adults as "excitement-seeking competitives."

All those years of watching television *National Geographic* documentaries and *Nova* programs have whetted the appetites of many people to see those special places themselves. Organized adventure-travel expeditions represent one of the fastest growing areas in the travel industry. They are marvelous opportunities to learn about diverse habitats, see and photograph rare forms of animal and plant life, and experience some of the most exotic parts of our world. Accompanying naturalists turn such trips into learning experiences through slide shows, lectures, and films that pave the way for a greater understanding of our world's wild places.

The world has never been more accessible. From the highest mountain to the deepest caverns, we can get there, and we do, in ever increasing numbers. Bob Citron, founder of the American Adventurers Association, agrees. "Today's travelers," he insists, "can ride a wagon train across the Plains with the pioneers, trek and canoe through the Northwest with Lewis and Clark, dogsled across the Greenland ice cap with Scott, scuba dive with Cousteau, fly a hot-air balloon with Montgolfier, and sail around the world with Magellan."

Larry Abramson, a lawyer from Boston, recalls a trip he and his wife made several years ago: "I travel to learn, to meet people, and see new cultures. I try not to have a boring sightseeing trip. Our last trip was a month-long trek across Nepal. We were among the first outsiders to visit areas which had been closed for hundreds of years."

For many travelers the major advantages of signing on to an organized adventure travel trip through an operator are the stimulating companions and great dinner-table conversations they can expect to enjoy. The typical participant possesses a college degree, a keen interest in the outdoors, and a strong commitment to environmentalism. "We offer our clients an opportunity to explore the earth in a supportive environment with compatible trip members and a caring, knowledgeable leader," insists David Roderick, the founder of Nature Expeditions International of Eugene, Oregon.

But there are other important benefits to traveling with a group on an organized adventure travel trip. Planning a trip on your own to a remote part of the Third World can often be a frustrating and stressful experience for the individual unfamiliar with the intricacies of distant government bureaucracies. By letting a knowledgeable operator handle all such details, the traveler is then free to focus on the experience itself without the host of distractions the solitary adventurer must endure.

The general public may naively think of adventure travel as the exclusive preserve of the younger generation. But adventure travel has nothing to do with age and everything to do with spirit. Most adventure-travel trip operators know that seniors frequently constitute a majority of their clientele and often put their younger counterparts to shame when it comes to patience and good spirits if events take an unexpected turn for the worse. "I have often noticed that older people have an extra reserve of energy," observes Sven-Olaf Lindblad, the president of Special Expeditions.

On the other hand, the field has become so popular that many of the larger operators now offer trips designed for families with small children. Overseas Adventure Travel, of Cambridge, Massachusetts, for years has offered special family trekking expeditions in Nepal. When a youngster gets too tired to walk, he or she can ride in style in a special basket on the back of a Sherpa porter.

Adventure travel will always appeal as long as there is a Walter Mitty buried within us, or a Tom Sawyer struggling to be set free and eager to explore the wonders of McDonougal's Cave.

ADVICE FOR THE NOVICE ADVENTURER

Adventure travel is for people in good health who have open minds, enjoy the outdoors, and want to explore remote and exotic parts of our planet. If that describes you, then you should consider an adventure-travel vacation. The basic ingredient necessary is an inquisitive, adventuresome mind. Having this, prospective adventurers should consider the following advice:

• Start off with an overnight camping experience, perhaps with a local chapter of the Sierra Club.

• Remember that adventure trips are not deluxe tours and often lack certain creature comforts, especially if camping is involved.

• Book your trips through reputable outfitters, who provide experienced guides with special expertise.

• Investigate the challenges you will face on the trip. Some operators rate adventures on a scale of I through V in terms of difficulty. Properly evaluating the fitness requirements—and making certain you meet them—can make the difference between the adventure or the fiasco of a lifetime. If in doubt, describe your physical condition to the operator and ask his/her advice. If you are not in great shape, then consider an expeditionary cruise or a barge trip along a French canal. Most operators insist that people do a pretty good job of evaluating their own condition and few get in over their heads.

• Be safety-conscious and prudent at all times. Adventure travel can be as safe or as dangerous as you want to make it. The surest way to cut the risk to a minimum is not to do it on your own but rather go with a reputable operator. Major operators will handle hundreds of clients every year and not have one serious injury. They have excellent safety records because with each group they send competent guides who know the areas and the risks involved and work to minimize them. Of course, some kinds of adventure travel (white-water kayaking, for instance) inherently involve more risk than others (such as tall-ship cruising in the Caribbean). If you have any questions about the risks involved, talk to the operator and ask for the names of previous participants whom you can call.

• And finally, always strive to maintain a flexible attitude when traveling through wilderness areas and Third World countries. Understand that no operator can guarantee you real adventure and accept the fact that the farther off the beaten path you go, the less predictable your journey will be.

HOW TO USE THIS BOOK

The Big Book of Adventure Travel is divided into two sections, land and water adventures. Each section is divided further into activities offered within that category. In turn, each activity is divided into major geographic regions. All seven continents are used for these divisions, as well as the major oceans and seas, such as the Pacific and the Caribbean. These are listed alphabetically by country. The United States and Canada are treated as distinct geographic areas and are subdivided into states or provinces.

PRICE: All trips are listed as inexpensive, moderate, or expensive, depending upon their cost per day. The breakdown is as follows:

Inexpensive: under $75 a day

Moderate: between $75 and $150 a day

Expensive: over $150 per day

COUPONS: Most of the operators listed here offer *The Big Book of Adventure Travel* readers a five or ten percent discount. Many have extended this discount to include all the trips in their catalogs. In order to qualify for this reduction, readers must submit the original operator's coupon (found in the back of the book) when they reserve space on a trip. In most cases, the operator will then give them a credit toward their final payment. Each coupon can be used only once and for only one person. Couples will have to purchase two copies of the book. Readers should contact the individual operators to see what restrictions, if any, apply to their coupons.

IMPORTANT NOTICE

Readers must understand that many forms of adventure travel involve a certain amount of risk. Neither James C. Simmons nor John Muir Publications has a financial interest in any of the operators whose trips are described in this book. Therefore, neither the author nor the publisher can assume any responsibility whatsoever for the operators and the quality of their trips, nor for any injury, death, loss, or property damage brought about by any reader's participation in the trips described in *The Big Book of Adventure Travel*. Readers take these trips at their own risk.

LAND ADVENTURES

"The adventurer is within us, and he contests for our favor with the social man we are obliged to be."

WILLIAM BOLITHO,
Twelve Against the Gods

1
BACKPACKING, TREKKING, AND HIKING EXPEDITIONS

Trekkers on a Hiking Holidays trip in the Blue Ridge Mountains pass through some of the finest mountain scenery on the Eastern Seaboard

Hiking Holidays

"Know how to tramp and you know how to live," insisted Stephen Graham in his classic 1926 book, *The Gentle Art of Tramping*. "Know how to meet your fellow wanderer, how to be passive to the beauty of nature and how to be active to its wildness and its rigor. Tramping brings one to reality."

Walking is the first thing a child learns and the last thing an older person wants to give up. Few forms of exercise provide greater enjoyment or more benefits. Hiking and walking today are more popular than ever before. In America, the opportunities for exploring wilderness by foot are virtually unlimited.

Our national park system boasts over 12,000 miles of scenic trails, while the U.S. Forest Service maintains another 100,000 miles. The most ancient form of travel known to man, hiking offers the most intimate means by which one can explore new cultures and environments.

Today in the organized adventure travel industry, hiking refers primarily to a walk between inns or huts, in which the participants carry only light packs or none at all. For longer trips, treks are now the most popular form of travel; porters or pack animals carry all the expedition's baggage and supplies, leaving participants free of heavy burdens to enjoy the trail and scenery. Independent hikers usually prefer backpacking, carrying on their backs everything they need to make themselves self-sufficient in the wilderness.

AFRICA

MOROCCO

Trek to the Heart of the High Atlas

Operator:
Himalayan Travel, Inc.,
P.O. Box 481,
Greenwich, Conn. 06836;
(800) 225-2380 or
(203) 622-6777.
Price: Inexpensive.
Season: July and
September.
Length: 15 days.
Accommodations: Local
homes and tents.
Five percent discount
with BBAT coupon.

The highest mountain range in North Africa, the Atlas offers huge escarpments, deep gorges, and flat-topped summits. The villages of the Berbers— a hardy, fiercely independent people—cling to the steep hillsides. After two days in Marrakech, members of this expedition start their trek from the lush, green Mizzane Valley, following ancient mule trails into the higher elevations. Nights are often spent in the characteristic stone, wood, and mud houses of typical Berber villages. Expedition members share their friendly hosts' food and accommodations, sipping their ubiquitous green mint tea and observing their traditional dances. The highlight of the trip is a climb to the top of Mount Toubkal, at 13,670 feet the highest peak in North Africa. Mules carry all baggage.

TANZANIA

The Kilimanjaro Trek

Operator:
Mountain Travel-Sobek,
6420 Fairmount Ave.,
El Cerrito, Calif. 94530;
(800) 227-2384 or
(510) 527-8100.
Price: Expensive.
Season: Throughout
the year.
Length: 16 days.
Accommodations: Tented
camps and mountain huts.
Five percent discount with
BBAT coupon.

Few of the world's mountains enjoy the majesty and mystique of Kilimanjaro, at 19,340 feet the highest mountain in Africa. The grueling, non-technical climb to its summit tests minds as well as bodies. This expedition includes a seven-day climb along the popular Marangu route, staying nights in mountain huts. Porters carry all the gear. Partici-pants are not required to have any technical climbing skills. One day is spent on the enormous summit, crowned with no fewer than 15 glaciers flowing off three ice fields. Before the trek, the group spends several days visiting Manyara and Ngorongoro Crater National Parks, remarkable places to see the full realm of East

A walking safari offers great potential for the close observation of some of Africa's biggest game

James Sano/Geographic Expeditions

African wildlife. Trekkers also make a warm-up hike to the top of Mount Meru Crater.

ZIMBABWE

The Hunters and the Hunted: A Foot Safari through the African Bush

For those travelers tired of landscapes flooded with garishly painted vans converging on hapless wildlife, this is a chance to experience Africa as the early British explorers did, by an expeditionary foot safari through the bush. Groups on these adventures are strictly limited to six people plus the guides, men who once worked as professional hunters and know the animals and countryside intimately. Trekkers carry their own backpacks and walk in the cool hours of the morning. The heat of the day is spent at watering holes to observe the wildlife there. Five days are spent in Matobo National Park, tracking rhinos, visiting Bushman caves with their colorful wall paintings, and climbing to remote black-eagle breeding sites. Another five days are then spent trekking through Hwange National Park, home to 40,000 elephants and large numbers of cape buffalo and lions along with 400 species of birds. Nights are spent sleeping in the open.

Operator: Geographic Expeditions, 2627 Lombard St., San Francisco, Calif. 94123; (415) 922-0448.
Price: Expensive.
Season: September and October.
Length: 18 days.
Accommodations: Lodges and tented camps. Five percent discount with BBAT coupon.

ASIA

BHUTAN

Trek through the Dragon Kingdom

Operator:
Journeys International,
4011 Jackson Rd.,
Ann Arbor, Mich. 48103;
(800) 255-8735
or (313) 665-4407.
Price: Expensive.
Season: Spring and fall.
Length: 14 days.
Accommodations: Hotels
and camps. Five percent
discount with
BBAT coupon.

Of the handful of kingdoms still existing today, only one is genuinely medieval. In Bhutan, the last true Buddhist kingdom in the Himalayas, both the king and his subjects wear the same simple robes. Here, in a country so isolated that even nails are still a novelty, the visitor finds preserved the most traditional Buddhist lifestyle in Asia. Participants on this trek beneath snow-covered Himalayan peaks explore the "Land of the Dragon," passing through a society virtually free of discontent, hunger, and crime. Numerous visits are made to ancient *dzongs*, temple-fortresses perched high upon the flanks of mountains. Trekkers on the spring departure will find themselves hiking across a richly colored carpet of alpine wildflowers. Porters carry all luggage.

On one of Journeys International's family treks, children who get tired of walking can ride in a porter's basket while enjoying views of the nearby mountains

Journeys International

"We live and learn, and big mountains are stern teachers."

H. W. TILMAN,
TWO MOUNTAINS AND A RIVER

CHINA

Treasures of China: Terra Cotta Warriors and the Great Wall

This trekking and cycling adventure focuses on two of China's major cultural treasures, the Great Wall (the only man-made object recognizable from outer space) and the 7,500 life-size clay soldiers that were buried for 22 centuries with real war chariots and weapons of wood and bronze to guard the tomb of China's first emperor, Qin Shi Huangdi. The clay soldiers are painstakingly detailed, down to the last rivet in their body armor. Participants have ample time for bicycle-exploring of Xi'an, famous in medieval Europe as the beginning and end of the Silk Road and still possessing a rich selection of historic sites. In Beijing participants will cycle 35 miles east to the town of Jixian, situated near the Great Wall. The next day they begin a three-day trek along the Great Wall. Porters carry all supplies and set up camp each night.

Operator:
REI Adventures,
P.O. Box 1938,
Sumner, Wash. 98390;
(800) 622-2236 or
(206) 395-8111.
Price: Moderate.
Season: June and October.
Length: 15 days.
Accommodations: Hotels, inns, and guesthouses. Five percent discount with BBAT coupon.

INDIA

Trek through Northern India to Ladakh

Hidden away in the extreme northern corner of India, between Pakistan and China, lies Zanskar, cut off from the rest of the world by several of the greatest mountain ranges in the world. The people of this secret kingdom, rarely visited by outsiders, embody a cultural extension of Tibetan Buddhism which expresses itself in their colorful dress, the spectacularly sited cliffside monasteries, and the exquisitely carved *mani* walls lining the trails. Participants on these lengthy expeditions spend 21 days on the trail traversing level plains, rivers, gorges, and several passes through a region few foreigners have ever penetrated. The trek concludes in Ladakh, in the town of Leh, where several days are spent in a comfortable, traditional Central Asian yurt (tent) camp. Considerable time is allowed for interaction with the local people.

Operator:
Wilderness Travel,
801 Allston Way,
Berkeley, Calif. 94710;
(800) 368-2794 or
(510) 548-0420.
Price: Moderate.
Season: June through August.
Length: 34 days.
Accommodations: Tent camps and hotels. Five percent discount with BBAT coupon.

MALAYSIA

Trekking, Caving, Rafting, and Kayaking on Borneo

Operator:
Outer Edge Expeditions,
45500 Pontiac Trail,
Walled Lake, Mich. 48390;
(800) 322-5235 or
(810) 624-5140.
Price: Moderate.
Season: April and
September.
Length: 16 days.
Accommodations: Hotels
and lodges. Five percent
discount with BBAT
coupon.

Once famous for its fierce headhunters, Borneo is an almost-mythical island with a richness of natural and cultural treasures few other Asian regions can match. Participants on these expeditions can expect to have their arduous traveling rewarded with sights and experiences few travelers have known. They begin with a two-day climb of Mount Kinabalu, at 13,455 feet the highest peak in Southeast Asia. Later adventures include an exploration of the rain-forest canopy by means of a walkway high above the jungle floor below; white-water rafting the Padas River's Class IV rapids; two days of underground exploration in the Clearwater Cave, the largest system in Southeast Asia; kayaking another stretch of the Padas River rich in wildlife; and two days in a jungle longhouse with Iban tribespeople, once notorious for their headhunting.

NEPAL

Mount Everest the Easy Way

Operator:
REI Adventures,
P.O. Box 1938,
Sumner, Wash. 98390;
(800) 622-2236 or
(206) 395-8111.
Price: Moderate.
Season: March and June,
October through
December.
Length: 18 days.
Accommodations: Hotels,
tent camps, and Sherpa
homes. Five percent dis-
count with BBAT coupon.

Trekking is *the* Nepalese adventure. There are so few roads that one must hike the country to know it. Participants on this popular trek travel at elevations considered moderate by Nepalese standards: between 11,000 feet and 13,000 feet. Most of the trekking takes place within Sagarmatha National Park. (*Sagarmatha* is the Nepalese name for Mount Everest and translates as "Mother Goddess of the World.") Stops are made at Khumjung village, famous for its large population of Impeyen pheasants, the national bird of Nepal; the village of Thame, home to one of the oldest monasteries in the country; and the village of Namche, which boasts a fine bazaar. Participants on the October departure will observe, as an added benefit, the full-moon festival at Thangboche Monastery. Porters and yaks carry all camping supplies.

Trekkers through the Nepalese high country find both spectacular mountain scenery and an abundance of local culture

R. Brennan/ REI Adventures

Classic Trek Around Annapurna

The tenth-highest mountain in the world, Annapurna-I (26,540 feet) is actually just one of several awesome monuments bearing the same name scattered along a 64-mile-long massif. This lengthy expedition, which includes 24 days of strenuous hiking, begins in the lush valley of the Marsyandi River (first opened to foreigners in 1977) and follows ancient Tibetan-Nepalese trade routes through Hindu and Buddhist hill villages. In the Manang Valley, trekkers encounter gypsy traders of Tibetan origins whose villages are picturesque clusters of medieval stone huts. The women wear their wealth in chunks of turquoise or lumps of coal. From Manang, the trail climbs abruptly from dense forests to alpine pastures. The expedition crosses north of the Annapurna massif at Thorong La pass (17,771 feet) and descends past many Hindu and Buddhist shrines. Sherpa porters and pack animals carry all personal baggage.

Operator: Mountain Travel-Sobek, 6420 Fairmount Ave., El Cerrito, Calif. 94530; (800) 227-2384 or (510) 527-8100.
Price: Moderate.
Season: April and November.
Length: 31 days.
Accommodations: Hotels and tent camps. Five percent discount with BBAT coupon.

UZBEKISTAN, KYRGYSTAN, AND TADJIKISTAN

Trekking in Central Asia

Operator:
REI Adventures,
P.O. Box 1938,
Sumner, Wash. 98390;
(800) 622-2236 or
(206) 395-8111.
Price: Moderate.
Season: July and August.
Length: 15 days.
Accommodations: Hotels
and tent camps.
Five percent discount
with BBAT coupon.

Central Asia is a land of giant mountains, idyllic hidden valleys, and ancient cities steeped in the lore of the Silk Road. Trekkers on this expedition explore an area rarely visited by outsiders before the collapse of the Soviet Union. Eight days are spent in the Aksu Valley of Uzbekistan, hiking among the mountains of the Turkestan Range, which thrust upward toward 18,000 feet. Kyrgyz herders have grazed their flocks of sheep and horses there for centuries. Pack animals carry all supplies. At the end two days are spent in Samarkand, which played a central role in the turbulent history of the region, first as an important link on the Great Silk Route and later as Tamberlane's illustrious capital.

VIETNAM

Trekking in Northern Vietnam

Operator:
Geographic Expeditions,
2627 Lombard St.,
San Francisco, Calif.
94123; (415) 922-0448.
Price: Expensive.
Season: November.
Length: 14 days.
Accommodations: Tents and
village longhouses.
Five percent discount with
BBAT coupon.

Members on these expeditions explore the hill country of the northern borderlands, a region where Westerners rarely venture. Trekkers can expect considerable cultural contacts with a variety of ethnic groups, including the Muong, Hmong, and Thai, as they walk through a landscape of rice paddies, bamboo groves, clusters of farm buildings, and isolated villages. Porters carry all gear. An extended visit is also made to Cuc Phuong National Park, a primary tropical forest that is home to 137 species of birds and 64 species of animals.

"I love not Man the less, but Nature more."
LORD BYRON

AUSTRALASIA

AUSTRALIA

Hike through Central Australia

To most visitors Ayers Rock is Australia, far more so than Sydney's Harbor or its Opera House. Timeless, enigmatic, and awesomely immense, the rock is the premier tourist attraction in central Australia. Participants on these trips use foot and four-wheel-drive vehicles to explore three of the geological wonders of Australia's Red Center: Ayers Rock, the nearby Olgas (a cluster of 30 smooth-faced, dome-shaped monoliths separated by deep ravines), and King's Canyon (the region's most spectacular canyon complex). Days are taken up with bushwalks. Participants have an opportunity to climb Ayers Rock (about 75 percent of the visitors do) for the most spectacular view in all Australia.

Operator:
Worldwide Adventures,
36 Finch Ave. W.,
North York, Ont.,
Canada M2N 2G9;
(800) 387-1483 or
(416) 221-3000.
Price: Moderate.
Season: May through
October.
Length: 5 days.
Accommodations: Cabins
with one night camping.
Five percent discount
with BBAT coupon.

NEW ZEALAND

Walking with the Maori

Hikers on this nature safari explore New Zealand's North and South Islands by foot, gaining unsurpassed opportunities for photographing scenery and studying wildlife. They begin with an overnight stay on Tiritiri, an isolated sanctuary for New Zealand's rarest birds, then hike and camp along the Whakatane River in Urewera National Park, the traditional home of the Maori people. A Maori guide leads the group through virgin forests of rimu and rata trees and along the shores of wilderness lakes. The highlight is a three-day trek on The Routeburn, one of the world's greatest walks, featuring native red-beech forests and mountain streams and waterfalls. They also explore Franz Joseph and Fox glaciers, walk alongside Lake Matheson, and visit the world's only breeding ground of the largest burrowing petrel. A naturalist accompanies each group.

Operator:
Nature Expeditions
International,
P.O. Box 11496,
Eugene, Ore. 97440;
(800) 869-0639
or (503) 484-6529.
Price: Expensive.
Season: February and
November.
Length: 15 days.
Accommodations: Hotels,
lodges, and tents.
Five percent discount
with BBAT coupon.

CANADA

BRITISH COLUMBIA

Heli-Hiking in the Bugaboos

Operator:
Tauck Tours,
P.O. Box 5027,
Westport, Conn. 06881;
(800) 468-2825 or
(203) 226-6911.
Price: Expensive.
Season: June through
August.
Length: 8 days.
Accommodations: Lodges.

The use of helicopters to transport day hikers into virgin wilderness promises to transform backpacking and hiking. Helicopters mean freedom and easy access to wilderness areas hitherto considered too remote for most people to experience. They also mean a chance once again for older people to hike the high country as they did in their youth. Heli-hiking's appeal stems partly from the fact that it offers the best of both worlds. Nights are spent in the comfort of luxurious ski lodges, while each day brings two or three drops by helicopter into some of the most beautiful and unspoiled high country on the North American continent. Participants on these trips may find themselves exploring a high-altitude glacier in the morning, roaming a pristine mountain meadow in the afternoon, and watching a sunset from atop a mountain peak in the evening.

Helicopters allow day hikers the opportunity to visit remote alpine scenery while nights are spent in comfortable lodges

James C. Simmons

NEW BRUNSWICK

Hiking the Maritime Coast of the Bay of Fundy

Located just over the border from Maine, the enormous Bay of Fundy stretches for 94 miles and is 32 miles wide at its mouth. The bay is famous for its swift tidal currents, with 70-foot tides occasionally recorded. Settled in the 1660s, the coast offers hikers unmatched scenery and huge flocks of migrating shorebirds. Participants on these trips visit Fundy National Park; hike a portion of the Canadian Coastal Trail; and explore the beach at St. Mary's Point, a resting spot for hundreds of thousands of the migrating shorebirds.

Operator: Hiking Holidays, P.O. Box 711, Bristol, Vt. 05443; (800) 537-3850 or (802) 453-4816.
Price: Expensive.
Season: July and September.
Length: 5 days.
Accommodations: Quaint inns in fishing villages. Five percent discount with BBAT coupon.

NORTHWEST TERRITORIES

High Arctic Backpacking on Ellesmere Island

This expedition penetrates the heartland of Ellesmere Island National Park. A land of rugged mountains and immense glaciers, this is a true Arctic desert, receiving only 2 more inches of precipitation annually than the Sahara. Members backpack through the Hazen Plateau, an oasis in the polar desert, along routes used 4,000 years ago by ancient Inuit cultures. The area abounds in wildlife—mammoth musk-oxen, Arctic hares by the hundreds, the rare Peary caribou, polar bears, wolves, and numerous species of birds. Because of the region's extreme isolation, many of the animals lack an instinctive fear of humans and approach closely to satisfy their curiosity.

Operator: Black Feather, 1960 Scott St., Ottawa, Ont., Canada K1Z 8L8; (800) 574-8375 or (613) 722-9717.
Price: Expensive.
Season: July.
Length: 16 days.
Accommodations: Tent camps.

"A voyage to a destination, wherever it may be, is also a voyage inside oneself; even as a cyclone carries along with it the centre in which it must ultimately come to rest."

LAURENS VAN DER POST,
VENTURE TO THE INTERIOR

EUROPE

AUSTRIA

Inn-to-Inn Hiking in the Austrian and Swiss Alps

Operator:
New England Hiking
Holidays, P.O. Box 1648,
North Conway, N.H. 03860;
(800) 869-0949 or
(603) 356-9696.
Price: Expensive.
Season: July and August.
Length: 8 days.
Accommodations: Traditional
inns. Ten percent discount
with BBAT coupon.

Participants on these popular trips spend their nights at inns in scenic towns, while their days are given over to hikes along the excellent network of trails in the eastern ramparts of the Alps. The route travels from the Appenzellerland in Switzerland between the Bordensee and the Alpstein mountains, to the Rhine Valley on the Swiss–Austrian border, and then to the lovely Bregenzerwald Mountains of Vorarlberg and Austria's high Alpine peaks of Montafon. A highlight is the Bregenzerwald, where the charming houses in the villages sport colorful shutters and windows trimmed with handmade lace. The women in this region still wear the handsome, stiffly starched folk dresses of their ancestors. On their final day, hikers walk through the spectacular gorge of Rappenlochschlucht, to an idyllic Alpine village, and then up to a peak that offers views of the Rhine Valley.

BRITAIN

The Devon Coast and Moors

Operator:
New England
Hiking Holidays,
P.O. Box 1648,
North Conway, N.H. 03860;
(800) 869-0949 or
(603) 356-9696.
Price: Expensive.
Season: June, July, and
September.

This popular trip combines almost everything England has to offer: medieval villages, bucolic farmlands, flower-filled gardens, winding footpaths, and one of the most impressive coastlines in Europe. Hikers follow the Devon Coast Path, visiting the picturesque towns and villages on England's southwest peninsula, past castles and ancient ruins, and through hamlets where many of the cottages date back to the 15th century. Hikers have a full day to explore the stark beauty of Dartmoor's high moorlands, then spend three days hiking the coast around Dartmouth. A support van carries all luggage.

"To live is to travel."

HANS CHRISTIAN ANDERSON

Length: 8 days.
Accommodations: Historic hotels, including the 14th-century Rising Sun Hotel in Lynmouth, where the poet Shelley spent his honeymoon and novelist R. D. Blackmore wrote *Lorna Doone.* Ten percent discount with BBAT coupon.

Classic Coast-to-Coast Trek Across England

"The Coast-to-Coast Walk is simply the finest long-distance, cross-country walk in the British Isles," Bill Birkett insists in his *Classic Walks in Great Britain.* This trip passes through three of Britain's most celebrated National Parks: the Lake District, the Yorkshire Dales, and the North York Moors. Hikers begin at the St. Bees Head lighthouse overlooking the Irish Sea, then head inland along a well-marked trail into the Lake District National Park, through countryside celebrated by such great Romantic poets as Wordsworth and Coleridge. In Westmoreland, they travel along an ancient Roman road and easy paths formed by generations of sheep. The 12th day takes hikers through the valley of Swaledale, better known as "Herriot Country," after the writings of British veterinarian James Herriot, who lived there. On the 15th day trekkers pass through the mythical countryside of the Yorkshire Moors, made famous by the novels of the Brontë sisters. The trek concludes at the quaint fishing village of Robin Hood's Bay on the North Sea. Full-day excursions are also made to the medieval cities of Durham and York.

Operator:
Wilderness Travel,
801 Allston Way,
Berkeley, Calif. 94710;
(800) 368-2794 or
(510) 548-0420.
Price: Moderate.
Season: May through August.
Length: 16 days.
Accommodations: Village inns. Five percent discount with BBAT coupon.

Walk through the Lake District

The Lake District contains some of the best-loved scenery in England. For almost two centuries its combination of craggy mountains, serene lakes,

Operator:
REI Adventures, P.O. Box 1938, Sumner, Wash. 98390; (800) 622-2236 or (206) 395-8111.
Price: Moderate.
Season: June.
Length: 9 days.
Accommodations: Small hotels, guesthouses, and bed and breakfasts. Five percent discount with BBAT coupon.

and green valleys has attracted more visitors than any other part of the country. The Romantic poets William Wordsworth and Samuel Taylor Coleridge both lived here and found the area an inspiration for some of their most famous poems. The self-guided nature of these walking tours make them ideal for families, couples, or solo travelers, who hike off the beaten track but always have a choice of routes. For example, on the third day they can hike to the village made famous by Beatrix Potter or follow a path through forest far from any habitation. A car carries all luggage.

Guided Walks through Magical Cornwall

Operator:
Above the Clouds Trekking, P.O. Box 398, Worchester, Mass. 01602; (800) 233-4499 or (508) 799-4499.
Price: Moderate.
Season: July and September.
Length: 8 days.
Accommodations: Country inns. Five percent discount with BBAT coupon.

The Cornish are an independent lot. Their peninsula was one of the last Celtic refuges from the invading Saxons. As late as the 18th century, the Cornish people still spoke their own Celtic language. Even today, many continue to maintain traditional lifestyles. The proximity of the Gulf Stream moderates the climate and gives the region its lush vegetation, including palm trees. Hikers on these trips spend their days exploring the sights with local guides. The walks average 5 miles each day and cover the North Coast's towering cliffs and sandy dunes as well as Bodwin Moor, rich in local history and legend and studded with Bronze Age hut circles and other prehistoric structures.

Day-hikers make their way through a tranquil woodland past a sheltered bay along the Cornish coast
Above the Clouds Trekking

Hiking the Scottish Highlands

The operator offers several hikes through the sparsely populated Scottish countryside. From the lochs, wild moorlands, and rolling mountains, to the craggy shores interspersed with beaches and tiny fishing villages, the scenery is pristine and unspoiled throughout. The hike at Ullapool is more moderate, while that in the Kintail and Skye area is more rigorous. The Ullapool excursion, for example, offers excellent day hikes along a glorious coastal area that's home to numerous seals and gannets. Ullapool is a busy fishing village. Partici-pants make two trips to offshore islands, rich in birdlife, for day hikes.

Operator:
Above the Clouds,
P.O. Box 398,
Worchester, Mass. 01602;
(800) 233-4499 or
(508) 799-4499.
Price: Moderate.
Season: Year-round.
Length: 9 days.
Accommodations: Hotels.
Five percent discount with BBAT coupon.

FRANCE

French Alps Llama Trek

Although llamas have been a staple of pack treks in the United States for over a decade, they are largely unknown in Europe. One exception is southeastern France, where a French company has pioneered llama trekking. The itinerary for these trips leads through a remote and charming section of the French Alps rarely visited by tourists. Traveling along footpaths and small roads, participants explore the high mountain valleys in the Queyras Regional Park, just west of the Italian border, in a corner of Europe almost forgotten amid the vastness of the Alps. This region is known among French travelers for its spectacular mountain scenery and historic Alpine villages. The trip begins in Montdauphin, a fortress built in 1692 by order of Louis XIV. Highlights of the trek include visits to Chateau Queyras, a 14th-century fortification erected on a glacial vantage point; Saint Veran, the highest village in Europe; and Briancon, famous for its fortifications dating back to the early Middle Ages.

Operator:
Hurricane Creek Llama
Treks, 63366 Pine Tree Rd.,
Enterprise, Ore. 97828;
(800) 528-9609 or
(541) 432-4455.
Price: Moderate.
Season: June through
September.
Length: 7 days.
Accommodations: Hotels
and hikers' huts with
indoor plumbing and
hot showers. Five percent
discount with BBAT
coupon.

Undiscovered France: Hiking in Diois

Operator:
Above the Clouds,
P.O. Box 398,
Worchester, Mass. 01602;
(800) 233-4499 or
(508) 799-4499.
Price: Expensive.
Season: May and June.
Length: 9 days.
Accommodations: Hotels.
Five percent discount with
BBAT coupon

Despite its location between Provence and the Alps, Diois—as the region around Die in the Drôme Valley is called—is virtually unknown to tourists and the French alike. Die gained significance as the third-century capital of Roman Gaul and later as a Catholic stronghold during the religious wars. Today it languishes in obscurity, still moving to the rhythms of an earlier time. The walks on this trip include a hike up Diois' holy mountain, la Glandasse, a tabletop populated by thousands of Provençal sheep. Other walks visit a medieval abbey, numerous villages hidden away in the mountain recesses, and several vineyards. A special feature of the June departure is la Fête de la Transhumance, which culminates in a parade of sheep through the town of Die while craftspeople, jugglers, magicians, and dancers crowd the sidewalks.

Inn-to-Inn Hiking along the Dordogne River

The Dordogne River Valley offers hikers an unparalleled mixture of archaeological, historical, culinary, and scenic delights. During the Middle Ages control of the region passed back and forth between the French and English, who constructed numerous fortresses. The center of

Great Achievements in Adventure Travel

On July 3, 1981, five blind climbers with Braille maps, one man with an artificial leg, an epileptic, and two deaf adventurers completed a joyful three-day trek to the snowcapped summit of 14,410-foot-high Mount Rainier. The nine climbers cheered and applauded as they unfurled flags and hugged one another in triumph over what they called the mistaken notion that the horizons of the handicapped are limited. Jim Whittaker, the first American atop Mount Everest, led the expedition.

The 1981 expedition's base camp at 11,500-foot-high Ingraham Flats was near

French prehistory, the Dordogne Valley has spectacular cave art, some dating back over 30,000 years. Hikers on these trips visit several of these rock-art galleries to see drawings of wild oxen, ibex, mammoths, bears, and bison, sketched with amazing grace and beauty by Cro-Magnon artists. Other attractions include the 15th-century Chateau de Puymartin with its magnificent Renaissance furnishings; Sarlat, a fully restored medieval town with narrow streets; and the picturesque ruins of the 12th-century Chateau de Commarque. A van carries all luggage.

Operator: Progressive Travels, 224 W. Galer Ave., #C, Seattle, Wash. 98119; (800) 245-2229 or (206) 285-1987.
Price: Expensive.
Season: May and June, September and October.
Length: 7 days.
Accommodations: Hotels. Five percent discount with BBAT coupon.

Trek through the High Pyrenees

An imposing barrier of mountain peaks, some rising to 11,000 feet, the Pyrenees have historically proved an effective barrier between France and the sunbaked expanse of the Iberian Peninsula. The range is notable for its many streams, waterfalls, and distinctive, deep, steep-walled amphitheatric cirques at the upper ends of its valleys. This trip devotes 12 days to trekking the high country between the magnificent Cirque de Gavarine and the Val d'Incles in the tiny mountain state of Andorra, a route which encompasses the two highest peaks in the range, the Posets and Maladeta. Hikers pass through an

Operator: Himalayan Travel, Inc., 112 Prospect St., Stamford, Conn. 06901; (800) 225-2380 or (203) 359-3711.
Price: Inexpensive.
Season: July and August.
Length: 15 days.
Accomodations: Tent camps and mountain huts. Five percent discount with BBAT coupon.

an 80-foot crevasse and a quarter of a mile away from the place where an icefall had killed 11 climbers ten days before. For the sighted climbers, the views were stunning—Mount Adams, Mount Baker, and steam-spewing Mount St. Helens. For the blind members Whittaker stopped regularly, tracing the route on the Braille maps and describing the surroundings.

Richard Rose of Vancouver, Washington, strode onto the summit, shouting, "There's one for epileptics!" Chuck O'Brien of Philadelphia, who had lost his leg in the Vietnam War, said that the climb had really "tore up" his artificial leg. "But I'll make it," he insisted. "My spirit is really up." Before reaching the summit, O'Brien received word by radio that his wife had given birth to twins.

alpine landscape of forested slopes, high meadows, streams, and jagged limestone peaks. Several days are spent hiking through the Spanish section of the Pyrenees. Vehicles transport all luggage.

Backpacking through Corsica

Operator: Himalayan Travel, Inc., 112 Prospect St., Stamford, Conn. 06901; (800) 225-2380 or (203) 359-3711. *Price:* Moderate. *Season:* June through September. *Length:* 15 days. *Accomodations:* Tent camps. Five percent discount with BBAT coupon.

The whole of Corsica sometimes seems like one enormous mountain, 114 miles long, rising 8,943 feet from the blue waters of the Mediterranean. Running the length of the island's interior is the Grand Rondonee, a maintained 177-mile-long hiking path that follows ancient shepherds' trails. The route crosses only three roads and passes through just one village. The operator offers two different treks, one covering the southern portion of the Grand Rondonee and the other the upper portion. On both trips trekkers walk through impressive wilderness scenery of fir and beech forests, jagged peaks, and rushing mountain rivers. Both are vehicle-supported, although participants can expect to carry backpacks for about four days.

The Adventure Travel Hall of Fame: GEORGES-MARIE HAARDT

Given the popularity of overland expeditions from Europe to Asia in the years before the Soviet invasion of Afghanistan, it is sometimes hard to realize that the first such expedition took place just over 50 years ago. Frenchman Georges-Marie Haardt found himself challenged by Asia's vastness. In 1923 he led the first Trans-Africa Motor Expedition, crossing the Sahara Desert and proceeding to the East African coast. Then he decided to mount the first overland expedition from Europe to Asia since the days of Marco Polo.

For vehicles, Haardt used specially designed half-track automobiles from Citröen. He determined to follow ancient pilgrim and trade routes and to record

GREECE

Exploring the Gorges of Central Greece

Central Greece is a complex region of high forested mountains broken up by powerful rivers, which have cut deep canyons on their circuitous route to the sea. Many of these gorges are almost inaccessible, gashed deep into limestone rock and enclosed by towering cliffs, with high waterfalls breaking up the riverbeds. Others are slightly wider, allowing the sun to penetrate the turquoise waters of their meandering rivers. Participants on these canyoneering trips explore five very different gorges. Two are large canyons with relatively flat beds, where the group treks along the river bottom, walking, wading, and swimming downstream. The other three are much steeper and narrower, with drops as great as 100 feet in some places. Hikers then rappel down the sheer cliffs from one level to the next. All the gorges offer hikers ample opportunities to swim and shower under waterfalls. The operator firmly states this is not a technically demanding trip, and no previous experience in any kind of rock-climbing is necessary.

Operator:
Worldwide Adventures,
36 Finch Ave. W., Toronto,
Ont., Canada M2N 2G9;
(800) 387-1483 or
(416) 221-3000.
Price: Moderate.
Season: May through
August.
Length: 7 days.
Accommodations: Small
hotels in nearby mountain
villages. Five percent discount with BBAT coupon.

with still cameras and movie film the sights and sounds of a changing Orient. The expedition started in Beirut. Ahead lay Himalayan passes, bandits, and warlords. The difficulties were enormous. To cross the Roof of the World above Hunza and Gilgit, the expedition had to disassemble each automobile; carry it piece by piece over the narrow, twisting trails across the mountains; and then reassemble it on the opposite side.

The expedition arrived in China during a vicious civil war. Nervous Chinese soldiers repeatedly fired on Haardt's vehicles but, miraculously, no one was injured. Finally, at noon on February 12, 1932, the Citröen-Haardt Trans-Asiatic Expedition reached the grounds of the French legation in Peking. The journey had lasted ten months and covered a grueling 7,370 miles. A month later, Georges-Marie Haardt was dead from pneumonia.

Trekking the Mountains and Monasteries of Peloponnese

Operator: Worldwide Adventures, 36 Finch Ave. W., Toronto, Ont., Canada M2N 2G9; (800) 387-1483 or (416) 221-3000. *Price:* Moderate. *Season:* May through September. *Length:* 7 days. *Accommodations:* Small hotels. Five percent discount with BBAT coupon.

Just a step away from the familiar ancient sites of the northern Peloponnese is a hidden world of wild mountain ranges, foaming rivers, and vast forests. These mountains were a part of ancient Arcadia, the original paradise of the gods, where Hercules slew the man-eating Stimfalian birds and Achilles was immortalized in the waters of the Styx. More recently, the region's many villages and age-old monasteries inspired revolution against the Turkish occupation. Trekkers on these popular trips cross the remote and little-visited ranges of Mount Ziria and Mount Helmos, visiting several monasteries and numerous isolated mountain villages along the way. A vehicle carries all baggage.

Trek Across Crete

Operator: Himalayan Travel, Inc., 112 Prospect St., Stamford, Conn. 06901; (800) 225-2380 or (203) 359-3711. *Price:* Inexpensive. *Season:* April and September. *Length:* 15 days. *Accommodations:* Small hotels and tent camps. Five percent discount with BBAT coupon.

Although Crete is one of the most popular Greek islands for tourists, it is still possible to escape the crowds and enjoy deserted beaches, rarely visited fishing villages, and unspoiled mountain vistas. Participants in this trek start their adventure at the ancient Cretan capitol of Chania and hike along paths from village to village. Highlights include the ancient thermal baths, mosaics, and necropolis of Siesta; the spectacular gorges of Samaria, one of Crete's most beautiful landscapes; and the 1,000-year-old chapel of Agios Pavlos. Several days are spent hiking and swimming along the coast. All baggage is carried by vehicle.

"There is no moment of delight in any pilgramage like the beginning of it, when the traveller is settled simply as to his destination and commits himself to his unknown fate and all the anticipations of adventure before him."

CHARLES D. WARNER,
BADDECK AND THAT SORT OF THING

ITALY

The Lakes of Italy

The Italian Lake District has long been a favorite with poets, artists, and discriminating travelers, drawn by the region's sumptuous Renaissance villas, flower-bedecked alpine meadows, and elegant villages. Hikers on these trips walk along scenic country trails and lightly traveled roads with occasional rides on ferries, cable cars, and funicular railways. Three days at the village of Bellagio offer walks along the spectacular promontory that divides Lake Como and Lake Lecco and along the shore to the splendid gardens of the extravagant Villa Serbelloni and Villa Melzi in San Giovanni. A support vehicle accompanies the group.

Operator:
Euro-Bike Tours,
P.O. Box 990,
DeKalb, Ill. 60115;
(800) 321-6060 or
(815) 758-8851.
Price: Expensive.
Season: June and September.
Length: 8 days.
Accommodations: Hotels. Five percent discount with BBAT coupon.

Hike through Tuscany

This hike follows paths established by Vallombrosan monks in the 11th century, through a Tuscan countryside saturated in history and dotted with castles and vineyards. Tuscans regard themselves as the most civilized of all Italians, insisting that their culture is the oldest and their Italian the purest. Participants start their hike from a 17th-century farmhouse in Greve, in the heart of Chianti country. Hikers follow trails that lead past many delights, including the birthplace of Giovanni da Verrazzano, the discoverer of New York Harbor. They then proceed at a leisurely pace through Gaiole to Siena. A full day is devoted to a walking tour of Siena's burnt-colored, narrow medieval streets. Time is allowed for visits to the most important artistic, architectural, and historical sites, such as the Palazzo Pubblico with its 14th-century frescoes by Simone Martini. The trip ends in the town of Volterra, a perfect example of a medieval Italian fortress city, which also boasts important Etruscan and Roman ruins. A van carries all personal luggage.

Operator:
Ciclismo Classico,
13 Marathon St.,
Arlington, Mass.;
(800) 866-7314 or
(617) 646-3377.
Price: Expensive.
Season: May, June, and September.
Length: 8 days.
Accommodations: Hotels. Five percent discount with BBAT coupon.

Hikers follow paths laid down by medieval monks through a sun-drenched landscape in Tuscany

Lauren Hefferon/Ciclismo Classico

NORWAY

Inn-to-Inn Trek through the Mountains and Fjords

Operator: Above the Clouds Trekking, P.O. Box 398, Worchester, Mass. 01602; (800) 233-4499 or (508) 799-4499. *Price:* Expensive. *Season:* July and August. *Length:* 10 days. *Accommodations:* Country inns. Five percent discount with BBAT coupon.

These popular treks focus on central Norway in the heart of the mountains, a region rich in culture, history, and splendid scenery. The trip begins at the enormous Hardanger Jokulen Glacier, where trekkers don crampons and explore the tongue of ice. Another trek takes hikers along an ancient cart-track at the edge of a river, which leads them to the shore of the magnificent Sognefjord. They also visit a well-preserved Viking farm inside a fortification and enjoy a two-hour cruise along the Sognefjord. Each day, participants are offered a choice of two routes: a shorter, easier hike and a longer, more demanding one. A local guide accompanies each group. Daily hiking distances range from 7 to 15 miles.

SWITZERLAND

The Haute Route: Chamonix to Zermatt

The great high-altitude Alpine traverse between Chamonix and Zermatt known as the Haute Route is one of the world's classic mountain treks. The quality of the traverse, its height, its sustained nature, and its continuity of aesthetically pleasing scenes explain the unparalleled reputation of this crossing. The route is even more fascinating because of its history, for it was here during the last century among the glaciers, ridges, precipices, and summits that the sport of mountaineering was born. Hikers on this expedition pass below the Alps' two most famous peaks, the Matterhorn and Mont Blanc.

Operator:
Geographic Expeditions,
2627 Lombard St.,
San Francisco, Calif. 94123;
(415) 922-0448.
Price: Expensive.
Season: September.
Length: 13 days.
Accommodations: Mountain huts. Five percent discount with BBAT coupon.

Berner Oberland Trek

The Berner Oberland range bisects Switzerland east to west and includes some of Europe's most celebrated mountains. Hikers on this trek go inn-to-inn from Interlaken through the fabled mountain villages of Grindelwald, Wengen, Murren, the Kiental, and Kandersteg. Participants wend their way among a dazzling array of peaks, passes, glaciers, lakes, and waterfalls. A highlight is Lauterbrunnental, arguably the most beautiful valley in Switzerland, where waterfalls plunge over sheer, 3,000-foot cliffs. Trekkers have plenty of time along the way to admire the wildflowers, appreciate folkways in the more remote villages, and snap pictures fit for a calendar. Hiking distances average less than 12 miles a day. A support vehicle carries all luggage.

Operator:
Ryder-Walker Alpine Adventures,
P.O. Box 947,
Telluride, Colo. 81435;
(970) 728-6481.
Price: Expensive.
Season: August.
Length: 7 days.
Accommodations: Hotels and inns. Five percent discount with BBAT coupon.

The Engadine Trek

This inn-to-inn trek covers the length of the Inn River Valley almost from the Austrian to the

Operator:
Ryder-Walker Alpine
Adventures,
P.O. Box 947,
Telluride, Colo. 81435;
(970) 728-6481.
Price: Expensive.
Season: July.
Length: 7 days.
Accommodations: Hotels and
inns. Five percent discount
with BBAT coupon.

Italian border. This is a moderately strenuous hike which passes from the gentler terrain of the lower Engadine, through the upper Engadine with its majestic, glaciated peaks, and into Val Bregaglia and its wild and dramatic granite spires. The villages along the way range from tiny, antique Guarda and Soglio to pristine Sils Maria and the pleasant resort town of Pontresina. Participants hike along ancient footpaths that link tiny villages, ruins, and lively towns; climb to passes and summits; and traverse the valley above sparkling lakes before plunging into Val Bregaglia with its spectacular Sciora range. A support van transports all luggage.

LATIN AMERICA

ARGENTINA

Hiking the Towers of Paine and Fitz Roy

Operator:
Geographic Expeditions,
2627 Lombard St.,
San Francisco, Calif. 94123;
(415) 922-0448.
Price: Expensive.
Season: February and
November.
Length: 16 days.
Accommodations: Tent
camps. Five percent discount with BBAT coupon.

This expedition combines hiking and camping to explore two of the world's most magnificent mountain regions: Fitz Roy and Cero Torre in Argentina's Parque de los Glaciares (a World Heritage Site) and Chile's Torres del Paine National Park. The trip begins in Rio Gallegos (where in 1905 Butch Cassidy and the Sundance Kid robbed the town's one bank) for five days of hiking and camping in nearby Torres del Paine National Park. Its most striking geologic features are the Paine Towers, vertical spires over 2,500 feet high that seem to pierce the sky. After a six-hour drive across the pampas to Argentina, travelers visit the Moreno Glacier, one of the fastest-moving in the world, before heading to Fitz Roy for a series of day hikes from a base camp.

An Indian guide shows hikers secrets of the Amazonian rain forest on a wilderness expedition
Markham Johnson/Wilderness Travel

COSTA RICA

Coast-to-Coast Trek

Trekkers on these expeditions cross the width of Central America, hiking from the Atlantic to the Pacific Ocean. Along the way they experience the many scenic, natural, and cultural attractions the country offers, including rain forests, rivers, jungles, volcanoes, and beaches, each with its own unique flora and fauna. The expedition begins with a morning rafting excursion through the jungle down the Pacuare River and its Class IV rapids. Next, participants drive to Chirripó National Park and begin their ascent to the highest point on the country's Continental Divide; from the top they can see both the Atlantic and Pacific Oceans. On following days they trek down from the forests of tropical evergreen, fern, and bamboo into the lower-altitude rain forests. Along the way they can expect to see tapirs, giant anteaters, ocelots, and jaguars. The final two days are spent at a beach resort on the Pacific Ocean. Pack horses carry all the gear and camping supplies.

Operator:
Above the Clouds,
P.O. Box 398, Worchester,
Mass. 01602;
(800) 233-4499 or
(508) 799-4499.
Price: Moderate.
Season: Year-round.
Length: 11 days.
Accommodations: Tent camps. Five percent discount with BBAT coupon.

"A true adventure begins with the proverbial small step and never really ends."

DANIEL TERRAGNO

ECUADOR

Amazon Trekking Expedition

Operator:
Wilderness Travel,
801 Allston Way,
Berkeley, Calif. 94710;
(800) 368-2794 or
(510) 548-0420.
Price: Expensive.
Season: Year-round.
Length: 14 days.
Accommodations: Open-sided houses set on stilts.
Five percent discount with
BBAT coupon.

This natural history adventure provides the most intimate experience of Amazonia's biodiversity. Participants trek camp-to-camp for 40 miles along a trail in a virgin rain forest, through Cofan Indian lands on a remote stretch of the border. The hiking is done from mid-morning to mid-afternoon, saving the early morning and late afternoon hours for wildlife observation led by Cofan Indian guides. The region is particularly rich in birdlife, home to over 1,400 species (as compared to 850 for all of North America and Mexico). One leader of this adventure is Randy Borman, born in Ecuador of American missionary parents, who has lived his entire life in Indian villages in the Amazon.

MEXICO

Trekking with the Tarahumara Indians in Copper Canyon

Operator:
Remarkable Journeys,
P.O. Box 31855,
Houston, Tex. 77231;
(800) 856-1993
or (713) 721-2517.
Price: Moderate.
Season: Year-round.
Length: 5 days.
Accommodations: Tent
camps. Five percent discount with BBAT coupon.

Mexico's Barranca del Cobre, the largest and deepest canyon complex in North America, is still largely undiscovered by the world's visitors. Of the 50,000 travelers who visit the rim each year, only a handful make it to the Tarahumara Indians' home at the bottom of the canyon. The most traditional of the North American Indian tribes, some 60,000 Tarahumaras inhabit the canyons, insulated from the modern world by isolation and the intractability of the landscape, and leading a late–Stone Age lifestyle that has not changed in centuries. The operator offers three different treks into the canyons. The most ambitious is a five-day hike across the complex, allowing participants to see ancient mines, cave-dwelling Tarahumaras, exotic birdlife, and some of the most spectacular scenery in Mexico. A layover day is spent at a beautiful swimming hole and beach in the heart of the canyon. Stock animals carry all camping gear.

Trekkers on a Journeys International expedition cross the isthmus of Panama through uninhabited rain forest in the footsteps of vanished tribes and famous explorers

Journeys International

PANAMA

Darien Trek

Participants on this challenging expedition trek the vast, essentially unexplored Darien Rain Forest, the only section of Central America not penetrated by the Pan-American Highway. The continent's greatest diversity of birds, animals, and plants survive unaffected by human culture in this area. Trekkers visit numerous Indian villages and wade through shallow streams where gold nuggets can be found. Activities along the way include bird-watching, fishing, nature photography, and gold-panning, as well as numerous opportunities to interact with the local Indian tribes and observe their lifestyles (including dances). This may just be the best adventure available in Central America.

Operator: Journeys International, 4011 Jackson Rd., Ann Arbor, Mich. 48103; (800) 255-8735 or (313) 665-4407.
Price: Moderate.
Season: December through January.
Length: 14 days.
Accommodations: Jungle camps. Five percent discount with BBAT coupon.

PERU

Classic Trek along the Inca Trail to Machu Picchu

Operator:
Wilderness Travel,
801 Allston Way,
Berkeley, Calif. 94701;
(800) 368-2794 or
(510) 548-0347.
Price: Expensive.
Season: Year-round.
Length: 12 days.
Accommodations: Hotels and
tent camps. Five
percent discount with
BBAT coupon.

This 35-mile trek follows a centuries-old highway once used by Incan royalty for their pilgrimages. Hikers take five days to reach the fabled "Lost City of the Incas," allowing ample opportunity to explore the remnants of the New World's greatest Indian civilization. The trek begins at the small village of Chilca on the banks of the Urubamba River. Climbing steadily to 13,776 feet, the trail passes the ruins of ancient terraces, aqueducts, frontier outposts, stone baths, and tombs. Porters carry all baggage. Two days are spent at Machu Picchu exploring the finest complex of Indian ruins in the Western Hemisphere. On the day before the start of the trek, visitors raft the Urubamba.

MIDDLE EAST

TURKEY

Trekking the Turkish Highlands

Operator:
Geographic Expeditions,
2627 Lombard St., San
Francisco, Calif. 94123;
(415) 922-0448.
Price: Moderate.
Season: July and August.
Length: 17 days.
Accommodations: Tent
camps and inns. Five
percent discount with
BBAT coupon.

This expedition focuses on the beautiful Kackar Mountains, with their lush forests, meadows carpeted with flowers, and villagers dancing to the music of bagpipes. The green terraces of Kackar's lower slopes recall Nepal; and the lakes, forests, and jagged peaks suggest Switzerland. The heart of the trip is a six-day trek through countryside rarely visited by Westerners. Chamoix, wild ibex, foxes, golden eagles, and wild boar all abound in the area. The moderate treks each day offer numerous opportunities for cultural exchanges. Pack horses carry all gear, while a crew sets up tents and prepares the meals. A special stop is at one of Cappadocia's mysterious underground cities, vast cave complexes inhabited by early Christians who fled underground when invading Arab armies swept through the region in the sixth century.

UNITED STATES

ALASKA

Backpacking through the Arrigetch Wilderness

Known to the Eskimos as "the fingers of the hand outstretched," the imposing granite peaks of the Arrigetch range stab skyward from the Gates of the Arctic National Park. This expedition begins above the Arctic Circle with a floatplane ride from Bettles to an isolated lake within the park. Participants then backpack along animal trails for two days, set up a base camp in the very palm of Arrigetch, and spend several days exploring nearby spires and glacial valleys. The region abounds in Dall sheep and bears. The June departure concludes with a raft trip down the Alatna River, which meanders gently through scenic mountains.

Operator: Sourdough Outfitters, P.O. Box 90, Bettles, Alaska 99726; (907) 692-5252. *Price:* Expensive. *Season:* June and July. *Length:* 8 days. *Accommodations:* Tent camps. Five percent discount with BBAT coupon.

CALIFORNIA

Backpacking in the Ansel Adams Wilderness

The Ansel Adams Wilderness may be one of the best-kept secrets of the high Sierra. Located on the southern border of Yosemite National Park, it has mile upon mile of sweeping granite ridges, spectacular vistas, and excellent trout-fishing in the many sparkling high-mountain lakes. Meadows are blanketed in subalpine flora such as aster, cow parsnip, lupine, and mule ears. These trips begin and end at Bass Lake. All food and camp supplies are packed in on mules, leaving trekkers free to carry only day packs. A base camp is set up in the middle of the high Sierra, from which day trips are made to surrounding areas. Warning: these trips are popular, so book early!

Operator: Southern Yosemite Mountain Guides, P.O. Box 301, Bass Lake, Calif. 93604; (800) 231-4575 or (209) 658-8735. *Price:* Moderate. *Season:* July through September. *Length:* 7 days. *Accommodations:* Tent camps. Ten percent discount with BBAT coupon.

Hikers through the Ansel Adams Wilderness
soon discover why the great photographer
Ansel Adams found this area so appealing

Mike Maciaszeks/Southern Yosemite Mountain Guides

COLORADO

Rocky Mountain National Park Rambler

Operator: Roads Less Traveled, P.O. Box 8187, Longmont, Colo. 80501; (800) 488-8493 or (303) 678-8750. *Price:* Expensive. *Season:* July through September. *Length:* 6 days. *Accommodations:* Grand Lake Lodge and the Baldpate Inn, two historic structures. Five percent discount with BBAT coupon.

Colorado's most popular park presents visitors with a dazzling array of snowy peaks, rugged ridges, and massive cirques. Its famous Trail Ridge Road enjoys a reputation as America's highest highway, topping 12,000 feet as it crosses the Continental Divide. The park has more than 355 miles of trails. Hikers on this trip explore far off the beaten track, enjoying the remote corners of the park. One day is spent hiking past echoing waterfalls to enter the barren landscape of Glacier Gorge, a stunning testimony to the mighty forces of nature. Another day hike, above treeline in the tundra country above Trail Ridge Road, passes through what looks like an acres-wide bonsai garden. With a growing season measured in weeks, these stunted trees and plants have struggled for centuries to attain their Lilliputian size.

HAWAII

Hiking on Kauai, Molokai, and Hawaii

Participants begin this trip with three days of exploring the natural wonders of the lush island of Kauai, a jewel of the sea, boasting a landscape more varied than any other Hawaiian island. One day hikers travel along the edge of 3,600-foot-deep Waimea Canyon, known as the "Grand Canyon of the Pacific," and on another day hike the cliff trail of the spectacular Na Pali coast to visit unforgettable Hanakapiai Falls. The highlights of the two days in Maui are treks through the lush tropical forest of West Maui Mountain and the moon-like landscape of Haleakala Volcano. The big island of Hawaii offers a visit to Volcanoes National Park; a hike across the crater floor of Kilauea, one of the world's most active volcanoes; and a morning hike into uninhabited Pololu Valley. Hikers have plenty of chances to swim and snorkel at some of Hawaii's most idyllic beaches.

Operator:
Journeys International,
4011 Jackson Rd.,
Ann Arbor, Mich. 48103;
(800) 255-8735 or
(313) 665-4407.
Price: Moderate.
Season: Year-round.
Length: 11 days.
Accommodations: Small lodges. Five percent discount with BBAT coupon.

MAINE

Hiking through Acadia National Park

The Maine coast through Acadia is a place where mountains tumble to the Atlantic and end in battered cliffs, where breakers claw into coves and inlets, and where hikers can fish with one hand and sample blueberries from a wind-stunted bush with the other. These popular trips focus on Mount Desert Island, exploring every corner by means of well-maintained trails. Some wind their way along the shore line to sandy beaches, hug the many lake shores, or follow the more gentle carriage paths that John D. Rockefeller Jr. constructed in the 1920s.

Operator: New England Hiking Holidays, P.O. Box 1648, North Conway, N.H. 03860; (800) 869-0949 or (603) 356-9696.
Price: Moderate.
Season: June through mid-October.
Length: 5 days.
Accommodations: Historic inns at Northeast Harbor and Bar Harbor. Ten percent discount with BBAT coupon.

MICHIGAN
Hike and Bike the Porcupine Mountains

Operator:
Michigan Bicycle Touring,
3512 Red School Rd.,
Kingsley, Mich. 49649;
(616) 263-5885.
Price: Moderate.
Season: June through early
September.
Length: 5 days.
Accommodations: Lodges.
Five percent discount with
BBAT coupon.

Located in the extreme western portion of the Upper Peninsula, Porcupine Mountains State Park is Michigan's largest and least-civilized park, a place so remote that even the merciless lumber barons of the last century left it untouched. Its 58,000 acres offer some of the wildest and most spectacular landscape in the Midwest and are home to a rich selection of wildlife, including deer, black bear, and bald eagles. Participants on this tour explore the park's backcountry by both foot and bicycle. Special attractions include the waterfalls in Black River Canyon, old mining towns, and the largest stand of virgin pine and hemlock east of the Mississippi. Two days are for hikes, three for biking.

MONTANA
Hiking Glacier and Waterton National Parks

Operator:
Backcountry,
P.O. Box 4029,
Bozeman, Mont. 59772;
(800) 575-1540 or
(406) 586-3556.
Price: Expensive.
Season: August.
Length: 6 days.
Accommodations: Lodges.
Five percent discount
with BBAT coupon.

The ancient ice sheets are long gone; only a few dozen small glaciers remain. Yet the broad, bathtub-shaped valleys of western Montana's Glacier National Park offer hikers more than 700 miles of trails. With day pack on back, in a few hours a hiker can be alone in some of the most dramatic, unspoiled wilderness in the country. Participants on these trips do a series of day hikes through the backcountry wilderness of Glacier National Park, viewing alpine meadows, turquoise lakes, ice caves, and waterfalls. The last day is spent hiking in Waterton National Park, just across the Canadian border.

"Surely the gods live here. This is no place for man!"

RUDYARD KIPLING,
UPON HIS FIRST SIGHTING OF THE HIMALAYAN MOUNTAINS

NEW HAMPSHIRE

White Mountains Weekend Hiking Trips

New Hampshire's White Mountains are a major tourist destination. Yet travelers willing to do a little day hiking can easily lose the crowds in the splendid wilderness of one of New England's most scenic areas. Participants on these weekend escapes discover the waterfalls, lakes, cliffs, and mountain peaks of Crawford Notch, Pinkham Notch, and other spots within the Mount Washington Valley, and also visit an Appalachian Mountain Club Hut. Those on the three-day trips range a little farther afield and explore the scenic splendor of Franconia Notch. The operator also offers five-day trips.

Operator:
New England Hiking
Holidays, P.O. Box 1648,
North Conway, N.H. 03860;
(800) 869-0949 or
(603) 356-9696.
Price: Expensive.
Season: May, September
through mid-October.
Length: 2, 3, and 5 days.
Accommodations: Nights are
spent at the gracious Inn at
Thorn Hill (1895). Ten
percent discount with
BBAT coupon.

NORTH CAROLINA

Inn-to-Inn Trekking in the Blue Ridge Mountains

This five-day trip begins near Mount Mitchell, the highest point east of the Mississippi, and heads north along the backbone of the Blue Ridge Mountains. These treks have been scheduled to take advantage of spring wildflower displays and fall foliage. A highlight is a hike to Linville Gorge, one of the East's most spectacular wild canyons. The ascents and descents are generally moderate. Trekkers also stop at the Penland School of Arts and Crafts, celebrated for its students' outstanding productions. A van carries all personal luggage.

Operator:
Hiking Holidays, P.O. Box
711, Bristol, Vt. 05443;
(800) 537-3850 or
(802) 453-4816.
Price: Moderate.
Season: April, May, and
October.
Length: 5 days.
Accommodations: Lodgings
range from a farmhouse to
an elegant stone inn. Five
percent discount with
BBAT coupon.

"What we get from adventure is just sheer joy. And joy is, after all, the end of life."

GEORGE LEIGH MALLORY, MOUNTAINEER

Over the past decade llamas have gained in popularity for use as pack animals, allowing trekkers to explore isolated wilderness areas in greater comfort

Stanlynn Daugherty/Hurricane Creek Llama Treks

OREGON

Llama Trekking in Northeastern Oregon

Operator: Hurricane Creek Llama Treks, 63366 Pine Tree Rd., Enterprise, Ore. 97828; (800) 528-9609 or (541) 432-4455. *Price:* Moderate. *Season:* June through August. *Length:* 5 days. *Accommodations:* Tent camps. Five percent discount with BBAT coupon.

Llama treks have increased in popularity since people have discovered the advantages of these gentle ruminants as pack animals over the more traditional horses and mules. Llamas are easier to handle, require almost no care, step lightly on the trails, and are great for people over 50 who still enjoy camping in remote wilderness areas but no longer want the burden of 60-pound backpacks. These popular trips visit the Eagle Cap Wilderness Area, Oregon's largest. Uncrowded and unspoiled, the region was carved by glaciers and features rugged granite peaks that reach 10,000 feet. The area's forests are home to mule deer, elk, bighorn sheep, and mountain goats. These are great trips for children.

UTAH

Backpacking through the Escalante Wilderness

The lower canyons of the Escalante River form the heart of one of the West's most remote areas. This is a landscape of colorful sandstone cliffs, arches, and alcoves; water trickling into inviting pools; and the greenery of cottonwood trees. In the company of a naturalist guide, backpackers on this trip explore the natural wonders of this rarely visited region of the Glen Canyon National Recreation Area. Average daily hiking distance is 7 miles. The schedule includes two rest days to allow participants an opportunity to explore the Escalante's hidden side canyons, hanging gardens, and rock arches. Special attractions are the cliff dwellings, storage wells, ceremonial kivas, and pictographs created by the Anasazi Indians more than 600 years ago. The operator supplies all camping equipment.

Operator: Wild Horizons Expeditions, West Fork Rd., Darby, Mont. 59829; (406) 821-3747.
Price: Moderate.
Season: May; other departures by special arrangement.
Length: 7 days.
Accomodations: Tent camps. Five percent discount with BBAT coupon.

VERMONT

Villages and Covered Bridges of Southeast Vermont

This tour invites hikers to experience a cross-section of southern Vermont that evokes Norman Rockwell's America. The trip begins and ends in Proctorsville, located in the midst of an unspoiled, bucolic countryside of apple orchards, dairy farms, covered bridges, and log cabins. Day hikes are made to scenic Hamilton Falls; the summit of Little Ball Mountain; the home of Augustus Saint Gaudens, one of America's premier turn-of-the-century sculptors; and the small village of Plymouth, birthplace of President Calvin Coolidge. Hikers walk along old carriage roads through forests and fields. A support van carries all luggage.

Operator: Hiking Holidays, P.O. Box 711, Bristol, Vt. 05443; (800) 537-3850 or (802) 453-4816.
Price: Expensive.
Season: Late May through early October.
Length: 5 days.
Accommodations: Country inns. Five percent discount with BBAT coupon.

WASHINGTON
Backpacking Mount Rainier

Operator:
REI Adventures,
P.O. Box 1938,
Sumner, Wash. 98390;
(800) 622-2236 or
(206) 395-8111.
Price: Moderate.
Season: July through
September.
Length: 7 days.
Accommodations: Tent
camps. Five percent dis-
count with BBAT coupon.

Mount Rainier National Park's 378 square miles have something for everybody. Located just a short drive from Seattle, the park draws almost 2 million visitors each summer. At 14,410 feet, Mount Rainier is the crown jewel in the Cascade Range and boasts the largest glacier system in the lower 48 states. More than 300 miles of trails probe the wilderness haunts of deer, bear, elk, bobcat, and mountain goat. Backpackers on these trips hike among alpine meadows, lush forests, and glacier-fed lakes in the shadow of Mount Rainier. Their route includes the Northern Loop Trail and portions of the famous Wonderland Trail that circles Washington's highest peak.

WYOMING
Llama Trek through Yellowstone National Park

Operator:
Yellowstone Llamas,
Box 5042, Bozeman,
Mont. 59717;
(406) 586-6872.
Price: Moderate.
Season: July to mid-
September.
Length: 3, 4, and 5 days.
Accommodations: Tent
camps. Five percent dis-
count with BBAT coupon.

The patriarch of our national parks, Yellowstone is the oldest and, outside of Alaska, the largest American park. These treks avoid all the usual tourist spots in favor of backcountry wilderness areas rarely visited by outsiders. Accompanied by their llamas, which carry all gear and supplies, hikers average 5 miles a day along game trails, traveling into the heart of the park, among herds of elk, across meadows ablaze with wildflowers, and past thermal areas. A llama trek is the perfect way to experience the natural wonders of this great park. Avid fisherfolk will think they have died and gone to heaven.

PROFILE
WILLIAM READ AND JAMES SANO
GEOGRAPHIC EXPEDITIONS

A reflective William "Al" Read, both the executive vice-president of Geographic Expeditions in San Francisco and the president of Exum Mountain Guides in Grand Teton National Park, leans back in an easy chair in his summer home in Moose, Wyoming. In his younger days he made the first ascent of Mount McKinley's East Buttress and led the first expeditions to the summits of the Himalayan peaks of Gaurishankar and Cholatse. He was one of five survivors of the 1969 American expedition, which was attempting an ascent of the unclimbed southeastern ridge of the Nepalese peak Dhaulagiri when an avalanche killed seven members of the team. He recollects the early days of trekking in Nepal, the role of the legendary Jimmy Roberts in the development of that industry, and his own contributions over the past 20 years.

"Mountain Travel was the original trekking company set up by Jimmy Roberts, a former British army officer who single-mindedly developed the trekking industry in India and Nepal," Read says. "In the 1930s and 1940s he made countless first ascents in India and the Karakoram Range, using any excuse to leave his Gurkha regiment to get to the mountains, and basically throwing away a promising military career. I got to know Jimmy in 1972, when I was transferred to Kathmandu as a career Foreign Officer in the American embassy there.

"Jimmy had retired and gotten involved with trekking in 1964 as a means of providing assistance to the Sherpas. He developed the concept of sending in groups of walkers who were supported by teams of Sherpas. He insisted that the problem of the lack of tourist facilities in the mountains could be solved by the Sherpas, who take such good care of their charges, carrying their gear, setting up their tents, and handling all the camp chores. That is what he started. Then it grew into this thing we now call 'trekking.' In fact, he was the first to use the Boer word 'trek' to describe an organized walking expedition into the Nepalese high country. He ran the first 'treks,' as such.

"I was torn between the mountains and my career as a diplomat. In 1975 I realized that I had to choose. Did I want to be a diplomat for the rest of my life, going from embassy to embassy all over the world? Or did I want to get back to my first love, the mountains? Fortunately, at that time Jimmy wanted to step down from Mountain Travel. So I took over as managing director and ran the company from 1975 to 1984. When I started, he had already started a partnership with Leo Le Bon at Mountain Travel/U.S.A. that continued until the early 1980s. Leo was our American agent and provided about a third of our clients. The rest were British, German, and Australian travelers we recruited ourselves. (In 1975 there were only six trekking companies in Nepal. Today there are over 300!) I spent eight months of the year in Nepal and the summer months in Wyoming working with Exum Mountain Guides in the Grand Tetons National Park. For me that was an ideal life."

In 1984 a lawsuit over the company name ended Mountain Travel/Nepal's relationship with its American namesake. But well before then Read saw the necessity of establishing a new company in the United States to act as their agent. In 1981 he and several partners founded Inner Asia Expeditions in San Francisco. Their early focus consisted of specialized travel programs in Central Asia. James Sano, the company president since 1988, proudly sums up the early achievements:

"We were the first American company to negotiate protocols with the Chinese government to operate expeditions in Tibet and Xingjiang Province. We were the first across the remote Turugart Pass, crossing from the former Soviet Union into China. We pioneered tourism in Tannu Tuva. And we were the first to trek in northern Vietnam, to the Great Bend of the Tsangpo, and to Tibet's holy Lake Lhamo Lhatso. Our clients made rare first ascents in the Bhutan Himalayas. We developed a reputation as a company able to achieve seemingly impossible border crossings in remote areas between countries which do not have open borders with one another. Not a year goes by that we don't push the travel envelope a little further."

In 1996 the company changed its name to Geographic Expeditions to reflect the broader range of its current trips. The company's growth has held steady around 25 percent annually during the past five years. It now offers more than 250 departures and moves 4,500 clients a year. According to Sano, 61 percent of these are repeaters or referrals, a level that is the envy of many in the industry. The most popular destinations remain western China and Tibet, with Geographic Expeditions sending more travelers into those areas than any other company, according to Chinese authorities.

Geographic Expeditions also acts as a consultant on the development of tourism to the governments of China, the former Soviet Union, Nepal, Bhutan, Mongolia, Pakistan, and Laos. In recent years it has expanded into location consultation for film, television, and video production companies; publishing houses; advertising agencies; and magazines.

Sano points out what he considers to be his company's major distinction: "Unlike other companies, instead of having a product planning group, a sales group, and a customer service group all functioning separately, our hierarchy rests on country directors. Their job is to live and breathe a country. They all have extensive experience in the countries for which they design our trips. They plan trips to that area, select the leaders, and are intimately involved in discussing the trips with prospective clients. There is only one person overseeing the entire process. When a client has a specific question about how far they have to trek on an average day or whether their sleeping bag is suitable for a particular trip, that client will speak directly to the person who planned the trip and knows the region intimately. This is very different from having a sales force answer such important questions."

About 55 percent of Geographic Expedition's annual client list consists of custom trips to remote regions. Many of these are for families or groups of friends who seek an itinerary that reflects their own group interests. These clients include both film and television celebrities. Some time ago the company handled all the logistics for former president Jimmy Carter's trek into Nepal.

World-renowned photographer Galen Rowell also works closely with Geographic Expeditions. His recent book on Antarctica was based on two of the company's expeditionary cruises into that region. Rowell and the company have combined talents on several trips for serious photographers, on which Rowell was the group leader. Sano recalls:

"Galen wanted to get to the North Pole by sea for a picture book he was working on. We found a Russian icebreaker capable of plowing through 10 meters of ice. We put together a trip in which avid photographers could accompany him to the North Pole and at the same time help subsidize the expenses of the expedition. Some 75 people signed up for that trip. It was a great success."

The company's demographics reveal that the majority of its clients are in the 45- to 60-year age bracket. As Sano observes, "Those travelers over 45 have the money to travel. Their idea of a vacation is not the same as their parents.' They may have been to some of these places when they were younger but were then in a backpacking or youth-hostel mode. Now they would like to go back to those same areas but not stay in lice-ridden hotels. So they come to us here at Geographic Expeditions."

Sano is proud of the fact that no Geographic Expeditions' client over the years has suffered death or serious injury. He attributes this track record to the company's rigorous screening of its clients. He insists:

"We do not accept everyone who wants to go on our trips. We do serious health screening of our potential clients who apply for our more rigorous expeditions. We ask them to get a clearance from their personal physician. And we also check to see if they have any mental-health problems which might jeopardize the well-being of the group. By conducting extensive conversations with our clients, we can usually get a handle on their personal anxieties and, if need be, diplomatically steer them away from those expeditions which we think might not be suitable for them. For many people travel is a stressful experience. And when you're on a lengthy trip, the chemistry of the group is all-important."

Like Read, Sano came to the company from a mountaineering background. He was the leader of a 1983 American Mount Everest expedition and four other major Himalayan expeditions. Before joining Geographic Expeditions in the spring of 1988, he was the executive assistant to the superintendent at Yosemite National Park. His duties included overseeing park naturalist programs, search and rescue operations, and the Yosemite General Management Plan.

In 1994 Geographic Expeditions expanded into Africa, offering a selection of trips ranging from the classic tented Kenyan safaris to game-viewing spectaculars in Zimbabwe, Botswana, Zambia, and rarely visited Namibia.

"A challenge we faced in setting up our African trips is that so many people's notions are framed by the media in general and by such films as *Out of Africa,*" observes Sano. "Most people go into Africa with companies that put them into Land Rovers and run them through the backcountry to collect their species. This is mass tourism with its big buses, big lodges, and we'll-have-ten-minutes-to-flashbulb-that-cheetah-out-of-its-wits approach. We offer a vastly different experience. For example, in Zimbabwe we have a popular 18-day safari, limited to just six clients, which includes two five-day treks led by men who once worked as professional hunters. They know the animals and countryside intimately and are superb trackers."

Read reflects on the question of whether there are any truly exploratory treks left in Nepal. "Most people don't realize that there are untold places in Nepal where there are virtually no foreigners," he says. "The Ganesh Himal north of Kathmandu has some very remote country, isolated villages, and great mountains. What it really takes is just asking, because we can get people into those areas if they want to go."

What about the charge that trekking has caused ecological damage to the Nepalese countryside? Read is quite emphatic in his denial:

"I disagree. The alternative to trekking or tourism in the Himalayan

Mountains is smokestacks—industrialization. Each step foreigners take in those mountains earns critical hard currency, and there is a spin-off at the local level in income and development. Trekking is still a pretty localized phenomenon in Nepal, and, by far, most deforestation occurs away from areas where foreigners go. The deforestation we do see in some areas is caused by trekking lodges and the independent trekkers who use them. The lodges burn wood for heat and cooking. Treks operated by responsible trekking companies don't use lodges and don't burn wood. Certainly that is how all our treks operate now."

2

BICYCLE TOURING

"The bicycle is the most civilised conveyance known to man," British novelist Iris Murdoch once insisted. "Other forms of transport grow daily more nightmarish. Only the bicycle remains pure in heart."

Many Americans agree. A Gallup poll several years ago found that bicycling is the second most popular recreational sport in America. Some 10 million serious cyclists ride regularly, keeping their muscles, hearts, and lungs in top form.

More and more people have discovered in the bicycle the perfect vehicle for long-distance traveling: swift enough to satisfy their urge to "get somewhere" and slow enough to let them enjoy the countryside in the process. In the past decade, bicycle touring has mushroomed into a big business. Two-wheeled vacations are one of the fastest growing areas within the adventure travel field. Their appeal is obvious: bike tours promise an invigorating mixture of adventure, scenic beauty, camaraderie, and hard work—plus all the advantages of the packaged tour in which the operator handles arrangements for accommodations and meals.

There are other benefits as well. Operators can generally provide a selection of rental bikes, which means no hassles at airports. A van with special bike racks accompanies the group, carrying all luggage, picking up weary cyclists, and making instant road repairs when a bicycle breaks down. Groups are small, usually fewer than 20 members. Cyclists ride at their own pace and often have a choice of routes from easy to challenging, to suit their physical abilities. And at the end of the day, they can always look forward to a fine meal in a comfortable country inn.

The Bicycle Travel Association estimates that mountain bikes comprise more than half of all bikes now sold in the United States. The new popularity of these rugged off-road bikes indicates that many cyclists are seeking a much more adventuresome biking experience. With these machines they can strike out from paved roads along primitive, rarely used logging roads and park trails into their favorite wilderness areas.

"Bike riders are close to all of nature," 62-year-old William Quinn observed during his 1979 solo bike journey across the United States. "They know what a mountain really is, or what a 30-knot wind means, or how far 50 miles stretches out."

Amen to that, William.

AFRICA

MOROCCO

Biking Expedition to Desert Oases and Mountain Valleys

Few cycling adventures are more exotic than this expedition through the interior of the Arab country most accessible and hospitable to Western travelers. The operator uses Land Rovers and short plane flights to shrink the distances between the highlights. The trip begins in the legendary city of Casablanca and then moves quickly to Zagora, the great southern oasis of the Moroccan pre-Sahara, which becomes the base for three days' exploration of the region. On one day cyclists exchange their bikes for camels for a ride to the dunes of M'hamid, where they spend the night in a Berber camp, dining on tangerines and couscous while Berber dancers entertain just beyond in the shadows. The next day Land Rovers carry expedition members into the Atlas Mountains to rarely visited Berber villages, where inhabitants lead traditional lives of Biblical simplicity. Another highlight is the coastal city of Essaouira, with its robed merchants in labyrinthine souks, where musicians Cat Stevens and Jimi Hendrix hung out more than 20 years ago.

Operator: Butterfield & Robinson, 70 Bond St., Toronto, Ont., Canada, MSB 1X3; (800) 678-1147 or (416) 864-1354.
Price: Expensive.
Season: October through April.
Length: 9 days.
Accommodations: Hotels.

"The meaning of travel is to know the unknown. I'm not very good at accepting other people's word for what's out there. If I have half a chance, I want to see what the middle of Greenland looks like, see what Las Vegas looks like. And oddly enough, traveling gives me a greater sense of security. It's the opposite of the stay-at-home-because-you-might-get-killed view of life. The more I know about the world and the people around me, the safer I feel."

MICHAEL PALIN, FORMER MONTY PYTHON COMIC, *OUTSIDE*, FEBRUARY 1993

ASIA

CHINA

Cycling through Scenic Southwestern China

Operator:
Asian Pacific Adventures,
826 S. Sierra Bonita Ave.,
Los Angeles, Calif. 90036;
(800) 825-1680 or
(213) 935-3156.
Price: Expensive.
Season: April through
November.
Length: 22 days.
Accommodations: Hotels.
Five percent discount with
BBAT coupon.

In a country of 1 billion bicycles, what better way to travel is there? This bike tour has been designed to allow participants a rare opportunity to experience a southern China of friendly people in rustic villages as yet untouched by modern tourism. The group cycles along unpaved back roads through some of China's most photogenic scenery. Stops are made at Guilin, celebrated as one of China's most scenic areas, where oddly shaped, solitary hills rise from a flat plain; the walled city of Dali, flanked by the majestic Changshan Mountains on one side and the deep blue waters of Lake Erhai on the other; Lijiang, located on a bend of the Yangtze River, for a visit to the Jade Peak Temple; and the Stone Forest, to see the bizarre karst terrain. A support van accompanies each group.

"The traveler is active; he goes strenuously in search of people, of adventure, of experience. The tourist is passive; he expects interesting things to happen to him. He goes 'sight-seeing.'"

DANIEL J. BOORNSTEIN,
THE IMAGE

Cyclists on an Asian Pacific Adventures trip pedal through the dramatic karst landscape near Yangshuo in southwestern China

Asian Pacific Adventures

INDIA

South India Cycle

This lengthy trip combines cycling with wildlife viewing and a two-day barge trip. Ten days are spent cycling along the backroads of southern India, through villages set amidst rice paddies, and past ornate Hindu temples. The principal crops grown in this region are rice, sugar cane, and coconut palms. Cyclists can expect numerous opportunities to mingle with the local Indian residents. A support vehicle accompanies all departures. Two days are spent at the Nagarhole Wildlife Sanctuary, home to a rich collection of Indian bison, monkeys, sambar deer, wild dogs, elephants, and many species of birds. Then participants drive to Cochin, one of the busiest and most colorful ports on the western coast, for a two-day barge trip along canals through a landscape of palm-thatch houses and coconut plantations, with stops at rural villages.

Operator: Worldwide Adventures, 36 Finch Ave. W., Toronto, Ont., Canada M2N 2G9; (800) 387-1483 or (416) 221-3000.
Price: Moderate.
Season: December, January, and March.
Length: 22 days.
Accommodations: Tents and hotels. Five percent discount with BBAT coupon.

INDONESIA

Inn-to-Inn Biking around Bali

One of the world's most beautiful and legendary islands, in recent decades Bali has succumbed to the inevitable cultural pollution that comes on the heels of rapid overdevelopment of a country's tourist industry. Two-wheeled adventurers, however, can easily escape the tourist ghettoes of Sanur, Kuta, and Denpensar, and lose themselves among hundreds of small villages where a traditional Balinese way of life still prevails. Cyclists on this trip

For the rural residents of Bali, the bicycle provides much of the local transportation
Tom Hale/Backroads

Operator:
Backroads, 801 Cedar St.,
Berkeley, Calif. 94710;
(800) 462-2848 or
(510) 527-1555.
Price: Expensive.
Season: April, May, and
October.
Length: 9 days.
Accommodations: Inns and
hotels. Five percent dis-
count with BBAT coupon.

head inland over the central mountain chain to
the black-sand beaches at Lovina Beach and
Kubutambahan. Two days are spent on the rims of
Bali's lake-filled volcanoes, Gunung Bratan and
Gunung Batur. The group spends another five
days exploring the tranquil, palm-thatched villages of Bali's eastern province and its excellent
beaches. A highlight there is the lovely village of
Ubud, Bali's craft center. Cyclists average 30 miles
a day. A support vehicle accompanies the group.

TIBET

A Mountain-Bike Expedition across the Tibetan Plateau

Operator:
Worldwide Adventures,
36 Finch Ave. W., Toronto,
Ont., Canada M2N 2G9;
(800) 387-1483 or
(416) 221-3000.
Price: Moderate.
Season: May.
Length: 25 days.
Accommodations: Tents and
small hotels. Five percent
discount with BBAT
coupon.

This is challenging expeditionary cycling of the first
order. Participants traverse the vast Tibetan Plateau
over high and demanding passes that link Llasa
with the historic towns of Gyantse, Shigatse, and
Shegar. Pedaling against a background of snow-covered mountain ranges, cyclists enjoy ample opportunities to visit historic forts, octagonal stupas,
monasteries, picturesque villages, and other sights
along the route. Five days are spent in an off-road
ride to Rongbuk Monastery and its spectacular view
of the entire north face of Mount Everest. A support
vehicle accompanies all departures.

VIETNAM

A Mountain-Bike Tour of the Vietnamese Countryside

Perhaps no better way exists for foreign visitors to
meet the people of Vietnam than from the seat of
a bicycle—after all, bicycles are the preferred
means of travel of most rural Vietnamese.
Participants on these tours explore many of the
scenic, cultural, and historic sights of this country,
where the people are among the friendliest in all

Asia toward Americans. The itinerary includes Ho Chi Minh City (formerly Saigon), where bike tourers pedal along wide boulevards designed by the French; Cu Chi, the amazing tunnel complex built during the war; a ride along the South China Sea coast past pagodas, beaches, old French villas, and quaint fishing villages; Hoi An, a 16th-century town preserved just as the early European traders found it; and Hanoi, far more traditional than its southern sister city, Ho Chi Minh City.

"The thing about my bicycles I want to remember is the way I rode them, and what I thought while I rode them, and the music that came to me."

WILLIAM SAROYAN,
THE BICYCLE RIDER IN BEVERLY HILLS

Operator:
Asian Pacific Adventures, 826 S. Sierra Bonita Ave., Los Angeles, Calif. 90036; (800) 825-1680 or (213) 935-3156.
Price: Moderate.
Season: Year-round.
Length: 17 days.
Accommodations: Hotels. Five percent discount with BBAT coupon.

AUSTRALASIA

AUSTRALIA

Cycle Tasmania

Popular with the thousands of Australians who visit each year but almost unknown to American travelers is Tasmania, anchored in the Tasman Sea off Australia's southern coast. Proclaimed a World Heritage Site, the island offers dramatic peaks and mirror-like lakes, incomparable beaches and seascapes, rare temperate rain forests, and a spectacular wild river, the Franklin. Tasmania is, as the Australians say, a "two-lane island," which makes it the perfect place for bicycle touring. These tours focus on the northeastern section, where cyclists pedal through rolling farmlands, picturesque fishing villages, and spectacular coastal scenery. A highlight is Freycinet National Park, where visitors explore its secluded bays, sheer granite cliffs, and white-sand beaches. A support van accompanies the group.

Operator:
Worldwide Adventures, 36 Finch Ave. W., North York, Ont., Canada M2N 2G9; (800) 387-1483 or (416) 221-3000.
Price: Moderate.
Season: November through April.
Length: 8 days.
Accommodations: Tent camps. Five percent discount with BBAT coupon.

NEW ZEALAND

South Island Odyssey

Operator:
Backroads, 801 Cedar St.,
Berkeley, Calif. 94710;
(800) 462-2848 or
(510) 527-1555.
Price: Expensive.
Season: December through
March.
Length: 14 days.
Accommodations: Hotels,
lodges, and private homes.
Five percent discount with
BBAT coupon.

This tour has been carefully tailored to include some of New Zealand's most celebrated wilderness attractions, including the spectacular Southern Alps. Participants cycle along beautiful Marlborough Sound, through fertile wine and apple country, and into the magnificent Buller Gorge. For six days they follow the wild western coast past numerous deserted gold-mining towns, an area reminiscent of America's Old West. Several days are spent in Westland National Park exploring the Fox and Franz Josef Glaciers. In Wanaka, riders take a break from cycling for a ski-plane ride over nearby glaciers and a boat cruise on Milford Sound. Total cycling distance is 700 miles. A support van accompanies the group.

CANADA

ALBERTA

Inn-to-Inn Tour through the Canadian Rockies

Operator:
Backroads, 801 Cedar St.,
Berkeley, Calif. 94710;
(800) 462-2848 or
(510) 527-1555.
Price: Expensive.
Season: June to mid-
September.
Length: 5 days.
Accommodations: Hotels and
lodges. Five percent dis-
count with BBAT coupon.

Along the western edge of Alberta lies one of North America's greatest bicycling roads: the spectacular Icefields Parkway. Cyclists on this tour ride wide-shouldered roads, along relatively flat country between two magnificent mountain ranges, into the heart of the Canadian Rockies. They travel from Banff to Jasper, stopping along the way to explore such major attractions as Moraine Lake, Lake Louise, and the massive Columbia Icefield. This is a wilderness rich in black bear, elk, and moose. A support van accompanies each group.

PRINCE EDWARD ISLAND

Prince Edward Island by Bicycle

Participants on these tours pedal around this scenic southeastern Canadian island on uncrowded roads through a gentle terrain perfect for bicycling. PEI also has seaside cliffs, long stretches of white-sand beaches, and colorful fishing villages. Other attractions include Green Gables, the house that inspired Lucy Maud Montgomery's classic *Anne of Green Gables*; Prince County, where the descendants of the hardy Arcadian settlers from 200 years ago still maintain their French language and traditions; and the Micmac Indians of Lennox Island. A support van accompanies each group.

Operator: Classic Adventures, P.O. Box 153, Hamlin, N.Y. 14464; (800) 777-8090 or (716) 964-8488. *Price:* Expensive. *Season:* July and August. *Length:* 7 days. *Accommodations:* Country inns. Five percent discount with BBAT coupon.

EUROPE

CZECH REPUBLIC

Cycling through Bohemia

This cycling expedition begins and ends in Prague. Participants pedal along deserted country lanes through a bountiful agricultural region, an area of well-manicured farms and gently rolling wooded hills. Ample opportunity is allowed for leisurely visits in the enchanting villages, castles, and cathedrals along the way. In Kutna Hora cyclists don hard hats and take flashlights in hand to explore the narrow tunnels of one of the famous old silver mines that produced wealth for the region in earlier times. Two nights are spent at the town of Cesky Krumlov, the crown jewel of southern Bohemian towns, built along the serpentine banks of the upper Vltava River. A support van accompanies each group.

Operator: Kolotour Holidays, P.O. Box 1493, Boulder Creek, Calif. 95006; (800) 524-7099 or (408) 338-3101. *Price:* Expensive. *Season:* July. *Length:* 14 days. *Accommodations:* Hotels and pensions. Five percent discount with BBAT coupon.

DENMARK

Island Cycling in Scandinavia

Operator:
Euro-Bike Tours,
P.O. Box 990, DeKalb, Ill.
60115; (800) 321-6060 or
(815) 758-8851.
Price: Expensive.
Season: July.
Length: 15 days.
Accommodations: Hotels.
Five percent discount with
BBAT coupon.

These tours begin and end in Copenhagen and encompass both idyllic islands remote from the usual tourist haunts and popular sights on the mainland of both Denmark and Sweden. The first two stops are the small islands of Aerø and Taasinge, where cyclists pedal through old fishing villages and tranquil farm communities. Favorite stops include Faaborg, an ancient walled village that is popular with local artists, and Odense, the birthplace of Hans Christian Andersen. Back on the mainland, cyclists travel through Jutland's peaceful Lake District before crossing the Baltic Sea to Skåne, Sweden's southernmost province, which boasts such an abundance of sandy beaches that it has earned itself the nickname of the "Swedish Riviera." A support wagon accompanies all groups.

"Our nature lies in movement; complete calm is death."

PASCAL, *PENSÉES*

The Adventure Travel Hall of Fame:
RICHARD HALLIBURTON

Like Ulysses, the American Richard Halliburton was one of those travelers who gave the impression that he kept moving because only then did he feel fully alive. His popularity in his day as an author, lecturer, and traveler exceeded that of most film stars, and was due in large part to the success

with which he realized personally those urges for adventure latent in the public at large.

In late 1929 Halliburton purchased a Stearman two-seat biplane with an open cockpit, painted it bright scarlet, named it the "Flying Carpet," and hired a pilot. Their first destination was Timbuktu, which had captured Halliburton's imagination as a symbol

FRANCE

A Food- and Wine-Lover's Tour of Provence

Cycling through the south of France is a sybarite's dream of châteaus, Chardonnay, and friendly smiles. This tour of Provence's most celebrated vineyards, restaurants, and hotels is well worth pumping for. The clear, dazzling light and Mediterranean landscapes of the region inspired the finest paintings of van Gogh and Cézanne. The tour begins with a ride through the valley of the Gardon River and the bustling medieval village of Uzès. The second day starts with a private walking tour of the exquisitely preserved Pont-du-Gard, part of a three-tiered, 31-mile aqueduct built by the Romans in the year 19 B.C. The road to Rasteau passes several vineyards and medieval villages clinging precariously to the rocky outcroppings. A support van accompanies all groups.

Operator:
Vermont Bicycle Touring,
Box 711, Bristol, Vt. 05443;
(800) 245-3838 or
(802) 453-4811.
Price: Expensive.
Season: May through mid-October.
Length: 7 days.
Accommodations: Hotels, ranging from elegant rural retreats to small village hotels. Five percent discount with BBAT coupon.

A Wine-Tasting Tour of Burgundy

This tour takes participants through one of the major wine areas of France—Burgundy, the grand dame of French wine-making. A highlight is

of remoteness. After a hazardous flight across the Sahara Desert they arrived at the legendary West African city, which proved to be a dreary collection of mud buildings. He visited the slave market and bought two youngsters for $5 each, selling them back at a loss several days later. Then he and his pilot flew back across the Sahara to Sidi-bel-Abbes, Algeria, for the centennial celebration of the founding of the French Foreign Legion. Halliburton donned a Legionnaire's uniform and marched with the soldiers to a remote mountain outpost that had recently withstood a fierce siege by desert warriors. In the Middle East, he followed in the footsteps of Alexander the Great. In Nepal they flew around Mount Everest, where Halliburton almost fell out of his plane while trying to photograph the mountain. In Borneo they lived with headhunters for a week, and Halliburton departed with a gift of 12 human heads from the local chief.

Operator:
Progressive Travels,
224 W. Galer Ave., #C,
Seattle, Wash. 98119;
(800) 245-2229 or
(206) 285-1987.
Price: Expensive.
Season: June through
September.
Length: 6 days.
Accommodations: Hotels,
including a restored
Renaissance residence.
Five percent discount
with BBAT coupon.

organized wine-tasting sessions at several of the region's most celebrated vineyards, including the Château de Meursault with its famous 15th-century cellars. There is also an optional hot-air balloon ride above the vineyards near Beaune. Historical highlights include the medieval walled town of Beaune, the ancient monastic town of Tournus, and a 15th-century hospital still in use. A support van accompanies the group.

"The first love, the first sunrise, the first South Sea island are memories apart."

Robert Louis Stevenson

Tour along the Dordogne River Valley

Operator:
Progressive Travels,
224 W. Galer Ave., #C,
Seattle, Wash. 98119;
(800) 245-2229 or
(206) 285-1987.
Price: Expensive.
Season: May through
October.
Length: 8 days.
Accommodations: First-class
hotels. Five percent dis-
count with BBAT coupon.

Between the world-famous wine regions of Burgundy and Bordeaux lies the Dordogne River Valley, perhaps France's most beautiful rural land-scape. Participants on these tours cycle from the medieval town of Roumegouse to Les Eyzies-de-Tayac, the capital of French prehistory. Along the way they visit the picturesque amphitheater over-looking the Autoire River; Rocamadour, a medieval pilgrimage site; and Château Beynac, a castle once captured by Richard the Lionhearted. In the cav-erns of Font-de-Gaume near Les Eyzies, cyclists tour a 35,000-year-old Cro-Magnon art gallery where magnificent murals depict prehistoric mam-moths and great bisons. A support van accompa-nies the group.

Classic Bicycle Tour of the Loire

Long known as the "Garden of France," the Loire Valley is synonymous with magnificent châteaus, gastronomic adventure, and light-bodied wines. Francois I, Leonardo da Vinci, and Joan of Arc are three who made their home here. Cyclists on these tours pedal along flat roads through a peaceful countryside, among lavish palaces and stately manor houses mirrored in the waters of the France's longest river. The historical stops include Amboise, where da Vinci lies buried; the Château de Chenonceaux, a famous castle constructed across the Cher River; and Chambord, with its great château built by Francois I. A support vehicle accompanies each group.

Operator: Europeds, 761 Lighthouse Ave., Monterey, Calif. 93940; (800) 321-9552 or (408) 372-1173. *Price:* Expensive. *Season:* June through September. *Length:* 6 days. *Accommodations:* Hotels. Five percent discount with BBAT coupon.

Cahors-to-Carcassonne Cycle

On these trips cyclists pedal from France's best-preserved medieval bridge, the Pont Valentré, spanning the Lot River in Cahors, to the best-preserved medieval walled city in all of Europe, Carcassonne. Their route takes them through the little known regions of Quercy, Aveyron, Tarn, and Aude. They follow the Lot upstream, where magnificent limestone cliffs frame an intimate valley and picturesque villages hug the vertical rock faces. Additional sights along the way include the ruins of a medieval fortress overlooking the Aveyron River; Albi, where the famous painter Toulouse-Lautrec was born, a city of 50,000 with a red-rose cathedral; and Castres, with its magnificent Musée Goya, home to a large collection of Spanish art. A support wagon accompanies all groups.

Operator: Europeds, 761 Lighthouse Ave., Monterey, Calif. 93940; (800) 321-9552 or (408) 372-1173. *Price:* Expensive. *Season:* July and October. *Length:* 7 days. *Accommodations:* Hotels. Five percent discount with BBAT coupon.

GERMANY

Cycling the Mosel Valley

Castles and steep-roofed villages cling to vineyard-clad hillsides above Germany's Mosel Weinstrasse. The Mosel River snakes in gentle loops, as giant sundials point to the sky amidst

Operator:
Euro-Bike Tours, P.O. Box 990, DeKalb, Ill. 60115; (800) 321-6060 or (815) 758-8851.
Price: Expensive.
Season: June, July, and Sept.
Length: 5 days.
Accommodations: Hotels. Five percent discount with BBAT coupon.

plantings of bright green Riesling grapes. Cyclists on these adventures pedal through half-timbered medieval villages to Koblenz on the mighty Rhine River. A highlight is Zeltingen, with its narrow streets little changed since the days of chivalry, elegant figures of knights carved on wooden gables, frescoes painted on houses, and cheerful flower boxes. A support vehicle accompanies the group.

Monks from the Greek Orthodox Church greet cyclists on a Classic Adventures tour of coastal Greece

Classic Adventures

GREECE

Coastal Tour of Classical Greece

Operator:
Classic Adventures, P.O. Box 153, Hamlin, N.Y. 14464; (800) 777-8090 or (716) 964-8488.
Price: Expensive.
Season: May, June, September, and October.
Length: 14 days.
Accommodations: Small hotels. Five percent discount with BBAT coupon.

This popular tour is the perfect match for lovers of history and antiquities. It is also an excellent opportunity to meet the friendly and hospitable Greek people who live in small villages along the route. Although Greece is largely a mountainous country, this tour follows a flat coastal route. Several days are spent cycling the western island of Zakinthos, with ample free time to explore the sights or just lounge on the beaches. Other highlights include Olympia, the site of the ancient Olympic games, and a cog-rail train ride to the imposing gorge of Kalavrita. A support van accompanies the group.

HOLLAND

Tulip and Spring-Flower Bike Tour

The art of bulb-growing is a Dutch specialty. The Dutch imported the first tulips from the Himalayas in the late 16th century; within a few years tulip-mania swept through Europe. Every spring the Dutch countryside bursts into a riot of color no painter could duplicate. These trips focus on the tulip-growing region, pedaling in a flat-terrain circle along bike paths and next to canals starting in Leiden, the city of Rembrandt. Attractions along the way include the town of Gouda, with its architecturally striking church and town hall as well as the celebrated cheese market; and Delft, a city of gabled houses, canals, and humpbacked bridges. A support van follows the group.

Operator: Classic Adventures, P.O. Box 153, Hamlin, N.Y. 14464; (800) 777-8090 or (716) 964-8488. *Price:* Expensive. *Season:* May and June. *Length:* 7 days. *Accommodations:* Hotels. Five percent discount with BBAT coupon.

IRELAND

Cycling the Western Shores

A ride through western Ireland is an enchanting journey through charming villages filled with warmly hospitable people and across gently rolling

Cyclists on the Easy Rider trip through western Ireland spend a day on Inishmore, the largest of the Aran Islands, where a traditional Irish lifestyle still prevails

James C. Simmons

Operator: Easy Rider Tours, P.O. Box 228, Newburyport, Mass. 01950; (800) 488-8332 or (508) 463-6955.
Price: Expensive.
Season: May through July.
Length: 10 days.
Accommodations: Small hotels. Five percent discount with BBAT coupon.

green fields studded with medieval castles and abbeys. Cyclists on these tours explore the tranquil countryside and rugged coasts of Counties Clare and Galway, pedaling through a land steeped in ancient ruins and history that covers the many layers of human settlements over the centuries from Stone and Bronze Age people to Picts, Celts, Romans, and Vikings. One day is set aside for a visit to Inishmore, the largest of the Aran Islands, where cyclists will pedal through a landscape of rock—rock houses, rock walls, and rock fields. The highlight is Dun Aengus, the finest surviving prehistoric fort in Europe, which sits in silent splendor on the edge of a sheer 300-foot sea cliff. A support van accompanies all groups.

ITALY

Giro D'Italia, the Ultimate Italian Cycling Experience

Cyclists on this popular trip pedal along some of Italy's most beautiful roads and through seven of her most fascinating regions. From the canals of storybook Venice to the roughly hewn mountain towns of Abruzzo, this itinerary provides participants with an amazing variety of Italy's scenery, gastronomy,

The Adventure Travel Hall of Fame:
WILLIAM AND FANNY WORKMAN

William and Fanny Workman —he was British, she American —were a husband-and-wife team who spent 15 years abroad from 1896 to 1910 cycling through remote parts of the world and writing books about their adventures. They started off with an easy 1,500-mile tour of Spain and followed

that with a more strenuous bicycling trip through the Atlas Mountains of Morocco. In the early 1900s they traveled to Asia to explore off the beaten track.

Their most arduous trip—and one of the most epic bicycle journeys ever undertaken—occurred in 1903–1905, when the Workmans pedaled over 14,000 miles along

culture, and history. Stops are made at such celebrated Italian treasures as Ravenna, Florence, Arezzio (a well-preserved medieval city which once boasted great wealth), Spoleto (set amidst a countryside rich with Roman antiquities), and Popoli, where a visit is made to the ghostly, abandoned Rocca Calasio, a medieval castle. At trip's end cyclists can unwind and relax on the Island of Ischia in the Bay of Naples, famous for its spas and natural springs. A support vehicle accompanies each group.

Operator:
Ciclismo Classico,
13 Marathon St.,
Arlington, Mass. 02174;
(800) 866-7314 or
(617) 646-3377.
Price: Expensive.
Season: May, June, and September.
Length: 15 days.
Accommodations: Hotels.
Five percent discount with BBAT coupon.

Bike Across Italy

Bikers on this coast-to-coast tour pedal through four of Italy's most beautiful regions—Le Marche, Umbria, Lazio, and Tuscany, each known for its charming hill towns, lush landscapes, and unique cuisines. Riders begin their adventure at Fano, a small resort town on the Adriatic coast, and pedal to Urbino, a thriving cultural center; then cycle along rivers at the bottom of deep gorges through lush mountains. At Genga they explore the spectacular Grotte di Frasassi, Italy's largest cave system, and continue on to Fabriano, the medieval birthplace of paper-making. Other stops include Assisi, the birthplace of St. Francis; Todi, a hilltop town

Operator:
Ciclismo Classico,
13 Marathon St.,
Arlington, Mass. 02174;
(800) 866-7314 or
(617) 646-3377.
Price: Expensive.
Season: May through October.
Length: 11 days.
Accommodations: Hotels.
Five percent discount with BBAT coupon.

dirt roads through India. Their principal goal was to visit and photograph the thousands of temples, palaces, forts, and tombs scattered the width and breadth of India, to prove to Europeans that "at a time when the greater part of Europe was slumbering in the darkness of barbarism, civilization existed in India that produced remarkable monuments."

The Workmans scoured the mountains, jungles, forests, plains, and caves of India,

cataloguing and photographing thousands of architectural and artistic relics, many of which had never before been seen by Europeans. To this end they endured impossible road conditions, an utter absence of accommodations (except in the major cities), temperatures in excess of 120 degrees Fahrenheit, floods, plague, famine, and robbers. In many of the smaller communities, the Workmans were the first whites the people had ever seen.

famous for its Etruscan, Roman, and medieval walls; and Saturnia, the oldest city in Italy, where the hot springs still draw visitors. A support vehicle accompanies each group.

"I craved a little risk, some danger, an untoward event, a vivid discomfort, an experience of my own company, and, in a modest way, the romance of solitude."

PAUL THEROUX,
THE OLD PATAGONIAN EXPRESS

Tuscany Wine Country of Central Italy

Operator: Progressive Travels, 224 W. Galer Ave., #C, Seattle, Wash. 98119; (800) 245-2229 or (206) 285-1987. *Price:* Expensive. *Season:* September and October. *Length:* 7 days. *Accommodations:* First-class hotels, including a 14th-century fortified monastery. Five percent discount with BBAT coupon.

Bicycling in Italy is both sport and religion—cyclists can be found along every road. This tour from Florence to Sinalunga explores the distinctive landscape, culture, cuisine, and architecture of Tuscany. On the second day, cyclists pedal through a countryside of olive groves, orchards, and vineyards to arrive in the heart of Chianti Classico. Wine-tasting sessions at several leading vineyards allow participants to sample this universal favorite among red wines. Historical sights include Etruscan ruins, walled medieval villages, ancient castles, and stately villas. A full day is spent enjoying the art, architecture, and culture of Siena. Cyclists should know that Tuscany is perhaps the hilliest region in Italy. A support vehicle accompanies the group.

PORTUGAL

Cycling the Costa Azul

Cyclists pedal south from Sesimbra, just 25 miles south of Lisbon, along the Portuguese Riviera through a landscape of unspoiled beaches, turquoise waters, and picturesque harbors bustling with colorful fishing boats. Participants take a half-day cruise on an antique wooden sailboat to the Tróia Peninsula, where they continue their route through endless dunes and beaches. A layover day in Zambujeira do Mar allows plenty of time for enjoying the area's secluded crescent beaches tucked among the cliffs. Dinners feature the seafood dishes for which the region is famous. A support van accompanies all groups.

Operator:
Easy Rider Tours,
P.O. Box 228,
Newburyport, Mass. 01950;
(800) 488-8332 or
(508) 463-6955.
Price: Expensive.
Season: May through July.
Length: 9 days.
Accommodations: Small hotels and the 400-year-old Castelo de Milfontes. Five percent discount with BBAT coupon.

SPAIN

Cycling through Andalucia

Nowhere in the Iberian peninsula is the Moorish influence more pronounced than in "Al-Andalus," the last stronghold of the Arabs before they were banished by Ferdinand and Isabella in 1492. Participants on these trips pedal from Seville to Grenada through a region noted for its excellent wines and local cuisine. A highlight is the Córdoba, famous for the Mezquita (Spain's most beautiful mosque) and a magnificent 16-arched Roman bridge. The tour ends in Grenada, where cyclists will tour the Alhambra, a vast structure straight out of *The Arabian Nights,* and enjoy some of the finest flamenco dancing in all Spain. A support van accompanies all groups.

Operator:
Easy Rider Tours,
P.O. Box 228,
Newburyport, Mass. 01950;
(800) 488-8332 or
(508) 463-6955.
Price: Expensive.
Season: May through July.
Length: 10 days.
Accommodations: Hotels and a graciously restored 16th-century monastery. Five percent discount with BBAT coupon.

SWITZERLAND

Cycling the Swiss Lake Country

Switzerland may be Europe's most mountainous country, but these trips feature some of the easiest cycling on the continent. Participants use trains and boats to cover the difficult terrain. The rest of the time they pedal along easy bicycle paths and secondary roads, in flat valleys, from one small village to another. The trip begins with a cycle ride

A tandem bicycle provides
the perfect means for a
couple to enjoy the Alpine
scenery of Switzerland
Vermont Bicycle Touring

Operator:
Vermont Bicycle Touring,
Box 711, Bristol, Vt. 05443;
(800) 245-3838 or
(802) 453-4811.
Price: Expensive.
Season: June through
August.
Length: 7 days.
Accommodations: Five-star
hotels. Five percent dis-
count with BBAT coupon.

along the fertile Rhône Valley over gentle terrain,
while incredible mountain peaks dominate the
horizon. Other highlights include a cycle along the
shores of Lake Thun in German-speaking
Switzerland; a ride around Lake Brienz, one of the
country's most scenic bodies of water; and two
nights in the lakeside resort of the five-star Hotel
Waldstatterhof, with its fine beaches, peaceful terraces, and formal dining room. A support vehicle
accompanies the group.

LATIN AMERICA

VENEZUELA

Andes Mountain Biking

The Venezuelan Andes are a real treat for mountain bikers seeking spectacular scenery, plenty of
sunshine, and crisp, clean air. This mountain
region is crisscrossed by scenic roads and trails that
provide excellent routes, ranging from jungle-like
tropical cloud forest to sparsely inhabited alpine

country. These popular trips begin in Merida, the historical capital of the Venezuelan Andes. The highlight may well be the ride from Mucuchies, a high-mountain town dating back to 1596, along the magnificent Trans-Andean Highway to the Sierra Nevada National Park. About 60 percent of the pedaling is on paved road, the rest on dirt trails. A support vehicle accompanies the group.

Operator:
Lost World Adventures,
1189 Autumn Ridge Dr.,
Marietta, Ga. 30066;
(800) 999-0558 or
(404) 971-8586.
Price: Moderate.
Season: Year-round.
Length: 5 days.
Accommodations: Small hotels. Five percent discount with BBAT coupon.

A cyclist takes a rest amidst beautiful scenery on a mountain-bike trip through the South American Andes

Lost World Adventures

UNITED STATES

ALASKA

Cycling the Richardson Highway from Fairbanks to Valdez

This 345-mile bike ride is Alaska's most popular cycling trip. The Richardson Highway is the oldest in the state, dating back to 1899. Avoiding most of

Operator:
Alaskan Bicycle Adventures,
2734 Iliamna Ave.,
Anchorage, Alaska 99517;
(800) 770-7242 or
(907) 243-2329.
Price: Expensive.
Season: June to mid-Sept.
Length: 8 days.
Accommodations: Hotels,
with one night camping.
Five percent discount with
BBAT coupon.

the heavily touristed areas, it is the most scenic, low-traffic, paved highway in the state. Cyclists on these trips pedal a straight line from the center of the state to the edge, passing through different climate zones and past mountains and river basins. The trip begins in Anchorage with a ride on the Alaska Railroad past Mount McKinley. The cycling starts the next day in Fairbanks with a cruise across Prince William Sound. A support van accompanies all groups.

Denali Mountain Biking

Operator:
Alaskan Bicycle Adventures,
2734 Iliamna Ave.,
Anchorage, Alaska 99517;
(800) 770-7242 or
(907) 243-2329.
Price: Expensive.
Season: July and August.
Length: 6 days.
Accommodations: Cabins and
small lodges. Five percent
discount with BBAT
coupon.

Alaska's other great pedal for cyclists is the Denali Highway, constructed in the early 1950s as an access road into Denali National Park. However, a 133-mile stretch of the road was abandoned in 1972, when the Parks Highway was completed. While the crowds of tourists ride shuttle buses along this newer highway, just to the east lies one of the state's great mountain-bike experiences. The unpaved two-lane road skirts the south side of the Alaska Range for its entire length, and most of the highway is above treeline (about 2,500 feet). Cyclists on this trip enjoy stunning views of the mountains, lakes, and wildlife. A support van accompanies all departures.

"Travel can also be the spirit of adventure somewhat tamed for those who are no Frobishers ready to find new straits, but who desire to do something they are a bit afraid of. You can feel as brave as Columbus starting for the Unknown the first time you decide to enter a Chinese lane full of boys laughing at you, when you risk climbing down into a Tibetan pub for a meal smelling of rotten meat, or simply addressing a witty taxi driver in Paris."

ELLA MAILLART,
"MY PHILOSOPHY OF TRAVEL"

The Denali Highway offers cyclists some of the finest mountain biking in Alaska

Alaskan Bicycle Adventures

ARIZONA

A Mountain-Bike Ride along the Grand Canyon's North Rim

Few of the millions of tourists who visit the Grand Canyon each year experience the North Rim. Rain on the plateau to the north drains into the canyon; as a result, the North Rim has been cut back twice as far and is 1,000 feet higher than the South Rim, where water drains away from the canyon. The Arizona Trail, a mix of single-track and dirt roads, traverses this remote wilderness and eventually will run from Utah to Mexico. Riders on these trips pedal across a landscape of rolling hills and open meadows surrounded by aspen, pine, and juniper forests. Part of the route runs along the edge of the canyon. Wildlife is abundant. A support vehicle carries all gear.

Operator:
REI Adventures,
P.O. Box 1938,
Sumner, Wash. 98390;
(800) 622-2236 or
(206) 395-8115.
Price: Moderate.
Season: June.
Length: 6 days.
Accommodations: Camping.
Five percent discount with
BBAT coupon.

CALIFORNIA

Weekend Mountain-Bike Trip in Yosemite National Park

Operator: Southern Yosemite Mountain Guides, P.O. Box 301, Bass Lake, Calif. 93604; (800) 231-4575 or (209) 658-8735.
Price: Inexpensive.
Season: May through October.
Length: 3 days.
Accommodations: Chalet on Bass Lake. Ten percent discount with BBAT coupon.

This adventure has proven enormously popular with residents from the nearby San Francisco Bay Area eager to explore the wealth of seldom-traveled mountain bike trails in the Sierra National Forest. Cyclists pedal through thickly carpeted forests of pine and fir; down a thrilling 4,000-foot descent; over clear, tumbling alpine streams; and across granite slickrock ridgelines with spectacular views of the High Sierra. The trails are a combination of scenic fire road and rugged four-wheel-drive trails. On the second day the group lunches at "The Amphitheater," a granite phenomenon with 100-mile views of the high country. From this 7,000-foot level cyclists then head downhill for the 4,000-foot, 25-mile descent to beautiful Bass Lake. A four-wheel-drive SAG vehicle accompanies all groups and carries all necessary repair tools.

Inn-to-Inn Ride through the California Wine Country

The operator bills this as "the most luxurious bicycle inn tour in America." The popular trip through

A cyclist with a Backroads group pedals through the California wine country

Tom Hale/Backroads

the Napa Valley wine country is as much a connoisseur's tour of country inns as it is of California wineries. Cyclists spend their first night at Madrona Manor, a Victorian mansion that gives Falcon Crest a run for its money. A 26-mile ride the next day ends at the historic Mount View Hotel, where riders enjoy a mudbath or soothing massage before sampling the nouvelle cuisine in the hotel's famous restaurant. Participants have plenty of time for wine-tasting at the many celebrated wineries that make Napa Valley America's premiere wine-producing region. Cyclists then travel the Sonoma Valley, past its historic Spanish mission to the Sonoma Mission Inn, Northern California's finest health spa. The trip concludes at the Inn at the Tides, where the rooms look out over the blue Pacific.

Operator: Backroads, 801 Cedar St., Berkeley, Calif. 94710; (800) 245-3874 or (510) 527-1555.
Price: Expensive.
Season: Mid-March through mid-November.
Length: 5 days.
Accommodations: Five-star inns and health spas. Five percent discount with BBAT coupon.

A jubilant cyclist pauses atop the Funeral Mountains while on an REI Adventures mountain-bike trip through Death Valley National Park

Stephen Kasper/REI Adventures

Death Valley Mountain-Bike Tour

Operator: REI Adventures, P.O. Box 1938, Sumner, Wash. 98390; (800) 622-2236 or (206) 395-8115. *Price:* Moderate. *Season:* March and April. *Length:* 7 days. *Accommodations:* Tent camps. Five percent discount with BBAT coupon.

The newest of America's national parks, Death Valley is a big-picture affair—half again the size of the state of Delaware and more than 100 miles long. The valley is also a blast-furnace example of nature at its outer limits—with a record high summer temperature of 134 degrees set in 1913 and an average rainfall of less than 2 inches. The valley is in the record books as the lowest (280 feet below sea level), hottest, and driest place in North America. The region's seldom-traveled backcountry offers a variety of cycling conditions for the off-road enthusiast: narrow, winding canyons, table-flat dry lake beds, and challenging mining trails. Departures for these trips are timed to include the blooming of the spring wildflowers.

COLORADO

Hut-to-Hut Mountain Biking through the Rockies

Operator: Roads Less Traveled, P.O. Box 8187, Longmont, Colo. 80501; (800) 488-8493 or (303) 678-8750. *Price:* Moderate. *Season:* August. *Length:* 6 days. *Accommodations:* Comfortable trail huts. Five percent discount with BBAT coupon.

Named after a U.S. Army ski troop that trained in Colorado during the Second World War, the Tenth Mountain Division Trail stretches from Aspen to Vail, passing through a spectacular wilderness setting remote from the usual summer crowds. The 300 miles of single-track and forest trails constitute this country's most extensive hut-served trail network. The huts are actually spacious, two-story log cabins in the style of French chalets, featuring vaulted ceilings, varnished pine furniture, woodstoves, a large sundeck, and photovoltaic lighting. Bikers on these adventures follow a circuitous route through the rugged Holy Cross Wilderness, pedaling a mix of old mining roads, abandoned railway grades, forest trails, and single tracks. Along the way they explore remote ghost towns and hike to secluded alpine lakes and summits.

Cyclists on Colorado's Tenth Mountain
Division Trail can look forward to spending
their nights at comfortable log cabins in
the heart of alpine wilderness
Roads Less Traveled

MAINE

Penobscot Bay

The Maine coast offers well-maintained, quiet roads ideal for bike touring, along with an excellent mix of scenery. This tour's itinerary allows cyclists to visit small fishing villages, craft shops, antique stores, art galleries, lighthouses, and museums while cycling the scenic shoreline. The picturesque towns of Blue Hill and Castine anchor the itinerary, as cyclists explore the surrounding countryside. The road connecting the two passes through a collage of white clapboard houses, saltwater marshes, farms, and blueberry fields. The first day is given over to a cycling excursion around the island of Isleboro. A support van accompanies all groups.

Operator:
Vermont Bicycle Touring,
Box 711, Bristol, Vt. 05443;
(800) 245-3838 or
(802) 453-4811.
Price: Expensive.
Season: July through
September.
Length: 5 days.
Accommodations: Historic
inns, such as the Jed Prouty
Inn (1793), which is on the
National Historic Register.
Five percent discount with
BBAT coupon.

MARYLAND

Exploring the Shoreline of Chesapeake Bay

Operator:
Vermont Bicycle Touring,
Box 711, Bristol, Vt. 05443;
(800) 245-3838 or
(802) 453-4811.
Price: Expensive.
Season: May through July,
September and October.
Length: 5 days.
Accommodations: Historic
inns. Five percent discount
with BBAT coupon.

"Heaven and earth never agreed better to frame a place for men's habitation," Captain John Smith wrote enthusiastically in 1607. One of the great natural resources of the eastern United States, Chesapeake Bay is perhaps most celebrated for its unrivaled boating opportunities. But the mixture of historic sites, beautiful scenery, and well-maintained flat roads make the region a paradise for cyclists. Cyclists on these relaxing trips pedal through numerous picturesque villages set in a verdant countryside. One highlight is the fishing village of Rock Hall, where the group boards a skipjack bound for St. Michaels, home of the Chesapeake Bay Maritime Museum.

MASSACHUSETTS

Bike Tour of Martha's Vineyard and Nantucket Islands

Operator:
Vermont Bicycle Touring,
Box 711, Bristol, Vt. 05443;
(800) 245-3868 or
(802) 453-4811.
Price: Expensive.
Season: June through
October.
Length: 5 days.
Accommodations: Local inns.
Five percent discount with
BBAT coupon.

Cyclists on this tour divide their time between the two most famous islands in New England, both of which offer ideal bicycling conditions because of limited traffic, excellent roads, and gentle terrain. On Martha's Vineyard, riders stay at a 17th-century inn and explore at leisure secluded beaches and the Victorian villages of Edgartown, Chappaquid-dick, and Oak Bluffs. Evening options include a production at one of the excellent local theaters or perhaps dancing at a trendy nightspot. Next stop is Nantucket, for 200 years the home port of a great whaling fleet. Cyclists explore the island's quiet moors and cranberry bogs, numerous wildlife refuges, and the tiny village of 'Sconset, which looks like a set for the musical *Brigadoon*.

MICHIGAN

Mackinac Wayfarer

Michigan boasts some of the most beautiful, lightly traveled yet well-kept backroads in the country. Participants on this tour explore the northern portions of the state's lower peninsula, skirting the scenic coast of Lake Michigan from Charlevoix through hilly countryside toward Petoskey on Little Traverse Bay. Much of the cycling is through lightly settled farmland. At Mackinaw City, riders take a ferry to Mackinac Island, a bicyclist's dream, where horse-drawn buggies and bikes are the only traffic. (Automobiles are prohibited.) Two nights are spent on Mackinac, Michigan's most popular tourist attraction and a location for the 1979 film *Somewhere in Time.* A support van accompanies the group.

Operator:
Michigan Bicycle Touring, 3512 Red School Rd., Kingsley, Mich. 49649; (616) 263-5885.
Price: Expensive.
Season: June, August, and September.
Length: 5 days.
Accommodations: Inns. Five percent discount with BBAT coupon.

Biking through the Upper Peninsula

Across the majestic Mackinac Bridge is Michigan's Upper Peninsula, a world apart. This tour explores the unspoiled wilderness of the Keweenaw Peninsula, the 1843 scene of one of America's first mining booms. Cyclists ride along miles of rugged Lake Superior shoreline, past ghost towns, abandoned mines, and many waterfalls. Other highlights include Fort Wilkins (1844), the last remaining original wooden fort east of the Mississippi River, and the picturesque Copper Harbor Lighthouse (1866). A support van accompanies the group.

Operator:
Michigan Bicycle Touring, 3512 Red School Rd., Kingsley, Mich. 49649; (616) 263-5885.
Price: Moderate.
Season: June through mid-September.
Length: 5 days.
Accommodations: Inns and cabins. Five percent discount with BBAT coupon.

"We, like the eagles, were born to be free. Yet we are obliged, in order to live at all, to make a cage of laws for ourselves and to stand on the perch."

WILLIAM BOLITHO,
TWELVE AGAINST THE GODS

A large part of the appeal of Classic Adventures' Southern trips is the opportunity for cyclists to see firsthand some of the important historic sites of the Old South

Classic Adventures

MISSISSIPPI

Cycling through the Antebellum South

Operator: Classic Adventures, P.O. Box 153, Hamlin, N.Y. 14464; (800) 777-8090 or (716) 964-8488. *Price:* Expensive. *Season:* April, May, and October. *Length:* 7 days. *Accommodations:* Inns. Five percent discount with BBAT coupon.

"We are a ghost-ridden people," novelist William Faulkner once observed about Southerners. Cyclists on these popular trips experience a ghost-ridden landscape as they pedal from Nashville, Tennessee, to Natchez, Mississippi, past sprawling cotton plantations, Civil War battlefields, and stately mansions straight out of *Gone with the Wind*. The route is the Natchez Trace, which dates back several hundred years to its first use by Indians and later by pioneers as a shortcut to the Ohio Valley. In 1806, Congress made it a National Road. The northern section of the route tends to be cooler and hillier, while the southern section is flat and warmer. The tour ends at the historic city of

Natchez, which boasts over 500 antebellum buildings still standing, including scores of stately mansions and plantation homes. A support vehicle accompanies all groups.

MONTANA

Pedaling through Glacier National Park

This northern Montana park boasts a superb glacier-carved mountain wilderness that is quite similar in climate, flora, and fauna to central Alaska, along with 50 glaciers and 200 lakes. Cyclists on this popular trip pedal the grand loop of both Glacier and Waterton Lakes National Parks. A highlight is the ride along the spectacular Going-to-the-Sun Highway and over Logan Pass (6,046 feet), past glacial snowfields, waterfalls, and spectacular vistas at every switchback. On the third day the group cycles across the border into Canada for a visit to Waterton Park, spending the night at the famous Prince of Wales Hotel overlooking the lake. The return is along the sparsely traveled eastern perimeter of Glacier National Park, for two evenings at the grand Glacier Park Lodge. On their day of rest, cyclists have the option of a half-day of white-water rafting on the Flathead River or numerous fine hiking excursions. A support vehicle follows the group.

Operator:
Timberline Bicycle Tours, 7975 E. Harvard, #J, Denver, Colo. 80231; (800) 417-2453 or (303) 759-3804.
Price: Moderate.
Season: June through mid-September.
Length: 7 days.
Accommodations: Lodges. Five percent discount with BBAT coupon.

"Adventure travel is a revelation of the world and of the self. All revelation is private and personal, and the most meaningful travel is that which reveals the most to us. Adventure travels reveals more than tourist travel because it uncovers more novelty, often throwing a subtle light onto an age-old theme, or shining on it from a different angle."

RICHARD CURTIS, "FINDING NEW ADVENTURE," *ADVENTURE TRAVEL* MAGAZINE, APRIL 1981

NORTH CAROLINA
Coastal Odyssey

Operator:
Vermont Bicycle Touring,
Box 711, Bristol, Vt. 05443;
(800) 245-3868 or
(802) 453-4811.
Price: Expensive.
Season: May and
September.
Length: 6 days.
Accommodations: Country
inns. Five percent discount
with BBAT coupon.

Take towering waves, whipped to a boil by frequent Atlantic gales, against a fragile barrier of lonely islands. Add the ghosts of pirates and the hulks of hundreds of decaying shipwrecks. Season with wheeling seabirds, scrappy game fish, dunes sculpted by the winds, shells, and sunsets in rainbow hues. What you have is Cape Hatteras and the other barrier islands that make the North Carolina coast one of the most spectacular in the nation. These tours explore the best parts of this magical area. Of special interest are elegant Tryon Palace, the home of North Carolina's colonial governor; historic Ocracoke Island, which boasts some of the finest beaches on the Eastern Seaboard; and the Cedar Island Wildlife Refuge, where over 300 bird species have been spotted. A support van accompanies all groups.

OREGON
Cycling Around Crater Lake

Operator:
Backcountry,
P.O. Box 4029,
Bozeman, Mont. 59772;
(800) 575-1540 or
(406) 586-3556.
Price: Expensive.
Season: May through
September.
Length: 6 days.
Accommodations: Lodges.
Five percent discount with
BBAT coupon.

Six thousand five hundred years ago, 12,000-foot-high Mount Mazama erupted with a titanic roar and then collapsed into a crater 1,932 feet deep. Over the centuries this filled to form Crater Lake, the deepest (and bluest!) lake in the United States and the seventh-deepest in the world. Cyclists on these adventures pedal on well-maintained paved roads through old-growth forests on a leisurely ride around the 33-mile caldera rim. This is one of the most scenic bike rides in North America, with impressive views of volcanic peaks in every direction. One day is spent hiking along the Rogue River to view deep canyons and lava tubes.

Most operators provide a support vehicle to accompany each group of cyclists

Doug McSpadden/Backcountry

PENNSYLVANIA

Cycling Through Pennsylvania Dutch Country

This tour of Lancaster County in the heart of the Pennsylvania Dutch country has been designed as a showcase for a traditional Amish and Mennonite way of life in which the horse and buggy are still the transportation of choice. Cyclists pedal through a bucolic countryside of beautifully maintained farms where covered bridges still grace many rivers. Ample time is allowed to explore such centers of Amish culture as Intercourse, with its colorful farmers' markets and quaint craft shops. Cyclists also visit Lititz, the pretzel capital, where the first pretzel in America was made, and the Nissley Estate Winery for a tour of the vineyard. A support van accompanies all groups.

Operator:
Vermont Bicycle Touring, Box 711, Bristol, Vt. 05443; (800) 245-3838 or (802) 453-4811.
Price: Expensive.
Season: May through July, September and October.
Length: 2, 3, and 5 days.
Accommodations: Historic inns. Five percent discount with BBAT coupon.

"Something hidden. Go and find it.
Go and look behind the Ranges—
Something lost behind the Ranges.
Lost and waiting for you. Go!"

RUDYARD KIPLING,
"THE EXPLORER"

UTAH

Biking Bryce and Zion National Parks

Operator:
Backcountry, P.O. Box
4029, Bozeman, Mont.
59772; (800) 575-1540 or
(406) 586-3556.
Price: Expensive.
Season: May through
September.
Length: 6 days.
Accommodations: Lodges.
Five percent discount with
BBAT coupon.

These lodge-to-lodge cycling trips focus on two of the Southwest's most spectacular parks. Zion is a perpendicular country of deep canyons, sheer cliffs, and dizzying elevations, with Zion Canyon being the crown jewel, a beautiful gorge carved by the North Fork of the Virgin River. The smaller Bryce Canyon National Park is a geologic wonderland, a bewildering landscape of heavily eroded red-rock pinnacles sculpted by wind and rain into hundreds of fantastical shapes. Cyclists pedal along the paved roads and dirt backroads of both parks.

Mountain-Biking the Kokopelli Trail

Operator:
Roads Less Traveled
Adventures, P.O. Box 8187,
Longmont, Colo. 80501;
(800) 498-8493 or
(303) 678-8750.
Price: Moderate.
Season: May and
September.
Length: 5 days.
Accommodations: Tent
camps. Five percent dis-
count coupon with BBAT
coupon.

Linking Grand Junction, Colorado, and the fat-tire mecca of Moab, Utah, the legendary Kokopelli Trail is a tough but rewarding adventure that traverses dramatic canyon country and high-mountain scenery. The route is a 140-mile roller coaster of jeep roads and trails that include some 8,000 vertical feet of climbing in the snowcapped La Sal Mountains. Few who ride the Kokopelli will forget the trail's finale—a 4,000-foot, heart-pounding descent that winds through high-country pine and aspen, then juniper and piñon, and finally the sandstone domes of Moab's renowned Slickrock Trail. An off-road vehicle carries all supplies.

VERMONT

Champlain Valley

The locals jokingly refer to their Lake Champlain Valley as "New England's West Coast." And in a sense it is—a west coast composed of the sixth-largest body of fresh water in the United States. Long and slender, it stretches 110 miles along two-thirds of the

Cyclists on Vermont Bicycle Touring trips through the Vermont countryside may feel they have suddenly pedaled into a Norman Rockwell painting

Vermont Bicycle Touring

Vermont–New York border. Cyclists pedal through the Champlain Valley between the Green Mountains and the Adirondacks on one of the most scenic rides in New England. Starting in the small town of Danby and riding north through pastoral farmlands and fragrant orchards and across covered bridges, along the way cyclists visit the famous Morgan Horse Farm and take a cable-drawn ferry ride across Lake Champlain to New York's Fort Ticonderoga, where Vermont's Revolutionary War hero Ethan Allen outfoxed the British in 1777. The trip ends in Middlebury, the picturesque college town. A support van accompanies all groups.

Operator:
Vermont Bicycle Touring, Box 711, Bristol, Vt. 05443; (800) 245-3868 or (802) 453-4811.
Price: Expensive.
Season: June through mid-October.
Length: 5 days.
Accommodations: Historic country inns. Five percent discount with BBAT coupon.

VIRGINIA
Shenandoah Valley

Operator:
Vermont Bicycle Touring,
Box 711, Bristol, Vt. 05443;
(800) 245-3838 or
(802) 453-4811.
Price: Expensive.
Season: July through
September.
Length: 5 days.
Accommodations: Historic
inns. Five percent discount
with BBAT coupon.

Jeremys Run. Matthews Arm. Thornton Gap. The
old names recall the old times when settlers
cleared homesteads, planted corn and tobacco,
and hunted squirrel and deer. Since Shenandoah
National Park was established in 1935, nature has
reclaimed these ancient Blue Ridge Mountains.
Hardwood forests again cover the slopes, and
wildlife is abundant. Cyclists on these popular
trips explore this popular park along roads that
take them far from the madding crowds.
Highlights include visits to the Jordan Hollow
Farm, a 200-year-old working horse farm; Luray
Caverns, where the lovely sights are all underground; and a tour of Belle Grove Plantation.
Departures are timed to take advantage of the
spring wildflower bloom and the autumnal profusion of color. A support van accompanies each
group.

WASHINGTON
Biking the Islands of Puget Sound

Operator:
Backroads, 801 Cedar St.,
Berkeley, Calif. 94710;
(800) 245-3874 or
(510) 527-1555.
Price: Moderate.
Season: July through
September.
Length: 6 days.
Accommodations: Country
inn and health resort. Five
percent discount with
BBAT coupon.

Some 768 jade-green islands lie scattered across
Puget Sound, sheltered by the magnificent
Olympic Mountains. This popular tour travels by
ferryboat to savor some of the best sights that the
Pacific Northwest offers. Cyclists spend several
days each on two of the most popular and scenic
islands. On big San Juan Island they cycle along
quiet roads past hidden bays and secluded
beaches. Next they travel to Orcas Island's peaceful villages, lovely Cascade Lake, and lush forests.
They also make a day trip to nearby Lopez Island
for some leisurely cycling and swimming. Cycling
distances are short.

WISCONSIN

Cycling the Lake Michigan Shoreline

Door County, Wisconsin's thumb-shaped peninsula, has long been popular with travelers seeking a secluded haven without much development. Cyclists on these tours pedal the entire length of the peninsula, sampling waterfront villages, orchards, and turn-of-the-century lighthouses. One entire day is spent bike-exploring Washington Island, the country's largest Icelandic settlement. Participants have plenty of time for swimming and sunning at some of the prettiest beaches in the upper Midwest. A support wagon follows the group.

Operator: Vermont Bicycle Touring, Box 711, Bristol, Vt. 05443; (800) 245-3868 or (802) 453-4811.
Price: Expensive.
Season: July.
Length: 5 days.
Accommodations: Country inns. Five percent discount with BBAT coupon.

WYOMING

Grand Teton Adventure

The special appeal of the Tetons lies in the way they rise so precipitously from the lake-studded valley of Jackson Hole, the tallest peak clawing the sky at nearly 14,000 feet. One of the largest herds of elk in North America migrates from the valley floor each summer to the high country where they

Cyclists pedal along quiet paved roads pass the majestic Grand Teton Mountains
Doug McSpadden/Backcountry

Operator:
Backcountry, P.O. Box
4029, Bozeman, Mont.
59772; (800) 575-1540 or
(406) 586-3556.
Price: Expensive.
Season: July to mid-
September.
Length: 6 days.
Accommodations: Park
lodges. Five percent dis-
count with BBAT coupon.

fatten, raise their calves, and frolic in the cool alpine meadows. Participants on this popular trip bike, canoe, horseback-ride, and raft through Grand Teton National Park's many attractions. This easygoing trip is perfect for families.

"I wanted to keep going forever, to never stop, that morning when the truck picked me up at five a.m. It was like a drug in me. As a traveler I can achieve a kind of high, a somewhat altered state of consciousness. I think it must be what athletes feel. I am transported out of myself, into another dimension in time and space. While the journey is on buses and across land, I begin another journey inside my head, a journey of memory and sensation, of past merging with present, of time growing insignificant."

MARY MORRIS,
NOTHING TO DECLARE

Cycling the Yellowstone Country

Operator:
Timberline Bicycle Tours,
7975 E. Harvard, #J,
Denver, Colo. 80231;
(800) 417-2453 or
(303) 759-3804.
Price: Moderate.
Season: June through August.
Length: 7 days.
Accommodations: Park
lodges. Five percent dis-
count with BBAT coupon.

This popular trip focuses on two of our country's most celebrated national parks, Yellowstone and Grand Teton. Cyclists assemble in Jackson Hole and the next morning start pedaling along the Lewis River. Their route takes them over the Continental Divide and down into the geyser basins, where Old Faithful is the star performer, and on toward Grand Teton National Park. Daily mileages are sufficiently modest to allow cyclists plenty of opportunities to explore the wonders of the area by foot and observe its wildlife. A support wagon follows the group.

PROFILE

WILLIAM PERRY
VERMONT BICYCLE TOURING

"I believe that Vermont is the best state for a bicycling touring company," declares William Perry, the president and owner of Vermont Bicycle Touring. "Our population is extremely rural, living for the most part in small villages dotted with country inns. That way you can pedal from village to village and never feel you are out in the middle of nowhere. The state possesses an excellent network of well-maintained secondary roads. We also have all that glorious scenery, usually with mountains in the distance. There are no billboards along any of our roads, thanks to a state law prohibiting them. And, finally, all this is just a day's drive from the major population centers of the East Coast."

One of the three top bicycle-touring companies in North America, the company in 1996 celebrated its 25th anniversary in business by carrying its 150,000th client. Each year it sends out 500 departures while a second company, Hiking Holidays, offers another 100. All trips go inn-to-inn, and the group size is kept to 20 or fewer. With the guidance of trained leaders, riders make their way from one quaint country inn to the next along carefully chosen routes.

"We have been at this for a long time and enjoy a good reputation for delivering well-organized, fun tours that represent great value," stresses Perry. "Our trips are reasonably priced, and the clients get a lot of value for the money they are paying. That is particularly true of our European trips, which now account for 25 percent of our business. These European trips are booming. This year all of our departures there went out fully booked."

Perry runs his company out of a renovated farmhouse and dairy barn outside Bristol, within sight of the White Mountains. The house is the administrative complex, with modern office partitions creating work space from the country rooms. The refurbished yellow barn, which he calls the "technical center," has seven floors for the storage and maintenance of the company's 700 domestic bicycles, while another 500 are stored in Europe. (The company purchases a new fleet of bicycles every three years.) In his office Perry reflects upon his company's philosophy:

"At Vermont Bicycle Touring we don't think of what we do as cycling, but rather as sightseeing by bicycle. The world is filled with so many wonderful things that people in a rush never get to see—like the friendly smile of a farmer as he proudly offers you a taste of homemade cheese, the reflection of a gorgeous tree or mountain in a crystal-clear lake, or the way the road curves to reveal a breathtaking view. Our clients are people who bicycle for recreational purposes. Most are in reasonably good shape, physically. Some may not have cycled for five years. But they all like the idea of doing something different for their vacation travel. They're not intimidated by our itineraries because we offer them three to five route options every day, ranging from the easy to the more challenging in terms of distance and difficulty. Of course, a support van accompanies each group so people can ride if they get exhausted. The atmosphere on all our trips is one of noncompetitiveness. People stop and look around in the villages and visit the sights. And at night we always put them up at pleasant country inns or smaller, fine hotels abroad."

Perry's background before his acquisition of Vermont Bicycle Tours in 1985 was one of business mixed with outdoor recreation. While he was earning his business degree at the University of Colorado, he was a member of the ski team. Later he went on to coach the likes of Olympic notables Bob Beattie and Billy Kidd. He then joined the Olin Ski Company and worked there for 12 years, ending as the firm's vice-president of marketing. He left Olin in 1982 to become president of Daiway, a Japanese sporting-goods company based on the West Coast. After three years he missed his roots in New England and returned to look for a small business to purchase.

"I wanted something that was not just an attractive business but would also provide an enjoyable lifestyle," he recalls today. "I was very lucky to find Vermont Bicycle Touring. It's a real business, and the lifestyle it provides is terrific."

In 1985 Vermont Bicycle Touring was a small company specializing exclusively in bicycle tours in Vermont. It had been founded in 1971 by a college professor who liked biking and thought that Vermont was a perfect place for weekend bicycle trips. He introduced the organized bicycle tour, pioneering the concept of guided inn-to-inn trips.

"When I bought Vermont Bicycle Touring, the emphasis in the company was on serious bikers," Perry remembers. "There was little concern about the amenities of food and shelter. Where you biked was of primary importance. Where you stayed was secondary. The standard accommodation then was four people to a room. A married couple had to pay extra to get a room to themselves. We've come a long way since then! There has been a major evolution because of the client demand for higher qualities of lodging and restaurants. Instead of bunkhouse-style rooms, cyclists now enjoy four-star inns and gourmet meals. Over the years competitors watched what we were doing and saw it was a good idea. As a result, this has become the norm for the industry."

Perry immediately began reorganizing the company, introduced computers, and diversified the range of trip offerings beyond Vermont's borders. Within two years he was running trips in Maine, New Zealand, and England. Gradually, he expanded into the Mid-Atlantic states and Europe.

In 1987 Perry began Hiking Holidays. "It was a logical expansion to our business. Hiking Holidays is the same concept as Vermont Bicycle Touring. We stay at country inns. It's a guided, escorted vacation. We take care of everything for our clients. The difference is that they are hiking and walking. The people who sign up for those trips are usually older and prefer a slower pace than our cyclists. At the start we had just Vermont trips—in fact, these are still our bread-and-butter trips. But today Hiking Holidays offers a broad range of trips. In 1997 we introduced walking trips abroad in Italy, Austria, Spain, Costa Rica, and New Zealand."

Perry then acquired Travent International, a bicycle-touring company that focused on upscale European trips built around the finest hotels and châteaus in the different regions and went head-to-head in competition with Butterfield & Robinson. In 1997 he redefined the company to handle private, luxury European biking vacations after learning that people in that high income bracket like to travel with their friends on their own terms and add special features to their trips not normally available.

Perry relaxes at his office desk and reflects on the satisfactions of his life. "I've been pretty lucky, getting to mix business with pleasure," he says. "What pleases me the most are all the letters I receive from clients, and 97 percent are enthusiastic about the good time they experienced with us. I think this happens because we, as a company, have absorbed a lot of Vermont values over the years. Vermonters have an image as reliable, trustworthy people who do things the old-fashioned way with an emphasis on hard work and character. That describes perfectly this company and the people who work here."

3
WILDLIFE AND NATURAL HISTORY EXPEDITIONS

"There is something about safari life that makes you forget your troubles and feel the whole time as if you had drunk half a bottle of champagne—bubbling over with heartfelt gratitude for being alive," Isak Dinesen wrote in *Out of Africa.*

Wildlife and natural history expeditions offer marvelous opportunities to learn about diverse habitats, see and photograph rare forms of animal and plant life, climb unusual geological formations, and travel through exotic worlds. Naturalists often accompany these trips, turning them into learning experiences that pave the way for a greater understanding of the world's wild places.

East Africa is the world's premiere destination for wildlife safaris. Every year the game-thronged plains of Kenya and Tanzania draw record numbers of visitors who book safaris by Land Cruiser, hot-air balloon, camel or horseback, foot, and raft. Each offers its own unique advantages. A park such as Masai Mara takes on an entirely different perspective when viewed by foot instead of from the inside of a vehicle.

The world offers countless Edens waiting to be explored. The Galapagos Islands and Antarctica are two other major areas with superb wildlife. But the options are virtually unlimited. Adventure travelers can kayak with orcas off British Columbia, observe active volcanoes and geysers in Iceland, boat through the great Amazonian rain forest, watch tigers from atop an elephant in India's Kanha National Park, pet a gray whale in Baja California, and canoe through the Okefenokee National Wildlife Refuge.

AFRICA

BOTSWANA

Botswana Camping Safari

Botswana is roughly the size of Kenya but with only 1 million inhabitants. Its Okavango Delta region offers a magnificent profusion of wildlife with some of the finest game-viewing in all Africa. This expedition starts in Zimbabwe with a visit to Victoria Falls, then crosses the border into Botswana for stays in Moremi and Chobe National Parks, which have some of the largest concentrations of elephants still left in Africa. The days here are taken up with game drives and bush hikes. Several days are spent in the legendary Okavango Delta, a 9,000-square-mile network of lagoons and waterways similar to Florida's Everglades. One of the most unique and pristine wildlife areas in Africa, it supports a veritable garden of exotic and colorful flora and fauna.

ETHIOPIA

Exploring in the Simien Mountains

After many years of civil strife, Ethiopia is now open to the world again, permitting outside travelers the opportunity to experience one of Africa's most fascinating countries, its numerous historical sites, and exotic wildlife. Travelers spend a full week trekking through the mysterious Simien Mountains, the fourth-highest range in Africa, a stupendous collection of pinnacles, plateaus, chasms, cliffs, and tabletopped mountains. The area supports numerous rare species, including the Gelada baboon, which has a shaggy mane like a lion, and the Simien fox, found nowhere else on earth. Trekkers have the chance to climb Ras Dashen (at 15,157 feet, Ethiopia's highest peak) and Buhait (number two, at 14,796 feet). Mules carry all camping equipment and supplies. Pre- and post-trek visits are made to Lalibela, the isolated village where numerous Coptic churches have been carved out of bedrock; Gondar, with its impressive medieval castles and churches; Lake Tana, the source of the Nile, where several ancient monasteries on some of the remote islands will be visited; and finally the Awash River, for a day-long rafting trip down easy white water.

Operator:
Mountain Travel-Sobek, 6420 Fairmount Ave., El Cerrito, Calif. 94530; (800) 227-2384 or (415) 527-8100.
Price: Expensive.
Season: May through September.
Length: 18 days.
Accommodations: Tented camps. Five percent discount with BBAT coupon.

Operator:
Geographic Expeditions, 2627 Lombard St., San Francisco, Calif. 94123; (415) 922-0448.
Price: Expensive.
Season: November.
Length: 18 days.
Accommodations: Tent camps and hotels. Five percent discount with BBAT coupon.

"A lion chased me up a tree, and I greatly enjoyed the view from the top."

Confucius

KENYA

Classic Kenya Tented Safari

Operator:
Journeys International,
4011 Jackson Rd., Ann
Arbor, Mich. 48103;
(800) 255-8735 or
(313) 665-4407.
Price: Moderate.
Season: Year-round.
Length: 17 days.
Accommodations: Tented
camps. Five percent dis-
count with BBAT coupon.

Participants on this 17-day safari visit a variety of
Kenyan game parks. These include an afternoon
visit the first day to Nairobi National Park, an excellent place to see rare black rhinos; Samburu
National Reserve and the northern frontier district; El Karama Ranch on the western slope of
Mount Kenya, one of the few ranches taking an
active role in the preservation of wildlife; magnificent Lake Nakuru, where hundreds of thousands
of flamingos can be seen bathing and courting;
Hell's Gate National Park, where the volcanic
steam jets are an unforgettable sight; and the Masai
Mara Game Reserve, for game-viewing from a hot-
air balloon. Group hiking opportunities are provided in the more remote areas.

Deluxe Safari for Disabled Travelers

Operator:
Directions Unlimited,
720 N. Bedford Rd.,
Bedford Hills, N.Y. 10507;
(800) 533-5343 or
(914) 241-1700.
Price: Moderate.
Season: Year-round.
Length: 13 days.
Accommodations: Lodges
and hotels.

The operator has experience escorting groups of
disabled travelers on safari in Kenya. One seat is
removed from a nine-passenger minibus to accommodate four people and their wheelchairs comfortably. A professional assistant for the disabled
also accompanies the group. The safari itinerary
includes the Masai Mara, Lake Nakuru, and
Amboseli National Parks, with stops at the Karen
Blixen Homestead and Museum and the Mt. Kenya
Safari Club.

NAMIBIA

Namibia Explorer

This amazing corner of southern Africa is one of
the continent's last frontiers and is virtually unvis-
ited by American travelers. Namibia is a vast,
sparsely inhabited land, dry and silent, which

A highlight in rarely visited Namibia is the vast collection of red sand dunes in the Central Namib Desert
Journeys International

nonetheless supports a rich variety of wildlife. Members of this safari travel by minivan to the major wilderness areas. Highlights include visits to the enormous sand dunes of the Central Namib Desert; the Damaraland Wilderness Reserve, famous for its desert-dwelling elephants; Etosha National Park, home to one of the richest and most diverse collections of wildlife in Africa; and Mudumu National Park, where three days are spent exploring this fragile wetland system by boat and foot. The safari ends with visits to Chobe National Park in Botswana and Victoria Falls in Zimbabwe.

Operator: Journeys International, 4011 Jackson Rd., Ann Arbor, Mich. 48103; (800) 255-8735 or (313) 665-4407. *Price:* Moderate. *Season:* February through November. *Length:* 18 days. *Accommodations:* Tent camps and lodges. Five percent discount with BBAT coupon.

TANZANIA

Tanzania Off the Beaten Path

Participants on this mobile tented safari first spend a week visiting the better-known destinations, such as Lake Manyara, the Serengeti, and the celebrated Ngorongoro Crater. Then they set out for two of East Africa's least-visited and most compelling national parks, starting with the remote Selous Game Reserve in southeastern Tanzania: 18,000 square miles of untouched bush, dense forest, and

Operator:
Geographic Expeditions,
2627 Lombard St.,
San Francisco, Calif.
94123; (415) 922-0448.
Price: Expensive.
Season: August and
December.
Length: 18 days.
Accommodations: Tented
camps. Five percent dis-
count with BBAT coupon.

dramatic river gorges virtually devoid of human visitors. It supports one of Africa's greatest concentrations of big game, including 45,000 elephants.
The handful of travelers to the Selous get around
by foot safari along game trails or by small boats
down the Rufiji River. Then expedition members
visit Ruaha National Park, second in size to
Serengeti but largely unknown except to a few
visitors who like to view their game in undeveloped
parks, away from the crowds. The wildlife selection
and variety in Ruaha matches or exceeds most of
the other, more celebrated parks. For travelers
eager to experience East Africa as it was 50 years
ago, Selous and Ruaha are the places to go.

UGANDA

The Ultimate Gorilla Safari

Operator:
Mountain Travel-Sobek,
6420 Fairmount Ave.,
El Cerrito, Calif. 94530;
(800) 227-2384 or
(415) 527-8100.
Price: Expensive.
Season: February, June, and
August.
Length: 18 days; operator
also offers 6- and
8-day trips.
Accommodations: Tent
camps and hotels. Five percent discount with BBAT
coupon.

"There is more meaning and understanding in
exchanging a glance with a gorilla than with any
other animal I know," David Attenborough once
observed. Few people have ever seen mountain
gorillas at close range in the wild. The participants
on this safari begin with a sampling of several of
Uganda's finest parks, including legendary
Murchison Falls National Park, for a boat trip on
the Nile River to see its large populations of crocodiles and hippos. They then head to the Virunga
Mountains' lush equatorial jungle. Guided by
rangers, they hike through the dense rain-forest
vegetation to an area where several gorilla family
groups have become habituated to the presence of
nearby human beings. Two days are spent watching
these extraordinary animals, often from a distance
of only a few feet. A typical family group includes
an enormous silverback male, females with babies,
and young gorillas.

ASIA

INDIA

India Wildlife Expedition

With one of the finest systems of parks and sanctuaries in Asia, India offers an exciting alternative to African wildlife safaris. Accompanied by a naturalist, members of this safari begin their trip outside Delhi at Bharatpur, a bird sanctuary where over 100 species can easily be observed in a day. Next is a visit to Bandhavgarh National Park and nearby Kanha National Park in central eastern India, where participants mount elephants for game drives through the grassland meadows to search for Royal Bengal tigers and leopards. Three days are spent in Kaziranga National Park, perhaps the finest wild-animal park east of Kenya, established to preserve the rare one-horned Indian rhinoceros. Here again, game is viewed from atop elephants. Visits are also made to Agra, the Taj Mahal, and the celebrated temples of Khajuraho.

Operator:
Nature Expeditions International, P.O. Box 11496, Eugene, Ore. 97440; (800) 869-0639 or (541) 484-6529.
Price: Expensive.
Season: November through March.
Length: 16 days.
Accommodations: Lodges and hotels. Five percent discount with BBAT coupon.

"Travel, especially if one travels alone, can make the mind peculiarly alive. Meanings and dangers flow by like colors, like smells, the fluid nuances of place. Real travel is work and may profit from an edge of danger. . . . The final point of travel is always individual and indefinable: it makes the neutrons glow in a new way, It excites possibilities. People and scenery mean worlds they cannot mean except when we come to them for the first time as strangers. It is always oneself that one encounters in traveling: other people, of course, other parts of the world, other times carved into stone now overgrown with jungle—but still, always, oneself."

LANCE MORROW,
TIME, MAY 31, 1982

AUSTRALASIA

AUSTRALIA

Untouched Australia

Operator: Natural Habitat Adventures, 2945 Center Green Court S., Boulder, Colo. 80301; (800) 543-8917 or (303) 449-3711. *Price:* Expensive. *Season:* July and November. *Length:* 20 days. *Accommodations:* Hotels and bush camps. Five percent discount with BBAT coupon.

When the Aborigines arrived in Australia over 40,000 years ago, they found an isolated continent with an odd variety of animal life that exists nowhere else in the world. These expeditions focus on those wild parts of the continent overlooked by most travelers, including Cape Tribulation National Park, an excellent place to observe nocturnal animals; Lakefield National Park in the Outback, with its large populations of kangaroos, crocodiles, parrots, and pythons; Hamilton Island, one of the outer islands in the Whitsunday group, heavily covered with a pine forest, where the group will spend two days snorkeling and diving on the Great Barrier Reef; the rain forest of Eungella National Park, which supports a substantial population of duck-billed platypus; and Kangaroo Island, with its rich collection of kangaroos, koalas, echidnas, fairy penguins, sea lions, and fur seals.

Camel Safari in the Red Center

Operator: Outer Edge Expeditions, 45500 Pontiac Trail, Walled Lake, Mich. 48390; (800) 322-5235 or (313) 624-5140. *Price:* Moderate. *Season:* April, May, August, and September. *Length:* 10 days. *Accommodations:* Bush camps. Five percent discount with BBAT coupon.

The epitome of the Australian Outback, the Red Center is an uncharted red-sand desert—open, sunbaked, and vast. The ancient, tilted Macdonnell Ranges offer a splendid panorama of eroded escarpments, gorges, valleys, and dry riverbeds. Participants explore this wilderness from atop camels, experiencing a nomadic lifestyle almost forgotten elsewhere in the world. Daily activities include visits to Aboriginal rock paintings, explorations of unusual geologic formations, and swims in remote water holes. The area abounds in wildlife, including kangaroos, brumbies, dingoes, wild camels, and a profusion of colorful birds.

CANADA

A kayak becomes the best viewing platform from which to observe the activities of orcas off Canada's western coast

David Arcese/Northern Lights Expeditions

BRITISH COLUMBIA

Eye-to-Eye with Orcas

Off the west coast of Canada, in the Inside Passage, is found the largest and most accessible concentration of orcas in the world. Each summer more than 200 of the big black-and-white killer whales gather, drawn by millions of salmon on the way to their spawning grounds. These expeditions use extremely stable 20-foot sea kayaks to paddle quietly among the pods of orcas, often coming within a few feet of their 6-foot-high dorsal fins. Hydrophones in the water capture orca vocalizations from as far as 5 miles away. The area abounds in sea lions, black bear, eagles, minke whales, deer, and porpoises. No previous kayaking experience is required. The operator provides all camping equipment.

Operator: Northern Lights Expeditions, P.O. Box 4289, Bellingham, Wash. 98227; (800) 754-7402 or (360) 734-6334.
Price: Moderate.
Season: Weekly departures from June through September.
Length: 6 days.
Accommodations: Tent camps on uninhabited islands. Five percent discount with BBAT coupon.

"It is not worthwhile to go around the world to count the cats in Zanzibar."

HENRY DAVID THOREAU,
WALDEN

An Inuit Eskimo examines the landscape at the North Pole on an Arctic Odysseys expedition

George Holton/Arctic Odysseys

MANITOBA

Polar Bear Expedition

Operator: Natural Habitat Adventures, 2945 Center Green Court S., Boulder, Colo. 80301; (800) 543-8917 or (303) 449-3711. *Price:* Expensive. *Season:* October. *Length:* 8 days. *Accommodations:* Hotels. Five percent discount with BBAT coupon.

To the Eskimo people, the polar bear symbolized wisdom and strength. But to early European explorers, the big bears were fearsome white ghosts that could easily kill a man or ravage his food caches. Participants on these expeditions travel to Churchill, the northernmost town in Manitoba, where large numbers of polar bears congregate each winter. Members ride across the frozen tundra in specially constructed vehicles to observe and photograph the behavior of these magnificent bears, and may also see Arctic foxes, rock and willow ptarmigans, and snowy owls.

NORTH POLE

Journey to the Top of the World

The North Pole has long held a curious fascination as the ultimate travel destination. This expedition is just the thing for amateur adventurers eager to do the "Great Pole Vault." Participants fly to Eureka, a Canadian weather station located at 80 degrees North latitude on the west coast of Ellesmere Island. Here they experience the life of an isolated research station while observing packs of Arctic wolves at close range. Weather permitting, they then depart on their chartered turboprop Twin Otter for the flight to the top of the world. A stop is made at Lake Hazen, the northernmost lake in the world, to take on fuel from a cache. The plane then lands at the North Pole for a visit of several hours. Three days are also spent at Grise Fiord, where members and their Inuit guides board snowmobiles to visit nearby glaciers and Eskimo villages.

Operator: Arctic Odysseys, 2000 McGilvra Blvd. E., Seattle, Wash. 98112; (206) 325-1977.
Price: Expensive.
Season: April.
Length: 7 days.
Accommodations: Hotels. Five percent discount with BBAT coupon.

NORTHWEST TERRITORIES

A Congregation of 1,000 Beluga Whales in the High Arctic

One of the last remote and unexplored areas of the globe is that of the far north. Members of these expeditions spend nights at a comfortable lodge on Somerset Island, 480 miles north of the Arctic Circle and only 900 miles south of the geographic North Pole. During the long Arctic days they explore the spectacular Arctic landscape, home to numerous mammals and bird species specially adapted to survive the harsh environment. The highlight is the congregation of 1,000 beluga whales at the mouth of a river just 15 minutes' walk from the lodge. The whales are in the height of their nursing season and can be observed rolling in

Operator: Natural Habitat Adventures, 2945 Center Green Court S., Boulder, Colo. 80301; (800) 543-8917 or (303) 449-3711.
Price: Expensive.
Season: July.
Length: 10 days.
Accommodations: Lodge. Five percent discount with BBAT coupon.

the gravel at the mouth of the river in an effort to remove their molting skin. Polar bears are also common in the area, as are the "unicorns of the sea," the famed narwhals. Participants also visit the grave sites of the ill-fated Franklin expedition and the famed seabird island of Prince Leopold.

The annual spring birth of thousands of harp seal pups is one of North America's greatest wildlife sights

Natural Habitat Adventures

QUEBEC

The Harp Seals of St. Lawrence

Operator: Natural Habitat Adventures, 2945 Center Green Court S., Boulder, Colo. 80301; (800) 543-8917 or (303) 449-3711. *Price:* Expensive. *Season:* March. *Length:* 6 days. *Accommodations:* Hotels. Five percent discount with BBAT coupon.

Every March some 250,000 harp seals enter the Gulf of St. Lawrence to bear their young on the vast floating ice fields just west of the picturesque Magdalene Islands. Known as "whitecoats," these adorable newborn pups shed their snowy-white fur and turn grey within three weeks. In 1987 Canada banned commercial hunting of whitecoats, and today is working toward the creation of a tourist industry to boost the local economy. Participants on these adventures travel by helicopter from their hotel to the nearby ice floes and walk among thousands of mother seals and their pups. The nature photography is superb.

Be careful going in search of adventure—it's ridiculously easy to find.

WILLIAM LEAST HEAT MOON,
BLUE HIGHWAYS: A JOURNEY INTO AMERICA

CARIBBEAN

DOMINICAN REPUBLIC

The Humpback Whales of the Silver Bank

In late winter and early spring hundreds of humpback whales congregate between the Grand Turk and the Dominican Republic, an area considered to be the primary mating and calving ground for the North Atlantic humpback whale. Over 1,000 of these big whales migrate to the shallow Silver Bank from their northern feeding grounds off Canada and Western Europe, providing divers with perhaps the finest whale-diving in the world. Some of these 60-foot-long animals weigh more than 50 tons. Large groups of males, called "rowdy groups," compete aggressively for receptive females. The result is a ceaseless line of challengers, almost constantly breaching, ramming, slamming, lob-tailing, or fin-slapping. Particularly captivating are the famed humpbacks' songs. Passengers will also have considerable opportunity to snorkel among these big whales, observing their behavior at close range.

Operator:
Natural Habitat Adventures,
2945 Center Green Court S.,
Boulder, Colo. 80301;
(800) 543-8917 or
(303) 449-3711.
Price: Expensive.
Season: February and
March.
Length: 10 days.
Accommodations: Shipboard
cabins on a motor yacht.
Five percent discount with
BBAT coupon.

LATIN AMERICA

BELIZE

A Naturalist's Odyssey into the Mayan Heartland

Largely overlooked by travelers to Latin America, Belize boasts an extraordinary diversity of flora and fauna—more than 500 species of birds, 250 varieties of orchids, and many of the last wild jaguars. This expedition visits rain forests, pine-covered mountains, Mayan ruins, waterfalls, caves, and the world's second-largest barrier reef. Participants

Operator:
Journeys International,
4011 Jackson Rd.,
Ann Arbor, Mich. 48103;
(800) 255-8735 or
(313) 665-4407.
Price: Expensive.
Season: December through
July.
Length: 8 days.
Accommodations: Hotels and
lodges. Five percent discount with BBAT coupon.

explore the Mountain Pine Ridge Forest Reserve, which boasts both Mayan ruins and the Rio Frio Cave in the Chiquibul rain forest, a site of ancient Mayan rituals; Tikal National Park across the border in Guatemala, which contains 3,000 separate Mayan ruins; the Che Chem Ha Cave with its cache of large pots dating back 1,500 years; a boat trip down the Macal River for the excellent birding; and finally, Southwater Cay on the Barrier Reef, for two days of snorkeling over the spectacular coral reef formations.

"Now at last I know with absolute certainty that we travel to find ourselves. By placing ourselves in all possible circumstances which, like projectors, will illuminate our different facets, we come to grasp all of a sudden which of our facets is fully, uniquely, ourselves."

ELLA MAILLART,
"MY PHILOSOPHY OF TRAVEL"

BRAZIL
Pantanal Wildlife Adventure

Operator:
Mountain Travel-Sobek,
6420 Fairmount Ave.,
El Cerrito, Calif. 94530;
(800) 227-2384 or
(510) 527-8100.
Price: Expensive.
Season: June, August, and
September.
Length: 13 days.
Accommodations: Lodges.
Five percent discount with
BBAT coupon.

This exciting expedition focuses on the Pantanal, the world's largest and least-known wetlands. Located in southwestern Brazil, its 54,000 square miles offer the traveler one of the most extensive and (unlike the Amazonian jungle) easily accessible displays of wildlife in all South America. The area teems with 600 species of tropical birds, caimans (the South American crocodile), capybaras (the world's largest rodent), ocelots, marsh deer, tapirs, and jaguars. Excursions are by hiking, horseback, and boat, all accompanied by bilingual researchers. The final stop is the celebrated Iguaçu Falls on the Brazil–Argentina border.

Amazon Expedition

There is no place like the Amazon, with its network of waterways sprawling across an area two-thirds the size of the United States. One-fifth of all the river water in the world spills from the Amazon's mouth into the Atlantic Ocean. The river supports some 2,000 species of fish, 1,800 species of birds, and 200 species of land mammals, including the world's largest ant (1.4 inches), longest snake (38 feet), and biggest rodent (4 feet from head to tail). Its vast jungle also harbors approximately 50,000 Indians who are largely untouched by civilization. Members of this expedition travel by plane, riverboat, and dugout canoe, covering 3,000 miles to experience the Amazon from its mouth near Belem to its tributaries in Peru. Highlights include a four-day cruise on a vintage Amazon riverboat and four nights at rustic jungle lodges in areas rich in wildlife. A naturalist accompanies each group.

Operator: Nature Expeditions International, P.O. Box 11496, Eugene, Ore. 97440; (800) 869-0639 or (541) 484-6529.
Price: Expensive.
Season: March, June, August, and October.
Length: 17 days.
Accommodations: Hotels, lodges, and riverboat cabins. Five percent discount with BBAT coupon.

COSTA RICA

Tropical Wilderness Explorer

The small country of Costa Rica boasts a world-class national park system with exceptional birdlife and flora that includes over 1,000 species of orchids alone, world-class rivers, white-sand beaches, lush mountain rain forests, and active volcanoes. Participants on this popular trip cover the full range of the country's natural attractions from pristine beaches to the tropical rain forests. They visit Arenal Volcano on Lake Arenal, a prime area for bird-watching; Monteverde Cloud Forest Reserve, perhaps the best place to view the resplendent quetzal, widely regarded as the most beautiful bird in the Americas; and Tiskita, a rain-forest reserve in the remote region of Golfito, on the southern Pacific coast overlooking a deserted tropical beach.

Operator: Journeys International, 4011 Jackson Rd., Ann Arbor, Mich. 48103; (800) 255-8735 or (313) 665-4407.
Price: Moderate.
Season: January through March.
Length: 10 days.
Accommodations: Comfortable lodges. Five percent discount with BBAT coupon.

ECUADOR

In the Footsteps of Charles Darwin

Operator:
Journeys International,
4011 Jackson Rd.,
Ann Arbor, Mich. 48103;
(800) 255-8735 or
(313) 665-4407.
Price: Expensive.
Season: Year-round.
Length: 11 days.
Accommodations: Shipboard
cabins, featuring air-
conditioned bunk-style beds
with private baths and
showers. Five percent discount with BBAT coupon.

"A separate center of creation," Charles Darwin marveled at the Galapagos Islands, the inspiration for much of his thesis on evolution. An archipelago of active volcanoes and arid, rocky terrain, long celebrated as home to some of the strangest and most wonderful wildlife imaginable, these islands are one of the world's greatest natural treasures. Participants on these expeditions travel aboard comfortable yachts to explore all the important islands in this exotic Eden. This is an environment devoid of natural predators, in which the mammal, bird, and reptile species exist peacefully side by side. Participants also have numerous opportunities to snorkel and dive.

MEXICO

Whale-Watching in Baja California

Operator:
Oceanic Society
Expeditions, Fort Mason
Center, Bldg. E, San
Francisco, Calif. 94123;
(800) 326-7491 or
(415) 441-1106.
Price: Expensive.
Season: February.
Length: 9 days.
Accommodations: Shipboard
cabins. Five percent dis-
count with BBAT coupon.

Located on the Pacific side of the Baja California peninsula, San Ignacio Lagoon offers the visitor nothing less than the finest whale-watching in the world. More than 2,000 gray whales are in residence there each winter. This is also the home of the "friendly," or "petting," whales. Whale cows, often with calves in tow, present themselves to the small boats filled with observers, patiently lie alongside, and expect to have their heads, backs, and sides massaged. Nowhere else can one see such a range of whale behavior, including courtship, copulation, birth, sleeping, spy-hopping, and breaching. There is also excellent birding in the nearby saltwater mangrove swamps. These trips depart from San Diego on a comfortable sport-fishing vessel and spend three days in San Ignacio Lagoon. Stops are also made at the remote and beautiful Mexican islands of Todos Santos, San Benitos, Cedros, and San Martin, each offering an abundance of wildlife.

San Ignacio Lagoon on the Pacific coast of Baja California is home to the friendly, or petting, whale phenomenon

James C. Simmons

The Monarch Butterfly Migration

Each year up to 100,000,000 monarch butterflies migrate from the United States and Canada to the mountains of Michoacán. At an elevation of 10,000 feet, the tall forest provides the perfect environment for their time of semi-dormancy. From November until spring they cluster atop one another, providing warmth and conserving energy for their migration northward. Participants on this expedition find themselves in a world of black and orange in which all the trees are draped from top to bottom with butterflies, sometimes in such numbers that branches break under their weight.

Operator: Remarkable Journeys, P.O. Box 31855, Houston, Tex. 77231; (800) 856-1993 or (713) 721-2517. *Price:* Expensive. *Season:* February. *Length:* 7 days. *Accommodations:* Hotel. Five percent discount with BBAT coupon.

PERU

A Birding Extravaganza at the Macaw Collpa on the Tambopata River

The focus of this adventure set deep in the Peruvian rain forest is the famous macaw collpa (or clay lick) on the Tambopata River. Every day this site attracts hundreds of macaws and parrots, representatives of nine different species. For birders this is one of the great spectacles in the Western

Operator:
Journeys International,
4011 Jackson Rd., Ann
Arbor, Mich. 48103;
(800) 255-8735 or
(313) 665-4407.
Price: Expensive.
Season: April, July, and
September.
Length: 7 days.
Accommodations: Jungle
lodge. Five percent dis-
count with BBAT coupon.

Hemisphere. At the beginning of the trip participants travel six hours by motorized canoes up the
Tambopata River to the Tambopata Research
Center. This serves as the base for a detailed exploration of the surrounding rain forest. The area is
rich in animal life, including giant river otters,
caiman, ocelots, turtles, and a vast variety of
birdlife. Nights are spent in a jungle lodge.

THE PACIFIC

MIDWAY

Midway Atoll: Natural and Maritime History

Operator:
Oceanic Society
Expeditions, Fort Mason
Center, Bldg. E, San
Francisco, Calif. 94123;
(800) 326-7491 or
(415) 441-1106.
Price: Expensive.
Season: Year-round.
Length: 8 days.
Accommodations: Rooms in
restored military barracks.
Five percent discount with
BBAT coupon.

Midway is a remote coral atoll located 1,250 miles
west-northwest of Hawaii. Best known as the staging
area for one of the fiercest battles of World War II, it
supports one of the most spectacular concentrations
of seabirds in the Pacific, including a half-million
nesting pairs of the Laysan albatrosses (better
known as gooney birds) and the second largest
black-footed albatross colony. Thirteen other species
of migratory seabirds nest there along with four
species of migratory shorebirds. The endangered
Hawaiian monk seal also utilizes the atoll. Off limits
to civilians for over 50 years, Midway welcomed its
first tourists in 1997. The U.S. Fish & Wildlife
Service has established strict guidelines to minimize
visitors' impact on the ecosystem. Activities include
snorkeling, scuba diving, bird-watching, historical
tours, swimming, and beachcombing.

MICRONESIA

Snorkeling Expedition in Palau

Travelers on this adventure explore at their leisure
one of the of most legendary atolls in the Pacific.

Palau is a giant coral lagoon filled with islands sheltering more species of marine life than any similar-sized area in the world. It's a snorkeler's paradise, with a dazzling abundance and array of rainbow colored fish, sponges, and corals. The famous rock islands are a maze of unsurpassed beauty, tropical gardens atop limestone ridges, set in glass-clear waters. A naturalist guide accompanies the group to Turtle Cove, Soft Coral Arch, Ngemelis Wall, Jelly Fish Lake, and the jungle-capped Rock Islands. Palau rates among the top three snorkeling destinations in the world.

Operator: Oceanic Society Expeditions, Fort Mason Center, Bldg. E, San Francisco, Calif. 94123; (800) 326-7491 or (415) 441-1106.
Price: Expensive.
Season: June and December.
Length: 10 days.
Accommodations: Hotel. Five percent discount with BBAT coupon.

UNITED STATES

ALASKA

A Half-Day Flight to See the Brown Bears of Kodiak

The grizzly bear is the largest and most dangerous carnivore in the world, reaching up to 9 feet when standing on its hind legs and weighing more than 1,200 pounds in old age. Generally, the big bears are viewed only from a remote distance. However, participants on these half-day trips fly on float-planes to pristine lakes, where bears can often be seen nearby on the shoreline, digging clams or grazing on seaweed and grass in the lush green meadows. The flights to and from the viewing areas cross fjord-like bays, glaciers, and meadows where elk, deer, and caribou graze. The operator guarantees bears or clients' money is refunded.

Operator: Uyak Air Service, P.O. Box 4188, Kodiak, Alaska 99615; (800) 303-3407 or (907) 486-3407.
Price: Expensive.
Season: June through September.
Length: 4 hours.
Five percent discount with BBAT coupon.

Marine Mammal Discovery

These sea-kayaking adventures focus on the marine mammals in the straits of the Point Adolphus area in the midst of the Tongass National Forest. The

Operator:
Alaska Discovery, 5449
Shaune Dr., Suite 4,
Juneau, Alaska 99801;
(800) 586-1911 or
(907) 780-6226.
Price: Expensive.
Season: June through
August.
Length: 6 days.
Accommodations: Tent
camps. Five percent dis-
count with BBAT coupon.

nutrient-rich waters there support large populations of humpback whales, sea otters, seals, and sea
lions. The distances are kept short to allow maxi-
mum viewing of the area's spectacular wildlife.
There is also great fishing and birding. Point
Adolphus is the favorite summer home of the
humpback whale. The deep water off the point
contains abundant food sources, and the whales
are the most active there. Two-person kayaks are
used; these have more room for storage and
greater stability. The trip begins and ends in the
small settlement of Gustavus in Glacier Bay
National Park.

Fall Caribou Migration

Operator:
Sourdough Outfitters,
P.O. Box 90, Bettles, Alaska
99726; (907) 692-5252.
Price: Expensive.
Season: August.
Length: 5 days.
Accommodations: Tent
camps. Five percent dis-
count with BBAT coupon.

The annual migration of the 180,000-strong
Porcupine caribou herd is North America's most
awesome wildlife spectacle, as close as we come to
the great Serengeti migration. Participants on this
expedition settle into a base camp at the start of the
Arctic fall, when the herds of caribou are on their
meandering march to their wintering grounds
south of the Brooks Range. The bands vary from
several large bulls to groups of a few hundred.
Instead of the rather moth-eaten spring caribou

The Adventure Travel Hall of Fame: STAN PRICE

"My grizzly bears make fine
pets," the old man said with a
laugh, looking much younger
than his 84 years. "I'd rather
have a bear than a dog. Of course, you can't
housebreak them. But then again there ain't no
thieves going to break into my cabin when I'm
away for a few days—not with all these grizzly
bears prowling around my place!"

The two of us conversed in July 1982
on the front porch of Stan Price's cabin,
located deep in the Alaskan wilderness
along the southwestern coast of Admiralty
Island. His nearest human neighbors were
200 Indians, 50 miles away. Since 1952 he
had lived as a frontier woodsman in this
terribly wild Garden of Eden, the perfect
embodiment of the romantic dream of

shedding their hair, these magnificent animals have fully grown antlers and lush winter coats.

ARIZONA

Arizona Sonora Desert Natural History Tour

Southern Arizona has an environment supporting three distinct desert ecosystems where some 30 cactus species flourish, ranging from the giant saguaro to the minuscule fishhook. Gila woodpeckers drill nest holes in cactus boles, and elf owls roost among their spines. Visitors to the remote wildernesses may also see bighorn sheep, mule deer, and the elusive peccary roaming the stark, sun-blistered mountains, rocky canyons, and sweeping outwash plains. The operator offers wildlife safaris throughout the most pristine of the wilderness areas. Sites visited include Ramsay Canyon Preserve, the best place in the United States to see hummingbirds; Cave Creek Canyon on the eastern slope of the Chiricahua Mountains, which the pioneers called "Wonderland of Rocks," where over 330 species of birds have been identified; and Sonoita Creek Preserve, an area rich in fossils. A naturalist accompanies all groups.

Operator:
Baja's Frontier Tours,
907 E. Freeman Pl.,
Tucson, Ariz. 85719;
(800) 726-7231 or
(520) 887-2340.
Price: Moderate.
Season: April through
January.
Length: 7 days.
Accommodations: Hotels.
Five percent discount with
BBAT coupon.

closeness to nature with little need for the products of civilization. One of Alaska's legendary figures, his reputation rested on his uncanny ability to befriend the great grizzly, the state's most dangerous animal.

Unlike other Alaskans, who usually carry rifles when they venture into the wilderness for fear of running into bears, Price had only his walking stick to protect him. "A little tap on the nose will do it every time," he said confidently. "That's a very sensitive area for a bear."

The woods around Price's cabin on Pack Creek are a refuge to several dozen of the big bears, many of them sows with cubs. "I know them all by name," Price said quietly. "I raised a lot of them from cubs after their mothers were killed, and then turned them loose. Each bear has its own personality. Some are more sociable than others. But most of the time we get along real well as neighbors. I never had any children. These bears are sort of like family to me."

Cross-Country Skiing along the North Rim of the Grand Canyon

Operator: Canyoneers, P.O. Box 2997, Flagstaff, Ariz. 86003; (800) 525-0924 or (602) 526-0924. *Price:* Moderate. *Season:* January through March. *Length:* 3, 4, and 5 days. *Accommodations:* Park lodge. Ten percent discount with BBAT coupon.

The North Rim in winter is one of the Grand Canyon's best-kept secrets. Tourists cannot drive there because the road is closed by deep snow. Access is only by specially constructed snow-vans with tracks, which operate out of the historic Kaibab Lodge. The open meadows surrounded by aspen, pine, and juniper trees and rolling hills make this an ideal area for cross-country skiing. Elk and deer are common in the winter months. Skiers have the option of day trips into Grand Canyon National Park—snow conditions permitting—to ski along the North Rim to various outlooks. The *Washington Post* described the North Rim as "one of the ten best ski areas in the country."

During the winter snows, cross-country skiers can enjoy the pristine beauty of the Grand Canyon with none of the summer crowds

Canyoneers

CALIFORNIA

Jeep Tours of the Desert Wilderness near Palm Springs

Most of the Palm Springs area's 3 million annual visitors come for its splendid golf courses, swimming pools, tennis courts, and palm-shaded avenues. However, nature-lovers seeking high adventure need not despair. Desert Adventures, an ecotour jeep company, enjoys exclusive tour rights

A jeep tour is the perfect way to explore Southern California's desert wilderness
James C. Simmons

to the Santa Rosa Mountains, recently declared a National Scenic Area, and the mysterious Mecca Hills wilderness area, a rugged landscape of deeply eroded canyons and cliffs straddling the San Andreas Fault. Naturalists turn each trip into a learning experience and pave the way to a greater understanding of the region's wild places. One highlight is the visit to the palm-canyon oasis on the Cahuilla Indian Reservation, Palm Springs' finest natural attraction. There, Indians once kept cool during summer in the lush, stream-filled canyons and bathed in the hot mineral springs during winter. Visitors can walk the canyons in the footsteps of these ancient Indians in the world's largest fan-palm oasis.

Operator: Desert Adventures, 67-555 E. Palm Canyon Dr., Suite A-104, Cathedral City, Calif. 92234; (619) 324-JEEP.
Price: Moderate.
Season: Year-round.
Length: 4 hours.
Ten percent discount with BBAT coupon.

An Out-of-Africa Experience in Southern California

Owned and operated by the world-famous San Diego Zoo, the Wild Animal Park is the only American facility of its kind—a rural preserve where different species mingle much as they do in the wild, and where rare and exotic animals on the edge of extinction are bred and studied in an incomparably inviting laboratory. Some 3,000

Operator:
San Diego Wild Animal
Park, 15500 San Pasqual
Valley Rd., Escondido,
Calif. 92027;
(619) 738-5022.
Price: Moderate.
Season: Several days a week
throughout the year.
Length: 3 and 4 hours.

animals, representing 450 species, inhabit 2,200 acres. For years, animal-lovers and photographers had to be satisfied with viewing the park's animals from the confines of a silent electric monorail that glides around its perimeter. Now, groups of ten people each are permitted into the park on flatbed trucks. Accompanied by keeper-guides, visitors spend up to four hours enjoying one of the greatest opportunities anywhere in the world for observing and photographing wildlife. Although still wild, the park's animals are accustomed to the trucks' presence; they go about their business of courting, breeding, feeding, and playing, unmindful of nearby photographers snapping off dozens of rolls of film.

GEORGIA

Camping on Cumberland Island

No other East Coast barrier island can match Cumberland for its diversity of habitat, profusion of wildlife, and richness of history. With some 36,000 acres, it is the largest of the "Golden Isles of Georgia." The National Park Service owns 85 percent of the island and permits only 300 visitors each day. Transportation around the 16-mile-long

The Adventure Travel Hall of Fame:
MATTHEW A. HENSON

The first black man to reach the North Pole, Matthew A. Henson was an indispensable member of Robert Peary's numerous polar expeditions. Peary met Henson in 1887 in a Washington, D.C., shop and hired him on the spot as his personal servant. Because of his skin color, the Eskimos of Greenland looked upon Henson as a brother and taught him such important survival skills as dogsledding, igloo construction, hunting, and ice-fishing. He, in turn, learned their language and even adopted an Eskimo boy as his son. Peary's

island is strictly by foot. In the company of a naturalist, participants on this camping trip explore the four ecosystems—the beach, dunes, maritime forest, and salt marshes—that support more than 300 species of birds and mammals. At the southern end of the island the imposing ruins of Dungeness Mansion, once a social center for the Carnegie family, stretch to the sky.

Operator:
Wilderness Southeast,
711 Sandtown Rd.,
Savannah, Ga. 31410;
(912) 897-5108.
Price: Inexpensive.
Season: May and
November.
Length: 4 days.
Accommodations: Tent camp.

HAWAII

Hawaii Natural History Odyssey

Members of this expedition explore the exotic natural beauty of the Hawaii of old. Avoiding crowded beaches and high-rise hotels, they journey instead to the "Big Island" of Hawaii for two days in Volcanoes National Park to visit Kilauea Crater (one of the world's most active volcanoes), Kipuka Puaulu (a densely forested bird sanctuary surrounded by recent lava flows), and the extensive lava flows, tidal pools, and historical sites along the fabled Kona Coast. On Maui, they view the humpback whales in the Auau Channel; visit the 10,023-foot-high summit of Haleakala to explore the unique environment of this monstrous volcano; and hike through rain forests. On Kauai, the oldest and most beautiful island in the

Operator:
Nature Expeditions
International,
P.O. Box 11496, Eugene,
Ore. 97440; (800) 869-0639
or (541) 484-6529.
Price: Expensive.
Season: Year-round.
Length: 8 and 15 days.
Accommodations: Hotels.
Five percent discount with
BBAT coupon.

final expedition included 24 men, 19 sleds, and 133 dogs. Henson headed the lead party and was largely responsible for maintaining a high morale among the many Eskimo assistants. On the morning of April 6, 1909, they finally became the first men to stand at the North Pole. "The Commander gave the word, 'We will plant the stars and stripes at the North Pole,'" Henson recalled later. "And it was done. Another world's accomplishment was done and finished." After two decades of polar exploration, he returned to America to work at a New York garage and then as a messenger for the government. He died in Harlem in 1955 at the age of 89.

Hawaiian archipelago, members hike through Waimea, the "Grand Canyon of the Pacific"; photograph the variety of marine birds at Kilauea Lighthouse; walk along the Na Pali cliff trail; and board a chartered helicopter for a flight along the island's spectacular coast. A naturalist accompanies each group.

MINNESOTA

Lodge-to-Lodge Dogsled Adventure

Operator: Boundary Country Trekking, 590 Gunflint Trail, Grand Marais, Minn. 55604; (800) 322-8327 or (218) 388-9972. *Price:* Expensive. *Season:* November through March. *Length:* 2, 3, 4, and 5 days. *Accommodations:* Lodges, cabins, and yurts. Five percent discount with BBAT coupon.

Dogsledding was perfected a century ago in the Yukon frontier by prospectors and homesteaders who needed a reliable means of transportation across the frozen landscape. The operator has been offering sled-dog trips since 1978 and believes its trips are the most dog-centered mushing experiences available. Participants drive their own sled and team of dogs the entire trip through the snow-covered wilderness just south of the Canadian border. Alaskan huskies are used exclusively. The dogs are powerful and accustomed to traveling many miles in a day. No previous mushing experience is necessary—the dogs and their keeper will train you.

WYOMING

A Half-Day Wildlife Safari into the Yellowstone Backcountry

Operator: Great Plains Wildlife Institute, P.O. Box 7580, Jackson Hole, Wyo. 83001; (307) 733-2623. *Price:* Inexpensive. *Season:* Year-round. *Length:* 4 hours.

The richest wildlife preserve in the "Lower 48," Yellowstone National Park finds its most popular attractions overwhelmed by mobs of tourists each summer. Now visitors seeking some sanity far from the madding crowds can do so easily, thanks to the Great Plains Wildlife Institute. It provides both early morning and late afternoon expeditions to the backcountry for some of the finest wildlife-viewing available anywhere. Clients can expect to see a wide variety of species, including moose, bison, bighorn sheep, elk, coyotes, bald eagles, trumpeter swans, beavers, and mule deer. Transportation is a comfortable safari vehicle equipped with opening roof-hatches and spotting scopes. A naturalist driver accompanies all groups. (The operator also offers a full-day expedition.)

PROFILE

BEN BRESSLER
NATURAL HABITAT ADVENTURES

"In March of 1987 I began running trips to the Magdalen Islands in eastern Canada to see the 250,000 harp seals that come out on the ice there each winter to bear their young," Ben Bressler, the founder of Natural Habitat Adventures, recalls at his office in Boulder, Colorado. "The pups, cute little things called 'whitecoats,' change from white to gray in about three weeks. At that time they were the center of a major environmental conflict because the Canadian government allowed local hunters with baseball bats to club 250,000 of these whitecoats to death annually for their skins.

"The International Fund for Animal Welfare had approached me about organizing trips to the harp seals. At that time no American operator was taking groups there. They were looking for a younger, smaller company that was ambitious and would try to build something out of nothing. We decided a solution might be organizing seal-watching trips which would provide the local hunters with a source of income other than the slaughter of the baby harp seals. These trips in 1987 proved a turning point in the history of Natural Habitat Adventures, pointing us in a whole new direction."

The early travelers in 1987 encountered considerable rudeness and angry shouting from the local residents, upset over the Canadian government's ban on seal hunts. Bressler patiently explained to the demonstrators that his people were not there to protest but rather to experience the seals firsthand out on the ice floes. He also pointed out they would leave money in the local community. In the third season he started hiring former seal-hunters as guides to accompany his groups and their naturalist on to the ice.

"Although the seal-hunters lack formal education in harp seal biology, they do possess an extraordinary understanding of the animals' behavior from their years of hunting," Bressler says. "Now they really enjoy taking my clients on to the ice floes and explaining what goes on there. Changes happened on both sides. My clients at the beginning had their own prejudices against the hunters, viewing them as crude barbarians. Today both groups have come to see the other side as human beings. That interaction has changed a lot of minds."

The seal trips proved a major turning point in the young company's fortunes. Because of their success Bressler decided to focus exclusively on trips oriented toward the observation of wildlife in the field. He also insists that all his trips now incorporate local people in some significant way. "On our

Shetland Islands research expeditions, for example, my groups spend an evening as the dinner guests of a local family," he declares. "This allows my clients the opportunity to have an exchange with the local islanders, while at the same time giving the locals a financial stake in the success of my trips. Ecotourism is just tourism unless you get the local people involved and benefiting from the activities."

Natural Habitat Adventures has evolved its niche by offering only trips dedicated to the observation and study of wildlife in the field. Every trip focuses on the wildlife of a particular region, often on just one species, such as gorillas, polar bears, harp seals, or dolphins. Groups are kept small, usually fewer than 15. And the company always strives for a unique itinerary. On its popular trip to see the polar bears at Churchill, Manitoba, Bressler's clients enjoy a much broader range of options than those provided by other operators. In addition to polar-bear observation, they visit a local research station, go farther out on the ice where mothers and cubs congregate, and take a helicopter ride to a more distant area where the bears hibernate in the winter, crawling inside an unused den. And one departure is always set aside for serious photographers.

This formula seems to have a strong appeal to travelers. The number of clients for Natural Habitat Adventures' trips has been growing at a 50 percent annual rate. The company now offers itineraries to 23 different parts of the globe. A naturalist who is also a major researcher in the field accompanies each departure and uses slide-show presentations, lectures, and field observations to turn each trip into a learning experience.

Bressler formed Natural Habitat Adventures in 1985, just one year after graduating from college. He had tried teaching American history in high school as a first career, but quickly found the classroom claustrophobic. He had already done a fair amount of nature-based traveling on his own—such as whale-watching off the East Coast and looking for moose in Maine—and knew that he was always happier in a wilderness activity. However, his original conception for the company was much broader and included such activities as ski trips to Switzerland and Utah and a cultural trip to France to see the Cro-Magnon cave paintings there.

As the years passed, Bressler began to expand into other areas which lent themselves to superior wildlife-viewing. He found himself particularly attracted to small-ship cruising because of the excellent platform the ships provide for the study of marine mammals, especially whales and dolphins.

"After we decided to make a big push in the field of expeditionary cruises, we saw our bookings jump by over 400 percent in just 18 months, while our offerings jumped from just three different cruises in 1993 to 14 for

1996," Bressler says. "Our clients have come to recognize that expeditionary cruises, as opposed to the more traditional big-ship cruises, do have strong appeal for the adventurous traveler. And we also offer our clients access to many areas not easily reached by land. Our dolphin-watch cruise in the Bahamas is the most popular. People love to swim with dolphins in the wild."

Bressler now offers his clients a selection of a dozen different expeditionary cruises, ranging from a circumnavigation of Baffin Island aboard a massive Russian icebreaker to a cruise of the legendary islands of Seychelles and Comoros in the Indian Ocean and a whale-watching expedition off the Azores, 950 miles west of Portugal.

Another big push in recent years has been into research expeditions. Today the company offers a broad selection of such trips, ranging from the study of sperm whales off the Azores to humpback whales in the Silver Bank area off the Dominican Republic, wolf packs in Jacques Cartier Park near Quebec City, polar bears in Churchill, and puffin rookeries on the Shetland Islands in northern Scotland.

"I got involved with research quite by accident," Bressler admits candidly. "In the summer of 1991 I was scouting the Shetland Islands for a possible trip when I discovered by chance a research facility there run by the Royal Society for the Protection of Birds. I accompanied some of their researchers into the field and found myself fascinated by their work. I also discovered they were perennially short of funds. At that point I decided to get involved. By sending in small groups of volunteers, I can help the scientists by providing them with eager assistants and additional money for their expenses."

Bressler also learned that research expeditions attract a much different client than his more usual trips. "We discovered that little crossover takes place on these two types of trips," he observes. "Those of our clients signing on for the research projects often have been on an Earthwatch project in the past. Most come from the field of education, especially at the high-school level. They are quite serious about the project at hand and willing to dedicate themselves to long hours and enduring more Spartan living conditions for the satisfaction of participating in scientific discovery."

For Bressler this is a major source of accomplishment. "Many of our travelers return to us because they feel we have made a firm commitment to the preservation of animals in their natural habitat," he says. "This is something of which we are very, very proud."

4

CULTURAL EXPEDITIONS

The people of the Mursi tribe along the Omo River Valley of southern Ethiopia are one of the most isolated groups in Africa

Irma Turtle/Turtle Tours

"If you reject the food, ignore the customs, fear the religions and avoid the people, you might better stay home," novelist James Michener once warned. "You are like a pebble thrown into water; you become wet on the surface but you are never a part of the water."

For the traveler lured by the giant heads of Easter Island, the crafts of Bali, the cave art of France, or the ways of the Masai people in Kenya, the great cultures of the world, both past and present, have never before been so accessible. Cultural expeditions are journeys of discovery with a strong emphasis on education. Many are led by authorities in the culture, history, and art of the regions being visited. Lectures, both formal and informal, are often a part of the daily schedules. Participants on these trips will find themselves immersed in a foreign culture, eating the local food, drinking the local beverages, meeting the local people, and visiting their homes.

"No man is an island entire of itself," wrote poet John Donne 300 years ago. The same is true of cultures. By breaking down our linguistic and cultural myopia, these trips reaffirm for us that valuable lesson.

"The adventurer is an outlaw. Adventure must start with running away from home."

WILLIAM BOLITHO,
TWELVE AGAINST THE GODS

AFRICA

All the Way from Morocco to South Africa

Operator:
Adventure Center/Guerba
Expeditions, 1311 63rd St.,
Suite 200, Emeryville, Calif.
94608; (800) 227-8747 or
(510) 654-1879.
Price: Inexpensive.
Season: Year-round.
Length: 29 and 33 weeks.
Accommodations: Tent
camps. Five percent discount with BBAT coupon.

Participants on these lengthy expeditions cross Africa the hard way, in custom-built vehicles specially designed to drive through every kind of road condition from sand to swamp. The trip begins in London, passes through 22 countries, and ends in Cape Town, South Africa, 13,000 miles later—after crossing the Sahara Desert, the Central African jungles, and the savannahs of East Africa. Adventures along the way include a two-day trek in the high Atlas Mountains, a dugout canoe trip in Zaire, a two-day trek to a Pygmy village, a trek to view mountain gorillas at Kahuzi-Biega Park, six days of game-viewing in East African parks, a stop at Victoria Falls, and an expedition by canoe through the famous Okavango Delta. The operator supplies all camping equipment. Participants are expected to help with camp chores.

CENTRAL AFRICAN REPUBLIC

Expedition to the Bayaka Pygmies

Operator:
Turtle Tours, Box 1147,
Carefree, Ariz.;
(602) 488-3688.
Price: Expensive.
Season: September,
November, and January.
Length: 16 days.
Accommodations: Tent
camps. Five percent discount with BBAT coupon.

Participants on these 16-day expeditions travel by boat and foot to the home of the Bayaka Pygmies, still living as hunters and gatherers in the Lobaye Forest. Considered the first inhabitants of Africa, these "little people of the forest" find refuge in this immense jungle and consider the forest their mother protector and provider. They have remained nomadic throughout the centuries, moving from camp to camp and living on the honey, roots, fruits, and leaves they gather as well as the game they hunt with their bows and arrows. Their cultural life is rich with dances and songs that recount the ancient legends of the forest. This is

The people of the Hamar tribe along the Omo River Valley of southern Ethiopia have had little contact with Westerners

Irma Turtle/Turtle Tours

still-pristine Africa, where tourism has yet to arrive. Participants journey to the Pygmies by boat down the Ugangi and Lobaye Rivers, visiting villages of other ethnic groups along the way. Porters carry all baggage during the treks.

ETHIOPIA

Overland Expedition to the Omo Valley Tribes

Spilling out of a mountainous plateau southwest of Addis Ababa, the mighty Omo is so isolated that it was not first explored until 1973, a century after Stanley found Livingstone. To venture into the Omo Valley today is to be transported instantly out of a human history measured in years, decades, and centuries and back into the timeless world of ancient Africa. Participants on these rigorous expeditions travel 1,200 miles by four-wheel-drive

Operator:
Turtle Tours, Box 1147,
Carefree, Ariz.;
(602) 488-3688.
Price: Expensive.
Season: February, August,
and November.
Length: 17 days.
Accommodations: Tent camps
and hotels. Five percent discount with BBAT coupon.

vehicles into a virgin environment where tourism is nonexistent and tribal traditions remain unchanged. The women dress in skins and pelts decorated with beads, cowries, and pieces of metal. The men still proudly wear the hair bun and scarification that denotes they have killed an enemy. Particularly fascinating are the Mursi tribespeople, whose women wear huge lip plates and whose men participate in ritualistic stick-dueling. The region is also home to a rich variety of wildlife.

MALI

Overland Expedition to Timbuktu

Operator:
Turtle Tours, Box 1147,
Carefree, Ariz.;
(602) 488-3688.
Price: Expensive.
Season: November through
February.
Length: 16 days.
Accommodations: Tent
camps and hotels. Five percent discount with BBAT
coupon.

For centuries the name Timbuktu has symbolized ultimate remoteness. In the 16th century it was a major commercial, religious, and intellectual center of the Muslim world and home to 100,000 people. But today Timbuktu is a mere shadow of its former glory. This rigorous expedition travels by four-wheel-drive vehicles through the land of the Bambara, Dogon, Tuareg, and Peul tribes. The Dogons are best known for their dances on stilts and villages of mud-walled huts built at the foot of sheer cliffs. Participants also visit Djenne, a former religious center with a mosque that is the largest clay building in the world; and Mopti, an important river port with colorful markets. At Kona, on the Niger River, they board a private pirogue for a three-day river journey to Timbuktu.

NIGER

Festivals of the Wodaabe and Tuareg Nomads

At the end of each summer the Wodaabe and Tuareg people stage spectacular festivals to cele-

The men of the Wodaabe tribe in Niger dress in ceremonial garb once a year for a major festival

Irma Turtle/Turtle Tours

brate the arrival of a plentiful rainy season after a long season of drought. For the handsome Wodaabe, nomadic herders of ancient origin, this is the moment of "Gerewol," a beauty contest in which the men compete with colorful makeup, flashing smiles, and elaborate costumes. For the Tuareg, this is the time for "Tindes," a festival involving dances, camel races, and marriages. Participants on these expeditions spend five days camping with the two groups and sharing their celebrations. For the next five days participants board four-wheel-drive vehicles for an adventure in the legendary Sahara, a region of volcanic mountains fringed by some of the most sublime desert landscapes in Africa. A highlight is a visit to the Tuareg oasis of Iferouane, home to many jewelers still practicing their centuries-old art.

Operator:
Turtle Tours, Box 1147, Carefree, Ariz.;
(602) 488-3688.
Price: Expensive.
Season: October.
Length: 17 days.
Accommodations: Tent camps. Five percent discount with BBAT coupon.

ASIA

Classic Overland Expedition from London to Kathmandu

Operator: Adventure Center/ Dragoman, 1311 63rd St., Suite 200, Emeryville, Calif. 94608; (800) 227-8747 or (510) 654-1879. *Price:* Inexpensive. *Season:* August departure. *Length:* 9, 13, and 15 weeks. *Accommodations:* Tent camps. Five percent discount with BBAT coupon.

Perhaps no other trip gives its participants such insights into history as these lengthy overland expeditions. They pass through the lands of the world's greatest empires, including those of the Greeks, Romans, Byzantines, ancient Persians, Egyptians, Arabs, Ottoman, Sikh, and Hindu Rajputs. Stops at major cities are sandwiched between visits to historic sites, both ancient and modern. Travel is by specially designed 16-ton Mercedes overland vehicles able to traverse all types of terrain quickly and efficiently, no matter how rugged.

Bhutan's many religious festivals mix devotion and gaiety in Chaucerian fashion
Brent Olson/Geographic Expeditions

BHUTAN

Festivals of Bhutan

Bhutan's festivals are joyous expressions of the country's Buddhist culture. Participants on the spring departure observe the grand Paro Tshechu, the year's largest celebration. In fall, they visit Wangdiphodrang's equally exuberant tshechu. Villagers, dressed in their finest and most colorful garments and jewelry, come from the surrounding valleys to attend these important celebrations. A major feature of these celebrations is the dances, which evoke the history of particular deities. The festivals are both important religious events and major social gatherings where people can see and be seen. The itinerary also includes many activities beyond the festivals, such as day hikes and visits to temples and villages.

Operator: Geographic Expeditions, 2627 Lombard St., San Francisco. Calif. 94123; (415) 922-0448.
Price: Expensive.
Season: April and September.
Length: 10 days.
Accommodations: Deluxe tents, hotels, and guesthouses. Five percent discount with BBAT coupon.

"Life is a journey, not a destination."

ANONYMOUS

BURMA

Cultural Exploration of Burmese Life

The newest frontier to open in Asia, Burma is far less visited than any other Indo-Chinese country. From the ancient ruins of Pagan to the extraordinary markets of Mandalay, to the floating farms of Inle Lake, the country provides fascinating wonders at every turn. Travelers on these trips use trains and air-conditioned minivans to explore one of the most exotic cultures in Asia. The itinerary includes as many local festivals and holiday celebrations as possible. Highlights include a boat ride up the Irrawaddy River, the country's chief highway between Mandalay and Rangoon, and a ride on Inle Lake in a picturesque long lakeboat past villages and farms perched over the water on stilts.

Operator: Journeys International, 4011 Jackson Rd., Ann Arbor, Mich. 48103; (800) 255-8735 or (313) 665-4407.
Price: Moderate.
Season: Year-round.
Length: 8 and 15 days.
Accommodations: Hotels. Five percent discount with BBAT coupon.

CHINA

Tibet Overland Odyssey

Operator: Journeys International, 4011 Jackson Rd., Ann Arbor, Mich. 48103; (800) 255-8735 or (313) 665-4407. *Price:* Moderate. *Season:* April through November. *Length:* 8 days. *Accommodations:* Small hotels. Five percent discount with BBAT coupon.

Tibet, the highest kingdom in the world, has been an ultimate destination for much of this century. Since the time of Marco Polo, the country has traditionally been forbidden to outsiders. Chinese authorities did not open its borders to travelers until 1985. These highly affordable trips begin and end in Kathmandu. Travelers spend two nights in ancient Lhasa, visiting the incomparable Potala Palace, a palace of 1,000 rooms and home to the Dalai Lama, and join Tibetans on the ancient pilgrimage trail around the seventh-century Jokhang temple. Then they venture out into the country to see such sights as the Kumbum stupa, Palkhor Monastery, and hilltop fort at the ancient village of Gyantse; and the gold-roofed Tashilhunpo Monastery, founded in 1447 and home to 600 monks. Participants return to Kathmandu by road, driving over the Lalung Leh Pass at 17,102 feet, where they enjoy outstanding views of the Himalayas, including Mount Everest.

The Adventure Travel Hall of Fame:

Wilfred Thesiger is perhaps the last and certainly one of the greatest of the British travelers among the Arabs. He has walked in the footsteps of T. E. Lawrence, Charles Doughty, and Sir Richard Burton, all of whom forsook their homelands and the companionship of their countrymen to immerse themselves in the Bedouin cultures of the Arabian Peninsula. Like them, Thesiger has striven to enrich his own life by living with others—on their own terms.

For the past 70 years Thesiger has been on the move, first throughout Ethiopia, where he was born and where he attended Haile Selassie's coronation in 1930 as a private guest. Later he traveled over 10,000

A highlight of any journey to
Tibet is a visit to the famous
Potala Palace in Lhasa
Journeys International

The Silk Road Less Traveled

The Silk Road of Central Asia was one of history's
great arteries of trade and culture. For centuries,
fabled caravans carried gorgeous silks, brocades,
and other riches to Europe, where the goods were
sold at fabulous prices to the few who could afford
them. Members of this lengthy expedition explore
off the common route taken by most modern travelers, visiting cultures little changed over the centuries. Traveling by four-wheel-drive vehicles, they
visit the Bayinbulak Preserve, a lush valley

*miles among the Bedouins in Arabia and twice
crossed the notorious Empty Quarter, probably the most dangerous desert in the world.
He also trekked in Afghanistan, Pakistan, and
Iran. For nearly seven years he lived among
the Madan people of Iraq.*

*Thesiger regards his journeys as personal
affairs, needing no justification in terms of
material gain. He goes to remote places to
experience the people. "It is always the people
rather than the places which matter," he wrote*

*in his third book, Desert, Marsh, and
Mountain, "people who have adapted
themselves to their surroundings and managed to compete with a very harsh environment." To this end he travels alone, prefer-
ring the companionship of local people to
that of his own countrymen.*

*"I have led a hard life," Thesiger
admits. "This was from choice. I would not
have had it otherwise nor asked for more."*

Operator: Geographic Expeditions, 2627 Lombard St., San Francisco, Calif. 94123; (415) 922-0448. *Price:* Expensive. *Season:* June. *Length:* 23 days. *Accommodations:* Hotels, yurts, and tents. Five percent discount with BBAT coupon.

surrounded by 13,000-foot-high peaks where Mongolian herdsmen keep vast herds of horses, cattle, and sheep; Kuqa, an intriguing oasis town, once the most important Buddhist center of learning in the region; the Kumtura Caves, where the walls are covered with Buddhist art; and Kashgar, which boasts both an important Islamic tomb, now a pilgrimage site, and a Sunday bazaar where dashing Tajiks race horses up and down a dusty lane and fiery-eyed Uzbeks haggle over Bactrian camels.

INDIA

Ladakh Cultural Odyssey

Operator: Journeys International, 4011 Jackson Rd., Ann Arbor, Mich. 48103; (800) 255-8735 or (313) 665-4407. *Price:* Moderate. *Season:* May through September. *Length:* 17 days. *Accommodations:* Small hotels and tents. Five percent discount with BBAT coupon.

Although Ladakh lies adjacent to Kashmir, these two neighbors in India's northernmost region are worlds apart in culture, geography, and climate. The people of Ladakh are more Tibetan than Indian in their culture, appearance, and religion. This trip combines extensive exploration of this arid land and its moon-like landscapes, monasteries perched atop hills, and ancient palaces clinging to sheer rock walls, with numerous opportunities for cultural exchanges with its people. After two days in Delhi, participants fly to Leh and transfer to the picturesque village of Temisgam and a campsite in an apricot grove beneath an ancient palace and monastery. Participants then make an easy trek to Ridzong Monastery, the most scholarly in the region, where two days are spent observing the monastic life and learning about Buddhism. Next, they hike along the banks of the Indus River to the famous monastery at Alchi to observe its fine collection of Buddhist wall paintings.

"Genuine wilderness exploration is as dangerous as warfare."

THEODORE ROOSEVELT, *THROUGH THE BRAZILIAN WILDERNESS*

Rajasthan Camel Safari and Pushkar Camel Fair

Few travelers to India know about the Thar Desert on the India–Pakistan border. In 1977 the first Westerners to cross the area discovered isolated villages inhabited by nomadic and pastoral tribes, some of whom had not seen an outsider in over a century. The people retain their traditional lifestyle, tending livestock and riding camels with colorful-tasseled saddles. Expedition members spend four days traveling by camel from village to village, camping at night. A highlight is the celebrated Pushkar Camel Fair, an annual event for the Rajasthan desert tribes, who come from great distances to buy and sell livestock and compete in camel races. No previous camel-riding experience is required for this expedition. The itinerary also includes visits to the Rajasthani cities of Jaisalmer, Jodphur, and Jaipur.

Operator: Wilderness Travel, 801 Allston Way, Berkeley, Calif. 94710; (800) 368-2794 or (510) 548-0420. *Price:* Expensive. *Season:* January and November. *Length:* 20 days. *Accommodations:* Four nights desert camping, four nights in tented camps, and other nights in luxury hotels. Five percent discount with BBAT coupon.

INDONESIA

Indonesian Cultural Odyssey

Few regions in Asia are as rich in cultural treasures as the islands of Indonesia. This lengthy expedition focuses on the islands of Sulawesi, Flores, and Sumba. Four days are spent in Torajaland in Sulawesi, famous for both its great natural beauty and its funerals. After the initial funeral, the bones of the deceased are dug up for a special ceremony. Buffaloes and pigs are slaughtered, and then the remains are placed in wooden coffins, which are deposited in sunken holes carved high up on cliffs with an effigy of the deceased placed nearby. Flores boasts a rugged ridge of mountains with several smoking volcanoes. Its people are famous for their fine music, for which instruments include bamboo slit drums, small gongs, pan pipes, and drums made from parchment stretched over the end of a hollow coconut trunk. The people on the flat, barren island of Sumba produce some of the finest fabrics in Indonesia. Both islands also offer fine dances.

Operator: Asian Pacific Adventures, 826 S. Sierra Bonita Ave., Los Angeles, Calif. 90036; (800) 825-1680 or (213) 935-3156. *Price:* Expensive. *Season:* May, July, and November. *Length:* 20 days. *Accommodations:* Hotels and village homes. Five percent discount with BBAT coupon.

Bali through an Artist's Eye

Operator: Asian Pacific Adventures, 826 S. Sierra Bonita Ave., Los Angeles, Calif. 90036; (800) 825-1680 or (213) 935-3156. *Price:* Expensive. *Season:* January, February, June, and September. *Length:* 15 days. *Accommodations:* A private home in Ubud, a mountain village famous for its artists. Five percent discount with BBAT coupon.

Perhaps on no other Asian island have the people developed such a broad selection of sophisticated arts over the past 500 years. For instance, a typical Balinese woman knows the designs of 100 or more different offerings required in the rich ceremonial life of her society. Groups on this trip are limited to six people, a number small enough to visit the studios of artists, woodcarvers, weavers, and basket makers and learn something of their private and religious ceremonies. Participants also visit numerous museums and temples and spend a day at Tenganan, the ancient walled village where many musical-instrument makers reside and the unique double-ikat *gerinsings* are woven.

Cultural Exploration among the Tana Toraja People on Sulawesi

Living in an isolated area and preserving their traditional customs, the Torajan people are noted among anthropologists for their unique starship-shaped houses with soaring roofs, centuries-old hanging graves, effigies to the dead, and massive megaliths. The departures are timed to coincide

Great Achievements in Adventure Travel

"There is nothing we need to invent," insisted Alain Gheerbrant, a French-born editor, poet, and anthropologist. "But we have everything to discover." To learn more about the world and its people, in 1948, at the age of 28, he organized an expedition with three other men to cross Venezuela to Brazil through territory that was largely unexplored.

The group spent two months in the jungles along the upper reaches of the Orinoco River with the Piaroa Indians, none of whom had ever seen a white man before Gheerbrant won their trust with a portable phonograph and a selection of Western music. The music of Mozart proved the bridge between these two radically different cultures. "Mozart seemed to exercise some

with the ceremonies called *marante sadan*, funeral festivals to honor the dead. After a lengthy celebration of dancing and feasting, the dead man is launched into the afterlife, his body placed in a cliff grave, and an effigy erected nearby on a stone balcony. The itinerary also includes trekking to outlying Torajan villages, white-water rafting down the Sa'dan River at the base of 3,000-foot-high mountains; and the final two days in Bali.

JAPAN

Islands of the Inland Sea

This trip has been specially designed as a cultural encounter, allowing participants to experience Japan as the Japanese do. Most nights are spent in *ryokan*, traditional Japanese country inns, where guests don kimonos, soak in hot tubs, and sleep on comfortable, quilted futons. Few foreign visitors ever make it to the Inland Sea, a scenic area dotted with over 3,000 pine-covered islands and islets, each with its own distinctive beauty. The area is now a national park. Travelers on this trip explore a variety of islands, including Shikoku and the impressive Matsuyama Castle, the legendary hot

Operator:
Outer Edge Expeditions, 45500 Pontiac Trail, Walled Lake, Mich. 48390; (800) 322-5235 or (810) 624-5140.
Price: Moderate.
Season: May and June.
Length: 13 days.
Accommodations: Village guesthouses and hotels. Five percent discount with BBAT coupon.

Operator:
Geographic Expeditions, 2627 Lombard St., San Francisco, Calif. 94123; (415) 922-0448.
Price: Expensive.
Season: May and November.
Length: 11 days.
Accommodations: Japanese country inns. Five percent discount with BBAT coupon.

---

magical influence on the Indians," he wrote later. "In his music there is a strange charm in the wildest sense of the word, some magical influence to which no Indian could remain insensible."

The Indian hosts soon adopted the four white men into their tribe, permitting them to observe and film their most secret rituals. One day they were invited to witness an initiation rite for young boys that culminated in an extraordinary test of the boys' courage and endurance. Elders wove into square pieces of wickerwork hundreds of massive black ants, 1.5 inches long, exposing their powerful pincers on the one side and their bee-like stings on the other. For upwards of ten minutes each boy was forced to endure—without crying out—a mat of several hundred angry ants repeatedly pressed against the tender parts of his body.

springs of Dogo Onsen, dating back over 3,000 years; 88 sacred temples of the Shingon sect of Buddhism; and the southern castle town of Kochi, famous for its Sunday market.

LAOS

River Odyssey in Laos

Operator:
Journeys International,
4011 Jackson Rd.,
Ann Arbor, Mich. 48103;
(800) 255-8735 or
(313) 665-4407.
Price: Moderate.
Season: Year-round.
Length: 11 days.
Accommodations: Hotels.
Five percent discount with
BBAT coupon.

Participants on this cultural exploration of Laos will find themselves traveling through a land populated by a gracious people who have long since consigned the most recent war to a long history of wars stretching back over 1,000 years. Paradoxically, Americans—more than any nationality—are now welcome in this country where tourism is still in its infancy. The highlight of this trip is a two-day cruise down the Mekong River with frequent stops for villages, nature walks, and temples. Travel is aboard a comfortable diesel riverboat, the most common craft on the river. Participants then visit Luang Prabang, a city of 8,000 famous for its collection of 30 temples, some dating back 600 years.

A Buddhist sculpture garden near Vientiane invites visitors
Journeys International

MALAYSIA

Headhunters, Hornbills, and Orangutans in Sabah, Sarawak, and Borneo

The third-largest island in the world, Borneo represents one of the last frontiers for adventure travel. This expedition focuses on both the anthropological and natural attractions of the island. A full day is spent at the Sepilok Orangutan Reserve, where orphaned primates are conditioned to be returned to the wild. One day is spent on beautiful Turtle Island, where green turtles lay their eggs, for fine snorkeling or scuba diving. And finally, participants board motorized longboats for a journey up the Engari River to an Iban village deep within the jungle. The villagers are former headhunters who are now friendly toward outsiders. Participants will join the Iban in daily activities and be allowed to observe their dancing, traditional games, and animist rituals. (The May group will witness the Gawai Dayak festival, which celebrates the harvest with dances and banquets.)

Operator:
Asian Pacific Adventures, 826 S. Sierra Bonita Ave., Los Angeles, Calif. 90036; (800) 825-1680 or (213) 935-3156.
Price: Expensive.
Season: May, July, August, and September.
Length: 13 days.
Accommodations: A traditional Stamang longhouse and hotels. Five percent discount with BBAT coupon.

"Freud suggested that men travel to escape the oppressions of their families and their fathers. Maybe that is why people left Vienna. But they travel with more energy to get a tan. People travel because it teaches them things they could learn no other way. Herodotus got his real education by traveling. Like Odysseus, he saw 'many cities of men.' Travel showed him the world and how it worked. Travel is an imperialism of the imagination, a process of acquisition: the mind collects cultures and experiences and souvenirs."

LANCE MORROW,
TIME, MAY 31, 1982

Participants on Mountain Travel-Sobek's elephant safari through northern Thailand travel in safety through dense jungle as they go from one village to another

Max Holland/Mountain Travel-Sobek

THAILAND

Elephant Safari through the Golden Triangle

Operator: Mountain Travel-Sobek, 6420 Fairmount Ave., El Cerrito, Calif. 94530; (800) 227-2384 or (415) 527-8100. *Price:* Expensive. *Season:* November through February. *Length:* 16 days. *Accommodations:* Houses of village chiefs. Five percent discount with BBAT coupon.

For centuries, the remote mountains of northern Thailand have provided a sanctuary for nomadic tribes. Here some 375,000 non-Thai-speaking minorities live in small scattered villages. To travel among the various hill tribes with their fantastic traditionally embroidered costumes and massive silver jewelry is to be immersed in a cultural and racial potpourri of wondrous diversity. Members of this cultural expedition spend two days riding elephants, through dense jungle alive with the sounds of birds and monkeys, to visit the villages of these friendly hill tribes. Other activities include two days in a remote Hmong hill-tribe village in the frontier region near the Laos border, and a longtail boat ride on the Mekong River.

VIETNAM

Hill Tribes of Northern Vietnam

The ethnic peoples of northern Vietnam are among the most colorful in Southeast Asia, with cultures that are largely uncontaminated by outside influences. Participants on these cultural expeditions journey out of Hanoi to Hoa Binh to meet the Thai, Muong, and Dao people. Dao women, for example, wear short skirts of batik material, hand-dyed indigo jackets, and head scarves. Other stops include Hmong villages near Moc Chau and Son La, where the Hmong and Thai ethnic groups live in the hills. In Sa Pa visitors observe an evening festival put on by the Dao, who still follow a nomadic way of life.

Operator: Asian Pacific Adventures, 826 S. Sierra Bonita Ave., Los Angeles, Calif. 90036; (800) 825-1680 or (213) 935-3156. *Price:* Moderate. *Season:* April through November. *Length:* 13 days. *Accommodations:* Hotels and guesthouses. Five percent discount with BBAT coupon.

The Hmong Montagnard, hill-tribe people of northern Vietnam, have had little contact with travelers from outside

Tovya Wager/Asian Pacific Travel

EUROPE

BRITAIN

Barge Cruise on the Thames River

Operator:
Fenwick & Lang,
100 W. Harrison,
South Tower, #350,
Seattle, Wash. 98119;
(800) 243-6244 or
(206) 216-2903.
Price: Expensive.
Season: April through
October.
Length: 7 days.
Accommodations: Shipboard
cabins.

A mere brook compared with such river colossi as the Nile, Mississippi, and Amazon, the 236-mile-long Thames is nonetheless one of the world's most celebrated waterways. To take a barge along the Thames today is to follow in the wake of countless royal processions through 2,200 years of British history. Such a cruise is a marvelous social holiday. Every bend and lock along the river promises opportunities to encounter interesting people. The *Actief,* a 100-foot Dutch cargo-carrying river barge that has been handsomely converted to accommodate 12 passengers and a crew of four, makes a leisurely cruise along the 50 miles of river between Windsor and Oxford. A highlight is the sleepy river village of Pangbourne, where Kenneth Grahame wrote his classic tale *The Wind in the Willows.* Ample time is allowed for shore visits to nearby villages, country houses, and museums.

Castles and Circles of Stone

Operator:
Far Horizons
Archaeological & Cultural
Trips, P.O. Box 91900,
Albuquerque, N. Mex.;
(800) 552-4575 or
(505) 822-9100.
Price: Expensive.
Season: September.
Length: 18 days.
Accommodations: Castles, elegant country homes, and small, centuries-old coaching inns. Five percent discount with BBAT coupon.

Participants on this tour explore important British prehistoric and historic sites in the company of a university archaeologist. Sites include Stonehenge and other prehistoric stone circles, a luxurious Roman palace, medieval monasteries and castles, stately homes, and the restored Viking village of York. Other activities include a day hike along Hadrian's Wall, built in A.D. 122 to guard the northern frontier of the Roman Empire; the ruins of Tintern Abbey, which inspired one of William Wordsworth's most famous poems; the well-preserved Roman baths at Bath; and a reconstructed Iron Age Celtic farm.

FRANCE

Barge Cruise in the South of France

Stretching from Bordeaux on the Atlantic coast to the Camargue and Rhône delta on the Mediterranean, the canals of southern France provide some 350 miles of the most beautiful and romantic inland cruising in all Europe. The Canal du Midi, the most famous of these canals and shaded for much of its length by pine and cypress trees, has great charm and follows a winding course beneath ancient, arched stone bridges and through curious oval-shaped locks. Opened in 1681, the Midi is one of France's oldest canals. Now, 300 years later, it remains virtually unchanged. *La Tortue*, a six-passenger hotel-barge, cruises leisurely between Castelnaudary and Beziers. In between, visits are made to Carcassonne, France's greatest medieval walled city; Lagrasse, a fortified hilltop village with a Benedictine Abbey dating back to 778; Minerve, the ancient capital of the Minervois vineyards and site of a 12th-century fort set dramatically in the middle of a deep gorge; and Narbonne, a lovely old Roman city, with its magnificent Cathedral of St. Just.

Operator:
Fenwick & Lang,
100 W. Harrison,
South Tower, #350,
Seattle, Wash. 98119;
(800) 243-6244 or
(206) 216-2903.
Price: Expensive.
Season: March through mid-November.
Length: 7 days.
Accommodations: Shipboard cabins.

By Hot-Air Balloon over the Loire Valley

Here in the French heartland stands one of the greatest collection of architectural wonders in all the world. Over 1,000 magnificent châteaus, castles, and manor houses dot a countryside of vineyards, meadows, orchards, and forests. Participants on these adventures board gaily colored hot-air balloons and float majestically at treetop level over one of the most scenic regions in France. From their serene platforms, travelers enjoy a marvelous opportunity to see details of architectural design and intricate formal gardening that cannot be observed from the ground. The itinerary includes tours of the interiors and parks of several of the most famous royal châteaus.

Operator:
The Bombard Society,
6727 Curran St.,
McLean, Va. 22101;
(800) 862-8537 or
(703) 448-9407.
Price: Expensive.
Season: June through October.
Length: 3 and 7 days.
Accommodations: Luxurious château-hotels.

GREECE

Greek Island Wanderer

Operator: Adventure Center/Explore, 1311 63rd St., Suite 200, Emeryville, Calif. 94608; (800) 228-8747 in California, or (415) 654-1879. *Price:* Inexpensive. *Season:* May through September. *Length:* 16 days. *Accommodations:* Small hotels. Five percent discount with BBAT coupon.

Participants on this popular trip island-hop across Homer's "wine-dark" Aegean Sea, exploring the Cyclades Islands of myth and legend. Stays of several days each are made on the islands of Syros, the capital of the Cycladic group; Paros, with its lovely fishing villages, Venetian fortress, and Valley of the Butterflies; Santorini, now believed to be the original Atlantis destroyed in 1500 B.C. when a massive volcanic explosion wiped out its Minoan cities; and Naxos, the largest and most beautiful island in the Cyclades. Travel is by interisland ferries; transportation about the islands is by local bus, taxi, or moped.

"Adventure is a category of experience about which we know less than other cultures have known. It represents a portion of the 'language' we no longer speak with skill."

PAUL ZWEIG,
THE ADVENTURER

ITALY

By Hot-Air Balloon over Tuscany

Operator: The Bombard Society, 6727 Curran St., McLean, Va. 22101; (800) 862-8537 or (703) 448-9407. *Price:* Expensive. *Season:* May through October. *Length:* 5 days. *Accommodations:* A 16th-century palace in Siena.

Participants on this adventure ride serenely in hot-air balloons over an Italian countryside steeped in Etruscan, Roman, medieval, and Renaissance history, flying in gentle winds over many ancient and charming villages, close to the ground—seldom over 500 feet—and often at treetop level. Several days are spent balloon-exploring the wine-producing valleys near San Gimignano, a small, 14th-century town. Participants make their base in Siena which, perhaps more than any other Italian city, still retains the look and spirit of the Middle Ages.

LATIN AMERICA

BELIZE, HONDURAS, AND GUATEMALA

Mundo Mayan Expedition

Reaching a peak between A.D. 600 and 900, the Mayas not only were the most intellectual of all the American Indian tribes and nations but also surpassed all the Old World peoples of antiquity as well in arithmetic, in astronomy, and in the accuracy of their calendar. They learned to use the zero long before the people of Europe borrowed it from the mathematicians of India. A religious people, the Mayas built sprawling ceremonial centers, grouping their enormous temples around open squares. This special cultural expedition studies ancient and contemporary Belize, Honduras, and Guatemala with a major emphasis on Mayan archaeology, art, history, textiles, crafts, and contemporary Indian life. The highlights of this expedition include spelunking (cave-exploring) in search of Mayan ritual sites; investigating the incredible 72-step hieroglyphic staircase in the ruins of Copan, Honduras; and watching colorful religious processions and traditional Indian dances in Guatemala.

Operator: Nature Expeditions International, P.O. Box 11496, Eugene, Ore. 97440; (800) 896-0639 or (503) 484-6529.
Price: Expensive.
Season: December.
Length: 15 days.
Accommodations: Hotels.
Five percent discount with BBAT coupon.

BOLIVIA

A Cultural Expedition to the Tiwanaku and Katari River Valleys and Lake Titicaca Basin

Participants on this expedition examine in depth Tiwanaku, one of the great centers of native Andean civilization, which endured for over 1,000 years. From A.D. 100 to 1000, this was the seat of power for an empire that stretched from present-day southern Peru to northern Argentina. The

Operator:
Far Horizons
Archaeological & Cultural
Trips, P.O. Box 91900,
Albuquerque, N. Mex.
87199; (800) 552-4575 or
(505) 343-9400.
Price: Expensive.
Season: August.
Length: 16 days.
Accommodations: Hotels, a
dormitory, and an inn. Five
percent discount with
BBAT coupon.

Aymara, descendants of the builders of Tiwanaku, still live in the region. Participants will have opportunities to meet local Aymara community leaders and observe indigenous ceremonies. After exploring the major archaeological sites of Lake Titicaca and visiting the village of Copacabana with its splendid 16th-century cathedral, participants visit Cochabamba, in eastern Bolivia, where the Incas managed productive agricultural lands. A well-preserved Incan fortress and temple still stand in the area. An archaeologist accompanies the group.

CHILE

Journey to Easter Island

Operator:
Far Horizons Archaeological
& Cultural Trips, P.O. Box
91900, Albuquerque,
N.Mex.; (800) 552-4575 or
(505) 822-9100.
Price: Expensive.
Season: February.
Length: 18 days.
Accommodations: Hotels.
Five percent discount with
BBAT coupon.

Easter Island enjoys the distinction of being the world's most secluded piece of inhabited land. No other people in history have endured such extreme cultural isolation, and yet Easter became home to the most sophisticated Polynesian culture in the Pacific basin. Among their many achievements, the ancient Easter Islanders carved 1,000 highly stylized stone statues, some 60 feet high and weighing more than 300 tons. Members of this expedition visit the island's major archaeological sites in the company of local anthropologists. Sites include the quarry at Rano Raraku, where work on 200 statues was abruptly halted; the ceremonial village at Orongo on the rim of Rano Kau volcano; and the restored statues at Ahu Akivi. Participants stay in the village of Hangaroa, where they experience a modern Polynesian culture. Several days at the start of the journey are spent in the northern Chilean villages of San Pedro de Atacama, the center of a paleolithic civilization that left impressive rock fortresses, and Iquique, where hundreds of enormous prehistoric geoglyphs decorate the hills.

The enormous statues of Easter Island, 2,500 miles off the coast of Chile, are impressive reminders of the most advanced Polynesian civilization in all the Pacific

James C. Simmons

MEXICO

Festivals of Oaxaca

Mexico's Oaxaca Valley cradled a civilization that lasted for more than 1,000 years. Magic and religion are blended in its festive ceremonies, and colorful markets are stocked with special foods for the rituals. Travelers on these trips explore the many important archaeological sites in the valley, including Yagul, a fortress with magnificent views of the countryside; Mitla, renowned for its spectacular mosaics; and Monte Alban, a major Zapotec ceremonial center. Also on the itinerary are visits to the valley's major crafts centers. The April departure coincides with the breathtaking pageantry of the Easter Week celebrations, while the November trip

Operator:
Baja's Frontier Tours,
907 E. Freeman Pl.,
Tucson, Ariz. 85719;
(800) 726-7231 or
(520) 887-2340.
Price: Expensive.
Season: April and
November.
Length: 9 days.
Accommodations: Small
hotel. Five percent discount
with BBAT coupon.

catches the Dia de los Muertos (Day of the Dead), an extraordinary festival combining Christian and ancient Indian traditions—local residents gather at their cemeteries for a joyous remembrance of their ancestors, complete with music and fireworks.

By Classic American Train to Copper Canyon

Operator: Sierra Madre Express, P.O. Box 26381, Tucson, Ariz. 85726; (800) 666-0346 or (602) 747-0346. *Price:* Expensive. *Season:* Year-round. *Length:* 7 days. *Accommodations:* Train sleeping compartments and lodges. Five percent discount with BBAT coupon.

The Sierra Madre Express is reminiscent of an era filled with travel lore and impeccable service. Dating from the 1940s, these restored railway cars carry up to 50 passengers in relative comfort through some of the most spectacular countryside in Mexico. All food and drinking water are brought from the United States. Starting and ending their trip in Tucson, participants spend three days in the remarkable Copper Canyon region, where individual canyons are both deeper and wider than our own Grand Canyon. A major attraction of the trip is the time spent among the Tarahumara Indians who live throughout the canyon complex. Known for their long-distance running, the Indians survive in their harsh environment on planted corn and beans and wild fruit. They hunt by running small game to exhaustion. Most Tarahumara make their homes in naturally formed caves hidden in large rock outcroppings. They are the largest—50,000 strong—tribe left in northern Mexico.

PANAMA

The Cuna Indians of the San Blas Islands

Famous for their colorful, embroidered molas, Panama's Cuna Indians strive to preserve their traditional lifestyle in the face of tremendous cultural, economic, and environmental pressures. For centuries they have lived on the archipelago of tropical islands known as the San Blas, an area essentially unspoiled by modern development. Participants on these cultural expeditions spend their nights at

The Cuna Indians on the San Blas Islands of Panama hold to their traditional ways against all encroachments of modern life

James C. Simmons

a rustic bamboo lodge on the island of Waguitupo, across the water from the Cuna island settlement of Achitupo. Cuna guides take guests by motorized dugout canoes to settlements on neighboring islands, a Cuna burial ground, and a coconut plantation on the mainland. Other options include snorkeling over nearby reefs.

VENEZUELA

The Yanomamo Indians of the Orinoco River

Bearing a name that means "the fierce people," the nomadic Yanomamo Indians are among the last truly primitive peoples left in the Amazonian region. Deep in the rain forest, along the great Orinoco River, they still maintain much of their traditional way of life. Most wear face-paint, feather ornaments, and plugs in their ears and noses. Each village is actually a single, enormous communal structure the size of a football field, which houses upwards of 100 people. Every three months the people shift their living quarters to another site in the forest. Participants on these challenging expeditions will have ample opportunity to accompany their hosts on fishing and

Operator:
Lost World Adventures,
1189 Autumn Ridge Dr.,
Marietta, Ga. 30066;
(800) 999-0556 or
(770) 971-8586.
Price: Moderate.
Season: Year-round.
Length: 3 and 4 days.
Accommodations: Rustic
lodge. Five percent discount with BBAT coupon.

Operator:
Turtle Tours,
Box 1147,
Carefree, Ariz.;
(602) 488-3688.
Price: Expensive.
Season: January, March,
and November.
Length: 14 days.
Accommodations: Jungle
camps and village houses.
Five percent discount with
BBAT coupon.

Travelers on a Turtle Tours trip to the Amazonian rain forest spend several days sharing the daily routines of the Yanomamo Indians

Irma Turtle/Turtle Tours

hunting expeditions, as well as to linger by the local hearth, participating in the routines and traditions of local daily life. This is probably the finest adventure available in South American anthropology.

MIDDLE EAST

EGYPT

Cruise on the Nile River from Luxor to Aswan

No other river has so captured human imagination as the Nile. For centuries this majestic river defied the explorers who sought its source. Passengers on this journey cruise back into history to explore the great monuments of ancient Egypt, the best-preserved collection of temples and tombs in the Middle East. In the company of an Egyptologist, they visit such famous sites as the Temple of Horus on Edfu Island, which has deteriorated only slightly in its 2,500 years; Karnak, the largest temple complex in Egypt, which includes the Great Hypostyle Hall with its 134 enormous columns; the tombs in the Valleys of the Kings, Queens, and Nobles; the Colossi of Memnon; and the unique Ptolemaic temple, with its exquisite wall paintings, at Kom Ombo. At the beginning of the trip, three days are spent exploring the antiquities and museums of Cairo.

Operator: Journeys International, 4011 Jackson Rd., Ann Arbor, Mich. 48103; (800) 255-8735 or (313) 665-4407.
Price: Moderate.
Season: Year-round.
Length: 10 days.
Accommodations: Hotels and shipboard cabins. Five percent discount with BBAT coupon.

JORDAN

An Expedition to Jordan's Ancient Historical Monuments

The kingdom of Jordan has excited the imagination of Westerners ever since T. E. Lawrence ambushed Turkish troop trains in the desert west of Amman during the First World War. Here the traveler finds some of the most dramatic scenery in the Middle East, plus a rich selection of ruins from the Nabatean, Roman, Byzantine, and Arab civilizations. This trip visits the well-preserved Roman city of Jerash and nearby Qulat al-Rabad Castle, which dates back to the Crusades; the breathtaking desert landscapes of Wadi Rum; the beaches, with their superb coral reefs, of the Red Sea off Aqaba; and finally Petra, the celebrated ancient city of the Nabateans, famous for its profusion of temples, tombs, and dwellings, all carved from rose, crimson, and purple limestone.

Operator: Himalayan Travel, 112 Prospect St., Stamford, Conn. 06901; (800) 225-2380 or (203) 359-3711.
Price: Moderate.
Season: Year-round.
Length: 8 days.
Accommodations: Hotels. Five percent discount with BBAT coupon.

TURKEY

Village-to-Village Hike in Turkey and Cyprus

This cultural adventure combines hiking with village home-stays and delicious local food, as

Operator:
Geographic Expeditions,
2627 Lombard St.,
San Francisco, Calif. 94123;
(415) 922-0448.
Price: Moderate.
Season: July and August.
Length: 17 days.
Accommodations: Country
inns, village homes, and
hotels. Five percent discount with BBAT coupon.

participants travel from exotic Istanbul to the mountains of Central Anatolia, the otherworldly terrain of Cappadocia, the Taurus Mountains of the south, and the rarely visited northern shore of Cyprus. The emphasis along the way is always on establishing local contacts and participating whenever possible in the customs and festivities to be found in the villages along the way. A typical day begins with a hike to Goreme, where locals keep pigeons in the caves dotting the canyon walls and use the guano (droppings) to fertilize their apricot orchards and vineyards. After lunch participants hike another 30 minutes to the village of Ortasihar, where spacious caverns below the village are still used to store the citrus crop harvested during the summer months.

UNITED STATES

ARIZONA, COLORADO, NEW MEXICO, AND UTAH

American Southwest Indian Country Safari

Operator:
Nature Expeditions
International,
P.O. Box 11496,
Eugene, Ore. 97440;
(800) 869-0639 or
(541) 484-6529.
Price: Expensive.
Season: May and September.
Length: 8 and 16 days.
Accommodations: Hotels.
Five percent discount with
BBAT coupon.

This trip provides an immersion in past and present Indian cultures, in the company of an anthropologist. Traveling by van, participants cover 2,500 miles through four states. Nights are spent in motels and lodges. Historic sites, such as Canyon de Chelly, Mesa Verde, and Chaco Canyon, are sandwiched between visits to contemporary Indian settlements such as ancient Acoma, an imposing pueblo that sits atop a 400-foot-high sandstone mesa and is the oldest continuously occupied settlement in the United States. Along the way participants observe traditional Hopi dances, visit the homes of leading Indian artists, and eat Navajo tacos with an Indian family near Gallup.

SOUTH DAKOTA

Exploring the Culture of the Sioux and Cheyenne Indians

The enormous popularity of the movie *Dances with Wolves* generated considerable sympathy and appreciation for the Plains Indians and their way of life. Participants on this six-day trip accompany an anthropologist and his Indian staff on an expedition of cultural discovery, while leading a lifestyle reminiscent of the Plains Indians of the 1800s: they lodge in tipis while visiting the homes of Indian people from the Cheyenne and Sioux tribes. The focus of this cultural expedition is Bear Butte, a place of healing and pilgrimage for the Sioux and Cheyenne peoples where both Crazy Horse and Sitting Bull received their visions. Participants learn the teachings and lifestyle of the Sioux people from a traditional Sioux family at a ranch at the base of Bear Butte.

Operator: Journeys into American Indian Territory, P.O. Box 929, Westhampton Beach, N.Y. 11978; (800) 458-2632 or (516) 878-8655. *Price:* Moderate. *Season:* September. *Length:* 6 days. *Accommodations:* Indian ranch house. Five percent discount with BBAT coupon.

"To awaken quite alone in a strange town is one of the pleasantest sensations in the world. You are surrounded by adventure. You have no idea of what is in store, but you will, if you are wise and know the art of travel, let yourself go on the stream of the unknown and accept whatever comes in the spirit in which the gods may offer it."

FREYA STARK,
BAGHDAD SKETCHES

PROFILE
WILL WEBER
JOURNEYS INTERNATIONAL

Areflective Will Weber, founder and president of Michigan-based Journeys International, traces the roots of his adventure-travel company to his years as a Peace Corps volunteer in Nepal in the 1970s. After teaching for two years, he extended his service to work with the Nepalese government in their National Parks and Wildlife Conservation Office, helping his host government establish a national park system. During that time he traveled to remote areas that few foreigners had penetrated, and sometimes found himself hopelessly lost for days at a time. He recalls today:

"I loved every day of the Peace Corps training and my two years as a high-school math and science teacher in a remote hill-tribe village in eastern Nepal. It remains my best job ever, and I think I may have had the most fantastic Peace Corps experience any volunteer can claim. Because I'm tall—6 feet 4 inches—there were no buildings in the village in which I could stand up. Part of my task was to build a house, which I found frustrating but satisfying. The construction costs on the house totaled $80. This project helped me to get to know not only the elite of the community but the tradespeople as well. I learned about so many values we have lost in our own society. And I came to understand what real culture means. I saw the importance of the role and value of traditions. In Nepal I was able to dispel many naive illusions while living in a fabulously beautiful, friendly, and hospitable community."

Those Peace Corps experiences ruined Weber for a more conventional life after his return to the States, and eventually shaped his concept of the kind of adventure-travel company he wanted Journeys International to be. He married and enrolled in a doctoral program in Natural Resources at the University of Michigan. But the pull of Nepal eventually overwhelmed his ambitions to become a college professor. "I had a real longing for Nepal when I was back in America and in graduate school," he admits today. "I missed the sense of being involved, of doing important things rather than academic pursuits which seemed, after my Peace Corps stint, too remote from the real world."

Weber completed his doctorate in 1980. But the course of his life had already veered in a sharply different direction. In the summer of 1978 he led a group of ten people from the University of Michigan to Nepal for a 30-day trek to the Everest base-camp area, and then added another five days in Chitwan National Park. The trip was a great success, and he saw the potential rewards in creating trekking trips that would also provide important cross-cultural learning experiences.

Upon his return to the States, Weber decided to found an adventure-travel company and offer trips specifically designed to wed cross-cultural adventures with nature expeditions, the kinds of travel experiences that he had found so satisfying during his Peace Corps years.

"My wife, Joan, and I sensed an opportunity to create a unique business," Weber recalls today. "At that time the only local company doing treks in Nepal was the original Mountain Travel/Nepal run by Col. Jimmy Roberts. The model for his trips was basically that of a military expedition. We created a different kind of trekking model, one that valued each American and Nepalese participant as an equal, eliminated status, and encouraged Nepalese of all castes to engage the Americans in conversation, eat together, sing together, and participate in the economic rewards according to the effort expended. It was a hard model to make work, and we still struggle with it. But it has succeeded in distinguishing us from other companies in Nepal. We have since improved upon our cross-cultural travel model and adapted it to our other destinations in Africa and Latin America. I think it's working well."

Weber pushed his concept long before the label "ecotourism" became a popular cliché. Believing strongly that simply bringing in groups of Americans without benefiting the local population was morally wrong and self-defeating over the long term, he set up Journeys offices in Ladakh (India), Kathmandu, and Rangoon, all staffed by locals. The Michigan office fronted the money for computers, fax machines, and filing fees; provided instruction in sound business practices; and carefully trained the local staff in the expectations of their American clients.

"By hiring members of minority groups and non-government-approved trip leaders, we have managed to gain access to remote villages that are often closed to other operators," Weber observes. "In Ladakh, for example, I insisted we go into partnership with Ladakhis rather than Kashmiris or Indians, who are the dominant business class there but lack the cultural sensitivity to provide our clients access to the villages."

The Peace Corps' goals have affected Journeys in other ways. In 1980 Weber set up the nonprofit Earth Preservation Fund, which sponsors hands-on work trips that allow travelers to leave tangible results—from planting trees in the deforested areas of Nepal to collecting trash left by the 6,000 less-considerate foreign trekkers along the Inca Trail in Peru each year. About 100 clients sign up for these projects annually.

Weber is extremely proud of the achievements of the Earth Preservation Fund, of which he is the director. "For one recent project we endowed a chair in astrology at a college in Ladakh," he says. "We did not do this because we believe astrology is a useful science. Rather, astrology is extremely important in the local culture. Astrologers compute the time when the people should hold their festivities. If they lose the skill of the astrologers, then the people will cease to celebrate their local festivals. So what we're doing is supporting local tradition and culture by just a small intervention."

This willingness to consider unorthodox solutions to problems has been characteristic of Weber since his youth. Lacking the funds to travel in high school and college, he generally relied upon his thumb and the kindness of strangers, hitchhiking more than 100,000 miles across North America. Over one college Christmas vacation he hitched 9,000 miles in just 11 days, a distance he insists today must be one for the record books.

"Even today I have this warm, fuzzy feeling whenever I see a Volkswagen Beetle," he admits. "They were the cars that could always be counted on to stop. Here was the smallest car on the road with the least room to spare, and their drivers were the people who always stopped for me. For me the VW Bug is an icon of my youth."

In recent years Weber has expanded his offering of wildlife trips, reflecting an interest he has had since boyhood. He recalls: "I have been a birder and nature enthusiast since receiving my first Golden Nature Guide at the age of 10. I have been active in a variety of ornithological groups, including an international raptor migration observatory near Windsor, Ontario, for which I was the founding president. I have taught birding for many years. The real challenge, however, is helping local people in remote places to learn to respect and enjoy nature rather than fear or destroy it. Increasingly, I find the pleasure of nature lies in the preservation as much as the observation. We are currently working with the Conservation International in Guatemala to help local villagers around the Maya Biosphere Reserve to understand, appreciate, and interpret the rain forest as a way to encourage more ecotourism."

As a tour company operator, Weber likes to think small. His company sends about 2,000 clients into the field each year, and he refuses to expand much beyond that figure for fear of compromising the quality of his trips. More than half of his travelers are repeaters, a percentage that's the envy of many of his competitors. When asked the reasons for Journeys' success, he reflects:

"We seek to give people a really personalized view of traditional cultures and unspoiled natural environments in remote places. We want our clients to return to this country with changed views of the world. We've had a good number of clients return and quit their jobs to take up other professions based on what they experienced on one of our trips. That, for us, is a sign of a successful trip."

5

RESEARCH EXPEDITIONS

Do your heroes include Howard Carter, Margaret Mead, and Louis Leakey? Do you dream about making a major scientific discovery—perhaps a new species of dinosaur in Utah or an Indian relic from the ruins of a pueblo—that will change what we know about early life in North America?

Historically, many areas of scientific research depended on the help of dedicated amateurs, who have made many of the most important scientific discoveries of modern times. In 1873 Heinrich Schliemann, a retailer who possessed no formal training in archaeology, discovered and excavated the fabled treasures of Troy. And Clyde Tombaugh, a 24-year-old former wheat-farmer with only a high-school education, located the planet Pluto in 1930—after professional astronomers had sought it in vain for decades.

For all those people addicted to National Geographic television specials, there is a way they can live out their fantasies and become a part of a scientific team. Organized research expeditions have grown in popularity over the past decade. Projects as diverse as the excavation of a Pharaoh's temple on the banks of the Nile and the study of moose/wolf dynamics on Isle Royale National Park, Michigan, are now open to untrained, enthusiastic volunteers willing to pay their own way. These are all definitely "working vacations," and living conditions in the field are often Spartan. The adventure they offer is of a more cerebral variety than that experienced when climbing a mountain or running a river. The thrill lies in participating in important scientific research and discovery.

Most of the projects team a scientist with a small group of volunteers. The work can sometimes be tedious—digging, sifting, measuring, and cataloging—and it is often physically demanding. The money each volunteer pays underwrites the cost of the project as well as the team's food, lodging, and supplies. An important side benefit is that all expenses, including travel to and from the site, may be tax-deductible.

But the rewards of scientific discovery often bring the volunteers back time after time. Gary Goshgarian, a professor of English at Northeastern University in Boston and veteran of numerous such expeditions, participated in an Earthwatch project searching for shipwrecks off the coast of Spain. One day, off the coast of Mallorca and 135 feet down, he suddenly came upon a pair of perfectly preserved Roman amphoras sitting on the sea bottom. "Imagine the privilege of finding those ancient vases," he recalled later. "Me, a plain old English teacher. I was almost afraid to touch them. It was an incredible moment of infinite discovery. It hit me that when that clay was soft, Bethlehem was just another dusty town and Hannibal was a current event."

AFRICA

ZIMBABWE

Saving the Black Rhino from Extinction

Operator: Earthwatch Expeditions, P.O. Box 403, Watertown, Mass. 02272; (800) 776-0188 or (617) 926-8200. *Price:* Expensive. *Season:* July through September. *Length:* 11 days. *Accommodations:* Tent camp.

This project is based in the magnificent Hwange National Park on the eastern border of Zimbabwe, an area which supports a profusion of wildlife. In 1970, Africa had 65,000 black rhinos. Today, because of losses from poaching, fewer than 2,500 survive. Volunteers on these projects assist in a census of the black rhinos in this corner of Africa in order to facilitate an effective strategy for the preservation of this important species. Volunteers get around the park by foot, recording spoor, tracks, and actual sightings of the animals. All large animals seen along the way are also recorded and classified.

ASIA

INDONESIA

Orangutan Research in Borneo

Indonesians once believed that orangutans could speak but had decided not to do so for fear that humans would put them to work. Today the widespread destruction of the jungle habitat of these primates threatens their survival. Much of our knowledge of these magnificent animals is the work of one woman. Over 20 years ago anthropologist Birute Galdikas began an intensive study of

Volunteers at a rain forest preserve in Borneo have the opportunity to get up close and personal with young orangutans
Bolder Adventures

wild orangutans, rehabituating former captive orangutans to the rain forest, educating local people about conservation, and working to halt the trade in captured primates. Volunteers follow orangutans through the rain forest and collect data on mother-infant relations, feeding patterns, and general social behavior. The surrounding area is rich in many species of exotic wildlife.

Operator:
Bolder Adventures,
P.O. Box 1279,
Boulder, Colo. 80306;
(800) 642-2742 or
(303) 443-6789.
Price: Moderate.
Season: Year-round.
Length: 11 days.
Accommodations: Dormitory.
Five percent discount with
BBAT coupon.

SRI LANKA

Monkey Politics

Volunteers on these expeditions spend their days in the dry evergreen forest of northern Sri Lanka, studying a population of 1,000 toque macaque monkeys which is divided into 30 social groups, each one exhibiting a stratified and sophisticated pecking order. Male macaques typically emigrate from their groups at an early age, leaving the females behind to run the family. Within groups, certain families overpower others. The most vigorous conflicts occur when two families confront each other over food or territory. Volunteers follow the different groups to learn how each uses its territory and how it fares in meetings with neighbors. Teams also chart home ranges and help examine

Operator:
Earthwatch Expeditions,
P.O. Box 403,
Watertown, Mass. 02272;
(800) 776-0188 or
(617) 926-8200.
Price: Moderate.
Season: January through
August.
Length: 17 days.
Accommodations: A field
station.

and measure anesthetized macaques. Volunteers also have time to visit the nearby ruins of the region's ninth-century capital.

CANADA

MANITOBA

Polar Bear Research Adventure

Operator:
Natural Habitat Adventures,
2945 Center Green Court S.,
Boulder, Colo. 80301;
(800) 543-8917 or
(303) 449-3711.
Price: Expensive.
Season: October.
Length: 9 days.
Accommodations: Rooms in
the local research center.
Five percent discount with
BBAT coupon.

Volunteers on these trips travel to Churchill, where over 1,000 polar bears congregate every October as they wait for Hudson Bay to freeze. Within the safety of giant tundra-buggies, the group journeys onto the tundra to observe the bears up close as they fight, play, and nurse. Participants work with University of Saskatchewan researchers studying the behavior of the polar bears, which feed intensively for two to three months, become obese, and then fast the rest of the year. Researchers seek to determine the health consequences of this unusual feeding behavior, as well as the effect of global warming upon the bears and their habitat.

Volunteers on a Natural Habitat Adventures research project travel to the Canadian Arctic to help researchers gain a greater understanding of these large bears

Natural Habitat Adventures

CARIBBEAN

BAHAMAS

Swimming with Dolphins

Donning snorkeling equipment, participants on this popular project spend several hours each day swimming with pods of Atlantic spotted dolphins who have come to enjoy human companionship. Because these cetaceans are quite friendly and curious about their human observers, volunteers can expect close personal interaction to occur. (Bring an old scarf to attract the dolphins for play.) Researchers use video and acoustic recording equipment to capture continuous sequences of human-dolphin interaction and communication patterns. The project's long-term goal is a better understanding of the system of communication employed by free-ranging dolphins in order to conserve their environment and better respect their needs.

Operator: Oceanic Society Expeditions, Fort Mason Center, Bldg. E, San Francisco, Calif. 94123; (800) 326-7491 or (415) 441-1106.
Price: Expensive.
Season: May through August.
Length: 8 days.
Accommodations: Shipboard cabins on the *Calypso Poet*, a 50-foot sailing trimaran. Five percent discount with BBAT coupon.

Lemon Sharks

Massive fishing over the past two decades has decimated the world's shark populations and threatens to upset the ecology of the oceans. And yet little is known about the behavior of most shark species. Volunteers on these expeditions to the Bimini Islands focus on the specific challenge of determining how lemon sharks are able to move with such great precision across broad reaches of ocean. For example, sharks are able to travel precise paths, such as from Miami to New York, and then return. Researchers fit sharks with ultrasonic transmitters, then release them and follow their movements. They also bait long lines to capture sharks; measure, sex, and tag the sharks; and collect environmental data such as water and ocean-floor samples. Volunteers must be able to swim.

Operator: Earthwatch Expeditions, P.O. Box 403, Watertown, Mass. 02272; (800) 776-0188 or (617) 926-8200.
Price: Expensive.
Season: June through August.
Length: 12 days.
Accommodations: A house on a lagoon.

U.S. VIRGIN ISLANDS

Saving the Leatherback Turtle

Operator:
Earthwatch Expeditions,
Box 403AT,
Watertown, Mass. 02272;
(800) 776-0188 or
(617) 926-8200.
Price: Expensive.
Season: April through June.
Length: 10 days.
Accommodations: Teams live
in beach cottages with
kitchens and bathrooms.

The deepest-diving breath-holding animal (to depths of 4,000 feet) and the largest of the turtles (weighing up to 1,500 pounds), the leatherback is the most threatened of the marine turtle species of the southeastern United States. It is most vulnerable during the months when the females come ashore at night to lay up to 100 leathery eggs in large pits on sandy beaches. Sixty days later the young turtles all hatch together and scurry toward the ocean. Volunteers on these expeditions make their base on idyllic St. Croix, where they engage in a variety of activities including measuring, tagging, and examining female turtles as they lay their eggs; moving unsafe nests to more secure areas; patrolling the beaches to guard against egg poachers; and protecting the hatchlings from predators and obstacles as they race toward the sea.

Over the last decade, Earthwatch volunteers have saved tens of thousands of leatherback turtle hatchlings and released them later into the ocean

Earthwatch

"Only those are fit to live who do not fear to die, and none are fit to die who have shrunk from the joy of life and the duty of life. Both life and death are parts of the same Great Adventure."

THEODORE ROOSEVELT,
"THE GREAT ADVENTURE"

Volunteers on a Natural Habitat Adventures research project in the Shetland Islands study the behavior and breeding patterns of the thousands of colorful puffins nesting there

Steve Morella/Natural Habitat Adventures

EUROPE

BRITAIN

A Puffin Watch in the Shetland Islands

Located some 90 miles north of the Scottish mainland and isolated by the Atlantic Ocean and the North Sea, the Shetland Islands are a haven for a vast variety of wildlife. Hundreds of thousands of seabirds (including the colorful and comical puffin) nest in enormous colonies on the rugged sea cliffs. The rolling moorlands, heaths, and countless lochs are the habitats of breeding birds such as snowy owls and Arctic skuas. Volunteers on these trips spend a week on lovely Fair Island, working on projects sponsored by the Nature Conservancy Council. These include the study of breeding puffins to determine their success rates and frequency of feeding, the monitoring of behavior, and

Operator: Natural Habitat Adventures, 2945 Center Green Court S., Boulder, Colo. 80301; (800) 543-8917 or (303) 449-3711.
Price: Expensive.
Season: July.
Length: 13 days.
Accommodations: Rooms in local research center. Five percent discount with BBAT coupon.

the banding of skua chicks. The remaining days are spent visiting the other Shetland Islands to see both the natural and archaeological sights.

IRELAND

Castles of County Clare

Operator:
University Research
Expeditions,
University of California,
Berkeley, Calif. 94720;
(510) 642-6586.
Price: Moderate.
Season: June to early
August.
Length: 12 days.
Accommodations: Rooms in
rented cottages.

Medieval Irish society was characterized by hundreds of chiefdoms, whose feuds, raids, and wars are recounted in the sagas of medieval poets. Irish aristocrats of the Middle Ages built tower-houses, the remains of which are still visible today. Dysert Castle in Corofin, County Clare, was the site of a major battle in the 14th century. Although a poet's saga provides considerable detail about the battle, little is known about how the people of the period actually lived. Volunteers on this project excavate an important ruin at this castle to shed light on the daily lifestyle of Irish aristocrats.

Medieval Churches of Aran

The Aran Islands off the west coast of Ireland were renowned during the medieval period for their monasteries. Such was the sanctity of the Aran

The Adventure Travel Hall of Fame:
ROY CHAPMAN ANDREWS

Roy Chapman Andrews, first the curator and then president of the New York American Museum of Natural History, was at once a resourceful explorer and hunter, a studious scientist, and a successful businessman. He was born at the end of the last century, a time when "rugged individualism" was still widely respected for its accomplishments. In the first three decades of this century, western China and particularly the area now known as Mongolia were largely unexplored by Western observers. Andrews proposed a series of expeditions into the area to collect specimens of both present and extinct species and

monasteries that the islands became known as "Aran of the Saints." No historical records exist for these monasteries, and little is known about how they functioned in their heyday. The focus of this project is Teampall Chiarain on the large island of Inishmore, where volunteers help map the extensive site and excavate the domestic structures located close to the 12th-century church. Participants also have time to explore the rest of the island by bicycle and foot.

PORTUGAL

Azores Whale Watch

The Azores, an isolated scattering of islands lying 950 miles west of Lisbon, are home to a wide variety of marine wildlife, including sperm whales, pilot whales, dolphins, and turtles. Volunteers on these projects travel among the islands on a sailing schooner and assist scientists from Oxford University in continuing vital whale research started more than a decade ago by the International Fund for Animal Welfare. Participants observe and identify whales, noting their markings and behaviors, and may even have an opportunity to swim with pods of socializing

Operator:
University Research Expeditions, University of California, Berkeley, Calif. 94720; (510) 642-6586.
Price: Moderate.
Season: June to early August.
Length: 13 days.
Accommodations: Rooms in a house close to the main town of Kilronan on the largest island of Inishmore.

Operator:
Natural Habitat Adventures, 2945 Center Green Court S., Boulder, Colo. 80301; (800) 543-8917 or (303) 449-3711.
Price: Expensive.
Season: June and August.
Length: 8 days.
Accommodations: Shipboard cabins. Five percent discount with BBAT coupon.

to test a major scientific theory of the day: that central Asia was "the incubating center for northern mammalian life." His group included top geologists, zoologists, topographers, and paleontologists.

China in the 1920s was a grim place. Racked by civil wars and periodic states of anarchy, the country presented very real risks to Andrews' people. Roving bandit gangs attacked them repeatedly—yet the first two expeditions into the Gobi Desert yielded the

largest collection of mammals ever taken from a single region in Asia. The Third Asiatic Expedition, in particular, proved significant and put Andrews on the front pages of newspapers around the world. After excavating numerous deposits of dinosaur skeletons (most of unknown species), his people discovered the first fossilized dinosaur eggs ever seen by modern people and thus answered one of paleontology's most perplexing riddles: how did dinosaurs come into the world?

sperm whales. The data from this project is used to protect these majestic animals.

SPAIN

Prehistoric Societies of Mallorca

Operator:
Earthwatch Expeditions,
P.O. Box 403,
Watertown, Mass. 02272;
(800) 776-0188 or
(617) 926-8200.
Price: Moderate.
Season: Year-round.
Length: 14 days.
Accommodations: Dorm style
in a farmhouse.

This popular Earthwatch project has continued for over 20 years and involved 1,800 volunteers. The results of their findings have changed the entire perspective on prehistory in the western Mediterranean basin. The target of this project is the numerous remains of a Copper Age people who settled this area about 2500 B.C. and developed a permanent, remarkably well-organized and sophisticated community. This was one of the longest continuously inhabited sites in Europe. Excavations have uncovered numerous tools, coins, pieces of pottery, and jewelry among the ruins of walls and pavements. Archaeologists have concluded that these ancient people were partly responsible for the spread of metallurgy throughout Western Europe.

LATIN AMERICA

BELIZE

Belize Archeology Project

The site of Lamanai lies in northern Belize. This great urban center of the ancient Maya was occupied continuously from 1500 B.C. until A.D. 1675 or later. Volunteers on these expeditions will aid in the excavation of a mound complex, consisting of three hills surrounding what may be a plaza. The area is littered with potsherds, flint debris from the manufacturing of stone tools, and structural remnants. Volunteers will help with the actual excavation of the sites, screen the material from the digs, wash and catalog the artifacts, and assist in the surveying and mapping.

Operator: Oceanic Society Expeditions, Fort Mason Center, Bldg. E, San Francisco, Calif. 94123; (800) 326-7491 or (415) 441-1106.
Price: Expensive.
Season: June through November.
Length: 8 days.
Accommodations: A comfortable jungle lodge. Five percent discount with BBAT coupon.

Volunteers with the Oceanic Society Expeditions project in northern Belize assist archaeologists in the excavation of Mayan ruins

Hal Markowitz/Oceanic Society Expeditions

Belize Howler Monkey Research Project

Black howler monkeys are found only in Belize, southern Mexico, and Guatemala. Additional information about their habitat needs, social behavior, and distribution must be gathered in order to create an effective program for their conservation. Howler monkeys live in groups of four to eight individuals, each troop usually consisting of an adult male and females with their young. The male has a distinctive roar which can be heard up to a mile away. The site of this research project is the jungle-covered Mayan ruins at Lamanai in northern Belize. Researchers on these expeditions have extra time for birding and wildlife observation in the jungle, canoeing in a nearby river, and swimming.

Operator: Oceanic Society Expeditions, Fort Mason Center, Bldg. E, San Francisco, Calif. 94123; (800) 326-7491 or (415) 441-1106.
Price: Expensive.
Season: March, May, October, and November.
Length: 8 days.
Accommodations: Lodge. Five percent discount with BBAT coupon.

Sea Turtle and Manatee Project

Operator:
Oceanic Society
Expeditions,
Fort Mason Center, Bldg. E,
San Francisco, Calif. 94123;
(800) 326-7491 or
(415) 441-1106.
Price: Expensive.
Season: August.
Length: 8 days.
Accommodations: Lodge.
Five percent discount with
BBAT coupon.

Just south of Belize City, along the coast at the end of a 15-mile dirt road, lies Gales Point, a settlement of 350 people who offer visitors a refreshing dose of rural Creole hospitality. The region is a critical habitat for the largest Caribbean manatee population in Central America, and its beach is the primary nesting site in Belize for the endangered hawksbill sea turtle. In 1992, residents created the Gales Point Manatee Community Sanctuary to protect the wildlife and develop an ecotourism program. Volunteers on these expeditions assist in a study of habitat use by resident manatees and a project for restoring and assessing the distribution of the turtles. Volunteers build cages over some of the 20,000 hawksbill eggs, which would otherwise be destroyed by local predators, and also excavate hatched nests to record the hatchlings and chaperone them as they make their way across the sand to the sea. Nights are spent in the town of Dangriga, whose residents are largely Garifuna, a closely knit people of West African and Caribbean Indian ancestry who first settled there in 1823.

"In wildness is the salvation of the world."

HENRY DAVID THOREAU

Great Achievements in Adventure Travel

In the summer of 1911, Hiram Bingham, a young professor of archaeology from Yale University, entered the jungle fastness of the Andes beyond Cusco, Peru, accompanied by two college companions, a Peruvian soldier, and a mule train. They sought the last great capital of the Incan Empire.

A few days out of Cusco the expedition entered the magnificent canyon of the Urubamba River. Cliffs loomed 2,000 feet overhead. Bingham questioned every Indian he met about ruins in the jungle and carefully investigated each rumor.

The small party camped one evening at the edge of the river at the foot of a mountain called Machu Picchu. A local Indian told Bingham of ruins high above on a ridge. The next morning Bingham set out

Dolphin Research on Turneffe Atoll

The Turneffe Islands comprise the largest of three atolls in the barrier reef that stretches for over 100 miles down the Belize coast. Most of its 35 small islands are covered with thick mangrove forests that provide a vital breeding area for many wildlife species, including numerous seabirds. Here, mangrove islands, seagrass beds, and coral reefs form one intricately related ecosystem. Bottlenose dolphins are plentiful in the area but have never been studied. Volunteers on these projects collect data on resident dolphins, observing them both above and underwater, and have plenty of opportunity to snorkel over some of the finest reefs in the Caribbean. A visit is also made to the famous Blue Hole on nearby Lighthouse Reef Atoll.

Operator: Oceanic Society Expeditions, Fort Mason Center, Bldg. E, San Francisco, Calif. 94123; (800) 326-7491 or (415) 441-1106.
Price: Expensive.
Season: Year-round.
Length: 8 and 10 days.
Accommodations: A small lodge on Blackbird Cay, a 4,000-acre tropical island. Five percent discount with BBAT coupon.

"The true traveler has in him something of the explorer's urge to discover. It does not matter that there is little scope left for original discovery. The important thing is that he should discover things that are new to him and be able to feel the same thrill and excitement as though they were equally unknown to everyone else."

M. A. MICHAEL,
TRAVELERS QUEST

with his Indian guide to climb the sheer cliffs to inspect the ruins. On all fours they pulled themselves up through slippery grass, digging their fingers into the soil to keep from falling. The heat was oppressive.

The two men reached a grass hut. The Indians there told Bingham that old houses were "a little farther on." He set out with a small boy to inspect them. He rounded a knoll and suddenly found himself facing tier upon tier of Incan terraces hundreds of feet long, rising like giant stairs up the mountainside.

"What settlement of Incas had needed a hundred such terraces in this lofty wilderness?" he asked himself in amazement.

Bingham soon discovered temples, plazas, houses, and scores of other buildings buried in the dense jungle. Only then did he realize that he had stumbled upon "the largest and most important ruin discovered in South America since the Spaniards had arrived."

CHILE

Wild Llama Research in Torres del Paine National Park

Operator:
Patagonia Research
Expeditions,
RR 6, Box 28,
Ames, Iowa 50014;
(515) 292-8384.
Price: Expensive.
Season: January.
Length: 16 days.
Accommodations: Tent camp.

The director has been conducting field research on guanaco behavior since 1976. Recently, he has shifted focus to the Patagonian puma and its predatory relationship with the wild guanacos. The study takes place in remote Torres del Paine National Park, home to thousands of free-ranging guanacos, the progenitor of the llama. Volunteers work on this project in mid-summer, that busy time when guanacos are divided into family and male groups, females are nursing newborn babies, males are defending territories, and the mating season is underway. Field activities include tagging and monitoring the wild guanacos with radio-collars.

COSTA RICA

Replanting Tropical Forests

Operator:
University Research
Expeditions,
University of California,
Berkeley, Calif. 94720;
(510) 642-6586.
Price: Moderate.
Season: July and August.
Length: 14 days.
Accommodations: Rooms in a
field station.

For years Costa Rica has been a leader in the preservation of its natural resources. Its park system, for example, is one of the most comprehensive in the Americas. However, deforestation still occurs at an alarming pace. Part of the problem is the willingness of local farmers to cut and burn the tropical forest to clear land for agriculture and cattle-grazing. Because the soil is poor in nutrients, the cleared areas are soon abandoned. Volunteers on this project replant native trees on cleared land and convert it to other uses, such as agroforestry. This should provide a financial incentive to farmers not to clear additional rain forest. The volunteers work on a 60-acre cattle pasture located in the southern part of the country at the 3,300 foot level, where they fence off cattle, take soil samples, measure runoff during rains, and plant trees.

MEXICO

Vanishing Rain Forests of Mexico

Every 30 minutes, 28 acres of the world's rain forest are destroyed. These complex yet shrinking ecosystems harbor 50 to 80 percent of all existing species of plants and animals, help stabilize the climate, and are an important source of human products, ranging from food to pharmaceuticals. At Los Tuxtlas are found the remaining remnants of the northernmost reaches of the Amazon rain forest. Only 15 percent of the original forest remains, and that in fragments. These isolated forest islands cannot support the high level of biodiversity that drive a nonfragmented rain forest. Volunteers on these expeditions survey these fragments, mesh-netting birds and bats, recording tree species, and capturing terrestrial mammals in an effort to determine how fragmentation has affected resident birds and mammals and whether these fragments can support these survivors.

Operator: Earthwatch Expeditions, P.O. Box 403, Watertown, Mass. 02272; (800) 776-0188 or (617) 926-8200.
Price: Moderate.
Season: June through August.
Length: 15 days.
Accommodations: Rooms in a research station.

Baja Island Predators

Like Darwin's Galapagos, each of the islands in the Gulf of California contains its own separate experiment in evolution and adaptation. On certain islands spiders, scorpions, lizards, or coyotes predominate, sometimes thriving in populations two to 100 times larger than those on the mainland. Volunteers on these expeditions seek to discover why these variances occur, working on some of the 30 offshore islands that fringe the pristine and beautiful beaches of Bahia de los Angeles. The local people live in small and peaceful communities. Teams capture, count, measure, observe, and determine the diets of lizards and spiders. The surrounding waters are an important nursery for whales, dolphins, sea turtles, and sea lions, while the small deserted islands are busy rookeries for seabirds. The trips begin and end in San Diego.

Operator: Earthwatch Expeditions, P.O. Box 403, Watertown, Mass. 02272; (800) 776-0188 or (617) 926-8200.
Price: Moderate.
Season: March, July, and October.
Length: 7 days.
Accommodations: Tent camps.

Digging Dinosaurs in the Chihuahuan Desert

Operator: Dinamation International Society, 550 Crossroads Ct., Fruita, Colo. 81521; (800) DIG-DINO or (970) 858-7282. *Price:* Expensive. *Season:* November and February. *Length:* 7 days. *Accommodations:* A small, three-star hotel. Five percent discount with BBAT coupon.

Paleontology in Mexico is still in its infancy. These seven-day expeditions allow volunteers to explore some of the richest unexcavated fossil sites in North America. Cretaceous fossils, such as hadrosaurs (duck-billed dinosaurs) and ceratopsians (horned dinosaurs), are common and often in such an excellent state of preservation that skin impressions can be found. They represent the most equatorial dinosaur fauna known in North America. Volunteers will work at two quarries, where dinosaur bones are abundant and scattered over the surface, and will also learn how to prepare the plaster jackets that protect the fossil material. Nights are spent in the colonial city of Saltillo, famous for its many preserved historical buildings and monuments.

PERU

Amazon Katydids

Operator: Earthwatch Expeditions, P.O. Box 403, Watertown, Mass. 02272; (800) 776-0188 or (617) 926-8200. *Price:* Moderate. *Season:* August and September. *Length:* 15 days. *Accommodations:* The Explorama Lodge near Iquitos.

Volunteers on these popular expeditions study the fantastic diversity of the 360 species of katydids found in the Peruvian Amazon. Known for their cricket-like nocturnal singing, these insects have evolved amazing adaptations to survive the bats, birds, monkeys, rodents, snakes, spiders, wasps, and ants which dine upon them. Camouflage artists, katydids mimic twigs, pieces of barks, leaves, lichen, and even bird droppings as they rest, otherwise defenseless, during the day. Volunteers collect data on katydid taxonomy, biology, ecology, and behavior. As part of the project, they spend time each day on a canopy walkway that runs for almost 3,000 feet along the top of the virgin rain forest. The area is also home to a rich assortment of tapirs, monkeys, sloths, and capybaras.

Research on River Dolphins in the Amazonian Rain Forest

Volunteers on these popular expeditions assist in a study of the Amazon's lively pink freshwater dolphins. These are the largest of the river dolphins and endemic to the Amazon River basin. There is a concern that they, like their cousins elsewhere, are at serious risk from human encroachment. Volunteers collect data on the dolphins' movements, social organization, and species communication, gathering the information necessary for the mammals' protection and conservation. Workers also have time to swim with the dolphins, explore the rain forest, and visit Indian settlements along the river.

Operator: Oceanic Society Expeditions, Fort Mason Center, Bldg. E, San Francisco, Calif. 94123; (800) 326-7491 or (415) 441-1106.
Price: Expensive.
Season: August and December.
Length: 8 days.
Accommodations: Cabins on a traditional wooden riverboat. Five percent discount with BBAT coupon.

THE PACIFIC

MIDWAY

Midway Monk Seals

The primary goal of this important endangered species recovery project is to restore the Hawaiian monk seal population at Midway Atoll. The National Marine Fisheries Service has placed a high priority on the recovery of this species. The goal of the project is to introduce young female monk seals to Midway in an effort to re-establish the population, and to monitor the entire resident population to determine survival and patterns of movement. Volunteers assist with all aspects of the recovery project, including data collection and seal reintroductions. In teams of two, workers patrol the beaches collecting data on seal beach-use patterns, mapping seal locations, reading tags of known seals, recording unusual markings of untagged seals, and collecting environmental data. Volunteers have free time to enjoy the incredible marine and birdlife of Midway.

Operator: Oceanic Society Expeditions, Fort Mason Center, Bldg. E, San Francisco, Calif. 94123; (800) 326-7491 or (415) 441-1106.
Price: Expensive.
Season: Year-round.
Length: 8 days.
Accommodations: Rooms in restored military barracks. Five percent discount with BBAT coupon.

Volunteers with Oceanic Society Expeditions monitor the 350,000 pairs of Laysan albatrosses nesting on Midway Atoll

Nanette Seto/Oceanic Society Expeditions

Midway Seabirds

Operator: Oceanic Society Expeditions, Fort Mason Center, Bldg. E, San Francisco, Calif. 94123; (800) 326-7491 or (415) 441-1106. *Price:* Expensive. *Season:* Year-round. *Length:* 8 days. *Accommodations:* Rooms in restored military barracks. Five percent discount with BBAT coupon.

Midway Atoll is home to the largest concentration of seabirds in the Pacific—over 1,000,000 birds nest there every year—and also shelters the world's largest colony of Laysan albatrosses. The highly endangered short-tailed albatross visits there regularly, along with 15 species of migratory seabirds. Under the direction of biologists from the U.S. Fish & Wildlife Service, volunteers will assist with monitoring the seabird populations of Midway Atoll. The results should yield valuable information on environmental change and fluctuation, since seabirds are considered an indicator species of oceanic resources. Volunteers will handle tasks such as population counts, nest monitoring, mapping of nesting areas, monitoring of chick hatching, marking nests, and banding of birds. Nights are spent at the old Navy base, which has been restored.

"Who valued life more highly, the aviators who spent it on the art they loved or the misers who doled it out like pennies through their ant-like days?"

CHARLES LINDBERGH,
WE

UNITED STATES

ALASKA

Alaska's Tropical Birds

Over the past 20 years an ominous trend has developed with regard to migratory songbirds. Many populations are in sharp decline, for reasons which are currently unclear. Volunteers on this research project will seek answers to this perplexing problem on the banks of remote Mother Goose Lake in the Becharof National Wildlife Refuge on the Alaskan Peninsula. Thousands of tiny warblers migrate there thousands of miles from tropical forests in order to nest. Helping to monitor songbird breeding and migration, volunteers can expect to assist in trapping the birds in mist nets, banding them, monitoring nests, and inventorying the small plants and mammals in the area. Moose, caribou, foxes, wolves, weasels, beavers and river otters also live there, along with 192 species of birds.

Operator:
Earthwatch Expeditions,
P.O. Box 403,
Watertown, Mass. 02272;
(800) 776-0188 or
(617) 926-8200.
Price: Moderate.
Season: June through mid-September.
Length: 16 days.
Accommodations: A three-room log cabin.

Wilderness Study in the Wrangell Mountains

Volunteers on this popular project spend their time in one of Alaska's most spectacular regions, the Wrangell-St. Elias National Park, the largest preserved wilderness area in North America. Established in 1980, the park is relatively new and uniquely mandated to preserve, as part of the natural system, the rural lifestyle of residents who live within the park boundaries. A major problem the volunteers study is the conflicts that a gateway community encounters as it works to sustain an Alaskan bush lifestyle in the face of increasing tourism and human activity. The itinerary includes two strenuous journeys into the backcountry: one a backpacking trip to the Kennicott Glacier to study the ice's movements and features; the other a 90-mile raft explo-

Operator:
Wildlands Studies/
San Francisco State
University,
3 Mosswood Circle,
Cazadero, Calif. 95421;
(707) 632-5665.
Price: Inexpensive.
Season: June through
August.
Length: 6 weeks.
Accommodations: Tent camps.

ration down the meltwater river born of the glacier, to study the diversity and adaptations of plants and animals to the stresses of a subarctic existence. The project carries nine units of college credit.

ARIZONA

Aboard the Trash Tracker on Lake Powell

Operator:
National Park Service,
Glen Canyon National
Recreation Area,
Box 1507,
Page, Ariz. 86040;
(520) 645-2471.
Price: No charge.
Season: April through mid-November.
Length: 5 days.
Accommodations: Cabins on a houseboat.

The world's second-largest man-made lake, 186-mile-long Lake Powell straddles the Arizona–Utah border and draws some 3.6 million visitors each year to its red sandstone-walled canyons. Volunteers commit to a five-day period aboard a houseboat for a minimum of 32 hours devoted to the removal of trash, debris, and waste from Lake Powell's 1,900-mile shoreline. The *Trash Tracker* carries four volunteers, captain, and first mate on weekly cruises to clean up the shoreline pollution left by less-considerate houseboaters. Volunteers provide their own food and personal gear, work in the heat, cold, and rain, and often travel great distances to take part in this program—and yet these trips usually book up one year in advance!

CALIFORNIA

Dolphins and Whales in Monterey Bay

Operator:
Oceanic Society
Expeditions, Fort Mason
Center, Bldg. E, San
Francisco, Calif. 94123;
(800) 326-7491 or
(415) 441-1106.
Price: Moderate.
Season: September and Oct.
Length: 7 days.
Accommodations: A Monterey motel. Five percent discount with BBAT coupon.

Volunteers on these popular projects work aboard a 55-foot motor vessel. Their primary task is to gather data on the behavior, ecology, communication, and distribution of the Pacific white-sided dolphins resident in the region. A secondary objective is to record all humpback and blue whales that enter the bay and to document their behavior. Both dolphins and whales will be photographed, and the pictures compared with those already in an identification file. The Pacific Ocean off Monterey harbors one of the richest and most diverse populations of marine mammals in the world. Pacific white-sided dolphins often swim in schools of more than 1,000 individuals.

Preserving California Wildlands

Team members take part in ecological investigations of the forested canyons, wilderness backcountry, and rugged coastal environments that form California's famed Big Sur wildlands. The focus of this project is the Landels Hill-Big Creek Reserve, 4,000 acres of largely undisturbed wilderness that is home to diverse flora and fauna. Team members help establish critical long-term studies to provide valuable information concerning changes in the status and composition of the Big Creek region and fresh insights into how the area is affected by major events such as fires, floods, and droughts. Teams work under the supervision of research biologists on a variety of projects: assessing the abundance and behavior of marine mammal populations, including sea otters and seals; taking part in fishery/stream-habitat investigations; and surveying and mapping the animal and plant communities found in the rich intertidal zone. Participants receive three college credits from San Francisco State University.

Operator:
Wildlands Studies/
San Francisco State
University,
3 Mosswood Circle,
Cazadero, Calif. 95421;
(707) 632-5662.
Price: Inexpensive.
Season: June and July.
Length: 14 days.
Accommodations: Tent camp.

COLORADO

Digging the Dinosaurs

Dinosaur-lovers seeking hands-on involvement in their favorite subject can join an actual dig under the supervision of paleontologists. The most popular of these are the five-day digging trips sponsored by Dinamation International Society. Unlike other digs located in remote desert areas of the West far from any amenities, these field projects lie within an easy drive of Grand Junction, Colorado, where participants are housed in a hotel instead of tents. These expeditions are particularly popular with youngsters. Volunteers work on a site that was once a water hole, excavating a jumble of skeletons that includes an apatosaurus, an allosaurus, and a nodosaur. Several years ago participants unearthed

Operator:
Dinamation International
Society, 550 Crossroads Ct.,
Fruita, Colo. 81521;
(800) DIG-DINO or
(970) 858-7282.
Price: Expensive.
Season: May through
August.
Length: 5 days.
Accommodations: Hotel. Five
percent discount with
BBAT coupon.

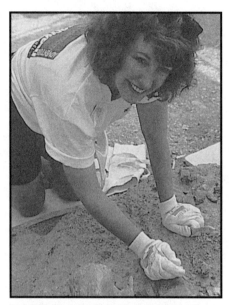

Volunteers on Dinamation International Society digs in Colorado have made several major discoveries
James C. Simmons

a new species of apatosaurus, the largest such animal ever found. One enormous vertebra of the animal measured 6 feet by 5 feet and weighed at least a ton.

Excavating an Anasazi Pueblo

Operator: Crow Canyon Archaeological Center, 23390 County Road K, Cortez, Colo. 81321; (800) 422-8975 or (970) 565-8975.
Price: Moderate.
Season: June through October.
Length: 7 days.
Accommodations: Comfortable dormitories.

The Anasazi domain once spread over an area larger than the state of California. They were compulsive builders who, without benefit of the wheel or beasts of burden, raised great apartment structures unequalled until the manufacture of structural steel centuries later. Some seven centuries ago the Anasazi people abandoned their cities and tilled fields, and moved into other regions of the Southwest to found the great Pueblo cultures in which many of their traditions and customs still survive. Working with trowels and whisk brooms, volunteers on this popular project excavate the sprawling, 350-room Sand

Canyon Pueblo, an Anasazi ruin forgotten and buried for at least 700 years. They also dig, wash, sort, and catalog artifacts in the laboratory. The site is located 10 miles from Mesa Verde National Park, in the heart of one of the most archaeologically significant regions in the United States.

An Earthwatch research project in Hawaii seeks to discover if dolphins can learn an artificial language

Earthwatch

HAWAII

Studying Humpback Whales

Of all the cetacean species, the gregarious humpbacks are particularly charismatic and delightful. This project focuses on the hauntingly beautiful songs (the most complex of any animal) the whales sing during their winter residence off the islands of Hawaii and Maui. The songs may go on for hours and are specific to groups and areas. Volunteers record the whales' songs and then play them back from underwater microphones to study the behavior they generate. Time is divided between a 17-foot Boston whaler (the playback boat) and an elevated shore station for observation and photography.

Operator: Earthwatch Expeditions, P.O. Box 403, Watertown, Mass. 02272; (800) 776-0188 or (617) 926-8200.
Price: Moderate.
Season: Jan. through April.
Length: 14 days.
Accommodations: A house on Maui and a tent camp on the Lanai beach.

Teaching Language to Dolphins

Operator:
Earthwatch Expeditions,
P.O. Box 403,
Watertown, Mass. 02272;
(800) 776-0188 or
(617) 926-8200.
Price: Moderate.
Season: Year-round.
Length: 14 and 28 days.
Accommodations: Ocean-
facing condominium.

Researchers at the Kewalo Basin Marine Mammal Laboratory in Honolulu have been teaching language to four bottlenose dolphins. Thus far, the dolphins have learned more than 600 sentences and can understand such grammatical distinctions as direct versus indirect objects. However, they cannot use their skills to communicate with one another because the emphasis in their training has been on language comprehension rather than language production. Volunteers on this popular project assist in the instruction of two young dolphins in an artificial language to see if they can learn to "speak" it. The long-term goal is to determine "the ability of dolphins to exchange information with trainers and amongst themselves." Volunteers serve as trainers in addition to helping with both the feeding of the dolphins and the weekly tank cleanings.

MONTANA

The Wolves of Yellowstone National Park

Operator:
Yellowstone Ecosystem
Studies,
P.O. Box 6640,
Bozeman, Mont. 59771;
(406) 587-7758.
Price: Expensive.
Season: May to early July,
December through March.
Length: 7 days.
Accommodations: Rooms in a
rented house. Five percent
discount with BBAT
coupon.

One of the major ecological stories of the past few years has been the return of wolves to Yellowstone 60 years after their elimination. Researchers will start an investigation of the ripple influence of the wolf's impact on the entire ecosystem, from plants and small animals to bison and bear. The particular focus is on the coyote and red fox, both of which will be forced to adapt to their changing environment. Volunteers monitor social ecology, including population density, pack and litter size, territorial behavior, and interactions with one another. The return of the wolf offers a rare opportunity to study the impact of a major predator on the balance of nature. The research takes place in the Lamar Valley and Blacktail Plateau regions of the park's Northern Range, an area often called the "Serengeti of North America."

Montana Wildlands Field Study

Volunteers on this project will join biologists in a unique biological study of the "micro" flora and fauna species in Montana's East Pioneer Mountains. The study area includes a rich variety of habitat types ranging from forests with relatively high human recreational use patterns to roadless high-country lands proposed for protected status. Baseline biological surveys of "micro" flora and fauna are now seen as being among the best ways to determine the biological diversity of an area and the overall health of the ecosystem. Once an initial survey has been completed, the health of the ecosystem can more easily be monitored by land managers and other resource specialists. The volunteers then backpack into a remote Rocky Mountain wilderness area to evaluate the area for inclusion in the Wilderness Preservation System. Participants receive nine college credits from San Francisco State University.

Operator:
Wildlands Studies/
San Francisco State
University,
3 Mosswood Circle,
Cazadero, Calif. 95421;
(707) 632-5662.
Price: Inexpensive.
Season: July and August.
Length: 6 weeks.
Accommodations: Tent camp.

"The pursuit and search for the buried treasures of knowledge calls for a unique combination of abilities, for the explorer-excavator must be traveller, detective, and scholar all at the same time. It is, perhaps, the most exciting of all intellectual pursuits."

JOHN GARSTANG,
"IN PURSUIT OF KNOWLEDGE"

Alpine Lakes Survey in Yellowstone National Park

Volunteers on these popular projects backpack into the Beartooth Plateau region of the park, a beautiful area boasting over 600 lakes. Previous research has concluded that these alpine lakes are quite sensitive and easily disrupted by such man-made pollution as acid rain. The study's goal is greater understanding of the delicate ecology of

Volunteers on a research project for Yellowstone Ecosystem Studies backpack into one of the park's most remote wildernesses to assess the status of several alpine lakes

Yellowstone Ecosystem Studies

Operator: Yellowstone Ecosystem Studies, P.O. Box 6640, Bozeman, Mont. 59771; (406) 587-7758. *Price:* Moderate. *Season:* July and August. *Length:* 12 days. *Accommodations:* Tent camps. Five percent discount with BBAT coupon.

this fragile and rare ecosystem. Daily activities include lake-chemistry sampling, lake mapping with satellite global positioning devices, and surveying for possible rare fauna. Volunteers spend five days at each of two base camps. Professional porters carry all camping supplies and food into the backcountry.

"Remaining for a long time at one place may be fatal to a traveler; for it weakens his energy and injures his health. Most of my attacks of fever and illness have occurred in the pauses between the journeys; whilst on the march I was generally well and in good spirits. Protracted spells of idleness in one place makes one prone to useless brooding and fancies."

DR. WILHELM JUNKER, *TRAVELS IN AFRICA, 1879–1883*

Volunteers on a long-lived Earthwatch project excavate the remains of more than 100 mammoths

Earthwatch

SOUTH DAKOTA

Excavating a Graveyard of Mammoths

Approximately 26,000 years ago, a steep-sided pool lured over 100 Ice Age mammoths to their death. Unable to escape, the huge animals drowned or starved to death, gradually filling the pool with their skeletal remains and creating the largest graveyard of mammoths in North America. Thus far, paleontologists have unearthed the bones of over 45 mammoths, as well as those of a great short-faced bear which stood 11 feet high. Volunteers wield trowels and dental picks to dig, map, record, and preserve the bones. The site lies within the city limits of Hot Springs, a retirement community.

Operator:
Earthwatch Expeditions,
P.O. Box 403,
Watertown, Mass. 02272;
(800) 776-0188 or
(617) 926-8200.
Price: Moderate.
Season: July.
Length: 14 days.
Accommodations: Dormitory rooms.

PROFILE

BIRGIT WINNING
OCEANIC SOCIETY EXPEDITIONS

J ayne Wise, a freelance writer on assignment for *National Geographic Traveler* magazine, had signed up for one of the Oceanic Society Expeditions' popular research projects in Belize to help assess the dolphin population. The country has the world's second longest barrier reef, which effectively protects the dolphins from attacks by such natural enemies as sharks and killer whales. The researchers' goal was an examination of the dolphins' social behavior, organization, and distribution in a Belize atoll, which is a different habitat from those previously studied. The data gathered would then be used by local environmentalists to persuade the government to designate the area as a marine sanctuary.

Wise was one of the first volunteers to enter the waters with the dolphins. "A dream about to come true, and I discover I'm nervous," she admitted later in her article. "Fumbling into flippers, mask, and snorkel, we ease underwater. And there, maybe ten feet away, we see them, a pair of dolphins hovering as if in suspension, backlit by sunbeams filtering through the blue sea. They've watched us enter their realm and now, curious, watch us move slowly toward them. Following weeks of anticipation, I search for a poetic reaction to this moment, an epiphany of oneness with dolphins, but in all honesty what strikes me is how familiar they look, like two frisky dogs, like bottlenose golden retrievers of the seas. After pausing a moment, they swim gently away from us in unison, twice looking back at us before they merge into the blue beyond. Above the crackling hum of snapping shrimp I hear their high-pitched squeaks, a sound so otherworldly in this watery vastness that I feel like a stranger in a strange land."

Like the thousands of other Oceanic Society Expeditions volunteers, Wise paid for the privilege of joining her project. With government and university funds for scientific projects in short supply, enthusiastic amateurs such as Wise often rescue enterprises that otherwise would have collapsed. The cost of each expedition is shared among the volunteers, and all these vacation marine scientists learn as they work. Before they leave home, they receive a packet of scientific information on their project. And once at the site, they gain a quick education in the intricate practicalities of their subjects. The scientists end up with money and workers, while the volunteers are rewarded with a valuable and exciting educational experience.

Oceanic Society Expeditions is a nonprofit organization dedicated to the twofold mission of undertaking research to protect aquatic habitats and promoting environmental education. Their current catalog lists 17 natural-history expeditions and 16 research expeditions. The latter are as diverse as collecting biological data on leatherback and green turtles as they come ashore on their nesting beaches of Surinam, expeditions to record the behavior and population distribution of the pink freshwater dolphins in the Amazon River Basin, and monitoring the monk seal population on Midway Atoll. Last year some 2,500 clients signed up for the extended international projects, while another 7,000 local people were involved on an outreach basis.

Sixty percent of the company's clients each year sign on to one of the research projects, the vast majority of which focus on sea mammals. These dedicated and energetic volunteers are responsible for the gritty day-to-day work that ultimately provides the basis for major discoveries. As Birgit Winning, the society's president, observes: "We use our volunteers not to interpret the behavior patterns observed but to collect and record the hard data that the researchers can then use to interpret the animals' behavior. For example, our volunteers on the dolphin projects will monitor the hydrophones and record the hard data on to the data sheets."

Oceanic Society Expeditions in its present form is the result of a vision that Winning brought to the organization when she became president in 1981. Born in Germany, she came to Canada at the age of 12 and four years later moved to the United States. She was a student of primates at San Francisco State University when she went to work for the Steinhardt Aquarium. "That experience really opened my eyes to the marine environment, so I changed directions in my studies and decided to go into the marine sciences," she remembers. Next she took a position as a zookeeper at the San Francisco Zoological Society and then went into administration. On the side she began to develop her skills as an underwater cinematographer and co-produced award-winning documentaries on marine mammals for public broadcasting and educational videos for Smithsonian Books.

Winning joined Oceanic Society Expeditions in 1981, when the emphasis was upon trips that offered a sailing experience, with wildlife observation secondary. Because of her background in marine biology, she shifted the emphasis toward using the sailing vessels as platforms for natural-history experiences. Then in 1984 she made a second major change, with the introduction of research expeditions.

Winning's first project grew out of a trip along the Grand Bahamas Bank, a shallow area with excellent visibility where a substantial population of spotted dolphins congregates at certain times of the year and has become habituated to the presence of human beings in the water. She immediately saw that the area presented special opportunities for researching dolphins, a species normally difficult to study in the wild. But the Grand Bahamas Bank proved to be a place where sizable populations can be counted upon a seasonable basis. The sea level is shallow, about 30 feet, with a sandy bottom, which means that the viewing area under water is exceptionally bright.

"We started our research project there because we felt we needed to look ahead at potential conservation issues," Winning says. "The area was already becoming popular with visitors eager for the opportunity to swim with dolphins. We were concerned that as the number of boats and people increased in the area, the dolphins might be displaced. So we started a long-term baseline project to examine the animals' behavior and their use of the habitat. The marine scientists and our volunteers soon acquired some useful data on the animals. We know now that they are a resident group and, using their natural markings, we have identified about 120 individuals we see year after year. They utilize the Grand Bahamas Bank for their newborn calves; they bring the calves there and rest themselves. We have also gathered considerable data about their social communication, correlating acoustic sounds with visual behavior. That had never been done before."

In 1988 Winning expanded the one project into a full-blown schedule of research programs. This happened as a result of several trips she made into the rain forest of the Amazon River Basin, where she encountered river dolphins. Many visitors to the region are astonished to discover dolphins so far from the sea. But the South American river systems support two species, one the amazing bufeo colorado (pink dolphin), so-called because of the color of the adults. As she recalls today:

"The Amazon in Peru was a major area I visited which inspired this change. I saw that considerable work was being done on the terrestrial species of the rain forest but little on marine species, especially the river dolphins. The local fishermen had just initiated gill net fishing in the rivers, a move which their own government had promoted. Officials had distributed the gill nets to enable the fishermen to increase their catch. But, of course, gill nets are indiscriminate. They capture dolphins and many other species which have no commercial value. I saw right away that the long-term consequence of gill nets would be the devastation of the populations of river dolphins.

"I checked around and discovered that no baseline data was being collected on the two freshwater dolphin species, so there was no way to evoke appropriate management guidelines and restrictions. Nor did any funding for this kind of research exist. That was when the Oceanic Society Expeditions became involved. Our objective from the first was to arm the local groups with the appropriate data to allow them to make an effective case to the government officials on behalf of the environment. We provided the funding, the expertise, and the labor, so that the local officials could take action on their own. The goal of the research was to determine the abundance and distribution of the dolphins for a management plan for this reserve in Peru. We committed then to a long-term study, which continues today."

Scientists from Oceanic Society Expeditions then established a third dolphin project, this one on Belize's celebrated barrier reef where the warm waters are highly conducive to surface and underwater studies of bottlenose dolphin behavior and distribution. Once again non-invasive research techniques are used to obtain observational, video, and acoustic data on wild dolphins. The objective of this third long-term project is, in the words of its mission statement, "to gather multi-generational data and to gain information on how and where dolphins feed, socialize, breed, and rest; to analyze the importance of their various habitats; to determine their reproductive rate; and to document behavior patterns, including social interaction." The year-round Belize dolphin project has proven to be the most popular, attracting over 400 volunteers each year.

On all its research projects, Oceanic Society Expeditions works closely with the local officials. This is a critical element in the success of many projects. As Winning has observed: "We have found with all our projects that the local officials have been quite supportive. This is because we have made an effort to involve them directly in our projects from the beginning. We continuously supply them with copies of all reports as they become available. In the past they complained that researchers from other organizations would come into their area and do the research, but never send back any of the information they had obtained. We always do. We support them, and they support us."

The Oceanic Society Expeditions research projects have yielded important discoveries over a wide range of projects. For example, researchers working with volunteers recently discovered a third humpback whale calving ground off the Pacific coast of Costa Rica. Humpback whales make seasonal migrations between calving grounds in low-latitude areas and high-latitude feeding areas. The wintering areas off Hawaii and Mexico had long been known, but the existence of a third area off Costa Rica confounded experts.

In 1996 Winning scored another major coup when she managed to secure exclusive rights for Oceanic Society Expeditions to take the first travelers in over 50 years to Midway Atoll in the Central Pacific. A remote coral atoll located some 1,250 miles west-northwest of Honolulu, it is best known for the pivotal sea and air battle fought nearby during the Second World War. But the island is also home to the greatest population of wildlife in the Central Pacific. More than 2 million birds visit there every year. The atoll supports the largest Laysan albatross (gooney bird) colony in the world, the second-largest black-footed albatross colony, at least 13 other species of migratory seabirds, and four species of migratory shorebirds. The endangered Hawaiian monk seal and short-tailed albatross, both species facing possible extinction, also use the atoll.

Midway was incorporated into the National Wildlife Refuge in 1988 through a cooperative agreement with the Navy. Officials with the U.S. Fish & Wildlife Service learned of Winning through her documentary on the recovery efforts on behalf of the Hawaiian monk seal. They were eager to secure funding for a series of research projects; however, no public money was available. Thus, the officials turned to Oceanic Society Expeditions. Starting in the fall of 1996, the company began offering one natural-history expedition and four research expeditions on frequent departures throughout the year. The research projects examine the Midway population of spinner dolphins, island habitat restoration, monk seal recovery, and the enormous seabird populations.

"Response to our Midway trips from both our previous and new clients has simply been overwhelming," Winning reports. "People have waited a long time to get into this special area. Now they can."

WATER ADVENTURES

*"An island pleases my imagination,
even the smallest, as a small continent
and integral part of the globe."*

Henry David Thoreau,
Walden

6
RIVER RAFTING EXPEDITIONS

The Brahmaputra River in northern India is one of the world's last frontiers of rafting

Steve Currey Expeditions

"Rivers are a constant lure to the adventurous instinct of mankind," Thoreau once observed. Some 3 million Americans agree. Each year that many climb into pontoon boats, paddleboats, dories, sportyaks, and motorized rafts to experience white-water adventure on the rivers of the world. They scream, shout, and hang on tight as their boats plunge over cataracts, fall into holes, and slam through giant waves on rapids boasting names like Hell's Kitchen, Nemesis, Satan's Gut, and Pure Screaming Hell.

Few of these trips require previous rafting experience. Most operators use inflatable oar-powered boats "driven" by expert boatmen who steer the craft using two long oars. The passengers simply hang on and enjoy the ride. Operators also supply all camping equipment and watertight metal boxes in which passengers stash their personal items during the day.

Rivers are the arteries of the world's wilderness areas and provide access to regions too remote and rugged to be explored by other means. River trips are the ideal way to experience great canyon systems. Many of these river trips offer rich experiences viewing wildlife and traditional cultures, and they teach new skills and build self-confidence at the same time they offer excellent opportunities for swimming, fishing, and hiking.

River-running can quickly become addicting. Most river buffs would agree with River Rat in Kenneth Grahame's classic story *The Wind in the Willows:* "Believe me, my young friend, there is nothing—absolutely nothing—half so much worth doing as simply messing about in boats."

AFRICA

ETHIOPIA

Rafting the Omo River

Operator:
Mountain Travel-Sobek,
6420 Fairmount Ave.,
El Cerrito, Calif. 94530;
(800) 227-2384 or
(510) 527-8100.
Price: Expensive.
Season: October.
Length: 30 days.
Accommodations: Tent
camps. Five percent discount with BBAT coupon.

This was the last pocket of unexplored territory in Africa when Sobek sent the first expedition down the Omo in 1973. Flowing out of the mountains of southwestern Ethiopia, the river offers an enormous variety of experiences: exciting white water; a 4,000-foot-deep canyon; an abundance of wildlife, including large populations of crocodiles and hippos; and primitive native cultures. This is Old Africa, as it was 150 years ago, before those hardy British explorers opened up the continent to the inquisitive eyes of the Victorian public. This lengthy expedition covers 250 miles in oar-powered inflatable rafts. Considerable time is allowed for hikes up tributary canyons to waterfalls, swims in quiet pools, and visits to native villages.

Mursi tribesmen greet members of a Mountain Travel-Sobek expedition on the Omo River in Ethiopia

James C. Simmons

ZAMBIA

Rafting the Zambezi

This expedition begins at the foot of spectacular Victoria Falls, twice as high as Niagara and a mile wide. One of the most violent rivers in the world, with six big drops larger than the famed Lava Falls on the Colorado, the Zambezi was first run by Sobek in 1981. The trip begins and ends at spectacular Victoria Falls. Expedition members use inflatable oar-powered rafts to navigate the treacherous white water at the bottom of a deep gorge. Along the way there are two river drops of 20 feet, which must be portaged. The area teems with wildlife, including crocodiles, hippos, baboons, and antelopes. Stops are also made at small fishing villages along the banks. This is a tough, dangerous trip for experienced river-runners only.

Operator:
Mountain Travel-Sobek,
6420 Fairmount Ave.,
El Cerrito, Calif. 94530;
(800) 227-2384 or
(510) 527-8100.
Price: Expensive.
Season: August through
November.
Length: 9 days.
Accommodations: Tent
camps. Five percent discount with BBAT coupon.

ASIA

CHINA

Rafting the Great Bend of the Yangtze River

The Yangtze received intense media coverage during the mid-1980s when groups of rafters vied to become the first to descend China's most famous river. A decade later this operator, which mounted the third expedition down the river, now runs the 200-mile stretch known as the Great Bend where the Yangtze spills out of the Tibetan plateau. Rafters on these trips enjoy a kaleidoscope of experiences, including Class IV white water, towering mountain peaks, beautiful sand beaches and dunes, and ancient stone towns and monasteries. A Chinese cook prepares all the meals from food native to the region. This is one of the finest adventures in all China.

Operator:
Earth River Expeditions,
182 Tow Path Rd.,
Accord, N.Y. 12404;
(800) 643-2784 or (914)
626-2665.
Price: Expensive.
Season: October and
November.
Length: 15 days.
Accommodations: Tent
camps. Five percent discount with BBAT coupon.

INDIA

Rafting the Brahmaputra River

Operator:
Steve Curry Expeditions,
P.O. Box 1574,
Provo, Utah 84603;
(800) 937-7238 or
(801) 224-6797.
Price: Expensive.
Season: February and
November.
Length: 19 days.
Accommodations: Tent
camps. Five percent discount with BBAT coupon.

Participants on these expeditions can expect to be pioneers. The Brahmaputra River (the name means "Son of Brahma") in northern India is one of the world's last frontiers for rafting. Originating in Tibet, the river cuts a deep gorge as it enters India. The first expedition on the river was mounted by this operator in late 1992; no expedition has ever (yet) run the entire river. Rafters can expect a warm welcome from the Adi tribe, a primitive and friendly people who live in bamboo huts along the banks. The 180-mile run is almost all white water, with over 100 Class III and IV rapids and approximately 20 Class V rapids.

AUSTRALASIA

AUSTRALIA

Running the Franklin River

Operator:
Worldwide Adventures,
36 Finch Ave. W., North
York, Ont., Canada M2N
2G9; (800) 387-1483 or
(416) 221-3000.
Price: Moderate.
Season: December through
March.
Length: 11 days.
Accommodations: Tent
camps. Five percent discount with BBAT coupon.

The Franklin River carves its spectacular way through the deep gorges and wild forests of southwestern Tasmania, a region designated as a UNESCO World Heritage Site (along with the Grand Canyon). Australia's most dangerous and challenging river, the Franklin has abundant stretches of white water that require great technical skill. Members of this expedition must be prepared for some extreme physical exertion, as three portages are required up steep paths. As a reward, a ride down the Franklin offers a kaleidoscope of natural beauty, including rocky crags, lush forests, and exotic wildlife.

Nymboida River Rafting

Probably Australia's most popular river for rafting adventure, the Nymboida in northern New South Wales flows through some of the continent's most breathtaking virgin wilderness. The white water is exhilarating, especially The Waterfall, a 4-foot drop encountered the first day. The highlight of these expeditions is a paddle on placid, deep water at the foot of towering cliffs through the impressive Nymboida Gorge. River days finish early to allow rafters time for swimming and hiking.

Operator: Worldwide Adventures, 36 Finch Ave. W., North York, Ont., Canada M2N 2G9; (800) 387-1483 or (416) 221-3000. *Price:* Moderate. *Season:* November through April. *Length:* 2 and 4 days. *Accommodations:* Tent camps. Five percent discount with BBAT coupon.

CANADA

BRITISH COLUMBIA

Rafting the Chilco, Chilcotin, and Fraser Rivers

Members of this expedition ride on oar-powered rafts down three swift rivers, each one feeding into the next, through a wilderness largely devoid of signs of human occupation. The Chilco runs through a landscape of forested ridgetops and valleys grassy with small cacti, which support large herds of bighorn sheep and mule deer. The Chilcotin drops into deep canyons and tumbles over impressive rapids. The Fraser drains 92,000 square miles with ten times the flow of the Colorado, hurling itself past relics of the 1858 gold rush and through Moran Canyon, whose sheer walls rise 2,000 feet high. The summer climate is ideal—hot, dry, and free of bugs.

Operator: Hyak Wilderness Adventures, 1975 Maple St., Vancouver, B.C., Canada V6J 3S9; (800) 663-7238 or (604) 734-8622. *Price:* Expensive. *Season:* July and August. *Length:* 6 days. *Accommodations:* Tent camps. Ten percent discount with BBAT coupon.

"A fantasy is a reality you're too chicken to live out."

FROM THE FILM *FIVE EASY PIECES*

British Columbia's Chilcotin River offers rafters
an abundance of white water excitement
Hyak Wilderness Adventures

One-Day Adventure on the Chilliwack River

Operator:
Hyak Wilderness
Adventures, 1975 Maple St.,
Vancouver, B.C., Canada
V6J 3S9; (800) 663-7238 or
(604) 734-8622.
Price: Inexpensive.
Season: May to mid-July.
Length: 1 day. Ten percent
discount with BBAT
coupon.

Located a quick one-hour drive from Vancouver, the fast-paced Chilliwack River offers exciting white-water rafting. It drains Chilliwack Lake in the Cascade Mountains, less than 5 miles from the Washington state border, then runs 30 miles to Cultus Lake. The river drops at a rate of 35 feet per mile, creating numerous lengthy rapids. Highlights of this trip are the famous Tamahi and Sawmill rapids, where the Canadian Kayaking Championships are held each spring. The Tamahi section is a 1-mile stretch of river with almost continuous Class III and IV rapids. Exciting but not too difficult, they can be enjoyed by both first-time and experienced rafters. The operator recommends and provides wet suits.

One-Day Adventure on the Thompson River

The Thompson is British Columbia's most popular river trip. A chief reason is that it flows through the desert region of the province's interior, where rafters can almost always count on warm, sunny weather. The river spills out of the western edge of Jasper National Park and rushes down the flank of the Rockies through the driest country in Canada, where the sun bakes the naked hillsides and little grows but cactus and sagebrush. The operator's one-day trip travels the 25-mile stretch through the lower Thompson Valley and White Canyon, a section which offers the best white water and most spectacular scenery. The Thompson becomes more challenging lower down, with rafters experiencing 19 major rapids in the last two hours of their ride. The operator also offers a two-day trip and return transportation from Vancouver for all trips.

Operator:
Hyak Wilderness Adventures,
1975 Maple St.,
Vancouver, B.C., Canada
V6J 3S9;
(800) 663-7238 or
(604) 734-8622.
Price: Inexpensive.
Season: July through Sept.
Length: 1 day. Ten percent discount with BBAT coupon.

QUEBEC

Rafting the Great Whale River

Participants on these trips will find a rafting experience that is rich in both white-water adventure and cultural interaction with the Cree Indians. These people have lived for the past 5,000 years in this remote stretch of northern Quebec and are now fighting an extended war with the provincial government which wants to build a series of dams and flood vast parts of their ancestral lands. As guests of the Whapmagoostui band of the Cree nation, rafters run one of their beautiful threatened rivers (which boasts numerous Class IV rapids), sleep in tipis under the magical pulsing light of the aurora borealis, share Indian customs, and learn firsthand of their struggle for survival. They will also see beluga whales, caribou, wolves, and rare freshwater seals.

Operator:
Earth River Expeditions,
182 Tow Path Rd.,
Accord, N.Y. 12404;
(800) 643-2784 or
(914) 626-2665.
Price: Expensive.
Season: August.
Length: 5 days.
Accommodations: Tipis. Five percent discount with BBAT coupon.

Rafting the Magpie River

Operator:
Earth River Expeditions,
182 Tow Path Rd.,
Accord, N.Y. 12404;
(800) 643-2784 or
(914) 626-2665.
Price: Expensive.
Season: August.
Length: 8 days.
Accommodations: Tent
camps. Five percent dis-
count with BBAT coupon.

Beginning on Newfoundland's Labrador Plateau in eastern Quebec, the Magpie River flows untouched through hundreds of miles of lake-dotted virgin forests of pine and multicolored moss, hurtling down steep granite gorges and off spectacular falls before emptying into the St. Lawrence River. Float planes provide access to this remote wilderness. Rafters on this trip explore a region which, aside from the occasional explorer, few people have ever seen. A highlight of the trip is Magpie Falls, where the river hurtles 80 feet off the Laurentian Plateau in a thunderous crescendo of spray and sound.

EUROPE

GREECE

White-Water Adventure in the Pindus Mountains

Forming the backbone of Greece, the Pindus Mountains rise to over 7,000 feet and are snow-

Great Achievements in Adventure Travel

No event did more to further the status of adventurous women than the 1978 ascent of Nepal's 26,504-foot Annapurna by a group of ten intrepid American women. Women had participated with men in major climbing expeditions but only in secondary roles. But the 1978 American Women's Expedition to Annapurna, which placed two of its members on the summit and set an altitude record for women, belonged to them alone. "We did not organize the Annapurna expedition to prove that women could climb high mountains," expedition leader Arlen Blum wrote later. "We knew that before we began. But the publicized success of the venture brought that message

capped for five months each year. As the snow melts, the rivers swell to foaming white torrents that rush down narrow gorges and forested valleys. This expedition focuses on two regions, Evritania in the southern Pindus and Grevena in the northern portion, and rafts two rivers in each section. The four descents, each lasting from three to four hours, range from Class II to Class IV rapids.

Operator: Worldwide Adventures, 36 Finch Ave. W., Toronto, Ont., Canada M2N 2G9; (800) 387-1483 or (416) 221-3000.
Price: Moderate.
Season: January through mid-April.
Length: 7 days.
Accommodations: Guest houses in nearby Greek villages. Five percent discount with BBAT coupon.

LATIN AMERICA

CHILE

Running the Bio-Bio

Following the Bio-Bio's torrents from the Andes through the rugged Chilean frontier, rafters

to people all over the world."

Planned and financed by American women climbers, the expedition made good its slogan, "A woman's place is on top." On October 15 they planted flags on the summit of the world's tenth-highest mountain and congratulated one another. "We are filled with deep feelings of camaraderie, of accomplishment, of gratitude to everyone who made our team's success possible," one exuberant climber wrote in her journal that

night. But the joy of being the first Americans to ascend Annapurna was soon tempered with grief. The next day the two women in the second team were killed in their attempt to reach the summit.

Operator:
Mountain Travel-Sobek,
6420 Fairmount Ave.,
El Cerrito, Calif. 94530;
(800) 227-2384 or
(510) 527-8100.
Price: Expensive.
Season: December through
February.
Length: 14 days.
Accommodations: Tent
camps. Five percent discount with BBAT coupon.

experience the finest white water in South America and a taste of the past. Richard Bangs calls the Bio-Bio, the second largest river in Chile, "the wildest river Sobek runs commercially." It makes a steep descent through a formidable mountain range of glaciated volcanic peaks and generates over 100 rapids, most comparable to the meanest the Colorado delivers in the Grand Canyon. One trip highlight is a day hike to the summit of Mount Callaqui, a smoking, 9,000-foot-high volcano that looms threateningly over the river. The expedition offers numerous opportunities to meet the farmers, cowboys, and Indians who live along the river. This is a dangerous trip, for experienced rafters only.

Chile's Futaleufu River serves up some of the most challenging white water in South America

James Beal/Earth River Expeditions

Rafting the Futaleufu River

Operator:
Earth River Expeditions,
182 Tow Path Rd., Accord,
N.Y. 12404; (800) 643-2784
or (914) 626-2665.
Price: Expensive.
Season: January through
March.
Length: 10 days.
Accommodations: Tent
camps. Five percent discount with BBAT coupon.

"The Rio Futaleufu is the gem of Chile," Lars Holbeck insists in his *Whitewater Guide to Chile.* The operator pioneered this river, which has in the past few years become a favorite with many international river-runners. The 100-mile-long "Fu" begins in the high Andes and then rushes toward the Pacific, slicing through deep canyons and past snowcapped peaks and towering spires. Tributaries tint the river a deep azure color. Long stretches of Class IV and V rapids abound, offering some of the best white-water adventure in the Western Hemisphere. These trips begin in the town of

Puerto Varas in the heart of the lovely Chilean Lake District. Forty-five minutes after putting in the boats, rafters run Inferno Gorge with a series of back-to-back Class V rapids bearing names like Wall Shot, Orgasm, and Exit. A layover day is scheduled at the scenic Zeta Rapids where rafters can hike, ride horses, kayak, or fish for trout. A classy touch is provided by the presence of a professional Chilean masseuse, who accompanies the entire trip.

COSTA RICA

Pacuare River Expedition

The Pacuare River is the most scenic rafting river in Costa Rica, plunging down the Caribbean slope through spectacular canyons and virgin rain forest. On this expedition paddlers make a full descent of this river, including a newly opened stretch through densely vegetated headwater gorges. The white water is perhaps the finest in Central America. The trip begins with a warm-up run down the Reventazon River, which drops 100 feet per mile for the first 3 miles to make one constant, powerful rapid. A major feature of the trip is the concentration of wildlife along the banks of these rivers. Costa Rica has more animal species than all of North America plus some 2,000 species of orchids alone.

Operator:
Mountain Travel-Sobek,
6420 Fairmount Ave.,
El Cerrito, Calif. 94530;
(800) 227-2384 or
(510) 527-8100.
Price: Expensive.
Season: December through February, June and July.
Length: 10 days.
Accommodations: Tent camps and hotels. Five percent discount with BBAT coupon.

MEXICO

Running the Mayan River of Ruins

For almost a thousand years, the Rio Usumacinta along the remote border between Mexico and Guatemala was a major avenue of trade for a flourishing pre-Columbian culture of several hundred thousand Mayas who thrived and raised ornate cities along its banks. Today the region has reverted to tropical wilderness, inhabited only by a handful of homesteaders and howler monkeys who keep

Operator:
Far Flung Adventures,
P.O. Box 377,
Terlingua, Tex. 79852;
(915) 371-2489.
Price: Moderate.
Season: January through
April.
Length: 10 days.
Accommodations: Shore
camps. Five percent discount with BBAT coupon.

watch over the ruins of this lost civilization. Members of this expedition spend seven days on the Usumacinta, paddling through dense jungle teeming with jaguars, tapirs, sloths, and ocelots. This is an ornithologist's paradise, where as many as 200 different species of birds can be counted in the course of the trip. But the real attractions are the jungle-covered, ghost-haunted ruins of palaces, plazas, and temples—unrestored, unexcavated, and unstudied. Mexico and Guatemala have plans for the joint development of this region, including the construction of a series of major dams to flood a 500-square-mile area that will inundate most of the major archaeological sites. So take this trip while the Usumacinta still runs free.

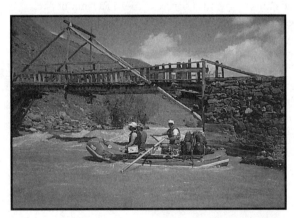

Rafters on a Mountain Travel-Sobek expedition down the Coruh River explore one of Turkey's most isolated wilderness areas

Dave Heckmann/Mountain Travel-Sobek

MIDDLE EAST

TURKEY

White-Water Excitement on the Coruh River

Spilling out of the sparsely settled northeastern corner of Turkey, the Coruh flows through the Black Mountains before finally reaching the Black

Sea. Members of this expedition ride oar-powered rafts through a densely forested canyon almost as deep as the Grand Canyon, past snowcapped peaks, Seljuk castles, ruins of ancient monasteries, and villages so remote they don't even appear on a map. The rapids are world-class. Participants also experience numerous cultural encounters along the way with the friendly shore people in their traditional costumes, few of whom had ever met an American before Sobek mounted the first expedition into the area. One highlight is a visit to the village of Isper, a center for traditional rug-weaving.

Operator: Mountain Travel-Sobek, 6420 Fairmount Ave., El Cerrito, Calif. 94530; (800) 227-2384 or (510) 527-8100.
Price: Expensive.
Season: June.
Length: 16 days.
Accommodations: Tent camps. Five percent discount with BBAT coupon.

UNITED STATES

ALASKA

Down the Tatshenshini

To raft the Tatshenshini through British Columbia to the Pacific is to experience nature on a grand scale. The river slices through mountains over 14,000 feet high and passes more than 20 glaciers. Splendid scenery, not white water, makes this one

Rafters on Alaska Discovery's trip down the Tatshenshini River travel past ice-covered mountains and glaciers, dodging icebergs along the way

Alaska Discovery

Operator:
Alaska Discovery,
5449 Shaune Dr., Suite 4,
Juneau, Alaska 99801;
(800) 586-1911 or
(907) 780-6226.
Price: Expensive.
Season: June through
September.
Length: 10 days.
Accommodations: Tent
camps. Five percent dis-
count with BBAT coupon.

of the world's premiere wilderness river trips.
Participants on this expedition experience one of
the richest concentrations of wildlife in Alaska,
including grizzly bears, Dall sheep, moose, and bald
eagles. A highlight is the layover day at iceberg-
studded Alsek Bay, so remote that no cruise ship or
tour bus has ever reached there. Rafters watch
bergs the size of tall buildings calve off the 7-mile-
wide Alsek Glacier; paddle among the scores of
floes, fantasy creations in blue ice; and hike up the
tongue of ice.

Rafting the Kongatut River

Operator:
Alaska Discovery,
5449 Shaune Dr., Suite 4,
Juneau, Alaska 99801;
(800) 586-1911 or
(907) 780-6226.
Price: Expensive.
Season: June.
Length: 10 days.
Accommodations: Tent
camps. Five percent dis-
count with BBAT coupon.

This expedition begins and ends in the Land of the
Midnight Sun, as participants paddle through the
imposing and remote wilderness of the Arctic
National Wildlife Refuge. The Kongatut flows
quickly, with few rapids, through the Brooks Range
foothills and tundra country ablaze with wildflowers. The major attraction is the profusion of
wildlife, including the annual migration of the
180,000-strong Porcupine caribou herd. Rafters
also can expect to see wolves, bear, Dall sheep, and
thousands of nesting birds. The fishing is excellent,
and the dinner menu often includes fresh char and
grayling. The final night is at the traditional
Eskimo settlement of Kaktovik.

ARIZONA

The Colorado River through the Grand Canyon

Ever since Teddy Roosevelt declared in 1903 that
the Grand Canyon is "the one great sight every
American must see," it has been the premiere
American natural attraction. "The canyon is at least
two things beside spectacle," naturalist Joseph
Wood Krutch wrote. "It is a biological unit and the
most revealing single page of earth's history any-

where open on the face of the globe." Each year millions of tourists arrive at the small village of Grand Canyon to stare off into the awesome gorge below, at its monumental buttes and erosion-scarred slopes. But only a handful experience its full impact, riding the muddy chaos of the Colorado for 300 miles through some 200 rapids. This is the world's supreme river trip, the standard against which all others are measured. The U.S. Park Service allows some 17,000 people a year to know the special enchantment of the canyon by seeing it from the bottom up, 1 mile below the distant rims. These visitors have a variety of options available.

Motorized Inflatable Boats

Most people ride the motor-driven pontoon boats that slam with a shock through the toughest white water. These big boats are virtually unflippable and provide the most stable ride through the major rapids. The trips travel the length of the Grand Canyon.

Operator: Canyoneers, P.O. Box 2997, Flagstaff, Ariz. 86003; (800) 525-0924 or (602) 526-0924. *Price:* Expensive. *Season:* April to mid-Sept. *Length:* 7 days. *Accommodations:* Shore camps. Five percent discount with BBAT coupon.

"Adventure is a human need. We recognize it as the daring thing which makes us bigger than our usual selves. Adventure is the curiosity of man to see the other side of the mountain, the impulse in him that makes him break his bonds with lesser things and frees him for greater possibility."

WHIT BURNETT,
THE SPIRIT OF ADVENTURE

Oar-Powered Inflatable Boats

Operator:
Dvorak's Kayak and Rafting Expeditions, 17921 U.S. Hwy. 285, Nathrop, Colo. 81236; (800) 824-3795 or (719) 539-6851.
Price: Expensive.
Season: May through September.
Length: The trip through the entire canyon takes 12 days, but the operator allows rafters to book shorter segments.
Accommodations: Shore camps. Five percent discount with BBAT coupon.

These trips all use smaller, oar-powered inflatable rafts which are free of the noise and smoke associated with outboard motors. Typically, five or six rafts launch together and travel as a group. Most operators limit group size to 25 people.

Small wooden dories offer the most exciting ride through the big rapids along the Colorado River at the foot of the Grand Canyon
Bert Sagara/O.A.R.S.

Wooden Dories

Operator:
Grand Canyon Dories, P.O. Box 216, Altaville, Calif. 95221; (800) 877-3679 or (209) 736-0805.
Price: Moderate.
Season: April through Sept.
Length: The trip through the entire canyon from Lee's Ferry to the Grand Wash Cliffs takes 20 days, but clients can book a variety of shorter segments.
Accommodations: Shore camps. Five percent discount with BBAT coupon.

For pure adventure and a nonstop rush of adrenaline, go with the 17-foot-long-by-7-foot wide wooden boats. These are small dories that ride low in the water and can easily capsize or break up against the rocks. This is the ultimate way to challenge Lava Falls and Crystal Rapid, two of North America's biggest drops.

Rafting through the Sonoran Desert

Generally overlooked in all the excitement over the Colorado River through the Grand Canyon, the Salt River flows out of the White Mountains through a series of stark granite gorges in the wilderness of the Sonoran Desert before ending in Roosevelt Reservoir. Participants on these 52-mile raft trips float through the White Mountain Apache Indian Reservation for part of the way. In early spring, the surrounding desert comes alive with blooming wildflowers. Numerous Class II and III rapids are punctuated by a half-dozen Class IV drops and, on the third day, one Class V rapid. Several short hikes are made up tributary canyons.

Operator:
Far Flung Adventures,
P.O. Box 377,
Terlingua, Tex. 79852;
(915) 371-2489.
Price: Moderate.
Season: Feb. through May.
Length: 5 days.
Accommodations: Shore camps. Five percent discount with BBAT coupon.

CALIFORNIA

Lower Klamath

These popular trips are ideal for families with young children seeking a scenic float on a warm, gentle section of the Klamath River flowing through the mountains and valleys of Northern California. This is California's second-largest river and one of the first rivers in the state to be granted National Wild and Scenic status. The Klamath runs free for 180 miles to the ocean. These easy trips offer an abundance of scenic beauty, diverse wildlife, and recreational opportunities. The rapids are exciting but not intimidating, perfect for young children.

Operator:
O.A.R.S., Box 67,
Angels Camp, Calif. 95222;
(800) 346-6277 or
(209) 736-4677.
Price: Moderate.
Season: June through October.
Length: 2 and 3 days.
Accommodations: Shore camps. Five percent discount with BBAT coupon.

Lower Kern

Located just a few miles from Los Angeles, the Lower Kern is a superb rafting challenge. These popular trips originate below Lake Isabella and end at Democrat Beach, traveling a distance of 20 miles. The river flows southwest through a deep gorge forested with willows, cottonwood, sycamore, and alder. Paddlers experience several fine stretches of white water, boasting such names as Oscar's Nightmare and Hari Kari.

Operator:
O.A.R.S., Box 67,
Angels Camp, Calif. 95222;
(800) 346-6277 or
(209) 736-4677.
Price: Moderate.
Season: June through September.
Length: 2 days.
Accommodations: Shore camps. Five percent discount with BBAT coupon.

Two-Day Adventure on the American River

Operator:
Action Whitewater
Adventures, P.O. Box 1634,
Provo, Utah 84603;
(800) 453-1482 or
(801) 375-4111.
Price: Moderate.
Season: Mid-May through
mid-September.
Length: 2 days.
Accommodations: Shore
camp. Ten percent discount with BBAT coupon.

Cascading through the scenic foothills of the historic Sierra Nevada Mountains, the South Fork of the American River is California's most popular river adventure and a near-perfect white-water run. This is the river where James Marshall's gold discovery started California's famous 1849 Gold Rush. Rafters put in near Chili Bar, 3 miles from Placerville. After an early lunch they arrive at Gold Discovery State Park where they spend several hours touring the historical buildings and artifacts associated with that exciting period of Western history. Night is spent at a riverside campground, where showers and modern toilets are available. The next day in the gorge, the river is squeezed between sheer rock walls where one rapid follows another as a grand finale to this 21-mile river run. The operator also offers a one-day rafting adventure on this river.

"Travel is the retrieval of a mislaid identity."

H.M. TOMLINSON, "OUTWARD BOUND"

The Adventure Travel Hall of Fame:
THEODORE ROOSEVELT

"On February 27, 1914, shortly after midday, we started down the River of Doubt into the unknown," Theodore Roosevelt wrote in his book Through the Brazilian Wilderness, an account of the most dangerous expedition ever undertaken by a president of the United States. The party numbered 22 men crowded into seven dilapidated wooden dugout canoes. Earlier, his friends had advised him against such a dangerous journey. The former president's reply was typical: "I have already lived and enjoyed as much of life as any nine men I know. I have had my full share, and if it is necessary for me to leave my remains in South America, I am quite ready to do so."

Soldier, statesman, politician—these are the aspects of Theodore Roosevelt on which biographers have focused. Almost lost in the shadows is another side of this remarkable man, his achievements as an explorer and naturalist. Roosevelt put the one in the service to the other. Both reflected his omnivo-

Gastronomic Adventure on the Tuolumne

Plunging down a gradient of 60 feet per mile, through the grandeur of an unspoiled Sierra mountain canyon, the Tuolumne has some of the finest white water in the West, secluded tributary streams, and relics from an earlier generation of gold-seekers. Eagles, river otters, and ring-tailed cats all call the nearby forests home. Dubbed the "California Roll," this expedition on oar-powered rafts blends high river adventure and haute cuisine. A top San Francisco chef prepares gourmet dinners, served with vintage wines, crystal, and white linens in a wilderness setting. "We invite you to discover how a 20-year-old bottle of California Cabernet safely descends the Class IV rapids of this wild river," teases owner/host Marty McDonnell. A typical five-course dinner includes artichoke hearts with roast leg of lamb, baby-chicken tamales with South Texas salsa, mesquite-grilled albacore tuna, and chocolate truffle cake. No less an authority than Craig Claiborne, the food guru of the *New York Times*, has pronounced the California Roll *"magnifique."*

Operator: Sierra Mac River Trips, P.O. Box 366, Sonora, Calif. 95370; (800) 457-2580 or (209) 532-1327.
Price: Expensive.
Season: June through October.
Length: 3 days.
Accommodations: Shore camps. Five percent discount with BBAT coupon

rous appetite for physical exertion, what he called "The Strenuous Life."

Roosevelt mounted his Brazilian expedition as a private citizen on behalf of the American Museum of Natural History. He was determined to penetrate the country's unexplored central region between the Amazon and La Plata river systems. When the expedition was finally completed, he had traversed a vast blank space as big as Nevada and explored a river the size of the Hudson. He had also collected for the museum 2,500 birds and 500 mammals along with hundreds of fish, insects, and reptiles, many representing newly discovered species.

But Roosevelt's expedition down the fearful River of Doubt almost proved his undoing. A bout of malaria, accompanied by a fever of 105°, nearly killed him and left his health permanently impaired. Other dangers included famine, terrible stretches of white water that drowned one man, and a boatman who went berserk and murdered another expedition member. When he returned to the United States in May 1914, a sick man, 55 pounds lighter than when he started, Roosevelt's days as an explorer and hunter were over.

White-Water Rafting School

Operator:
Sierra Mac River Trips,
P.O. Box 366,
Sonora, Calif. 95370;
(800) 457-2580 or
(209) 532-1327.
Price: Moderate.
Season: April and May.
Length: 7 days.
Accommodations: Motel. Five
percent discount with
BBAT coupon.

This intensive white-water week is designed for beginners to advanced rafters. The course covers the fundamental skills of reading white water and maneuvering boats. The instruction follows a written manual and is tailored to meet students' individual needs. Lectures cover safety procedures and equipment. Students also learn raft-rigging, maintenance and repair of equipment, and camp cooking. Field instruction takes place on a variety of California wild rivers, including the Main and Upper Tuolumne, Giant Gap, and North Fork of the American. At the end of the course each student receives a personal written evaluation.

COLORADO

A Classical Music Journey down the Dolores River

Operator:
Dvorak's Kayak and Rafting
Expeditions,
17921 U.S. Hwy. 285,
Nathrop, Colo. 81236;
(800) 824-3795 or
(719) 539-6851.
Price: Moderate.
Season: June.
Length: 8 days.
Accommodations: Shore
camps. Five percent discount with BBAT coupon.

Since 1985 the operator has brought professional musicians from major orchestras and their instruments into some of the wildest canyons of the West. They provide four scheduled performances on the trips, but rafters soon get used to hearing a Mozart quartet or a Vivaldi flute concerto while traveling down the river at the bottom of a deep canyon. The highlight is a formal recital in an immense amphitheater near the campsite. All this takes place on the Dolores River, a joy to run. This lovely alpine stream spills out of the southern San Juan range and rushes through the foothills and tablelands, cutting a canyon some 2,500 deep. With an average gradient of 20 feet per mile and one section approaching a 60-foot drop per mile, the Dolores offers an abundance of Class II and III rapids. Stops are made on these trips for hikes into tributary canyons, visits to Anasazi ruins, and fishing breaks. (The operator also offers a classical music journey down the Green River.)

Huck Finn, eat your heart out! Dvorak's
Kayak and Rafting Expeditions gives rafters
Mozart on the Dolores River

Dvorak Kayak & Rafting Expeditions

IDAHO

Snake River through Hell's Canyon

As the Snake River flows along the border between Idaho and Oregon, it carves Hell's Canyon, the deepest in North America. At one point the canyon drops 7,900 feet from the craggy heights of the Seven Devils Mountains to the churning rapids and eddies of the river below, eclipsing the Grand Canyon by 2,000 feet. Rafters on these expeditions ride through some of the wildest white water in the West—full-bodied, roller-coaster-style rapids. This is an area steeped in frontier history, from 8,000-year-old Indian sites and abandoned pioneer cabins to the gory Deep Creek, where in 1887 a group of cowboys brutally murdered 31 Chinese placer miners. The Snake also offers excellent fishing for rainbow trout, smallmouth bass, and steelhead.

Operator: Hughes River Expeditions, P.O. Box 217, Cambridge, Idaho 83610; (208) 257-3477.
Price: Expensive.
Season: Late May through September.
Length: 3, 4, 5, and 6 days.
Accommodations: Shore camps. Five percent discount with BBAT coupon.

Down the "River of No Return"

Operator:
Silver Cloud Expeditions,
P.O. Box 1006,
Salmon, Idaho 83467;
(208) 756-6215.
Price: Expensive.
Season: May through
September.
Length: 4 and 5 days.
Accommodations: Shore
camps. Five percent discount with BBAT coupon.

Idaho's celebrated Main Salmon River flows fast, cold, and rough through the second-deepest canyon in North America (the Grand Canyon is the third!). When the Lewis and Clark expedition saw the mile-deep canyon and raging rapids, they understood why the Indians called it the "River of No Return." Participants on these trips ride oar-powered inflatable rafts through some of the most legendary rapids in North America. Along the way they visit abandoned cabins, hidden waterfalls, hot springs, and Indian pictographs. Camps are set up on white-sand beaches. The surrounding forests abound in a wide variety of wildlife, including bighorn sheep, bear, cougars, and eagles.

A fly fisherman tries his luck on the Middle Fork of the Salmon River

Dave Miles/Rocky Mountain River Tours

The Middle Fork of the Salmon

The Middle Fork snakes its way through the heart of the 2.2-million-acre Salmon Wilderness Area in central Idaho, amid a spectacular blend of mountains, forests, and deep canyons. With an average drop of 27 feet per mile and more than 100 rapids, it offers a superb combination of thrilling white water, extraordinary scenery, and abundant wildlife. Rafters descend from an elevation of 5,700 feet to 3,000 feet, riding through dense forests to end in the rugged granite gorge of Impassable Canyon. Stops are also made at several abandoned homesteads, masterpieces of frontier handiwork with handmade furniture inside finely cut and fitted log cabins.

Operator: Rocky Mountain River Tours, P.O. Box 2552, Boise, Idaho 83701; (208) 345-2400; and in summer, P.O. Box 207, Salmon, Idaho 83467; (208) 756-4808.
Price: Expensive.
Season: Late-May through September.
Length: 6 days, with 4-day trips in the early season.
Accommodations: Shore camps. Five percent discount with BBAT coupon.

Rafting Owyhee Canyon

The Owyhee Canyon and Plateau are among the West's wildest and most remote areas. One of the longest wilderness rivers in the United States, the Owyhee rushes 190 miles from northern Nevada across southwestern Idaho into eastern Oregon. Because of the difficulty of its rapids, the few roads penetrating the area, and the short, unpredictable boating season, the Owyhee is one of the least-rafted and least-known wild rivers in North America. Yet it features unparalleled solitude, some of the finest white water in the northwest, magnificent canyon scenery, and excellent wildlife.

Operator: Hughes River Expeditions, P.O. Box 217, Cambridge, Idaho 83610; (208) 257-3477.
Price: Expensive.
Season: April and May.
Length: 5 days down the Lower Owyhee; 4 days on the isolated Middle Owyhee, where rafting parties rarely venture.
Accommodations: Shore camps. Five percent discount with BBAT coupon.

Through Bruneau Canyon

The Bruneau River twists through the Pacific Northwest's most dramatic desert canyon. Sheer basalt cliffs tower more than a thousand feet above the boats. The white water is excellent, the most celebrated stretch being "Five Mile Rapids" where the rapids hit with machine-gun frequency. Because of the river's difficulty the operator uses

Operator: Hughes River Expeditions, P.O. Box 217, Cambridge, Idaho 83610; (208) 257-3477. *Price:* Expensive. *Season:* May and early June. *Length:* 4 days. *Accommodations:* Shore camps. Five percent discount with BBAT coupon.

special small oar-powered boats, each one carrying only two passengers and a boatman. Bruneau Canyon is rich in mule deer, otters, birds of prey, and other types of wildlife. Short hikes are also made up tributary canyons to visit the remains of an old whiskey still, two hot springs, and several large caves. Although only a handful of people have experienced the Bruneau, it has become a favorite with river guides and boaters.

MAINE

One-Day Adventure on the Kennebec River

Operator: New England Outdoor Center, 240 Katahdin Ave., Suite 3, Millinocket, Maine 04462; (800) 766-7238 or (207) 723-5438. *Price:* Moderate. *Season:* April, May, June, and September–October. *Length:* 1 day. Five percent discount with BBAT coupon.

Huge waves crashing through a deep forested gorge, combined with the Class IV white-water excitement of Magic Falls, create a natural roller-coaster ride that makes the Kennebec an ideal rafting adventure. When the first rafter ran the river in 1976, he was told that he would never survive. He not only survived, he spawned a multimillion-dollar industry. More than 55,000 people now run the Kennebec each year on those days when the Yankee Nuclear Power Plant releases excess water from its dam. The flow of 6,000 cubic feet per second insures plenty of thrills for the 13-mile adventure, with the first 5 miles being one continuous white-water run. The rapids grow in a crescendo, each one bigger than the one before.

One-Day Adventure on the Penobscot River

Operator: New England Outdoor Center, 240 Katahdin Ave., Suite 3, Millinocket, Maine 04462; (800) 766-7238 or (207) 723-5438. *Price:* Moderate. *Season:* May through Sept. *Length:* 1 day. Five percent discount with BBAT coupon.

The west branch of the Penobscot challenges even the most experienced rafter. To make the river accessible to all rafters and to eliminate 1.5 miles of flat water, the operator begins the adventure on the lower, calmer stretch of the river. After a lunch break with a riverside cookout, paddlers are then bused upstream to the headwaters for the formidable run through the white water of Ripogenus Gorge. The big drops there sport such intimidating names as Exterminator (a Class V rapid), Staircase,

The Penobscot River in Maine offers rafters some of the most exciting white water in the northeastern United States

New England Whitewater Center

and Cribworks, with the latter considered the most challenging white water in the East.

MARYLAND

The Upper Yough

The Indians called it *Youghiogheny,* meaning "river which flows in all directions." With the steepest riverbed east of the Rockies, it starts in West Virginia, rushes through Maryland, and finishes in Pennsylvania. Appalachian Wildwaters runs an 11-mile section in western Maryland popularly known as the Upper Yough (pronounced "yok" to rhyme with "rock"). The 115-foot-per-mile gradient in the main section of the run and the nonstop nature of the rapids make the Upper Yough one of the most challenging stretches of white water anywhere. The names of the rapids—Triple Drop, Snaggle Tooth, and Meat Cleaver—hint at the violence of this stretch of the river. Trips in four-person paddle rafts are scheduled for Monday through Friday when a power company opens the floodgates of a dam and releases a rush of water. The Upper Yough is for experienced rafters only.

Operator: Appalachian Wildwaters, P.O. Box 100, Rowlesburg, W. Va. 26425; (800) 624-8060 or (304) 454-2475. *Price:* Moderate to expensive. *Season:* April through November. *Length:* 1 day. Five percent discount with BBAT coupon.

MONTANA

Running the Flathead River

Operator:
Glacier Raft Company,
P.O. Box 218,
West Glacier, Mont. 59936;
(800) 332-9995 or
(406) 888-5454.
Price: Expensive.
Season: June and July.
Length: 4 and 6 days.
Accommodations: Shore
camps. Five percent discount with BBAT coupon.

Montana's Flathead County has 219 miles, or 8.5 percent of the total river miles in the nation classified as wild, scenic, or recreational under the 1976 Wild and Scenic Rivers Act. They are beautiful stretches of unspoiled, unchecked river offering an unbeatable experience for those who run them. These expeditions travel by oar-powered and paddle rafts down the Upper Middle Fork and the Middle Fork of the Flathead River, which together provide the best white-water experience in the state. Participants ride in to the Flathead by horse through the Great Bear Wilderness Area. Soon they find themselves floating through some of the most magnificent scenery in the West, dwarfed by steep mountains and towering rock outcroppings. Day hikes are made to nearby lakes for excellent fishing. The native cutthroat trout and Dolly Varden sometimes run to 20 pounds. The Flathead drops an average of 34 feet per mile and is a favorite with white-water enthusiasts. The final two days are spent floating along the southern border of Glacier National Park.

NEW YORK

Hudson River Gorge

Here's a surprise. The vast, murky, congested waterway that begs comparison with an open sewer by the time it gets to Manhattan is a pristine wilderness river a few hours north. Born high in the Adirondacks at Lake Tear of the Clouds, the upper Hudson flows smoothly until it reaches Indian River and the Gorge. Like most spring runs, this one changes dramatically with the water level. The operator puts his paddleboats in at the Indian River for a 3-mile stretch that is almost continuous Class III and IV rapids. At the confluence with the

Hudson, the river funnels into the Blue Ledge Narrows, a tight, turbulent Class IV passage. From there it's 2 miles and two dramatic 90-degree bends to the quarter-mile-long Harris Rift, the run's most notable rapid, with two large hydraulics near the end known as Big Nasty and Soup Strainer. Wet suits are advised, and these can be rented from the operator.

"I do not know much about gods;
but I think that the river
Is a strong brown god—
sullen, untamed and intractable."

T.S. ELIOT,
"THE DRY SAVAGES"

Operator: Adirondack River Outfitters, P.O. Box 649, Old Forge, N.Y. 13420; (800) 525-7238 or (315) 369-3536. *Price:* Inexpensive. *Season:* April to mid-June; also September and October, but expect splendid fall foliage, low river volume, and tamed white water on these later departures. *Length:* 1 day. Five percent discount with BBAT coupon.

NORTH CAROLINA
The Nantahala River

Nestled in a deep gorge along the southern edge of the Great Smoky Mountains National Park, the Nantahala is the most popular river in the Southeast. More than 150,000 people each year succumb to its beauty and playfulness to run the river in paddleboats, canoes, and kayaks. The Nantahala is dam-fed, so its flow is consistent and dependable throughout the year. A float along this lovely river is quiet serenity, laced with some exciting Class II and III rapids so the ride is never dull. This is the perfect river adventure for families and novices. The trip covers 8 miles.

Operator: Nantahala Outdoor Center, 13077 U.S. Hwy. 19 W., Bryson City, N.C. 28713; (800) 232-7238 or (704) 488-2175. *Price:* Inexpensive. *Season:* Late March through October. *Length:* 4 hours. Five percent discount with BBAT coupon.

OREGON
The Rogue River

One of the original rivers protected under the National Wild and Scenic Rivers Act, the Rogue boasts a 40-mile section that flows through the

Operator:
Sundance Expeditions,
14894 Galice Rd.,
Merlin, Ore. 97532;
(541) 479-8508.
Price: Moderate.
Season: April through mid-
September.
Length: 4 days.
Accommodations: Operator
offers a choice of tent-camp
and lodge-based trips. Five
percent discount with
BBAT coupon.

rugged coastal Mountain Range in Oregon's south-eastern corner. The white water on this stretch contains numerous Class II and III rapids. Warm water, beautiful sandy beaches perfect for campsites, and a wild, nearly pristine landscape make the Rogue one of the Pacific Northwest's most popular rivers. The most fearsome cataracts are Rainie Falls, which drops a full 10 feet, and Blossom Bar, a gigantic rock garden below the boiling waters of Mule Creek Canyon. Be certain to visit the cabin where Zane Grey wrote many of his novels and fished for chinook salmon and steelhead trout. Participants have a choice of oar boats, paddle rafts, or inflatables.

SOUTH CAROLINA

The Chattooga River

Operator:
Nantahala Outdoor Center,
13077 U.S. Hwy. 19 W.,
Bryson City, N.C. 28713;
(800) 232-7238 or
(704) 488-2175.
Price: Inexpensive.
Season: Late March
through October.
Length: 6 hours, although
operator offers a 2-day
weekend adventure. Five
percent discount with
BBAT coupon.

A National Wild and Scenic River, the Chattooga became an overnight celebrity in 1972 with the release of the popular film *Deliverance.* Its dramatic story of the city boys' race for life down the raging river established the Chattooga as one of the supreme challenges for rafters. Today this beautiful, remote river along the border between South Carolina and Georgia is best known for its superb white water and stunning scenery. Spectacular rock formations create some of the most powerful and exciting rapids in the Southeast.

TENNESSEE

The Nolichucky River

Rafters have only recently discovered the action on the Nolichucky, which flows out of the Blue Ridge Mountains in North Carolina and rushes 150 miles through Tennessee. Thus it lacks the crowds often found on more-accessible and better-known rivers. Paddlers put in across from Polly's

Rafters on the Nolichucky River in Tennessee can look forward to as many as 25 Class II to Class IV rapids

Ciro Pena/Nantahala Outdoor Center

General Store in the tiny town of Poplar, North Carolina, and run the Nolichucky for 9 miles through the Pisgah and Cherokee National Forests, at the bottom of one of the most scenic gorges in the Southeast. Towering cliffs loom above the rapids. The banks are lined with wild flowering laurel and rhododendron. Boaters can look forward to as many as 25 Class II to IV rapids. No previous rafting experience is necessary.

Operator: Nantahala Outdoor Center, 13077 U.S. Hwy. 19 W., Bryson City, N.C. 28713; (800) 232-7238 or (704) 488-2175.
Price: Inexpensive.
Season: March through mid-July.
Length: 4 to 7 hours. Five percent discount with BBAT coupon.

TEXAS

Running the Rio Grande through Big Bend National Park

Big Bend may be the most rugged, the most remote, the most desolate national park in the continental United States. To anyone who loves extremes—and what sophisticated traveler doesn't?—it is among the most beautiful. The river that separates the United States and Mexico begins high in the Colorado Rockies and flows for 1,900 miles through remote areas where a century ago outlaws took refuge and Comanche and Apache war parties roamed. The Rio Grande cuts five major canyon systems in Big Bend National Park, an area about the size of Rhode Island and home to some 400 species of birds. Much of this is through country so rugged it can be viewed only

Operator: Far Flung Adventures, P.O. Box 377, Terlingua, Tex. 79852; (915) 371-2489.
Price: Moderate.
Season: Year-round.
Length: Operator offers a variety of 2- to 7-day oar-powered raft trips down the various segments.
Accommodations: Shore camps. Five percent discount with BBAT coupon.

from the river. Two major attractions are Santa Elena Canyon, where sheer limestone walls rise 1,500 feet above the river; and Pico del Carmen, a 7,000-foot tall-limestone pedestal which thrusts abruptly out of Boquillas Canyon.

UTAH

Rafting Expeditions for the Disabled

Operator: Dvorak's Kayak and Rafting Expeditions, 17921 U.S. Hwy. 285, Nathrop, Colo. 81236; (800) 824-3795 or (719) 539-6851. *Price:* Moderate. *Season:* Check with operator for dates. *Length:* Check with operator. Five percent discount with BBAT coupon.

Only recently, because of advances in equipment and the development of access points, has river-rafting become available to physically disabled people. Experts now recognize that certain adventure-travel experiences can provide important steps toward rehabilitation after a disabling injury. On the river, disabled participants find themselves free to explore their limits—and many discover that their sense of accomplishment can be more powerful than their sense of being "handicapped." Dvorak's Kayak and Raft Expeditions has been a leader in providing rafting trips for a wide variety of disabled adventurers, offering trips down several rivers, including a six-day expedition down the Green. Boats are specially rigged for safety, and camping sites are chosen for their accessibility. A trained nurse accompanies each group. Those taking these trips include people who use wheelchairs as well as those living with deafness, blindness, muscular dystrophy, cerebral palsy, and multiple sclerosis.

"There is in the nature of every man . . . a longing to see and know the strange places of the world. Life imprisons us all in its coil of circumstances, and the dreams of romance that color boyhood are forgotten, but they do not die."

FREDERICK O'BRIEN,
WHITE SHADOWS IN THE SOUTH SEAS

WEST VIRGINIA

White-Knuckled Excitement on the Gauley

Located 30 miles southeast of Charleston, the Gauley drops almost 100 feet a mile through spectacular scenery in one of the East's finest whitewater runs. In the autumn it guarantees 50 or more Class III to VI rapids with hair-raising names such as Pure Screaming Hell. The Upper Gauley requires previous experience. This river is runnable for only 21 days each autumn, when Summersville Lake is lowered to prepare for winter snows and spring thaws.

Operator:
Appalachian Wildwaters,
P.O. Box 100,
Rowlesburg, W. Va. 26425;
(800) 624-8060 or
(304) 454-2475.
Price: Moderate.
Season: March through Nov.
Length: The Upper Gauley run covers 15 miles and takes 6 hours; the Lower Gauley, 11 miles and 4 hours. Five percent discount with BBAT coupon.

The Gauley River gives rafters mad rushes of adrenaline as they make their way through some of the most formidable white water in the eastern United States

Appalachian Wildwaters

Challenging the Cheat

The 150-mile long Cheat River is one of the largest uncontrolled watersheds in the eastern United States. A major flood in 1985 rearranged some of the rapids, exposed ledges, and made some drops even steeper. New drops have been christened with names such as Terminator and Cyclotron, while at the same time, old menaces like Devil's Trap remain. During the spring runoff, rafters encounter Class III to V rapids. Few rivers offer such a challenging run for experienced paddlers. Autumn on the Cheat brings spectacular foliage.

Operator:
USA Raft, P.O. Box 277,
Rowlesburg, W.Va. 26425;
(800) USA-RAFT or
(304) 454-2475.
Price: Inexpensive.
Season: March through August.
Length: 7 hours. Five percent discount with BBAT coupon.

This 12-mile-long trip is for experienced white-water paddlers or those "willing to assume risks somewhat in excess of those inherent in any raft trip."

Paddling the Tygart

Operator: USA Raft, P.O. Box 277, Rowlesburg, W. Va. 26425; (800) USA-RAFT or (304) 454-2475. *Price:* Moderate. *Season:* March through August. *Length:* The trip covers 7 miles and takes 6 hours. Five percent discount with BBAT coupon.

Commercial river-running came late to the Tygart, but it has quickly established its popularity with experienced river buffs. The Arden section opens with stretches of gentle white water that build in size until paddlers hit such formidable rapids as Deception, Undercut, and Premonition. The grand finale is Seven Wells Falls, which the operator declares is "the most powerful runnable rapid in the Monongahela River Basin." The short but intense Valley Falls features a 25-foot water slide and a 14-foot vertical waterfall. Constant releases from the Tygart Lake Dam guarantee rafters a plentiful supply of water. Passengers ride in four- and ten-person rafts. No previous rafting experience is necessary.

The New: The Grand Canyon of the East

Operator: Appalachian Wildwaters, P.O. Box 100, Rowlesburg, W. Va. 26425; (800) 624-8060 or (304) 454-2475. *Price:* Moderate. *Season:* March through November. *Length:* The operator offers both half-day and 2-day trips. *Accommodations:* Shore camp. Five percent discount with BBAT coupon.

One of the most popular rivers in America with river-runners, the New is the white-water equivalent of a roller-coaster ride. The lower New features spectacular white-water runs at the foot of a deep gorge known as the "Grand Canyon of the East." This is run in ten-person paddle rafts. No previous experience is necessary. The upper New provides the perfect trip for beginners and families, being a gentle run through some of the state's most beautiful mountain scenery.

WYOMING

Grand Teton Raft and Kayak Adventure

The special appeal of the Grand Teton Mountains lies in their precipitous rise from the lake-studded valley of Jackson Hole, the tallest peak stabbing the sky at nearly 14,000 feet. For visitors fed up with the swelling tide of tourists at Jackson Hole, no better escape exists than these leisurely trips. Participants put in on the fast-flowing Snake River just south of Yellowstone and float on rafts into Grand Teton National Park through a game-rich wilderness teeming with moose, deer, bear, otter, beaver, eagle, osprey, and Canada geese. Three days are then spent paddling along the wilderness shore of Jackson Lake in stable, two-person sea kayaks. Participants have ample time to hike through flower-strewn meadows or fish for trout.

Operator: O.A.R.S., Box 67, Angels Camp, Calif. 95222; (800) 346-6277 or (209) 736-4677.
Price: Expensive.
Season: June through Sept.
Length: 5 days.
Accommodations: Tent camps. Five percent discount with BBAT coupon.

"In overstepping our limitations, in touching the extreme boundaries of man's world, we have come to know something of its true splendor. In my worst moments of anguish I seemed to discover the deep significance of existence of which until then I was unaware. I saw that it was better to be true than to be strong. The marks of the ordeal are apparent on my body. I was saved and I had won my freedom. This freedom, which I shall never lose, has given me the assurance and serenity of a man who has fulfilled himself. It has given me the rare joy of loving that which I used to despise. A new and splendid life has opened out before me."

MOUNTAINEER MAURICE HERZOG,
ANNAPURNA

The North Platte River through Northgate Canyon

Mark Twain once joked that if the North Platte were turned on edge, it just might make a respectable river. But he was talking about the lower sections. The upper North Platte is as beautiful a mountain river as can be run in the Rockies. The hundreds of boaters who paddle the rapids of Northgate Canyon, where the river drops 470 feet in 18 miles, know the river is not all sandbars and flat water. Fine scenery, excellent white water, and great trout-fishing make the upper North Platte a first-rate experience. Rafters on these trips cover 35 miles.

Operator: Dvorak's Kayak and Rafting Expeditions, 17921 U.S. Hwy. 285, Nathrop, Colo. 81236; (800) 824-3795 or (719) 539-6851.
Price: Moderate.
Season: May through July.
Length: 2 and 3 days.
Accommodations: Tent camps. Five percent discount with BBAT coupon.

PROFILE
ERIC HERTZ
EARTH RIVER EXPEDITIONS

"The Yangtze is one of the great river trips of the world," states Eric Hertz, the founder and president of Earth River Expeditions. "The four gems are the Yangtze, the Colorado through the Grand Canyon in Arizona, the Colca River in Peru, and the Futaleufu in Chile."

Portland attorney Jay Waldron and Bruce Bergey, a homebuilder from Hillsboro, Oregon, could not agree more. They recently returned from one of Earth River Expeditions' pioneering rafting trips down the Great Bend of the Yangtze River. The trip covered some 130 miles of Asia's most famous river where it has carved one of the world's deepest canyons just as it flows off a high Tibetan plateau.

"The rapids were huge and the current moved at 8 or 9 miles per hour," Waldron recalled. "We went down the Yangtze with one of the top river groups in the world. They made it look easy because of their professionalism. The river isn't nearly as dangerous as [previous expedition leaders] have painted it."

Bergey agreed. "We scouted every set of rapids, then sent the kayaks through to establish a line. They looked like toothpicks going through 20-foot waves. There were a few places where if you fell out or the raft entered wrong, you would have been dead. I don't think I would ever run the river again because this trip was so good. I feel like a teenager who falls in love for the first time."

Earth River Expeditions is a small operator, specializing in a handful of the wildest, most spectacular and inaccessible rivers in the world—the Yangtze in China; the Futaleufu and Bio-Bio in Chile; the Colca River in Peru; and the Great Whale and Magpie in Quebec, Canada. Many of these expeditions combine superb white-water rafting with intensive cultural experiences among the local people, many of whom have experienced only limited contact with the outside world. In 1991 Hertz founded the Earth River Fund, which has been at the forefront of the worldwide movement to promote the preservation of threatened wild rivers.

Born in 1955 and raised in White Plains, New York, Hertz first met his destiny his 16th year when he spent a summer in Idaho, trained as a river guide, and ran the Middle Fork of the Salmon. When he turned 18, he was licensed as a river guide and worked five summers on the Tuolumne River in California. He followed that with a lengthy stint as a river guide on the Colorado River through the Grand Canyon. He started Earth River Expeditions

in 1991, after several seasons on Chile's famed Bio-Bio River.

"My chief motivation was a fear that too many of the world's great rivers were threatened by dams," Hertz recalls today. "I thought that by forming my own rafting company, I could engage in preservation work for several of these rivers, especially the wild rivers of Chile. I was working on the Bio-Bio when the controversy over the proposed dam erupted. I was shocked that none of the American companies with trips on the Bio-Bio were involved with the struggle to stop that dam from being constructed. Here they were, making money running clients down the Bio-Bio but were unwilling to take an active role in preserving it. This struck me as both shortsighted and morally wrong. So I founded Earth River Expeditions as a vehicle for both river-running and conservation. My first commercial trip was down the Futaleufu River in Chile, which had never been run successfully before from top to bottom."

The Futaleufu (or "Fu," as Hertz fondly calls it), with its translucent, turquoise waters, quickly established itself as his own personal favorite. Alternating between granite cliffs, lush foliage, snowcapped peaks and towering spires, the Fu rushes dramatically through one of the most challenging Class V river canyons in the world.

"Imagine a river which combines the power of the Colorado River through the Grand Canyon with the steep descent of the Bio-Bio through the Nirreco Gorge, and you have the Fu," marvels Hertz. "It boasts one Class IV or V rapid after another. The river also offers rafters spectacular private river campsites.

"My own favorite is the Cave Camp where we always spend two nights and one full day. Located in the middle of the rugged upper canyon, this is a unique and diverse river camp. There's a large natural cave, formed by a massive overhanging granite slab, that's large enough to sleep 40 people and ride a horse inside. The floor is sand, and there is a fireplace that breathes smoke through a crack in the ceiling. Just outside the mouth of the cave is a gorgeous spring-fed pond of brilliant turquoise color where we keep kayaks for clients who wish to do some paddling. The cave lies a few hundred feet from the most spectacular rapid on the river, Zeta, a Class V Z-shaped flume cut into solid granite. Next to Zeta is a clover-shaped tub carved into the rock ledge. Using a special submersible wood stove, we can heat the water in the three-foot-deep natural tub to 105 degrees, thus creating a wonderful hot tub for up to nine people at a time. The ledge around the hot tub slopes gently into the calm water below Zeta, making it easy to go back and forth between the hot tub and the colder river. Our clients always find this Cave Camp to be one of the highlights of the trip."

A well-maintained trail used chiefly by horse-mounted locals parallels the river's flow on one bank. Hertz offers his clients the popular option of taking a break from the rafts to ride along the river on horses provided by a local rancher.

Writer Jon Bowermaster accompanied one of Earth River Expeditions' first departures down the Fu. Later he summed up his experience in an article for *Men's Journal:* "Majestic, translucent and little known outside southern Chile, the Fu is, at any level, in any season, considered by knowledgeable kayakers and white-water rafters to be among the toughest, most powerful, and potentially most dangerous rivers in the world. . . . To a certain clientele and the companies that cater to them, that makes a river like this almost irresistible."

Soon after Hertz first started running the first commercial trips on the Fu, he learned to his horror that a private Chilean company had plans to dam the 100-mile-long Fu to generate electricity. He spearheaded a movement to save his precious river. He organized a rafting trip consisting entirely of Chilean policy-makers and took them down the Fu to acquaint them firsthand with the threatened scenic beauties of the area. He mounted other trips with local Chileans to give them a personal interest in the survival of the wilderness beauties. He founded a guide school in the area to teach the local people how to run the Fu safely in order to stimulate them to start their own rafting companies.

And finally Hertz organized a land trust. Earth River Expeditions and a number of his clients purchased 6 miles of riverfront property. "Because the proposed dam would have been constructed by a private company rather than by a government entity, they would first have to buy all the land fronting the river in order to build," Hertz observes proudly. "But we've frustrated them because the investors in our land trust will never sell under any circumstances, no matter how good the company offer may be. I believe that the Fu is now safe from development for the foreseeable future."

Hertz's other major project of conservation at this time concerned the Great Whale River in Quebec, which supports major concentrations of both caribou and beluga whales and nourishes the hunting grounds of the native Cree Indians as it flows toward Hudson Bay. The area was already under siege from hydroelectric development when he went in to organize commercial operations on a remote stretch of the river. He quickly saw that the construction of Hydro-Quebec's proposed Phase II dam would obliterate the Cree's food sources, their lifestyle, and all their ancestral land. "As long as our land

is intact, our culture is intact," explains former chief Robbie Dick. "When we say the land is our life, the developers don't understand this."

Hertz joined with the Cree Indians in their effort to stop construction of the dam. Lawyers discovered language in the original contract that allowed Hydro-Quebec to build only if the Great Whale River had no commercial value to the Indians who lived along its way. Up to that point they did not. Hertz offered to teach them how to run organized rafting trips down their river which would, in turn, generate both a cash flow for the beleaguered people and raise public awareness of the threat to the region from the proposed dam.

Today the Great Whale River is one of Earth River Expeditions' major success stories. Hertz reflects on what this means personally: "Our work for the Cree Indians is all volunteer. We get no money from the trips we run. It all goes to the Indians to allow them to establish their own rafting operation. We handle the marketing and provide the river guides. Eventually we will have trained a sufficient number of Indian guides so they can handle all aspects of the trips themselves except for the marketing, which we will continue to do out of our office in New York. If they make a go of it, then the river will become important to the Cree community for economic development and the dam will not be built."

Earth River Expeditions' trips on the Great Whale River have been a major success. The close cultural exchanges between the rafters and the Cree Indians have given a special dimension to these experiences. "These raft trips you've organized have succeeded in putting a human face on the proposed destruction of one of North America's last great wildernesses," a grateful Matthew Mukash, one of the Cree chiefs, wrote Hertz. "It is a rare and special occasion when a group of visitors can develop such a rapport with the Cree community."

The Great Whale River project has taken on special significance for Hertz as a pilot program of the kind he hopes to organize across the United States on other Indian reservations. Numerous fine white-water rivers pass through some of these reservations, but no American Indian tribe has developed an interest in organizing rafting trips. Rather, outside operators take all the clients down these rivers.

"I would like to see this change," Hertz says. "If we could prove that such a program works on the Great Whale River with the Crees, then I will set up a Native American Adventure Travel Society to market trips into the wilderness areas located on many of these reservations, trips which will be run by the Indians themselves. This is now a major goal for Earth River Expeditions."

Hertz's other great passion beyond conservation is white-water safety. He deplores the fact that no safety statistics for white-water rafting are kept for river-runners to check if they are planning a particular trip. Nor are there any government regulations covering the industry. "For a sport this popular, it's unbelievable," Hertz complained to a writer from *Outside* magazine. "You just have to ask your outfitter some tough questions and get the answers in writing."

"What sets Earth River Expeditions apart from the scores of other rafting companies is that we have pioneered the safety issue in river running," Hertz states. "I personally developed the concept of adding foot cuffs to all my rafts to keep my people inside during even the most turbulent stretches of white water. And I also designed the customized safety catarafts we use on most of our trips. These are stable, oar-powered rafts made from two pontoons with small decks on top. These catarafts are nearly as fast and maneuverable as kayaks but are capable of rescuing far more swimmers. We employ two of them on all our high-volume rivers. They always go through the rapids first and then position themselves below in the calm water, one on either side of the river, just in case a client should fall out of the raft. We are the only company using these catarafts this way. Thus far, we have had a perfect safety record for all our clients: no injuries and no deaths."

That enviable record is surely helped by Hertz's insistence that all clients on his two most dangerous rivers, the Fu and Colca, must devote an entire day at the beginning to intensive schooling in safety and survival techniques. All the company's river guides are also certified instructors at river-running guide schools. They train the clients how to paddle, survive a flip, and reposition an overturned raft. They also give swimming tests to determine the students' strength at these tasks. "It's just like guide school," Hertz says. "Our clients really appreciate this. And by the end of that first day they feel much more confident about tackling the challenges ahead."

Hertz's plans for the future of Earth River Expeditions is to focus on a handful of the world's rivers which offer the special combination of challenging white-water rafting and a spectacular natural setting in a pristine wilderness where few travelers have ventured before. Today he is the only operator offering regularly scheduled departures on the famed Colca River through Colca Canyon in southern Peru. At 10,607 feet, it is twice as deep as the Grand Canyon. Condors nest in the steep canyon walls, soaring in twos and threes and swooping down to the river. The canyon is virtually devoid of vegetation and people. The only green oasis along its entire length is

Hacienda Canco, where several Indian families live in complete isolation from civilization. At the bottom of the gorge the Colca River, brutal and intimidating, rushes on its way. "What really sets the river apart are the imposing walls," observed Jon Bowermaster in an article in the Fall 1994 edition of Summit. "At points the river narrows to eight feet wide, with steep walls rising 12,000 feet on one side, 10,000 on the other."

In May of 1997 Earth River Expeditions will begin offering commercial trips on Peru's Cotahuasi River, which has never before been run. The canyon there is reputed to be even deeper than the famed Colca Canyon. Travelers experience both exciting white water and impressive Incan ruins.

Another river in the Earth River Expeditions' inventory is the remote Magpie which winds across Newfoundland's Labrador Plateau in eastern Quebec. Accessible only by floatplane, the Magpie flows untouched through hundreds of miles of lake-dotted virgin forests of pine and multicolored moss, hurtling down steep granite gorges and off spectacular falls before emptying into the St. Lawrence River.

"Something will have gone out of us as a people if we ever let the remaining wilderness be destroyed," Wallace Stegner pleaded some 30 years ago. "We need wilderness preserved—as much of it as is still left, and as many kinds, because it was the challenge against which our character as a people was formed."

Eric Hertz has taken Stegner's plea to heart and made his life's work the preservation of some of the world's wild rivers for his grandchildren to enjoy many decades from now.

7

CANOE EXPEDITIONS

"The movement of a canoe is like a reed in the wind," Sigurd F. Olson observed years ago in *The Lonely Land*. "Silence is a part of it, and the sounds of lapping water, bird songs, and the wind in the trees. . . . A man is part of his canoe and therefore part of all it knows. The instant he dips his paddle, he flows as it flows, the canoe yielding to his slightest touch and responsive to his slightest whim and thought."

The romance of the canoe tugs at our imagination in ways a raft or kayak can never do. The canoe has figured in history and adventure on the North American continent from the earliest days. Its design remains virtually unchanged since the 17th century when the legendary French voyageurs heaped steel knives, red wool blankets, tomahawks, mirrors, and other trade items into 35-foot-long birch-bark canoes and set out for the unexplored interior of North America.

Modern canoes are made of aluminum, magnesium, plastic and glass fibers, molded plywood, or canvas over wood frames. But they still allow the adventurous traveler to paddle into the American past on routes once taken by the voyageurs. In 1979 a newlywed couple from Bend, Oregon, made the first transcontinental canoe journey. Paddling an estimated 1 million strokes each, Cathy and Greg Jensen completed their canoe and portage journey from Astoria, Oregon, to Savannah, Georgia, in eight months.

Canoes are fast, light, and highly maneuverable. With each stroke you come to know your boat better until, after a time, it becomes an extension of your own body, as Olsen noted. Once you have mastered some of the basic skills and strokes, you can join any number of organized canoeing trips into wilderness areas inaccessible by other means. A guided canoe trip down a wild river differs in fundamental ways from a rafting experience. You, not the guide, are in charge. Your strokes, not those of the guide, count. Your skill with a paddle determines how you fare in white water and whether or not you collide with rocks or roll over in a hole. And a good guide provides solid instruction, allowing his or her people to raise their levels of paddling experience while building their self-confidence.

A swiftly moving river has long been a source of fascination, and the canoe a perfect way to indulge that fascination. "A canoe trip has become simply a rite of oneness with a certain terrain," John McPhee wrote in *The Survival of the Bark Canoe*, "a diversion of the field, an act performed not because it is necessary but because there is value in the act itself."

AUSTRALASIA

AUSTRALIA

Canoeing the Outback through Crocodile Dundee Country

Largely undiscovered by foreign visitors, Kakadu National Park, Australia's largest, offers a magnificent profusion of wildlife and an extraordinary selection of easily accessible Aboriginal rock and cave paintings. This is safari country, rich in Australia's nearest approach to big game—wild Asian buffaloes, crocodiles, feral pigs, kangaroos, and pythons. One-third of the country's bird species have been spotted here. Everywhere great termite mounds, some 25 feet high, stab at the skies. The popular film *Crocodile Dundee* was filmed nearby. Members of these expeditions canoe for three days down the magnificent Katherine River through the heart of Kakadu National Park, then transfer to four-wheel-drive vehicles for a safari through Koolpin Gorge to view the superb collection of rock paintings at Nourlangie.

Operator: Worldwide Adventures, 36 Finch Ave. W., North York, Ont., Canada M2N 2G9; (800) 387-1483 or (416) 221-3000. *Price:* Moderate. *Season:* May through October. *Length:* 8 days. *Accommodations:* Tent camps. Five percent discount with BBAT coupon.

CANADA

NEWFOUNDLAND

Newfoundland Sampler

Newfoundland is a land of magnificent contrasts, with its rugged coasts, majestic fjords, fast-running rivers, and open valleys. Paddlers on this trip explore from the picturesque fishing village of Burgeo to the dramatic landscape of Gros Morne National Park, spending three days leisurely paddling the coastline near Burgeo, a seascape of rocky islands, sandy beaches, and sheer cliffs where

Operator:
Battenkill Canoe,
P.O. Box 65, Historic Route
7A, Arlington, Vt. 05250;
(800) 421-5268 or
(802) 362-2800.
Price: Moderate.
Season: June to mid-Oct.
Length: 9 days.
Accommodations: Inns and
guesthouses. Five percent
discount with BBAT coupon.

an abundance of marine life can be observed in the crystal-clear waters. They then canoe the Lloyds River, for hundreds of years used by the local Indians for their seasonal migrations; the Humber River, a remote waterway rarely visited by outsiders; and the Grandy's River which ends in a breathtaking waterfall. A stay is also made in Gros Morne National Park, which was proclaimed a UNESCO World Heritage Site in 1987.

NORTHWEST TERRITORIES

The Ultimate Northern Canoe Trip

Operator:
Sunrise County Canoe
Expeditions, Cathance
Lake, Grove Post Office,
Maine 04638;
(800) RIVER-30 or
(207) 454-7708.
Price: Expensive.
Season: July and August.
Length: 9 days.
Accommodations: Tent
camps. Five percent dis-
count with BBAT coupon.

The Soper River on Baffin Island is the northernmost navigable river in the eastern Arctic, and it is navigable for only a short time each year. Flowing only during July to mid-August, the river is frozen the rest of the year. The first descent by canoe was not made until July 1990. Members of these expeditions paddle through spectacular and dramatic northern landscape—flowering tundra and narrow gorges, with thin wisps of waterfalls drifting off steeply terraced escarpments. The river also offers a fair amount of Class II and III white water. At the end of the trip, paddlers spend two days at Lake Harbour, an Inuit village renowned for the excellence of its soapstone carvings.

The Soper River on Baffin Island offers hardy paddlers the challenge of canoeing Canada's northernmost river

Martin Brown/Sunrise County Canoe

Canoeing the Nahanni River

On the northwestern edge of the great prairies at the border between the Yukon Territory and the Northwest Territories, the Nahanni River runs through a region so remote there are no roads and access is by bush plane or raft. In 1978 the United Nations chose Nahanni National Park as the first World Heritage Site, describing it as "an exceptional natural site forming part of the heritage of mankind." The South Nahanni country is a land of myth and mystery. When the headless bodies of several prospectors were found on its banks at the turn of the century, legends of fierce natives and mythical mountain men grew. The operator offers two separate expeditions, a shorter trip from the northern park boundary to Nahanni Butte, and a longer one which begins at the river's headwaters and offers lengthy stretches of exhilarating white water. This is one of the most memorable canoeing experiences in western Canada. Plenty of time is allowed for fishing and hikes.

Operator: Black Feather Wilderness Adventures, 1960 Scott St., Ottawa, Ont., Canada K1Z 8L8; (800) 574-8375 or (613) 722-9717.
Price: Expensive.
Season: June through August.
Length: 14 days for the lower Nahanni and 21 days for the upper Nahanni.
Accommodations: Tent camps.

QUEBEC

The Ashuapmushuan River

Sometimes called the Chamouchouane, the Ashuapmushuan River flows out of the Ashuapmushuan Reserve and picks up the flow of the Riviere du Chef to become a river of major proportions. This was the major means of access to the northern interior for 18th-century French explorers. Canoeists on this trip paddle just under 100 miles through a wilderness devoid of human signs. The white-water stretches are long and runnable, with the exception of a few Class IV and V drops that require portaging. A special treat is the Chauirere Falls which has several drops, the biggest 60 feet. (This is portaged.) The pike fishing is excellent. The operator runs this trip at the height of the summer blueberry season.

Operator: Allagash Canoe Trips, P.O. Box 713, Greenville, Maine 04441; (207) 695-3668.
Price: Moderate.
Season: August.
Length: 7 days.
Accommodations: Tent camps. Five percent discount with BBAT coupon.

The Bonaventure River

Operator: Sunrise County Canoe Expeditions, Cathance Lake, Grove Post Office, Maine 04638; (800) RIVER-30 or (207) 454-7708. *Price:* Moderate. *Season:* June. *Length:* 7 days. *Accommodations:* Tent camps. Five percent discount with BBAT coupon.

Thickly forested, with many lakes and rivers, the Gaspé Peninsula in southeast Quebec is suffused with French culture. Among its many attractions is one of eastern Canada's finest canoeing rivers. The Bonaventure rises out of the remote Chic Choc Mountains and runs through misty, dense spruce forests and magnificent gorges before finally spilling into the ocean. This is a technically demanding river, with long expanses of Class II and III rapids and an occasional Class IV drop. The Bonaventure supports a large population of Atlantic salmon.

EUROPE

ICELAND

Canoeing the Land of Fire and Ice

Operator: Sunrise County Canoe Expeditions, Cathance Lake, Grove Post Office, Maine 04657; (800) RIVER-30 or (207) 454-7708. *Price:* Expensive. *Season:* July and August. *Length:* 10 days. *Accommodations:* Tent camps. Five percent discount with BBAT coupon.

Iceland lies just south of the Arctic Circle, astride the great crack in the earth's surface known as the Mid-Atlantic Rift, and is famous for its active volcanoes, geysers, and glaciers. The vast, uninhabited, and intensely surreal interior is technically Europe's greatest wilderness and its only desert. This is a stark and imposing tundra, characterized by immense black lava fields, volcanic craters, snowcapped peaks, ice caves, and bizarrely shaped headlands. In Icelandic folklore this region was the home of legendary outlaws and an assortment of mythical creatures. Paddlers on these rigorous expeditions run two rivers, neither of which had been run before 1994—the lunar-like Tungnaa, which flows from Europe's largest glacier, and the Pjorsa, which features spectacular gorges and miles of moderate Class II white water.

LATIN AMERICA

COSTA RICA

Canoeing the Rain Forests

A beautiful, peaceful Central American country, Costa Rica is a gem of wonderful natural diversity. The country's rivers are the finest for canoeing in all the region. Participants on these trips experience a variety of rivers, beginning with a paddle down the Rio Penas Blancas through a river corridor carved out of dense rain forest. Next, they travel along the Rio Arenal, a quiet, isolated river dominated by a volcano. Other highlights include the Rio Frio through the Cano Negro Wildlife Refuge, a remote haven for birds, caymans, sloths, howler monkeys, and numerous other animals; the Rio San Juan, along the border with Nicaragua; and the Sarapiqui River, which flows through rain forest and farmland and offers a variety of small rapids. This is one of the best adventures going in Costa Rica.

Operator:
Battenkill Canoe,
P.O. Box 65,
Historic Route 7A,
Arlington, Vt. 05250;
(800) 421-5268 or
(802) 362-2800.
Price: Expensive.
Season: December through March.
Length: 10 days.
Accommodations: Lodges.
Five percent discount with BBAT coupon

Canoes offer visitors to Costa Rica an unparalleled way to explore the wonders of a tropical rain forest

Battenkill Canoe

UNITED STATES

ALASKA

Noatak River Canoeing

Operator:
Sourdough Outfitters,
P.O. Box 90,
Bettles, Alaska 99726;
(907) 692-5252.
Price: Expensive.
Season: June and August.
Length: 10 days.
Accommodations: Tent
camps. Five percent dis-
count with BBAT coupon.

The Noatak spills out of the Brooks Range and
flows 400 miles west to Kotzebue Sound, running
its entire length north of the Arctic Circle. These
expeditions begin with a bush-plane flight from
Bettles. Canoeists paddle the upper reaches of the
Noatak, which offers the most spectacular scenery.
Wildlife observation and fishing are excellent. The
late-August trip includes observing the Arctic caribou herd migrating to the south slope of the
Brooks Range. The sight of these animals thunder-
ing across the tundra and swimming the river is
one of North America's great wildlife spectacles.

FLORIDA

Northern Florida Rivers

Operator:
St. Regis Canoe Outfitters,
P.O. Box 318,
Lake Clear, N.Y. 12945;
(518) 891-1838.
Price: Moderate.
Season: March.
Length: 8 days.
Accommodations: Cabins and
lodges. Five percent dis-
count with BBAT coupon.

Far from the crowded tourist meccas of Orlando
and Miami, northern Florida offers a canoeist's
paradise with some 500 miles of free-flowing rivers.
Canoeists on these trips paddle a different river
each day and return to the comfort of a cabin or
lodge each evening. Often they find themselves traversing a wilderness area of ancient pine and
cypress trees where signs of people are rare. Along
the way they explore isolated sandy beaches, silent
swamps, and refreshing springs. The Santa Fe,
Itchetucknee, Suwanee, Oclockonee, Aucilla, and
Wacissa are the rivers paddled.

"He who does not travel does not know the value of men."

Moorish Proverb

By Canoe through Everglades National Park

Another of the country's unique ecosystems, the Everglades are characterized by hundreds of square miles of water slowly migrating through sawgrass prairies toward the sea. The largest subtropical wilderness in North America, it teems with wildlife, including over 300 species of birds. Paddlers on this expedition travel through the maze of mangrove islands, bays, and channels of the Ten Thousand Islands area of the park. Alligators and manatees are common in this area. This trip offers a perfect opportunity to persons seeking a greater understanding of the trials, tribulations, and fragile beauty of one of our finest national parks.

Operator: Wilderness Inquiry, 1313 Fifth St., SE, Box 84, Minneapolis, Minn. 55414; (800) 728-0719 or (612) 379-3858. *Price:* Moderate. *Season:* Jan. through March. *Length:* 6 days. *Accommodations:* Tent camps set up on the sandy beaches of subtropical keys. Five percent discount with BBAT coupon.

GEORGIA

Canoe Crossing of Okefenokee Swamp

These expeditions penetrate deep into Okefenokee National Wildlife Refuge in southeastern Georgia, a vast watery wilderness where wildlife lives in primeval splendor. Oozing with the unique life forms that

Great Achievements in Adventure Travel

On July 2, 1982, Larry Walters, a 33-year-old truck driver, departed from his girlfriend's backyard in San Pedro, California, riding in a lawn chair powered by 45 helium-filled balloons. After a leisurely 90-minute ascent he reached an altitude of 16,000 feet, where he startled first a TWA and then a Delta pilot. Next Walters shot out ten of the balloons with a BB gun and eventually landed in some power lines, blacking out a small section of Long Beach. The Federal Aviation Administration charged him with operating his lawn chair "without an airworthiness certificate," among other violations. "I wouldn't do it again for anything," Walters told reporters, "but I'd be happy to endorse Sears lawn chairs."

Operator:
Wilderness Southeast,
711 Sandtown Rd.,
Savannah, Ga. 31410;
(912) 897-5108.
Price: Moderate.
Season: Year-round.
Length: 5 days.
Accommodations: Nights are
spent in camps on raised
wooden platforms.

inspire myths—miles of thick reeds and floating peat, water lilies, croaking frogs, and alligators that lurk beneath the murky waters—Okefenokee Swamp offers an entirely different kind of paddling experience. The Indians called this "the land of trembling earth" because of the numerous floating islands. Here the alligator, some 10,000 strong, is king. Expedition members paddle their way through forests of knobby-kneed, bald cypress trees and past wading birds, carnivorous plants, watchful possums, and blooming orchids. They also explore on foot Floyd's Island, the site of a former Indian village, and Billy's Island, with its remains of a 19th-century logging town. A naturalist accompanies each group.

MAINE

St. John River

Operator:
Allagash Canoe Trips,
P.O. Box 713,
Greenville, Maine 04441;
(207) 695-3668.
Price: Moderate.
Season: May.
Length: 7 days.
Accommodations: Tent
camps. Five percent discount with BBAT coupon.

Many consider this the most magnificent paddle in the eastern United States. Almost every site along the 140-mile river is a place of historical interest, strewn with turn-of-the-century artifacts left by lumberjacks who lived, worked, and died in the wild Maine woods. Paddlers on this trip fly to the headwaters by floatplane from Moosehead Lake. With only a few miles of lake paddling at the start, the rest is all river travel, often interspersed with Class I and Class II rapids. The longest and wildest freeflowing river left in the eastern United States, the St. John is flanked by beautiful woodland abundant in wildlife.

Saint Croix River

Flowing out of a chain of wilderness lakes, the Saint Croix runs through the beautiful woodlands of eastern Maine along the border with Canada. Its long stretches of easy white water with only a few precipitous drops make this an ideal river for novices. In the last century the Saint Croix was popular with

A party of paddlers explores the Maine wilderness along St. John River

Allagash Canoe Trips

the timber industry for floating logs to the mills, but now nature has reclaimed the area. Bald eagles are common once again, and paddlers can expect to see moose, black bear, deer, and loons. The smallmouth bass-fishing is excellent. The operator specializes in instruction, including lessons in the long-forgotten art of poling. The most popular month to paddle the Saint Croix is September, when the trees are ablaze with color and thousands of migrating birds fill the skies overhead.

MINNESOTA

The Boundary Waters Wilderness

Dividing the United States and Canada along 200 miles of border, the Boundary Waters Canoe Area

Operator:
Sunrise County Canoe Expeditions, Cathance Lake, Grove Post Office, Maine 04638;
(800) RIVER-30 or
(207) 454-7708.
Price: Moderate.
Season: June through early October.
Length: 5 or 7 days.
Accommodations: Tent camps. Five percent discount with BBAT coupon.

Operator:
Wilderness Inquiry,
1313 Fifth St., S.E., Box 84,
Minneapolis, Minn. 55414;
(800) 728-0719 or
(612) 379-3858.
Price: Moderate.
Season: May through
September.
Length: 5 days.
Accommodations: Tent
camps. Five percent dis-
count with BBAT coupon.

(BWCA) encompasses a million acres and a thousand lakes. It is America's only wilderness canoeing
country. On the Canadian side of the border,
Ontario's Quetico Provincial Park adds another million acres of water wilderness to the area. In BWCA,
300-year-old pines shelter a host of wildlife, ranging
from moose and Canadian lynxes to black bear,
otters, bald eagles, and wolves. This magnificent
country is one of the last intact wilderness areas left
in the "Lower 48." Canoeists on these expeditions
journey into the heart of the wilderness, following in
the footsteps of 17th-century voyagers who traveled
these waters in massive, 35-foot birch-bark canoes.

A couple relaxes in camp in
the Boundary Waters Canoe
Area, America's only wilderness set aside for canoeists
Gunflint Northwoods Outfitters

Lodge-to-Lodge Canoeing in the Boundary Waters

Operator:
Gunflint Northwoods
Outfitters, HC 64, Box 750,
Grand Marais, Minn.
55604; (800) 328-3325 or
(218) 388-2296.
Price: Moderate.
Season: July through Sept.
Length: 7 days.
Accommodations: Lodges.
Five percent discount with
BBAT coupon.

Canoeists on these expeditions spend four nights
in lodges and two nights camping. The trip begins
at Gunflint Lodge on historic Gunflint Lake, the
place where early explorers launched their journeys deep into the interior of North America.
Guests stay in cabins, most with fireplaces. The
serene BWCA waterways offer quiet paddling, plentiful wildlife, and excellent fishing. The second
night is at Nor'Wester Lodge, a family resort dating
back to the 1930s and furnished with family heir-
looms and antiques. Canoeists then circle back to
Gunflint before running the famous Granite River,

actually a series of small interconnected lakes with numerous waterfalls and rapids. The operator provides all equipment, a guide, and camp cook.

MISSOURI

Canoeing the Big Piney River through the Ozarks

This paddle trip down a lazy Ozark Mountain river is perfect for the entire family. The Big Piney flows through the Mark Twain National Forest, cutting a channel through spectacular limestone bluffs and hardwood forests as it is fed by numerous natural springs. The area teems with whitetail deer, wild turkeys, otters, and eagles. The river also offers some of the best smallmouth bass–fishing in the Ozarks.

Operator: Wilderness Inquiry, 1313 Fifth St., S.E., Box 84, Minneapolis, Minn. 55414; (800) 728-0719 or (612) 379-3858.
Price: Moderate.
Season: June.
Length: 5 days.
Accommodations: Tent camps. Five percent discount with BBAT coupon.

MONTANA

Paddle Yellowstone National Park

Travelers on these expeditions paddle on Yellowstone Lake, the largest alpine lake in North America, in sturdy, 24-foot voyageur canoes, crossing the lake from West Thumb to

Clients with Wilderness Inquiry use 24-foot voyageur canoes for their crossing of Yellowstone Lake
Wilderness Inquiry

Operator:
Wilderness Inquiry, 1313
Fifth St., S.E., Box 84,
Minneapolis, Minn. 55414;
(800) 728-0719 or
(612) 379-3858.
Price: Moderate.
Season: July and August.
Length: 9 days.
Accommodations: Tent
camps. Five percent dis-
count with BBAT coupon.

the towering Promontory area. This boasts a spectacular setting with the Grand Tetons rising to the south and the Absaroka range to the east. Plenty of opportunity is allowed for trout fishing, day hikes, or just sunning on an isolated beach. At trip's end one day is spent visiting the parks most famous sites by van.

NEW YORK

Canoeing Adirondack Park

Operator:
St. Regis Canoe Outfitters,
P.O. Box 318, Lake Clear,
N.Y. 12945; (518) 891-1838.
Price: Inexpensive to
moderate.
Season: April through
mid-October.
Length: Check with operator.
Accommodations: Tent
camps. Five percent dis-
count with BBAT coupon.

Long a mecca for canoeists, New York's glorious Adirondack Park covers more than 6 million acres and boasts almost 3,000 lakes and ponds and 1,500 miles of rivers. Particularly popular are the Saranac Lakes and the St. Regis Canoe Wilderness area. This operator offers a dozen varieties of canoe expeditions through various regions of Adirondack Park, ranging in time from three to nine days, including both camping and lodge-to-lodge trips. Guides maintain a relaxed pace with stops for wildlife observation, short hikes into the forest, swimming, and fishing.

Great Achievements in Adventure Travel

Few of the millions who watched the late political commentator Eric Sevareid on the evening news knew that his career began with one of this century's most extraordinary canoe voyages. In 1930, 17-year-old Sevareid and a companion set out from Minneapolis for Hudson Bay in the Sans Souci, a secondhand, 18-foot, wood-and-canvas canoe. After 14

weeks, 2,250 miles, and 60 portages, the youths finally reached York Factory on Hudson Bay. They had made their journey through some of the most remote and forbidding wilderness in North America, traveling without benefit of motor, radio, or even adequate maps.

When they departed, Sevareid and his friend possessed few canoeing skills and only a rudimentary knowledge of wilderness

NORTH CAROLINA

Canoe School

The Nantahala Outdoor Center sponsors the country's finest and most comprehensive canoe school. White-water courses ranging from three days to a week are offered in five skill levels, from novice to expert. Special courses for women, people over 40, handicapped persons, and children are also scheduled. The beginners' five-day course includes three days practicing techniques in the slower waters of the Nantahala River, then two days of instruction in white-water canoeing. On the final day they make a run through a major rapid under instructors' watchful eyes. Other classes for intermediate and advanced canoeists are offered on the Chattooga and Ococee Rivers.

Operator:
Nantahala Outdoor Center,
13077 U.S. Hwy. 19 W.,
Bryson City, N.C. 28713;
(704) 488-2175.
Price: Moderate.
Season: March through Oct.
Length: Check with operator.
Accommodations: Rustic
motel near the Nantahala
Center or camping along a
river. Five percent discount
with BBAT coupon.

"The adventurer is an individualist and an egotist, a truant from obligations. His road is solitary, there is no room for company on it. What he does, he does for himself."

WILLIAM BOLITHO,
TWELVE AGAINST THE GODS

survival. The first stage—the Minnesota and Red Rivers—proved easy. But on Lake Winnipeg, one of the world's largest, they encountered storms, high waves, and chilling temperatures that almost killed them. The highlights included friendly hours spent with Cree Indians, many of whom still lived in tipis and hunted with bows and arrows.

"It was not so much a test of the body," Sevareid recalled later. "It was a test of will and imagination, and they at 17 have a power and potency which rarely return to a man in like measure. I would follow shock troops across a hundred invasion beaches before I would repeat that youthful experience of the rivers."

But Sevareid admitted that the voyage had shaped many of his values as a man: "I knew instinctively that if I gave up, no matter what the justification, it would become easier forever afterwards to justify compromise with any achievement."

Canoeists on the Rio Grande easily take a stretch of white water at the bottom of a canyon in Big Bend National Park

Martin Brown/ Sunrise County Canoe Expeditions

TEXAS

Rio Grande Canoeing

Operator: Sunrise County Canoe Expeditions, Cathance Lake, Grove Post Office, Maine 04638; (800) RIVER-30 or (207) 454-7708.
Price: Moderate.
Season: March and April.
Length: 7 days.
Accommodations: Tent camps. Five percent discount with BBAT coupon.

The Rio Grande marks the boundary between the United States and Mexico. Much of the time it flows through a haunted desert landscape of volcanic hills and mountains and deep gorges, an area now protected as Big Bend National Park. Canoeists on these expeditions paddle the lower canyons, the most isolated and spectacular section of all. The river flows between sky-scraping cliffs and past banks overgrown with tamarisk and bamboo. Stops are made for hikes up tributary canyons and soaks in hot springs. This trip appeals to both beginning and intermediate canoeists.

"A trip, a safari, an expedition is an entity different from all other journeys. It has temperament, personality, uniqueness. . . . No two are alike. We find after years of struggle that we do not take a trip; a trip takes us."

JOHN STEINBECK,
TRAVELS WITH CHARLEY

VERMONT

Vermont River Sampler

After bicyclists, hikers, and cross-country skiers discovered the delights of traveling inn-to-inn through Vermont, it was only a matter of time before the canoeists fell into step. What all seek is a spirited adventure vacation but not at the expense of luxury. Inns offer the twofold advantages of comfort and excellent food. Canoeists on these trips paddle down the Batten Kill River, a swift tributary of the Hudson River and an excellent river for beginners; the upper Connecticut, which runs through unspoiled rural New England scenery at its finest; the Lamoille River, with wide-open views of valleys and interesting geological rock formations; and the White River, an excellent mixture of flat water and quick water, with Class I and II rapids to spice up the paddling.

Operator:
Battenkill Canoe,
P.O. Box 65,
Historic Route 7A,
Arlington, Vt. 05250;
(800) 421-5268 or
(802) 362-2800.
Price: Expensive.
Season: May to early
October.
Length: 5 days.
Accommodations: Country
inns. Five percent discount
with BBAT coupon.

PROFILE

MARTIN BROWN

SUNRISE COUNTY CANOE EXPEDITIONS

"When I was a young boy, I saw the Hollywood science fiction film *Journey to the Center of the Earth,* which was filmed in Iceland," recalls Martin Brown, the burly, mustachioed, pipe-smoking owner of Sunrise County Canoe Expeditions. "From then on, I always wanted to visit that country. Finally, in August 1994 I got my chance when I led the first descents of two of Iceland's rivers, the Pjósá and the Tungnaá. I'm not easily impressed when scouting new rivers, but this blew me away. The landscape was completely alien, the closest I've ever come to extraterrestrial canoeing. From the air the one river we ran looked like braids of mud flowing across the surface of the moon. The other sliced through a bizarre outwash plain like something out of *Road Warrior.* Both rivers were unnavigated and unexplored. I was lucky to find two rivers that are both scenic and safe, since the majority of rivers in Iceland are glacial in origin—short, steep, and suicidal. Most Icelanders had never even seen a canoe before. We shipped our open canoes in sea containers. The notion of navigating rivers in these little boats seemed quite radical to most of the Icelandic population."

Freelance writer Larry Rice was a member of Brown's first canoeing expedition down the two Icelandic rivers. His article on the experience appeared in *Men's Journal.* "We glided past calderas and snowcapped peaks, and stopped to investigate secluded waterfalls and luminous blue, dripping-wet ice caves," he wrote. "Tents were pitched amid expansive moraines, always within view of the looming glacial cap. It was a visually stunning scene but a lifeless one. The landscape was virtually devoid of vegetation and wildlife. Three days after embarking, we reached the take-out, a volcanic crater lake a mile across, surrounded by a rugged moonscape covered in black cinder and ash."

For almost 25 years Brown's Sunrise County Canoe Expeditions has pioneered unusual river itineraries ranging from the Canadian Arctic to the American Southwest. The company, which employs a staff of 25 seasoned professional guides, carries some 400 clients a year on trips down 14 rivers in Maine, Quebec, New Brunswick, Baffin Island, the Northwest Territory, Texas' Big Bend National Park, and Iceland. No other outfitter offers such a wide range of itineraries. Some 45 percent of the clients are women.

Equally popular with its clientele is the company's style in regard to its

trips—keeping alive the heritage of the Maine Guide, which has been around since 1899. "Maine was the first state to license its guides," Brown, a licensed Maine Guide himself, observes. "Here you have people whose fathers and grandfathers were guides. It is a proud tradition in the state and part of its heritage." His style has been to meld this rich tradition with the most effective elements of modern river-running and expeditionary techniques.

From the start of Sunrise County Canoe Expeditions in 1973 the Saint Croix River in eastern Maine has been the company's bread-and-butter river. One of the state's true gems, the classically beautiful Saint Croix rises in an extensive chain of wilderness lakes, flowing through attractive woodlands and spacious natural meadows. Once used for driving logs, the river now enjoys protected status as a Canadian Heritage River. "This is a fine learning river, great for families, and lively without being intimidating," Brown notes. "The Saint Croix is the river by which many people have been introduced to us over the years."

Another popular river is the Bonaventure on the Gaspé Peninsula in Quebec. One of the most pristine rivers east of the Canadian Rockies, it flows out of the remote Chic Choc Mountains through a landscape of misty, dense spruce forests. The trip boasts forested gorges, dramatic views, and crystal-clear Class II and III salmon-filled white water.

Sunrise County Canoe Expedition is technically oriented in that the guides teach the clients, when they want, advanced paddling techniques. "We provide in-depth, comprehensive, thorough instruction for the clients who wish it," says Brown. "My guides can take a novice canoeist and turn him or her into a good solo canoeist in three days. We encourage people to learn solo canoeing, and about one-third of them choose to do so. Going solo gives you lots more freedom and control."

The company guides also offer instruction in the lost art of poling, which Brown revived almost single-handedly. As he explains it, "This is the old way the log drivers and trappers worked the Maine rivers in the 19th century. Poling is a utilitarian way of working the river which gives the canoeist ultimate control. It is best when the river is less than three feet deep. You work off the bottom and gain a fine sense of the river's subtleties and moods. Poling is not a difficult skill to learn. I was taught poling by an old Maine Guide in my late teens. For many years almost no one in Maine was doing poling. It has now had a comeback—today we even have poling competitions. I can claim a good deal of credit for this. Here at Sunrise County Canoe Expeditions we have been poling evangelists for the past 25 years."

In the past Brown's clients started with the easier rivers such as the Saint Croix, gathered technical expertise, and then moved up to the expeditionary rivers in the far north. But now he finds that many want to begin with the more challenging northern rivers, even when they have never canoed before. He insists this usually works out well, both for the client and the group.

"Contrary to popular opinion, our canoe expeditions do not require a great deal of technical expertise," Brown observes. "We keep the actual technical difficulty fairly modest so as not to discourage potential clients. We keep our northern trips in the Class II or an easy Class III category. And my river guides quickly turn novice canoeists into experts. However, if we think a client may not be suited emotionally for one of our more rigorous northern river expeditions, then we will gently steer him or her to our Maine river trips."

"Martin is thorough and detailed on each of his expeditionary trips," enthuses George Whitehouse, a Cambridge, Massachusetts, minister, who has been on five of Brown's trips, including his first runs of rivers on Baffin Island and Iceland. "He really does his homework. For our exploratory Iceland run he managed to get hold of military ground-surveillance photographs of our two rivers to augment the sketchy topographical maps that really didn't show much. He is also very safety conscious. If there's a chance something will go wrong, he will always err on the side of safety."

Brown grew up in upstate New York, where he learned how to canoe while in Boy Scouts. "I always related to moving water and loved to study the blue lines in remote areas on a good atlas," he recalls. " I knew from the age of 8 or so that I wanted to be either a river guide or an explorer when I grew up. Now with my expeditionary river trips I can be both. "

Brown also felt the tug of history whenever he was in his canoe. The American Indians had made canoes everywhere there was water to navigate, from 60-foot cedar dugouts in the Northwest to the elegant birch-bark canoes of the North Woods. When Europeans penetrated the wilderness to capture the fur trade, they did so in canoes. The legendary exploits of these earlier travelers captured the young boy's imagination.

Brown started guiding canoe trips in Pennsylvania during the summer when he was 17. At 19 he moved to Maine to work as a guide on the Allagash River. After a time he moved Down East, which was more of a frontier in some respects. He got his Maine guide license in 1972 and the next year started Sunrise County Canoe Expeditions. His first commercial trips were on the Saint Croix and Machias Rivers.

In 1979 Brown went expeditionary for the first time with the first commercial descent of the Moisie River on the north shore of Quebec. Flowing off the remote Labrador Plateau through an impressive series of gorges and

canyons, some 2,000 feet deep, the Moisie proved to be one of the most spectacularly beautiful rivers in all Canada.

In 1982 Brown started running trips down the lower canyons of the Rio Grande in Texas. These seven-day trips have become another staple for Sunrise County Canoe Expeditions. "Western rivers are different from eastern rivers," Brown explains. "They're canyon rivers with a different set of hydraulics. And the water is heavily laden with silt, unlike the clear-flowing eastern rivers. They present a different set of challenges."

Brown then branched out to other Quebec rivers, most of which had never been run commercially before. In 1985 he organized the first commercial run of the Baie du Nord, which proved to be an exceptionally challenging river. In five days his group covered just 25 miles, 15 of those in one day. The drop was 120 feet a mile. The group ended up on the coast in the middle of nowhere. "The Baie du Nord is a great memory, but I personally do not want to run it again," he admits today.

Brown then went farther west to the northern Yukon Territory to mount an expedition on the Snake River, which flows past glaciers and sharply sculpted, snowcapped peaks. He calls this "Canada's perfect white-water river, being one continuous, 250-mile-long Class III rapid." He operated there for seven years.

Then Brown set his sights on the Soper River on Baffin Island, "as far north as you can go and still find running water," as he puts it. The world's fifth-largest island, Baffin is a barren, desolate northern landscape which is relieved by color and wildlife along its Soper River Valley, characterized by lush and delicately flowered tundra, intimate gorges, and thin wisps of waterfalls. Canoeing was unheard of on Baffin Island until July 1990 when Brown organized the first descent of the upper Soper. Since then the company has run up to three departures a year during the island's short, four-week season. Access is with a twin-engine Otter, equipped with underinflated DC-3 tires. The plane's "landing strip" is a 500-foot-long island in the middle of the river.

Brown resists all temptations to broaden his spectrum of trips, refusing to expand into rafting and kayaking. "Open canoes give me an intimacy with rivers I could never get from a heavy raft or a kayak," he says simply, "so I am going to stick with them."

8

KAYAK EXPEDITIONS

In the world of water sports, few adventures can match the thrill and immediacy of paddling one's kayak through a stretch of boiling white water at the bottom of a deep canyon. "Kayaking is to rafting as skiing is to tobogganing," declares Dana Olson, head of the Snake River Kayak and Canoe School. "There's something about being under your own power, in control of your kayak or skis, that's a real rush."

Elegantly simple in design, these sleek boats were original created over 5,000 years ago by Eskimo hunters, who shrank seal or other animal skins over a wooden frame. The kayak transformed Eskimo culture, giving its hunters mobility in the ice-filled seas and enormously increasing their range.

In the 1860s people began using kayaks recreationally to run European rivers. In the 1920s, enthusiasts first ventured into coastal waters. Today, expeditions by sea kayak have become increasingly popular with adventurous paddlers. One expedition paddled the 3,852 miles from Lisbon to St. Thomas, and another voyaged 9,400 miles around the entire coast of Australia.

Learning to kayak is easier and less dangerous than most people realize. Numerous kayak schools exist throughout the country, where novices can master the basic skills in small groups and a safe environment.

When Mark Billington and three friends paddled sea kayaks from Seattle to Ketchikan in southeastern Alaska and back, they encountered high winds, heavy rain, and large waves. But afterwards he recalled, "Those days gave my life a little more meaning, brought my values into focus, back to the basics of man's existence, back to the values of our ancestors, of quest and survival."

Students in the Sundance Kayak School tackle Upper Black Bar Falls

Sundance Expeditions

ASIA

THAILAND

Sea Kayaking off Southern Thailand

Participants on these trips use a variety of means to explore some of Thailand's most exotic wilderness, rarely seen by Americans. Three days at the start are spent in Bangkok, visiting attractions far from the normal tourist routes. Paddlers then travel by train to Kaow Sok National Park, a region of striking karst mountains covered with heavy jungle. Nights here are spent in elaborate tree houses, straight out of *The Swiss Family Robinson*. Wildlife in this rain forest includes gibbons, elephants, tapirs, and the elusive Bengal tiger. Next, boaters spend six days exploring Thailand's beautiful coastal beaches and islands near Phuket. Sea kayaks will be used to visit karst islands that are riddled with tidal caves and grottoes. Plenty of time is allowed for sunning on the beaches, snorkeling, and swimming.

Operator: REI Adventures, P.O. Box 1938, Sumner, Wash. 98390; (800) 622-2236 or (206) 891-2631. *Price:* Moderate. *Season:* February and November. *Length:* 15 days. *Accommodations:* Shore camps and small hotels. Five percent discount with BBAT coupon.

VIETNAM

Sea Kayaking on Ha Long Bay

Strange and fanciful legends abound in Ha Long Bay. Its myriad islands are said to have been created by dragons that descended from heaven and scattered gems across the water. Even today, local fishermen claim to encounter sea monsters and attempt to placate them with offerings. This mysterious body of water has the surreal quality of ancient Chinese and Vietnamese paintings: sheer limestone islets rise from misty depths, dwarfing the sampans and junks that glide silently past. The sheltered bay is ideally suited for sea kayaking. Stretching over 100 miles in length, it harbors close to 2,000 islands. Some are fantastically shaped rock spires; others support

Operator: Mountain Travel-Sobek, 6420 Fairmount Ave., El Cerrito, Calif. 94530; (800) 227-2384 or (415) 527-8100. *Price:* Expensive. *Season:* April through July, November. *Length:* 15 days. *Accommodations:* Hotels and shore camps. Five percent discount with BBAT coupon.

ancient fishing villages and primeval forests. Paddlers on these expeditions can expect to encounter fishing families in their colorful floating villages.

AUSTRALASIA

AUSTRALIA

By Sea Kayak among the Islands of the Barrier Reef

Operator: Worldwide Adventures, 36 Finch Ave. W., North York, Ont., Canada M2N 2G9; (800) 387-1483 or (416) 221-3000. *Price:* Moderate. *Season:* March through October. *Length:* 7 days. *Accommodations:* Shore camps on remote beaches. Five percent discount with BBAT coupon.

The northern islands of the Great Barrier Reef are among the loveliest and most isolated. Kayakers paddle among a variety of these tropical islands, including majestic Hinchinbrook, with rugged granite peaks rising over 3,000 feet above the sea; the collection of tiny islets comprising the Family islands; and the resort island of Dunk. They travel through an area rich in marine life, including giant sea turtles, rare dugongs, manta rays, and dolphins. The opportunities for snorkeling and fishing are excellent. Members of this expedition use two-person sea kayaks. Group size is limited to 12 people.

NEW ZEALAND

Exploring the Bay of Islands by Sea Kayak

Operator: New Zealand Adventures, HCR 56, Box 575, John Day, Ore. 97845; (541) 932-4925. *Price:* Moderate. *Season:* December through April. *Length:* 5 and 10 days. *Accommodations:* Shore camps. Five percent discount with BBAT coupon.

Outside magazine calls New Zealand "an international hot spot for sea kayaking." These trips focus on the Bay of Islands, a 100-square-mile maritime park on the top of North Island, the homeland of the Maori civilization. Paddlers explore a vast, sheltered bay blessed with a balmy subtropical climate, white-sand beaches, warm water, abundant fish and birdlife, and a treasure trove of green islands sporting wild basalt formations, sea caves, and Maori ruins. An additional attraction is kayak surfing at several beaches. Paddlers also have plenty of opportunity to enjoy the area's excellent fishing.

Running Seven Wild Rivers

The rugged Kiwi backcountry has long been the domain of trekkers and campers. Kayakers have only recently begun to enjoy the opportunities offered by the variety of white-water rivers that spill out of the New Zealand mountain ranges. Unlike the United States, dams are fairly rare. And the water in nearly all of the country's wild rivers and lakes is still pure enough to drink, one more indication of their undeveloped state. Members of this expedition paddle seven rivers on both North and South Islands. These include the Motu, which starts flowing slowly through narrow rock canyons; the Rangitaiki, Rangitata, and Mohaka, all short but challenging paddles; the Kawarau, which boasts the Chinese Dogleg, the country's wildest rapid; the Shotover, which flows through historic gold camps before running into a mining tunnel, capped with a Class IV rapid; and finally the Landsborough, which requires a helicopter ride to reach its headwaters and the start of the paddle.

Operator: Dvorak's Kayak and Rafting Expeditions, 17921 U.S. Hwy. 285, Nathrop, Colo. 81236; (800) 824-3795 or (719) 539-6851.
Price: Moderate.
Season: November through February.
Length: 10 and 17 days.
Accommodations: Tent camps and hotels. Five percent discount with BBAT coupon.

"We only get one crack at life. It lasts but a snap of the finger. What a waste, what a damned shame, if you are lowered away, for all eternity, without once having your mortal soul purged with the emetic of High Adventure."

JACK WHEELER,
THE ADVENTURER'S GUIDE

CANADA
BRITISH COLUMBIA
A Lodge-Based Kayak Exploration of the Inside Passage

Located off the Canadian coast, Vancouver Island encompasses 10,000 square miles, most of it heavily wooded wilderness with 6,000-foot mountains. To the east, on the mainland of British Columbia, is

Operator:
Northern Lights
Expeditions, P.O. Box 4289,
Bellingham, Wash., 98227;
(800) 754-7402 or
(360) 734-6334.
Price: Expensive.
Season: September.
Length: 6 days.
Accommodations: A four-star
fishing lodge, the only
structure on a remote
island. Five percent dis-
count with BBAT coupon.

the rugged Coast Range—its highest peak reaching nearly 14,000 feet. In between lies a beautiful glacier-carved channel called the Inside Passage. With a maze of beautiful islands, placid waterways, and excellent weather, this is one of North America's finest areas for kayaking. Participants on these trips spend their daylight hours leisurely exploring the splendid scenery of the Inside Passage in their kayaks. Wildlife is abundant, with pods of orca whales a common sight for paddlers. Trip members are flown in by chartered seaplane.

Paddling through Canada's Galapagos

Located 500 miles north of Vancouver, the Queen Charlotte Islands are often called the "Galapagos of the North." One-fourth of all the nesting seabirds on the Canadian Pacific Coast are found here, as well as the second-greatest concentration of nesting eagles in the world. The Haida Indians settled the area centuries ago, built great long-houses, and carved giant totem poles out of cedar trunks. From misty alpine heaths through lush primeval forests, past rich intertidal areas to the open sea, the Queen Charlotte Islands are a virtual layer-cake of life zones, each distinct from the rest

Great Achievements in Adventure Travel

In 1953 John M. Goddard set out to paddle a 15-foot kayak the entire length of the legendary Nile River, the world's longest, from its headwaters in Uganda to the Mediterranean Sea 4,187 miles away. For the young graduate student of anthropology at the University of Southern California, this was the realization of a lifelong dream. Just before Goddard and two friends launched their kayaks, a local official warned them: "You chaps are committing triple suicide by kayak." Events nearly proved him right when disaster struck the next day. Raging rapids flipped one kayak, shattered another, and forced a two-week delay.

On following days, the three boatmen glided silently past herds of elephants, cape

and each one a great treasurehouse of biological marvels. The operator offers a variety of trips by sea kayak which allow paddlers to explore a myriad of bays, islets, channels, and the open coast with its wealth of natural and cultural history. Paddling distances are short, and paddlers have ample opportunity to visit important Indian sites, soak in hot springs, hike on picturesque alpine slopes, snorkel in clear waters filled with marine life, and fish for salmon. No previous experience with sea kayaks is required.

Operator: Ecosummer Expeditions, 936 Peace Portal Dr., P.O. Box 8014-240, Blaine, Wash. 98231; (800) 465-8884 or (604) 669-7741.
Price: Expensive.
Season: June through early September.
Length: 7 and 14 days.
Accommodations: Tent camps. Five percent discount with BBAT coupon.

CARIBBEAN

BAHAMAS

By Sea Kayak through the Exuma Islands

Located close to the southern coast of Florida, the Bahamas have long been a popular tourist destination. Many adventure travelers have stayed away, thinking that all the islands must be despoiled by high-rise hotels and crowds of Americans. However, scattered over 100 miles of ocean southeast of

buffaloes, waterbucks, and impalas grazing on the papyrus-lined banks. Hippos attacked without provocation. Enormous crocodiles swam menacingly after them. But Goddard and his companions enjoyed warm receptions from the river tribes. They cheerfully shared their food, which sometimes included roasted locusts and boiled termites. Some had never seen a white man before. One chief was so impressed with Goddard's kayak that he offered to trade one of his four wives for it. In northern Sudan, noontime temperatures often reached 125 degrees. In southern Egypt they visited Abu Simbel, the great cliff temple of Ramses II. Near Luxor, they paddled furiously to escape 30 river pirates in five high-masted feluccas, who shouted, fired their rifles, and chased after them. Finally, after nine months and over 1 million paddle strokes, they reached the Mediterranean Sea and their journey's end.

Operator:
Ecosummer Expeditions,
936 Peace Portal Dr.,
P.O. Box 8014-240,
Blaine, Wash. 98231;
(800) 465-8884 or
(604) 669-7741.
Price: Moderate.
Season: March and April.
Length: 7 and 14 days.
Accommodations: Shore
camps on secluded
beaches. Five percent dis-
count with BBAT coupon.

Nassau are the Exuma Islands, an archipelago of 365 islands devoid of tourist facilities. Recently the government created a national park to protect the area. The uninhabited islands offer idyllic paddling conditions—perfect weather, crystal-clear waters, and spectacular marine life for snorkelers to watch. Participants have a choice of expeditions through the islands, using two-person, folding sea kayaks and paddling an average of 10 miles a day. No previous sea-kayaking experience is required.

Skellig Michael Island's archaeological sites are just one of the attractions for paddlers on Trek & Trail's kayaking adventure along the Irish coast

James C. Simmons

EUROPE

IRELAND

Kayaking the Dingle Coast

National Geographic Traveler has called the Dingle Peninsula one of the most beautiful places on earth. This is a land of sheer cliffs, rounded hills, and lush lowland bogs, studded with medieval castles and abbeys. Ireland is virgin ground for sea kayaks. This small band of paddlers will explore uninhabited islands offshore, including a 9-mile open sea crossing to Skellig Michael Island to visit the well-preserved beehive stone cells of a sixth-century outpost of Christianity and observe thousands of nesting puffins. This adventure is for advanced kayakers only.

Operator:
Trek & Trail, P.O. Box 906, Bayfield, Wis. 54814; (800) 354-8735 or (715) 779-3320.
Price: Expensive.
Season: August.
Length: 9 days.
Accommodations: Tent camps on uninhabited islands and local bed-and-breakfast establishments at the beginning and end. Five percent discount with BBAT coupon.

PORTUGAL

Kayaking the Douro River

Flowing broad and languid through narrow gorges and scenic valleys, the Douro offers enjoyable flatwater kayaking, easy enough for even the most novice kayaker. The put-in point is near the Spanish border in an area where the country's port grapes grow. Small villages cling to rising valley walls, and vineyards flourish on the banks. Paddlers on these trips follow in the footsteps of the Barcos Rabelos, the traditional boats that once brought the port wine from the vineyards to the storage cellars in Porto on the Atlantic coast. Considerable time is allowed to explore the surrounding countryside and villages.

Operator:
Mountain Travel-Sobek, 6420 Fairmount Ave., El Cerrito, Calif. 94530; (800) 227-2384 or (510) 527-8100.
Price: Expensive.
Season: June through September.
Length: 10 days.
Accommodations: Hotels, wine farms, and manor houses. Five percent discount with BBAT coupon.

LATIN AMERICA

BELIZE

Belize Adventure Week

Operator: Slickrock Adventures, P.O. Box 1400, Moab, Utah 84532; (800) 390-5715 or (801) 259-6996. **Price:** Expensive. **Season:** January and February. **Length:** 10 days. **Accommodations:** Thatch-roof cabanas on the beach and screened cabins in the jungle. Five percent discount with BBAT coupon.

These trips are composed of a series of adventure sporting events leading the paddlers through many of the natural wonders that have made Belize famous. Participants begin with several days of sea kayaking from Glovers Atoll, the country's newest National Marine Reserve. They then take a charter boat to the mainland for a series of adventures, including a mountain-bike trip through the jungle on trails linking remote Mayan villages; visiting a newly discovered Mayan ceremonial cave; exploring the Mayan ruins at Xunantunich; running a Class IV section of the Macal River by kayak or raft; and ending up with a kayak exploration of the Caves Branch River through 5 miles of underground caverns.

HONDURAS

Sea Kayaking among the Bay Islands

Operator: Slickrock Adventures, P.O. Box 1400, Moab, Utah 84532; (800) 390-5715 or (801) 259-6996. **Price:** Moderate. **Season:** Late December through mid-April. **Length:** 8 days. **Accommodations:** Shore camps and a small lodge. Five percent discount with BBAT coupon.

Roatan is the best-known of this collection of small islands lying in the Caribbean off the Honduran coast. The rare visitor finds idyllic islands ringed with palm-shaded beaches, jungle-covered mountain peaks, and a diverse marine life. The focus of these trips is Barbareta Island, a protected nature preserve owned by the same American family for over 30 years. Jungle paths lead past a pre-Columbian Indian site to the sandy coves on the north side of the island. The island's rain forest provides a home to a rich assortment of tropical birds. Kayakers explore at their leisure the nearby cays and reefs. Other options include day hikes, horseback rides, and snorkeling.

MEXICO

Sea Kayaking the Sea of Cortez

Few areas offer novices a better opportunity to learn sea kayaking than the coasts of Baja. Calm waters, lovely sand beaches, and numerous bays make this a paradise for paddlers. These trips operate out of Loreto. Paddlers explore the coasts and make day trips to the offshore islands of Danzante and Carmen. The operator's focus is on marine mammals; whales, porpoises, dolphins, seals, and sea lions are common in the area. Plenty of opportunity is also allowed for snorkeling over pristine reefs and walks through the rugged desert wilderness with its rich assortment of flora and fauna. Paddlers may also encounter the elusive Sea Gypsies of Baja, a group of nomadic subsistence fishermen.

Operator:
Northern Lights
Expeditions,
P.O. Box 4289,
Bellingham, Wash., 98227;
(800) 754-7402 or
(360) 734-6334.
Price: Moderate.
Season: January through mid-April.
Length: 8 days.
Accommodations: Shore camps. Five percent discount with BBAT coupon.

Sea Kayaking among Gray Whales

Paddlers on this expedition explore the unusual environment of Magdalena Bay on Baja's Pacific side, winter home to hundreds of migrating gray whales. They travel over 5,000 miles to the warm waters of Baja where they mate and bear their young. Kayakers observe a wide range of whale behavior at close quarters, paddle through the channels of a mangrove swamp for excellent bird-watching, explore the dunes of the barrier island, and beachcomb along 50 miles of uninhabited shoreline.

Operator:
Baja Expeditions,
2625 Garnet Ave.,
San Diego, Calif. 92109;
(800) 843-6967 or
(619) 581-3311.
Price: Moderate.
Season: January through March.
Length: 8 days.
Accommodations: Shore camps. Five percent discount with BBAT coupon.

Kayaking the Yucatan Coast

The Mayan civilization reached its height in the Yucatan Peninsula. The carefully restored Mayan complexes there are among the most impressive in all the Americas. Kayakers on these popular winter trips explore a different aspect of this popular part of Mexico, one few tourists ever see: they have a

Operator:
Trek & Trail, P.O. Box 906,
Bayfield, Wis. 54814;
(800) 354-8735 or
(715) 779-3320.
Price: Expensive.
Season: January through
April.
Length: 8 days.
Accommodations: Villas over-
looking the sea. Five per-
cent discount with BBAT
coupon.

unique opportunity to paddle through the ancient
waterways of the Mayans. The mangrove channels
were once used by early traders from Belize and
Guatemala. Among the sites they visit are a remote
guardhouse ruin built of massive carved stones and
a complex of ruins at Chunyaxche, an inland seaport archaeologists believe dates back to the first
century. Participants also have ample opportunity
for visits to local markets, sightseeing the famous
ruins, long beach-walks, swimming, and sunning
on deserted beaches.

The Rivers and Ruins of the Veracruz

Operator:
Nantahala Outdoor Center,
13077 U.S. Hwy. 19 W.,
Bryson City, N.C. 28713;
(704) 488-2175.
Price: Moderate.
Season: October and
November.
Length: 9 days.
Accommodations: Tent
camps and hotels. Five per-
cent discount with BBAT
coupon.

The Gulf coast of Mexico packs more history into
its three states than any other coastal area in the
country except the Yucatan Peninsula. Hernando
Cortez began his conquest of Mexico here, and the
area has been the stage for many other dramatic
incidents in Mexico history. In Veracruz, one can
travel from the beaches to the summit of Mexico's
highest mountain in 100 miles. Much of the popular film *Romancing the Stone* was filmed in this area.
Members of this expedition run white-water
stretches of two rivers, the Rio Antigua and the Rio
Actopan, both of which offer Class II, III, and IV
rapids. The Rio Antigua, in particular, is technically
demanding, comparable to the Chattooga River.
Members also have time to explore the cultural

Great Achievements in Adventure Travel

In early August of 1928,
Richard Halliburton, the
legendary American trav-
eler, author, and lecturer,
hit upon the idea of
becoming the first man in history to swim the
length of the Panama Canal. An incredulous

governor gave him permission. Halliburton
set out from the Atlantic coast, accompanied by an Army sharpshooter in a rowboat
to protect him from the many sharks and
alligators infesting the waters. "It was a
whale of an adventure," he wrote his parents later. "I was at it ten days. The passage

and historic attractions of the region. This trip is for people with advanced kayaking skills.

THE PACIFIC

FIJI

Sea Kayaking in Fiji

These expeditions focus on the unspoiled and uninhabited outer islands. These are the fantasy islands of the popular imagination, boasting splendid sunsets, emerald lagoons, and idyllic white-sand beaches. The area is remote from the tourist routes, and paddlers often find they have the islands to themselves. Kayakers also have the option of snorkeling over pristine reef formations. The islands visited include Oamea, where a Fijian family runs a coconut plantation; the Yanucas, a cluster of seven islets surrounded by the beautiful Ringgold Reef; and Taveuni, a larger island with a range of 5,000-foot-high mountains covered with rain forest.

Operator: Wilderness Travel, 801 Allston Way, Berkeley, Calif. 94710; (800) 368-2794 or (510) 548-0420.
Price: Expensive.
Season: July, August, and October.
Length: 12 days.
Accommodations: Tents in shore camps. Five percent discount with BBAT coupon.

through the locks was a stupendous contrast. I was locked through alone with my little boat; 27 million cubic feet of water were used to lift me the 85 feet into Gatum Lake— and just as much mechanical labor, just as much expense, just as much everything, as to lift the biggest ship that passed through." *When he reached the Pacific, Halliburton was charged a toll according to his weight, just* *like any other user of the waterway. The charge came to 36 cents, the smallest toll ever collected in the history of the canal.*

TONGA ISLANDS

By Sea Kayak through the Kingdom of Tonga

Operator: Ecosummer Expeditions, 936 Peace Portal Dr., P.O. Box 8014-240, Blaine, Wash. 98231; (800) 465-8884 or (604) 669-7741. *Price:* Moderate. *Season:* November. *Length:* 14 days. *Accommodations:* Shore camps on deserted beaches. Five percent discount with BBAT coupon.

Scattered to the south of Samoa, the Tongan islands are a Polynesian kingdom largely forgotten by the 20th century. King Taufa'ahau Tupou IV has ruled benignly since his coronation in 1967. Tonga consists of three major island groups, totaling 270 square miles. Members of this expedition head for the beautiful Vava'u group of 34 high and thickly forested islands, most of which are uninhabited. Few tourists penetrate this area, where a traditional Polynesian culture still prevails. Paddling distances are short, and members enjoy considerable leisure time to snorkel over coral reefs, visit native villages, and explore the idyllic islands. The operator supplies two-person sea kayaks. No previous sea-kayaking experience is necessary.

UNITED STATES

ALASKA

Admiralty Island Wilderness Area

Operator: Alaska Discovery, 5449 Shaune Dr., Suite 4, Juneau, Alaska 99801; (800) 586-1911 or (907) 780-6226. *Price:* Expensive. *Season:* July and August. *Length:* 5 days. *Accommodations:* Tent camps. Five percent discount with BBAT coupon.

Located south of Juneau, Admiralty Island's 1,650 square miles support one of America's unique ecosystems. Towering spruce forests provide shelter to the largest concentrations of bald eagles and brown bears in North America. The ancient Tlingit village of Angoon is the island's only permanent settlement. The departures of these expeditions coincide with the salmon runs which bring out great numbers of bear and eagles. Participants paddle two-person kayaks in the quiet waters of the Inside Passage, between the beaches and thick kelp beds just offshore, past sheltered coves, from one salmon stream to the next. This trip provides an excellent opportunity to view bear, eagles, deer, seals, and humpback whales. Salmon-fishing on both trips is excellent.

With 16 active glaciers and a profusion of wildlife, Glacier Bay offers kayakers a wealth of experiences

Alaska Discovery

Exploring Glacier Bay by Sea Kayak

Since naturalist John Muir explored Glacier Bay in 1879, this scenic wilderness in southeastern Alaska has taught the world much of what it knows about the behavior of great glaciers. There are 16 active glaciers within the park's boundaries; everywhere visitors look are long ribbons of ice flowing to the sea, resculpting the land in the process. Most people view them from the deck of a luxury cruise ship, but they are much more impressive when approached in a two-person sea kayak. The glaciers loom high above the paddlers who glide among the icebergs. Seals slither off the ice floes and splash into the sea. A floatplane flies participants into a remote section of the park. Kayakers can expect to travel 10 to 20 miles a day, leaving plenty of time for day hikes, wildlife photography, and glacier climbs on these trips. No previous kayaking experience is required.

Operator: Alaska Discovery, 5449 Shaune Dr., Suite 4, Juneau, Alaska 99801; (800) 586-1911 or (907) 780-6226.
Price: Expensive.
Season: June through August.
Length: 8 days.
Accommodations: Tent camps on pristine beaches. Five percent discount with BBAT coupon.

One-Day Sea-Kayaking Adventure on Glacier Bay

Operator: Alaska Discovery, 5449 Shaune Dr., Suite 4, Juneau, Alaska 99801; (800) 586-1911 or (907) 780-6226. *Price:* Moderate. *Season:* Mid-May to mid-Sept. One-day trips depart daily; three-day trips depart weekly. Five percent discount with BBAT coupon.

In addition to their eight-day trip on Glacier Bay, Alaska Discovery offers a popular one-day adventure kayaking Bartlett Cove and Beardslee Islands. Each group, accompanied by a professional guide, ranges in size from two to 12 guests. The day begins with instruction in the necessary kayaking skills. The pace is leisurely with a focus on natural history, wildlife observation, and the park's scenic beauty. The operator also offers a popular three-day kayaking adventure that focuses on the Hubbard Glacier, Alaska's largest.

"Men who go looking for the source of a river are merely looking for the source of something missing in themselves—and never finding it."

CAPTAIN SIR RICHARD FRANCIS BURTON,
THE GREAT 19TH-CENTURY BRITISH EXPLORER AND ADVENTURER

ARIZONA

Kayaking the Grand Canyon

Operator: Nantahala Outdoor Center, 13077 U.S. Hwy. 19 W., Bryson City, N.C. 28713; (704) 488-2175. *Price:* Expensive. *Season:* September and October. *Length:* 13 days. *Accommodations:* Shore camps. Five percent discount with BBAT coupon.

The 226 miles of the Colorado River through the Grand Canyon stand as the Mount Everest of whitewater kayaking. The canyon's combination of spectacular scenery and exciting rapids make this the supreme challenge for all serious paddlers. Since 1978, the Nantahala Outdoor Center has offered the only regularly scheduled commercial kayak support trips available through the Grand Canyon. Instructors accompany each group to provide assistance and advice on the best routes through such legendary rapids as Lava Falls. Oar-powered rafts carry all camping equipment and supplies. This expedition is for advanced kayakers only, who should expect to paddle an average of 22 miles a day.

The Nantahala Outdoor Center offers the only expedition by kayak down the Colorado River through the Grand Canyon

Christopher Smith/Nantahala Outdoor Center

CALIFORNIA

The Klamath River

Located along the border between Oregon and California, the Klamath offers excellent white water, impressive canyons, moderate water temperatures, and abundant wildlife. The operator provides 10-foot, inflatable plastic kayaks which have proven their effectiveness with thousands of first-time paddlers since 1969. (Hard-shell kayaks, by contrast, can be tippy and require a longer training period.) After just a few hours, even beginners will find themselves eagerly anticipating rapids boasting such names as Hell's Corner, Satan's Gate, and the Caldron.

Operator:
Orange Torpedo Trips, P.O. Box 1111, Grants Pass, Ore. 97526; (800) 635-2925 or (541) 479-5061.
Price: Moderate.
Season: May through mid-September.
Length: 3 days.
Accommodations: Choice of camping or riverside lodges. Five percent discount with BBAT coupon.

COLORADO

The Dolores River

Operator:
Dvorak's Kayak and
Rafting Expeditions, 17921
U.S. Hwy. 285, Nathrop,
Colo. 81236;
(800) 824-3795 or
(719) 539-6851.
Price: Moderate.
Season: April through June.
Length: 12 days,
or 3 to 10 days.
Accommodations: Shore
camps. Five percent dis-
count with BBAT coupon.

Running north for 120 miles through near-wilderness country in southwestern Colorado, the Dolores is one of the major tributaries of the mighty Colorado River. The upper reaches flow through ponderosa pine and Douglas fir forests. Downstream the river enters the desert-like world of Slickrock Canyon, where walls of slick sandstone streaked with desert varnish rise straight out of the water. Here, paddlers have plenty of opportunity to explore Indian ruins and pictographs. Hanging Flume Canyon holds visible relics from an 1891 mining operation. Support rafts carry all camping equipment.

"There is no moment of delight in any pilgrimage like the beginning of it, when the traveller is settled simply as to his destination and commits himself to his unknown fate and all the anticipations of adventure before him."

CHARLES D. WARNER, *BADDECK AND THAT SORT OF THING*

The Gunnison River

Operator:
Dvorak's Kayak and Rafting
Expeditions, 17921 U.S.
Hwy. 285, Nathrop, Colo.
81236; (800) 824-3795 or
(719) 539-6851.
Price: Expensive.
Season: May through
September.
Length: 1 and 2 days.
Accommodations: Shore
camps. Five percent dis-
count with BBAT coupon.

Better known as the "Baby Grand," the Black Canyon of the Gunnison plunges 2,400 feet. Other canyons may be longer or deeper, but no other offers such an atmosphere of profound gloom. Boaters ride beneath looming cliffs of ebony-like schist. Boaters must hike a mile down a steep trail to reach the river's edge. (Pack horses carry all camping equipment and boats.) This lack of easy access makes the Gunnison a very private wilderness for those willing to take the extra effort. The river offers fine white water and excellent game-viewing. These expeditions are raft-supported.

GEORGIA

Exploring the Barrier Islands

Along the East Coast, some 300 sandy barrier islands defend the mainland from the ocean's waves and tides. Although in some places the islands are little more than sand bars, off Georgia they form a substantial chain called the Sea Islands or "Golden Isles." A handful have been heavily developed, but most remain unspoiled natural reserves. Members of these trips use sea kayaks to explore the barrier islands and saltwater marshes near the historic city of Savannah. A base camp is set up on Skidaway Islands State Park. The area is rich in wildlife, especially seabirds. Paddlers also visit important historic sites, such as the ruins of Fort Pulaski (1829) on Little Tybee Island, and Wormsloe, a partially restored colonial estate on the Isle of Hope. This trip is a delightful "step up" for novices to sea kayaking.

Operator: Nantahala Outdoor Center, 13077 U.S. Hwy. 19 W., Bryson City, N.C. 28713; (704) 488-2175.
Price: Moderate.
Season: November.
Length: 7 days.
Accommodations: Shore camps. Five percent discount with BBAT coupon.

IDAHO

The Lower Salmon

When Lewis and Clark were thinking about floating down the Salmon River, their Indian guides advised against it, saying they would never return. However, as thousands of modern river-runners can testify, you can come back from the River of No Return. Many return again and again to experience the thrills and spills the great river offers at every turn. Boaters on this trip cover 50 miles of river on the Lower Salmon, paddling 10-foot, inflatable plastic kayaks that allow even novice kayakers to enjoy themselves when taking a roller-coaster ride through the Class III rapids. They travel through a series of magnificent canyons—the Green, Cougar, Snow Hole, and Blue Canyons—before coming out into the Snake River. The trip concludes with a thrilling 52-mile jet-boat ride down the scenic Hell's Canyon of the Snake River to Lewiston. (Hell's Canyon is the deepest canyon in North America.)

Operator: Orange Torpedo Trips, P.O. Box 1111, Grants Pass, Ore. 97526; (800) 635-2925 or (541) 479-5061.
Price: Moderate.
Season: July and August.
Length: 4 days.
Accommodations: Tent camps. Five percent discount with BBAT coupon.

The top school of its kind in the United States, Sundance Expeditions offers beginning through advanced kayak instruction through its base on Oregon's Rogue River

Sundance Expeditions

OREGON

Kayak School on the Rogue River

Operator: Sundance Expeditions, 14894 Galice Rd., Merlin, Ore. 97532; (541) 479-8508. *Price:* Moderate. *Season:* May to mid-September. *Length:* 9 days. *Accommodations:* Dormitory rooms and tent camps. Five percent discount with BBAT coupon.

The oldest kayak school in the western United States, Sundance Expeditions' popular program for beginners opens with a deliberately unchallenging first day and concludes with a descent of the Rogue. Students spend their first five days working a 12-mile stretch of the river to learn the basics—paddling strokes, eddy turns, ferrying current, and the roll. Accommodations are in the comfortable Sundance River House located on the banks of the river. Boaters then test their new skills on a four-day, 40-mile wilderness kayak trip through the spectacular Rogue River Gorge. The off-water agenda includes swimming, hiking, and catching a tan while contemplating the river and rapids ahead. Rafts carry all camping equipment and personal baggage. (Sundance also offers special classes in intermediate and advanced kayaking techniques.)

WISCONSIN

Paddle through Time

The operator uses this popular paddle as an opportunity to teach the techniques of sea kayaking while giving paddlers the chance to explore the wonders of Lake Superior. They visit two historic lighthouses, hike along wilderness trails, and explore rugged sea caves and cliffs at San Island and Squaw Bay. The final day is spent visiting five spots in the Apostle Islands National Lakeshore, an archipelago of 22 islands known for its sea caves, sandy beaches, lighthouses, and sunken shipwrecks. These islands are close to the mainland and are protected from Lake Superior's swells.

Operator:
Trek & Trail,
P.O. Box 906,
Bayfield, Wis. 54814;
(800) 354-8735 or
(715) 779-3320.
Price: Moderate.
Season: June through August.
Length: 3 days.
Accommodations: Tent camps on uninhabited islands. Five percent discount with BBAT coupon.

"People need fear, adventure, and trial to keep them on the right track. Whenever I return to the city and remain too long, I am reminded of how very removed much of our society is from the values of the wilderness. It is nice to just to turn switches and have everything work, yet a sort of complacency results. The dynamics of energy in cities is diametric to the life forces of the forests."

ANNE LaBastille,
ENVIRONMENTAL CONSULTANT AND AUTHOR

PROFILE

DAVID ARCESE
NORTHERN LIGHTS EXPEDITIONS

Joel Rogers, a Seattle writer, was on one of Northern Lights Expeditions' seven-day sea kayak expeditions along the Inside Passage off Vancouver Island, British Columbia. These waters are home to the world's largest res ident population of orca whales, and kayakers often find themselves paddling alongside pods of a dozen or more of the large animals. On their last morning, Rogers and his fellow kayakers saw orcas approaching. They quickly counted five bulls, four cows, and the characteristic hook-shaped baby fins of two youngsters. The whales continued to advance toward the bobbing boats, displaying a distinctive cruising pattern of shallow dives of ten to fifteen seconds, duration. The kayakers waited patiently as the whales quickly approached. As Rogers recalled later:

"At 100 yards the orcas dove again and we went quiet, darting glances at one another. Paul, our guide, ordered us to stay put. One by one their dorsal fins rose into the air right in front of us—so close it looked like a sure collision. At less than 30 feet, a bull aimed right for me. But, surprisingly, I wasn't nervous—I was just trying to focus my camera. They dove, the male's 6-foot dorsal fin sinking with a subtle side-to-side movement. I realized then it's flexible, not knife-like, not a weapon. I looked into the depths of the channel for the passing of the 25-foot-long submarine shape, its dorsal fin faint in the watery darkness—5 tons of *Orcinus orca* beneath my 55-pound kayak. Each of us sensed what no one mentioned—what a grand finale to a week in the wilderness!"

Northern Lights Expeditions (NLE), one of the country's most successful sea-kayaking operations, is the creation of David Arcese. For three months of each summer some 500 of his clients, most of them novices at sea kayaking, paddle their way along the Inside Passage through a spectacular landscape of rocky coasts, sheer cliffs, lush rain forests studded with red cedars, and secluded beaches. The region abounds in a rich profusion of wildlife—harbor seals, Dall's porpoises, black bear, mink, Pacific white-sided dolphins, river otters, and bald eagles are as common as sparrows in the city.

But the major wildlife attraction remains the 350 resident and transient orca whales that congregate in the area, drawn by the summer salmon runs. At least once a season, one of NLE's groups will encounter a "super pod" of 100 or more orcas, which can grow up to 30 feet in length and weigh over 5 tons. As vulnerable as the kayaks may seem, in more

than ten years of operations the company has not had a single instance of an orca bumping a kayak.

Arcese came to sea kayaking in a roundabout way. "It seems, as with everything, you focus on one thing and it leads you into something quite different," he reflects from his Bellingham, Washington, office, "And where it leads you seems to be where you needed to end up anyway."

Arcese traces the roots of his current business back to the summer of 1965 when he was a 15-year-old boy living in an old cabin on the San Juan Islands and working on a commercial salmon fishing boat. The major news event in the local press then was the capture of an orca whale off the coast of British Columbia. Placed in a floating pen, towed to Seattle, and named Numu, the bull became the first of the so-called "killer" whales put on public display.

"Shortly afterwards I had my first of many sightings of the whales that went by offshore from my cabin," he recalls. "From the first I had a profound sense of the wrongness of capturing them for public display in marine parks. Those feelings have remained with me ever since and grown stronger through hundreds of encounters with orcas over the years."

Soon afterwards, Arcese enrolled at the University of Colorado in Boulder, where he studied Asian philosophy and the Japanese language. After graduation he eventually settled into a one-man business doing remodeling for homeowners in the Seattle area. Adventure proved a scarce commodity in his life during this period. One exception came in April of 1975 when, finding himself with an urge to go to Denver and only three dollars in his pocket, he boarded a freight car in the Seattle rail yard and rode the rails to his destination. The experience made a major impression upon him:

"I still remember that trip as one of the most rewarding I ever made. In order to ride the freights you have to be willing to give up control. From hour to hour you do not know if you will be kicked off, or if the railroad will switch your car to another train going in a different direction. You have to be very adaptable. In a curious way I found this lack of control both challenging and exciting. At one time I shared my freight car with an old man who had started riding the rails in the early 1930s after he had lost everything in the Great Depression. He had made it his life ever since."

Arcese's involvement in kayaking began almost accidentally in the winter of 1980. By chance, he read a book about the history and joys of kayaking; he decided he would try it. He built his own kayak from a kit, in the shop of a man who was himself an avid kayaker. On the evening he completed his boat, he took it home to his house on the banks of Lake Washington. The nighttime temperature was 30 degrees, but he knew he could not wait until

daybreak to test his boat. He launched it shortly before midnight and paddled contentedly on the lake. The magic of the moment completely captured
his imagination. Soon afterwards, he was kayaking every weekend. In 1982
he started guiding trips for a local operator. At the end of that season he
decided to form his own company, named it Northern Lights Expeditions, and
ran his first trips the following spring.

Today, Northern Lights Expeditions operates some 40 trips a season for
just over 500 clients. Arcese focuses on the Inside Passage off Vancouver
Island. Out of this evolved his business philosophy: "Concentrate on one
place, learn everything about it, and do it really well. The more you spread
yourself out, the more you dilute your expertise and limit your ability to do
each place well."

In 1996 in response to the demands from numerous previous clients for
a winter destination, Arcese began running sea-kayaking trips out of Loreto
on the Sea of Cortez in Baja California. After his office sent out the first
announcement of the new trips, his clients quickly booked up all 12 departures within a few weeks. These trips, like his summer ones, focus heavily on
the concept of using the sea kayak as a convenient platform for the observation of marine mammals in their natural habitat.

Arcese does little advertising, relying instead chiefly upon referrals
from past clients. He owns a fleet of 37 two-person, 21-foot sea kayaks fitted with custom seats. "In our kayaks you're always sitting comfortably," he
insists, "so even beginners can enjoy many hours on the water each day."
He is also quick to stress the ease with which novice kayakers learn the necessary skills to get about. "In all the years we've been in business, we have
never had a client tip over in one of our kayaks," he says. "They are
extremely stable."

And though his clients may have several encounters during a trip with
the large orca whales, there has never been an unpleasant incident. "I have
never heard of any orca ramming or tipping a kayak," Arcese observes. "The
whales are quite preoccupied with what they are doing, whether it's feeding,
sleeping, or playing. They act as though we don't even exist. I don't think we
offer them any excitement or stimulation. We're just there, like floating logs,
as far as the orcas are concerned. Should something happen to disturb them,
then the pod either dives and comes up at a distance or reverses direction
and leaves the area."

NLE's guides make clear at the beginning of each trip the rules of
engagement. The paddlers must stay together. No one approaches closer to
the orcas than the group. And no one must ever paddle a kayak in front of a

pod of approaching whales, for fear of disrupting their activity.

"We know from years of watching these orcas what their patterns of movements are and where they go," Arcese says. "We can almost always find them. We also carry hydrophones, which allow us to monitor their movements underwater by listening to their communications with one another. Remember, about 200 of these orcas are resident to this area. We see the same animals over and over. I can personally recognize at least 100 of these individuals by their markings alone. And yet, no matter how many encounters I have with these creatures, the magic of the experience never seems to diminish."

9

SAILING ADVENTURES

"I must go down to the sea again, to the lonely sea and sky/And all I ask is a tall ship, and a star to steer her by," British poet John Masefield wrote in 1902.

A century ago they filled the sea lanes. Their graceful forms, square-rigged and fast, inspired countless poets, novelists, and painters. They were the tall ships, bound for Singapore with cargoes of silk and spice, or fighting their way through the fierce seas around Cape Horn, carrying grain and coal between England and Australia. But where cargo delivery is involved, schedules are important; and the newly developed steamships made their own power—no need for the right winds, no worry about becalming. So the majority of tall ships, no longer essential, were "retired." The very few that remained intact became permanently docked maritime museums or, in some cases, naval training ships for a few nations of the world.

Today, however, the tall ships have returned—once again to inspire poets, novelists, painters, and dreamers. Modern travelers can choose from numerous sailing expeditions open to public participation, and can realize two of the most enduring fantasies of our time: the thrill of the ship's surge as a freshening wind fills her sails and she answers the call of her elements; and the exquisite joy of finding that certain atoll, that white-sand island with palm trees, coral reefs, and clear blue water, that existed (one thought) only in dreams.

The choice of ships for today's traveler spans the spectrum, ranging from square-rigged tall ships built at the turn of the century to fast racing sloops incorporating the most recent advances in design and technology. Some cruise the fjords of Norway while others hug the wild coasts of Chile or island-hop across Micronesia. Both the novice and the experienced sailor are welcomed on board. Life aboard is rarely passive, as most participants quickly join in the work of sailing the ship. Smaller vessels offer excellent opportunities for one-on-one instruction in sailing and navigation. And sailing on old schooners combines maritime traditions with an active adventure cruise.

"The sole cause of man's unhappiness is that he does not know how to stay quietly in his room."

PASCAL,
PENSÉES

ASIA

INDONESIA

Sailing the Savu Sea

The Savu Sea lies east of Bali and west of Timor, a region of Indonesia that few travelers ever penetrate. Participants on this adventure explore this exotic region with its hundreds of untouristed islands on board the two-masted tall ship *Adelaar,* which has eight air-conditioned cabins. A full day is spent on Komodo Island, home to the legendary Komodo dragons, the world's largest and most fearsome lizards. These carnivorous monitor lizards measure up to 10 feet in length and can weigh 350 pounds. Other ports of call include Flores, a long, narrow, rugged island dotted with active volcanoes, where three days will be spent exploring the rich sights; Lomblen Island, where the villagers still hunt sperm whales from small sailboats for their sole source of protein; and Savu Island, which offers visitors walled, unspoiled villages, lively rituals, traditional dances, and splendid handwoven textiles.

Operator:
Geographic Expeditions,
2627 Lombard St.,
San Francisco, Calif. 94123;
(415) 922-0448.
Price: Expensive.
Season: July.
Length: 17 days.
Accommodations: Shipboard cabins. Five percent discount with BBAT coupon.

REPUBLIC OF THE MALDIVE

Sail Expedition through the Maldive Islands

A chain of some 1,300 coral atolls located in the Indian Ocean 400 miles southwest of Sri Lanka, the Maldive Islands support a population of about 200,000 people. Only 200 of the islands are inhabited. Participants on these expeditions travel from atoll to atoll on a *dhow,* the traditional Arab sailing vessel. Days are spent visiting native villages, enjoying some of the best snorkeling in Asia, and

Operator:
Worldwide Adventures,
36 Finch Ave. W., Toronto,
Ont., Canada M2N 2G9;
(800) 387-1483 or
(416) 221-3000.
Price: Moderate.
Season: January, March,
and November.
Length: 7 days.
Accommodations: Nights are
spent on the *dhow* or
camped on shore. Five percent discount with BBAT
coupon.

beachcombing on palm-fringed islands. A Maldivian proverb says it all: "Here the world ends and paradise begins."

"Had we lived, I should have had a tale to tell of the hardihood, endurance, and courage of my companions which would have stirred the heart of every Englishman. These rough notes and our dead bodies must tell the tale, but surely, surely a great rich country like ours will see that those who are dependent on us are properly provided for."

CAPTAIN ROBERT F. SCOTT'S
*FINAL DIARY ENTRY FROM HIS ILL-FATED
1911–1912 EXPEDITION TO THE SOUTH POLE*

THAILAND
Adventure Sailing in Southern Thailand

Operator:
Wilderness Travel,
801 Allston Way,
Berkeley, Calif. 94710;
(800) 368-2794 or
(510) 548-0420.
Price: Expensive.
Season: January and March,
November and December.
Length: 15 days.
Accommodations: Shipboard
cabins and hotels. Five per-
cent discount with BBAT
coupon.

The focus of this exploration of the more offbeat parts of Thailand is a six-day sailing adventure through the Andaman Seas on a 60-foot yacht, *Suwan Macha*. Participants visit deserted islands, idyllic beaches, and picturesque, isolated fishing villages. Lots of time is allowed for swimming, snorkeling, windsurfing, and sailing, with shore visits every day. The trip begins with a stay of several days in the tropical forest of Khao Sok National Park, where activities include jungle walks, river-rafting, visits to coffee and rubber plantations, and sea trips aboard a swift Thai long-tail boat. One day is spent at the famous Kata Thani Beach Resort. At Phang Nga Bay the group boards sea canoes for a day of exploring lovely sculpted limestone islands with dozens of secret lagoons and caves.

The *Star Flyer* is a modern clipper ship capable of traveling at speeds of 15 knots in the open ocean

Star Clippers

ATLANTIC OCEAN

Trans-Atlantic Crossing

For serious sailors, the trans-Atlantic crossing is the epitome of sailing experiences. Following the trade winds in a 2,300-mile northeastern arc across the Atlantic, the *Star Flyer*, a modern clipper ship, is the first commercial sailing vessel in more than 120 years to carry passengers on regularly scheduled trips across the Atlantic. She makes two annual ocean crossings from Barbados to Cannes, France. She boasts a length of 360 feet, surpassing by 25 feet the *Great Republic*, the largest clipper ship of the past century. *Star Flyer* is also the world's tallest sailing ship, with four masts that tower 220 feet over the deck and fly 36,000 square feet of sails. On one trip she recorded 14.8 knots westbound off the Azores in 1991. For much of the voyage passengers never see land or another ship, only empty horizon in every direction. The staff offers daily classes in navigation and knot-tying.

Operator: Star Clippers, 4101 Salzedo Ave., Coral Gables, Fla. 33146; (800) 442-0551 or (305) 442-0550.

Price: Moderate to expensive, depending upon the cabin.

Season: April–May and September–October.

Length: 31 days, although passengers can book shorter segments.

Accommodations: Shipboard cabins. Five percent discount with BBAT coupon.

AUSTRALASIA

AUSTRALIA

Sail Cruise along the Barrier Reef

Operator:
Adventure Center,
1311 63rd St., Suite 200,
Emeryville, Calif. 94608;
(800) 227-8747 or
(510) 654-1879.
Price: Inexpensive.
Season: Year-round.
Length: 7 days.
Accommodations: Shipboard
cabins. Five percent discount with BBAT coupon.

Off the east coast of Australia lie islands of astonishing beauty, all the more remarkable for their accessibility. The larger ones have succumbed to development as resorts. But hundreds of the smaller islands are uninhabited and unspoiled. Members of this seven-day expedition board the *Coral Trekker,* a square-rigged Norwegian-built wooden ship, for a cruise among the deserted islands and coral reefs of the Whitsunday Passage off North Queensland. The days are filled with snorkeling, swimming, sailing, windsurfing, and island visits. A fully qualified dive master accompanies each group. Sail instruction is also available for those who wish it.

NEW ZEALAND

North Island Sailing Expedition

Operator:
Ocean Voyages,
1709 Bridgeway,
Sausalito, Calif. 94965;
(415) 332-4681.
Price: Moderate.
Season: October through
February.
Length: 10 to 21 days.
Accommodations: Shipboard
cabins. Five percent discount with BBAT coupon.

North of Auckland lie some of the Pacific's finest sailing locations, blessed with strong winds, spectacular natural settings, and fast yachts. A major attraction is the Bay of Islands Maritime and Historic Park, 86 islands and 500 miles of coastline, a sailor's paradise because of its sheer variety. The sun-washed cliffs around the islands are deeply cut by caves and arches and further highlighted with dramatic rock formations. The area also has excellent fishing and snorkeling. Participants on these trips have a choice of several vessels.

CARIBBEAN

VIRGIN ISLANDS

Windjamming on the Sir Francis Drake

The three-masted *Sir Francis Drake* was built in Germany in 1917 to carry copper from Chile to Hamburg. At the age of 71, she was rechristened and refurbished to handle 35 passengers in air-conditioned comfort on cruises through the American and British Virgin Islands. These gems of the sea were a favorite haunt of 18th-century pirates; according to tradition, Blackbeard marooned a mutinous crew on Dead Man's Cay. The brisk trade winds, numerous islands, secluded anchorages, and crystal-clear waters make the Virgin Islands a sailor's paradise. The trip's many options include excellent snorkeling and scuba diving, windsurfing, swimming, shelling, duty-free shopping, and evenings spent dancing to the rhythms of a steel-drum band. All cruises begin and end in St. Thomas.

Operator: Tall Ship Adventures, 1389 S. Havana St., Aurora, Colo. 80012; (800) 662-0090 or (303) 755-7983.
Price: Moderate.
Season: Year-round.
Length: 3, 4, and 5 days.
Accommodations: Shipboard cabins. Five percent discount with BBAT coupon.

Instructional Sail Cruise through the American and British Virgin Islands

The Annapolis Sailing School, the country's oldest and largest, offers sail cruises of the Virgin Islands out of its Christiansted office on St. Croix. These are not only tropical vacations with numerous opportunities for swimming, snorkeling, and beachcombing, but also instructional courses in which students learn the art of sail cruising by living aboard a yacht and sailing under the watchful eye of an expert instructor. The boats include a Gulfstar 50-foot ketch-rigged luxury yacht and a 24-foot Rainbow sloop.

Operator: Annapolis Sailing School, P.O. Box 3334, Annapolis, Md. 21403; (800) 638-9192 or (301) 267-7205.
Price: Moderate.
Season: Year-round.
Length: 5 and 7 days.
Accommodations: Shipboard cabins. Five percent discount with BBAT.

WEST INDIES

By Tall Ship through the Leeward Islands

Operator: Windjammer Barefoot Cruises, P.O. Box 120, Miami Beach, Fla. 33119; (800) 327-2601 or (800) 432-3364 in Florida. *Price:* Moderate. *Season:* Year-round. *Length:* 14 days. *Accommodations:* Shipboard cabins. Five percent discount with BBAT coupon.

The last of the great Portuguese Grand Banks schooners, the 248-foot *Polynesia* was featured in *National Geographic* articles and a book by famous sea captain Alan Villiers. Now completely refurbished, she unfurls her 11 sails from 192-foot masts and departs from St. Maarten on cruises, carrying 126 passengers to some of the loveliest islands in the Caribbean. Sailing distances are short, and passengers spend most of their days ashore, exploring the sights. On the first and third Mondays of each month the *Polynesia* sails for Saba, St. Barts, St. Kitts, and Statia; on the second and fourth Mondays she heads for Antigua, St. Barts, Montserrat, and Nevis.

By Tall Ship through the Grenadines

Operator: Windjammer Barefoot Cruises, P.O. Box 120, Miami Beach, Fla. 33119; (800) 327-2601 or (800) 432-3364 in Florida. *Price:* Moderate. *Season:* Year-round. *Length:* 6 days. *Accommodations:* Shipboard cabins. Five percent discount with BBAT coupon.

Perhaps the least-known but among the loveliest of the Windward Islands, the Grenadines consist of 100 islands and rocks scattered along a submerged ridge between Grenada and St. Vincent. Many are uninhabited, most have no airstrip, and they are all ignored by the big cruise ships. The islands boast exotic names like Bequia, Mustique, Petit St. Vincent, and Isles des Saintes. The Grenadines are the playground for the 72 passengers on the tall ship *Mandalay*, which sails among them. Originally built in 1923 for financier E. F. Hutton, in her day she was one of the most luxurious personal yachts in the world, flying more than 22,000 square feet of sail. The *Mandalay* arrives at each port early in the day, allowing passengers ample time for whatever activities beckon ashore.

"A fantasy is a reality you're too chicken to live out."

From the film *Five Easy Pieces*

Passengers on the 248-foot *Mandalay* experience sea travel from another era

Windjammer Barefoot Cruises

Sail Cruising in the Grenadines

In addition to great scenic beauty, lovely beaches, and friendly people, the Grenadines also offer excellent sailing conditions with consistent, moderate winds. These sail cruises are for people who want a more intimate experience with the boat, sea, and islands than is possible on a larger ship. Group size is kept small (between two and six). The yachts include the *Infinity*, a Danish-built 46-foot sloop designed for offshore cruising and racing. Their captains know the islands extremely well, and all are ready to give hands-on sailing instruction to

Operator: Ocean Voyages, 1709 Bridgeway, Sausalito, Calif. 94965; (415) 332-4681.
Price: Expensive.
Season: Year-round.
Length: 10, 14, and 21 days.
Accommodations: Shipboard cabins. Five percent discount with BBAT coupon.

participants who show an interest. A highlight of the cruises is always the Tobago Cays, a group of uninhabited coral atolls that offer some of the finest snorkeling in the Caribbean.

EUROPE

FRANCE

Sailing on a Clipper Ship to Sardinia and Corsica

Operator: Star Clippers, 4101 Salzedo Ave., Coral Gables, Fla. 33146; (800) 442-0551 or (305) 442-0550.
Price: Moderate to expensive, depending upon the cabin.
Season: June through Sept
Length: 7 days.
Accommodations: Shipboard cabins. Five percent discount with BBAT coupons.

The magnificent clipper ships were the most celebrated of the tall ships of the last century. They set speed records which still stand. The *Star Flyer*, a modern clipper that started service in 1991, boasts a length of 360 feet, surpassing by 25 feet the *Great Republic*, the largest clipper ship of the past century. She is also the world's tallest sailing ship: her four masts tower 220 feet over the deck and fly 36,000 square feet of sails. Each summer she is positioned on the Mediterranean coast of France for sailing trips to the exotic islands just to the south—Corsica, Sardinia, and Elba. Considerable time is allowed for shore visits at such places as Costa Smeralda, a

Great Achievements in Adventure Travel

In 1947 Thor Heyerdahl and five companions sailed 4,300 miles from Peru to Tahiti on the Kon-Tiki, a primitive balsawood raft, deliberately risking their lives to prove a theory that ancient Peruvians could have settled the South Pacific islands. The historic Kon-Tiki sits enshrined today in a museum in Oslo, Norway. Almost forgotten in the annals of sail adventures is La Balsa, a second balsa-log raft which, in 1970, took Mexican Vital Alsar and three companions from Ecuador to Australia, a distance of 8,565 miles in six months' time—the longest raft voyage in recorded history.

On May 29, 1970, La Balsa slowly made its way out of the harbor of Guayaquil. Inspired by Heyerdahl before him, Alsar was eager to prove that transoceanic voyages on

Sardinian enclave of private seaside resorts developed by the Aga Khan; Bonifacio, Corsica's almost-landlocked harbor and ancient citadel town perched high atop a granite cliff; and Portoferrai, Elba, where Napoleon waited out his first exile.

GREECE

Sailing the Greek Islands

One-quarter of Greece consists of islands dotting the Cretan, Libyan, Aegean, and Ionian Seas. With 2,000 islands and a coastline of tiny fishing villages, major historical sites, peaceful bays, and white-washed towns, Greece is a sailing paradise. Two air-conditioned sail yachts carry 20 passengers in ten double cabins on cruises of the Aegean Sea. The ports of call include the sacred island of Tinos, where every August thousands of pilgrims attend celebrations in honor of the Virgin Mary; Santorini, thought to be the source of the myth of Atlantis after a volcanic eruption 2,000 years ago devastated the island's Minoan civilization; Mykonos, a favorite resort long popular with artists and writers; and the Cycladian islands of Paros, Naxos, Ios, and Antiparos. Participants have ample

Operator:
Greek Islands Cruise Center, 4321 Lakemoor Dr., Wilmington, N.C.; (800) 341-3030 or (910) 350-0100.
Price: Expensive.
Season: April through Nov.
Length: 7 days.
Accommodations: Shipboard cabins. Five percent discount with BBAT coupon.

primitive rafts were possible for the pre-Columbian Hauncavilca Indians of South America. Bad luck shadowed the expedition from the first—but not the hurricanes, sharks, and uncharted reefs that the voyagers had expected would be their major dangers. Within a few days the raft's mascots died of parrot fever, a deadly and highly contagious viral disease carried by certain birds. Alsar himself was stricken and almost died from the fever. A French crew member fell into a deep depression and became catatonic before the others were able to cure his condition. West of the Galapagos Islands, in busy shipping lanes, they sailed into an enormous fog bank that took almost two weeks to cross and nearly caused them to be run over by passing vessels. The boredom and personal tensions built over the long days and ultimately proved as dangerous as any storm. In the end, perseverance won the day when La Balsa sailed triumphantly into the harbor at Mooloolaba on the eastern coast of Australia.

time for secluded beaches, shore excursions, and the lively taverna.

SWEDEN

Sailing through the Stockholm Archipelago

Operator: Ocean Voyages, 1709 Bridgeway, Sausalito, Calif. 94965; (415) 332-4681. *Price:* Moderate. *Season:* July and August. *Length:* 7 days. *Accommodations:* Shipboard cabins. Five percent discount with BBAT coupon.

The collection of islands known as the Stockholm Archipelago is unique in Europe. Consisting of more than 24,000 islands in every conceivable shape and size, this island world actually starts in Stockholm. The islands near the city are virtually suburbs of the Swedish capital. Other parts are uninhabited and still among the wildest areas in Europe. Some of the islands are forest-clad and rise sharply from the sea; others are low, naked slabs of rocks called "skerries." Because so few tourists visit the Stockholm Archipelago, there are no bars, souvenir stands, or facilities for mass tourism. These sail expeditions offer the ideal way to explore these fascinating islands. Participants travel in groups of six or fewer on 40-foot sailing yachts.

LATIN AMERICA

BELIZE

Exploring the Barrier Reef

Just off Belize lies the largest barrier reef in the Western Hemisphere, second in size worldwide only to Australia's. Scattered along the 100-mile length are scores of small islands, most with beautiful sandy beaches and swaying palm trees. Many support large rookeries of reddish egrets, frigate birds, herons, and red-footed boobies. Known throughout the world for its pristine beauty and diversity of marine life, the reef is shallow enough to allow even the most inexperienced snorkeler the opportunity to enjoy the myriad life forms.

Participants on these cruises travel on a 48-foot sailboat built by one of the last of Belize's traditional shipwrights. After leaving the historic harbor of Belize City, the group sails to the remote parts of the reef, visiting several of the most famous atolls, including Lighthouse with its spectacular Blue Hole. The options include snorkeling, sea kayaking, and beachcombing.

Operator: Ecosummer Expeditions, 936 Peace Portal Dr., P.O. Box 8014-240, Blaine, Wash. 98231; (800) 465-8884 or (604) 669-7741.
Price: Expensive.
Season: January through mid-April.
Length: 7 days.
Accommodations: Shipboard cabins. Five percent discount with BBAT coupon.

"The island is a dream come true, so that romanticists who are patient enough and adventurous enough may see vindicated their faith in lonely lands beyond the farthest horizon."
ROBERT DEAN FRISBIE,
THE BOOK OF PUKAPUKA

ECUADOR

Sailing the Untouched Galapagos

Participants on these expeditions board a luxury yacht for an itinerary focused on the more remote and rarely visited of the islands. Four days are spent on Isabela Island, the largest and most diverse of the Galapagos Islands. Five of the six volcanoes on the island are still active. The full range of the region's flora and fauna can be found in this imposing volcanic landscape. Other stops include Seymour Island with its magnificent frigate-bird colony; Santiago Island with its pahoehoe lava formations and penguin population; Tower Island, which has large nesting colonies of frigate birds, masked and red-footed boobies, and swallowtailed gulls; Isla Santa Fe with its tall forest of prickly-pear cactus and large land iguanas; and Floreana, with its famous Post Office Bay, where whalers left their mail 150 years ago.

Operator: Natural Habitat Adventures, 2945 Center Green Court S., Boulder, Colo. 80301; (800) 543-8917 or (303) 449-3711.
Price: Expensive.
Season: May and July.
Length: 18 days.
Accommodations: Cabins on a luxury motor yacht. Five percent discount with BBAT coupon.

MIDDLE EAST

TURKEY

Sailing Turkey's Turquoise Coast

Operator:
Geographic Expeditions,
2627 Lombard St.,
San Francisco, Calif. 94123;
(415) 922-0448.
Price: Moderate.
Season: May and June,
August and September.
Length: 17 days.
Accommodations: Shipboard
cabins. Five percent discount with BBAT coupon.

When Antony wanted to impress Cleopatra, he took her to the spectacular southern coast of Turkey lying between modern Bodrum and Antalya. Participants on this expedition follow in the wake of the Roman general and his Egyptian queen past isolated coves, spectral ruins, and small fishing villages. Their ship is the traditional Turkish gulet, air-conditioned for the comfort of modern travelers. Twelve days are spent on board, providing a leisurely exploration of this fabled coast with considerable time allowed for day trips to archaeological sites. The stops include Termessos with its extraordinary 2,000-year-old rock-hewn tombs; the Greek ghost town of Kayakoy, abandoned in 1923; Epheus, one of the richest Greco-Roman sites in the world; Myra, with its spectacular Lycian rock tombs hewn into a cliff above a fine late Roman amphitheater; and the sunken ruins of an ancient city off Kalekoy, which provide some of the most exciting snorkeling in the Mediterranean.

Passengers with Geographic Expeditions explore the fabled Turkish coast from the deck of a traditional gulet

Geographic Expeditions

Your own idyllic Pacific island is there, waiting to be discovered

James C. Simmons

THE PACIFIC

FIJI

Adventure Sailing through Fiji's Yasawa Islands

This 12-day sail cruise is particularly well suited for lovers of islands, for all of us who feel alienated from desk-bound lives and seek that unprofaned sanctuary, removed from human haunts, where we may dwell as beachcombers, if only for an afternoon, in tranquility, happiness, and security amidst a closeness to nature. The Yasawas are a chain of 16 volcanic islands stretching away from the west coast of Viti Levu, Fiji's main island. Participants travel aboard the yacht *Galaxie*, a 72-foot-long sailing ketch. The islands, with their white, sandy beaches topped by palm trees swaying in the sunshine, also become the starting points for snorkeling and diving expeditions to beautiful coral gardens alive with strange and beautiful creatures.

Operator: Wilderness Travel, 801 Allston Way, Berkeley, Calif. 94710; (800) 368-2794 or (510) 548-0420.
Price: Expensive.
Season: Year-round.
Length: 12 days.
Accommodations: Shipboard cabins. Five percent discount with BBAT coupon.

A sail yacht in French Polynesia provides a
perfect escape to the idyllic tropical island of
our dreams where we can dwell, if only for a
day, in tranquility, happiness, and security
amidst natural beauty

Ocean Voyages

FRENCH POLYNESIA

Sailing in the Wake of Captain Cook

Operator:
Ocean Voyages,
1709 Bridgeway,
Sausalito, Calif. 94965;
(415) 332-4681.
Price: Moderate.
Season: April through
December.
Length: 7 days.
Accommodations: Shipboard
cabins. Five percent dis-
count with BBAT coupon.

Few places excite the traveler's imagination more
than the fabled islands of French Polynesia, where
the sweet scent of tiare blossoms promises Edens
still uncorrupted. Novelist James Michener called
Bora Bora "the most beautiful island in the world."
The operator has several yachts for sails between
Huahine and Bora Bora with stops at Raiatea and
Tahaa. Sailing distances are short, allowing passengers ample time to snorkel over coral reefs, play
Robinson Crusoe on deserted motus, and experience a traditional lifestyle in villages where few foreigners ever go. The French skipper is ready to
teach passengers the skills of reef sailing. Sail on

the *Archipels* and discover the beauty of the South Seas. Others have had to mutiny for it.

MICRONESIA

Palau

This portion of Micronesia consists of hundreds of islands with secluded beaches and greenhouse vegetation, connected by channels of clear water. Palau is best known for its underwater life. The huge diversity of corals is perhaps unequaled by any other place in the world. More than 1,500 species of tropical fish have been documented in Palau. Many of these can easily be seen by snorkeling in 3 to 20 feet of water. The operator has the *Eclipse*, an attractive 48-foot sloop, positioned in these waters. The ship offers accommodations for up to six passengers and is equipped for scuba diving, and passengers' interests determine the itinerary. Options include snorkeling over reefs, climbing to marine lakes (including the acclaimed Jellyfish Lake), bird-watching, swimming, and beachcombing.

Operator:
Ocean Voyages,
1709 Bridgeway,
Sausalito, Calif. 94965;
(415) 332-4681.
Price: Expensive.
Season: Year-round.
Length: 1 or 2 weeks.
Accommodations: Shipboard cabins. Five percent discount with BBAT coupon.

PITCAIRN ISLAND

Sailing in the Wake of the Bounty Mutineers

Two centuries after young Fletcher Christian seized HMS *Bounty* from its hard-driving captain, Lt. William Bligh, the colony founded by nine mutineers and 19 Polynesians still survives on this remote Pacific island, located 1,200 miles southeast of Tahiti. Increasingly cut off from the outside world with each passing year, the islanders depend upon these sail expeditions to bring them much-needed supplies. Rising sheer from the depths of the sea, Pitcairn has no fringing reef, harbor, sheltered bay, or even a beach. Participants on these expeditions spend two weeks in the homes of the islanders, exploring this legendary Pacific island and getting

Operator:
Ocean Voyages,
1709 Bridgeway,
Sausalito, Calif. 94965;
(415) 332-4681.
Price: Expensive.
Season: Check with operator.
Length: 21 days.
Accommodations: Shipboard cabins and family homes on Pitcairn Island. Five percent discount with BBAT coupon.

to know her people. These trips begin and end from the island of Mangareva, just two days' sail from Pitcairn and boasting its own exotic history.

VANUATU

Classic Pacific Sailing Adventure

Operator: Wilderness Travel, 801 Allston Way, Berkeley, Calif. 94710; (800) 368-2794 or (510) 548-0420. *Price:* Expensive. *Season:* April through June. *Length:* 11 days. *Accommodations:* Ship's cabins. Five percent discount with BBAT coupon.

Located between Fiji and the Solomons, the former French colony of Vanuatu is a cluster of lush tropical islands which offer ideal cruising conditions for the truly adventurous; it's the setting for James Michener's *Tales of the South Pacific.* Although 50 years ago cannibalism was rampant on some islands, today the islanders enjoy a reputation for friendliness, leading primitive lifestyles on idyllic islands. Participants explore this area on board the *Galaxie,* a 72-foot luxury sailing ketch. They have plenty of opportunity to observe island rituals, hike to the tops of volcanoes, and dive and snorkel over pristine reefs. Every Saturday in April and May, the famous Pentecost jumps take place on Pentecost Island, where islanders leap off 100-foot towers with vines tied to their ankles. This harvest rite of passage is said to be the origin of our contemporary "bungee jumping."

UNITED STATES

ALASKA

Exploring the Inside Passage

Southeast Alaska has long been popular with thousands of travelers for its spectacular scenery, fantastic profusion of wildlife, splendid isolation, and numerous colorful towns, some of great historic interest. Avoiding most of the usual ports of call, participants on these cruises explore parts of the

Alaskan coast that are still untouched frontier. Wildlife viewing is superb. Grizzlies feeding on salmon, bald eagles riding the wind currents, and orcas splashing about are just some of the common sights. Fishing is excellent, with salmon, red snapper, cod, and halibut the catches of the day. Travel is on the elegant 70-foot motor yacht *Midnight Sun.*

Operator: Ocean Voyages, 1709 Bridgeway, Sausalito, Calif. 94965; (415) 332-4681. *Price:* Moderate. *Season:* June through August. *Length:* 7 and 14 days. *Accommodations:* Shipboard cabins. Five percent discount with BBAT coupon.

CALIFORNIA

California Dreaming on the Deck of a Tall Ship

The *Californian,* a 145-foot recreation of an 1840s revenue cutter, was built by the Nautical Heritage Society of California. The state's official tall ship, she is a gaff-rigged topsail schooner with two masts towering over 100 feet above the deck and nine sails sporting 7,000 square feet of canvas. She carries a dozen passengers on cruises from various ports in California. Each participant receives a manual, stands a "watch," and works closely with the professional crew in learning to sail and navigate the ship. Lectures on history, seamanship, and earth sciences are included.

Operator: Nautical Heritage Society, 24532 Del Prado, Dana Point, Calif. 92629; (800) 432-2201 or (714) 661-1001. *Price:* Moderate. *Season:* July through October. *Length:* 4 days. *Accommodations:* Shipboard cabins. Five percent discount with BBAT coupon.

Sailing among the Channel Islands National Park

These islands beckon, not with the sensuality of the South Seas but with dramatic mountaintops and jagged shorelines of awesome cliffs and deep caves. Teeming with wildlife, they have been called an "American Galapagos." Nearly half the world's 100,000-plus population of California sea lions visits San Miguel. Santa Barbara Island is a major seabird rookery and has perhaps the world's largest breeding colony of Xantus' murrelet and the only nesting place in America of the black storm petrel. Anacapa is the only breeding place

Operator: Ocean Voyages, 1709 Bridgeway, Sausalito, Calif. 94965; (415) 332-4681. *Price:* Moderate. *Season:* Year-round. *Length:* 7 days. *Accommodations:* Shipboard cabins. Five percent discount with BBAT coupon.

in the country for the California brown pelican. In the winter months it is possible to follow and photograph California grey whales during their migration between the Bering Sea and Baja California lagoons. Participants on these expeditions discover the wonders of the Channel Islands from the deck of the classic sailing yacht *Sea Maiden*.

FLORIDA

Instructional Cruise to the Dry Tortugas

Operator: Annapolis Sailing School, P.O. Box 3334, Annapolis, Md. 21403; (800) 638-9192 or (301) 267-7205.
Price: Expensive.
Season: November through April.
Length: 8 days.
Accommodations: Shipboard cabins. Five percent discount with BBAT.

Located 68 miles south of Key West, the Dry Tortugas have a gaudy history of pirates and boat-wreckers. Today they are bird sanctuaries to thousands of sooty and noddy terns, cormorants, and frigate birds. They also offer excellent snorkeling over coral reefs in crystal-clear water. It was here that treasure hunter Mel Fisher discovered *Nuestra Señora de Atocha*, perhaps the richest Spanish wreck in history. A major attraction is Fort Jefferson, a perfectly preserved hexagonal fort, built in 1860 and notorious after the Civil War as an American "Devil's Island" for its use as a federal prison. The Annapolis Sailing School offers instruc-

---

The Adventure Travel Hall of Fame: JOHN FAIRFAX

"All travel is a quest, a conscious or unconscious searching for something that is lacking in our lives or ourselves," Freya Stark once observed wisely. She might have been talking about her fellow Englishman John Fairfax, the first man to row across both the Atlantic and the Pacific Oceans. Each time, he suffered the ordeal as a personal test of his own ability to survive. His rowing technique was "nearly nonexistent" but he was "after a battle against nature at its most primitive and raw." He admitted later: "Personally, I don't even like rowing as a sport. The idea was to row because that is the ultimate, hardest way of crossing an ocean."

Fairfax trained on the Serpentine Pool

tional sail cruises for advanced students to the Dry Tortugas out of St. Petersburg. This is both a true open-water cruising course, providing instruction in nighttime sailing and watch-keeping, and a vacation with plenty of opportunity to enjoy these historic islands.

HAWAII

Sailing the Other Hawaii

"The loveliest fleet of islands that lie anchored in any ocean," Mark Twain wrote, after his residency there in 1866. There is another Hawaii, of coral reefs, quiet anchorages, jagged pinnacles of black lava rock, and deserted beaches, that lies far beyond the tourist haunts. With groups of eight or fewer, these expeditions cruise among the wild places of Lanai, Maui, Molokai, and Oahu. Strong winds on the channel crossings often mean exciting, fast sails. Days are filled with wilderness hikes, swims in quiet pools at the bases of waterfalls, snorkeling over coral reefs, and coastal sailing excursions. The winter months also offer excellent opportunities to observe humpback whales. Participants have a choice of several yachts.

Operator:
Ocean Voyages,
1709 Bridgeway,
Sausalito, Calif. 94965;
(415) 332-4681.
Price: Moderate.
Season: Year-round.
Length: 7 days.
Accommodations: Shipboard cabins. Five percent discount with BBAT coupon.

in London's Hyde Park before setting off across the Atlantic alone in January 1969. To combat the monotony of his daily routine, he sang operatic arias and befriended the schools of porpoises that accompanied his boat. He arrived at Miami in July, apparently none the worse for his experience. He insisted to waiting reporters that he would never row again.

Just two years later, however, Fairfax started planning a second rowing expedition, this time from California to Australia. On this trip he took along his girlfriend, Sylvia Cook,

who had answered his newspaper advertisement. They set off in a 35-foot rowboat from San Francisco in April 1971 and arrived 363 days later in Australia, having stopped at three islands along the way. They endured one typhoon, in which 30-foot waves almost swamped their small boat; a shark attack that left Fairfax with a nasty 6-inch gash on his upper arm; and near-collisions with passing ships that failed to see them.

MAINE

Windjamming on the Roseway

Operator:
Yankee Schooner Cruises,
Box 696,
Camden, Maine 04843;
(800) 255-4449 or
(207) 236-4449.
Price: Moderate.
Season: June through
September.
Length: 6 days.
Accommodations: Shipboard
cabins. Five percent dis-
count with BBAT coupon.

Built in 1925 in the tradition of Gloucester fishing boats, the 137-foot schooner *Roseway* flies 5,000 square feet of red sails as she cruises the Maine coast. For 32 years she belonged to the Boston Pilots Association, safely ushering her pilots to the shipping lanes. In 1975 she was refitted with 14 comfortable cabins to carry 37 passengers on six-day cruises. The winds and currents determine each departure's itinerary. The *Roseway* explores the rugged, hilly coast of rock and pine, its thousands of islands and many bays. Possible options include Soomes Sound on Mt. Desert Island, the only natural fjord in the eastern United States. Nights are spent at anchor in quiet harbors.

Windjamming on the Nathaniel Bowditch

Operator:
Schooner *Nathaniel Bowditch,*
Box 459,
Warren, Maine 04864;
(800) 288-4098 or
(207) 273-4062.
Price: Moderate.
Season: June through
September.
Length: 6 days.
Accommodations: Shipboard
cabins. Five percent dis-
count with BBAT coupon.

The *Nathaniel Bowditch* is a 108-foot gaff-rigged topsail schooner originally built in 1922. Today, fitted with 11 cabins, she carries 24 guests on cruises off the Maine coast. These windjamming cruises are always unstructured, their direction and pace dictated by the winds and currents. Passengers sail through Penobscot Bay, a 30-mile-wide waterway dotted with hundreds of islands, many etched in pink granite and covered with teal-colored forests, and stop at several whitewashed fishing villages. These may include Castine, rich in maritime history; Vinalhaven, for many decades the source of granite for some of America's greatest buildings; and Stonington, a picturesque fishing village. Another highlight is a lobster cookout on an uninhabited island.

"Adventures are to the adventurous."

BENJAMIN DISRAELI,
CONINGSBY

Sailing and Canoeing the Maine Coast

This special combination package shows off the best that Maine has to offer. The adventure begins with a four-day guided canoe and camping trip down the beautiful Saint Croix River in eastern Maine. Once used for logging, it is now a principal nesting area for bald eagles. Then passengers transfer to the *Mary Day*, a windjammer built especially for passengers and launched in 1962. She flies 4,500 square feet of sail, carries 30 passengers, and sports a 90-foot deck and a 23-foot beam. She sails every Monday from Camden to explore the coast, islands, and bays.

Operator: Sunrise County Canoe Expeditions, Cathance Lake, Grove Post Office, Maine 04657; (800) RIVER-30 or (207) 454-7708.
Price: Expensive.
Season: June through September.
Length: 11 days.
Accommodations: Tent camps and shipboard cabins. Five percent discount with BBAT coupon.

The oldest sailing school in the country, the Annapolis Sailing School offers a broad range of courses covering all aspects of sailing

Annapolis Sailing School

MARYLAND

Instructional Sail Cruises on Historic Chesapeake Bay

Perhaps no American body of water offers finer sailing opportunities than Chesapeake Bay, over 195 miles long and up to 30 miles wide. This was, of course, a major reason why the federal government located its naval academy there. The oldest sailing school in the country, with 120 boats and

Operator: Annapolis Sailing School, P.O. Box 3334, Annapolis, Md. 21403; (800) 638-9192 or (301) 267-7205.
Price: Moderate.
Season: April through Oct.
Length: 5 days.
Accommodations: Shipboard cabins. Five percent discount with BBAT.

over 100,000 students graduated to date, the Annapolis Sailing School offers instructional cruises. Students learn sail cruising not from classroom instruction but by living aboard a yacht and actually sailing, under the careful supervision of an expert instructor. These are vacations as well as courses, so students have time to explore the scenic harbor towns.

MICHIGAN

Windjamming on Lake Michigan

Operator: Traverse Tall Ship Co., 13390 S.W. Bay Shore Dr., Traverse City, Mich. 49684; (800) 678-0383 or (616) 941-2000.
Price: Moderate.
Season: June through September.
Length: 3, 5, and 6 days.
Accommodations: Ship's cabins. Five percent discount with BBAT coupon.

The 105-foot gaff-rigged *Manitou* is a traditional two-masted topsail schooner, measuring 114 feet in length and flying more than 3,200 square feet of sail. This six-sailed ship is the only one of its kind in all the Great Lakes. She has 12 double-passenger cabins and a wood-paneled main salon that accommodates all her guests at one sitting. The *Manitou* sails in northern Lakes Michigan and Huron. Winds and currents determine the route. The days are spent sailing, exploring secluded anchorages, and enjoying cookouts on deserted beaches. Passengers can also use the ship's kayaks to explore small, uninhabited islands. Fresh bread is baked daily in a wood-burning stove.

"Tigers, snakes, lovely but indignant nymphs, and headhunters are not the dangers. What kills men in the wilderness is anxiety, under-nourishment, and mosquitoes."

H. M. TOMLINSON

WASHINGTON

Sailing Among the San Juan Islands in Puget Sound

Numbering over 200 jade-green islands, the San Juans lie in the shadow of the magnificent Olympic Mountains. They offer idyllic sailing conditions with scores of peaceful harbors, excellent beaches, and picturesque villages. Passengers stop at a different island each day and have ample opportunity to explore ashore. Excellent opportunities exist to observe pods of killer whales. Passage is on the 42-foot sailing yacht *Northwind,* which has three private cabins. These are protected waters, so no need to bring your medicines for seasickness! The captain offers interested participants hands-on instruction in sailing and navigation.

Operator:
Sail the San Juans,
304 36th St., Suite 186,
Bellingham, Wash. 98225;
(800) 729-3207 or
(360) 671-5852.
Price: Moderate.
Season: May through Oct.
Length: 7 days, with a 3-day San Juan sampler.
Accommodations: Shipboard cabins. Five percent discount with BBAT coupon.

PROFILE

MARY CROWLEY
OCEAN VOYAGES

One hundred feet off our bow the water's surface exploded as scores of flying fish suddenly took to the air, skimming the indigo blue of the Hawaiian seas. Right behind them, flashing like a silver arrow in the bright sunlight, a barracuda gave chase. With the trade winds in our sails, our steel-hulled ketch fairly hummed as it cut through the water just off the western coast of the island of Lanai. Sheer cliffs, their bases pitted with dark sea caves, towered 150 feet above us. Jagged pinnacles of black lava rock thrust skyward like prehistoric fingers, recalling the mighty cataclysmic forces of less peaceful geologic eras. Giant breakers thundered and crashed against the rocks, their spray boiling up 20 feet or more.

For three hours we had been cruising this coast and had not seen one sign of humans—no roads, homes, or hotels. This was hardly the typical Hawaiian paradise promised by the travel posters. Instead I felt like one of those tiny figures in Japanese landscape paintings, put there by the artist as a measure of the immensity of the natural forces depicted and a reminder of the fragility of the human condition.

Our boat was the *Oz*, an 80-foot ketch. Her skipper, John Bill, sails it under charter to Mary Crowley's Ocean Voyages, the world's largest operator of sail cruises. Each year Ocean Voyages sponsors hundreds of trips especially geared for adventurous travelers who thrill at the thought of visiting clusters of tiny islands in remote corners of the world—or, as in the present case, unfamiliar parts of familiar islands. Most of the expeditions are restricted to fewer than ten participants. And they all offer excellent opportunities for novices to learn the fundamentals of seamanship and navigation under expert guidance.

"Sailing is such a joyful experience that I'd like to share it with everyone," states Crowley, who has logged over 60,000 miles in worldwide sailing. "Sailing puts people back in touch with their dreams and priorities. They return home filled with enthusiasm for pursuing whatever is important to them."

To put people in touch with their dreams, Crowley has lined up a fleet of 200 vessels with which she works on a regular basis and another 300 she uses on an occasional basis for special projects. Each year she sends legions of secretaries, executives, and other sedentary types on voyages of discovery from Maine to Micronesia. They can board a 48-foot catamaran in the Galapagos

Islands, a 59-foot yawl in the islands of Vanuatu, a 145-foot brigantine cruising the South Pacific, or a 49-foot ketch off the Turquoise Coast of Turkey. The current catalogue of Ocean Voyages lists over 100 sail cruises in as many different parts of the world.

"We are the largest sail-charter operation in the world, both in terms of the number of people and the number of programs," Crowley says. "We are unique in that we are a worldwide operation and not just restricted to the Caribbean or the Mediterranean. If someone wants a good boat in the Seychelles, Hong Kong, or New Caledonia, then we can provide one. We're also unique in that we are a full-service maritime agency, meaning that we deal in a full spectrum of boats from Spartan adventure sailing at reasonable prices to luxurious, multimillion-dollar ships that charter for $3,000 a day."

Crowley offers her clients two types of trips—those which emphasize sail training and navigation, and those in which participants spend as much time in port as at sea. Her clients often include both those who have sold their own vessels to escape the high costs of maintenance, and potential owners who want to try out a variety of ships before buying one. Each ship comes with a captain, cook, and crew. The passengers participate as much or as little in the actual sailing as they wish. Both experienced sailors and novices are welcome.

"The experience of being on a boat is valuable to anyone, whether they want to continue with sailing or enjoy just a one-time-only learning experience," Crowley says. We are sitting on the deck of her houseboat docked off Sausalito, California, which has served as her headquarters since the company was founded in 1979. "You learn about the environment by being on the ocean. You are living and working with other people on the crew, and you learn about what a community spirit means. And perhaps more important, you learn about yourself. It's much more than just going from here to there."

One of Crowley's most successful new programs has been longer sail cruises, lasting several months to a year. This developed in response to clients between careers, on sabbaticals, or retired with long periods of free time to devote to themselves. She explains: "A while back we had planned an interesting 30-month around-the-world cruise on one vessel with the idea that most people would join it for one-month intervals. In fact, most chose to come aboard for six months at a cost of $18,000. That may seem like a lot at first. But you have to consider that it is much less than what most people pay for six months living in the States, and certainly much less than what six months of air and land travel with hotels and meals would cost if people were simply to take off and travel on their own. That trip taught us there is a strong market for much longer cruises."

Crowley developed her interest in sailing at an the early age of 4 when her grandfather began taking her out in his small sailboat. "From the beginning, I loved it!" she recalls. "When I was a little older, I was always off in my 12-foot dinghy traipsing around Lake Michigan near Chicago, where we lived. I was very interested in long-distance sailing. I read every book in the library about around-the-world sail voyages."

In 1968 Crowley moved to Sausalito. Unable to make up her mind about pursuing a career in law or university teaching, she fell into the boat-delivery business. If someone bought a boat in Sydney, Australia, but wanted it brought to San Francisco, she and her colleagues delivered it. The experience taught her a great deal about ocean sailing. A few years later she worked for nine months as a teacher aboard the *Staatsraad Lehmkuhl*, a 320-foot, square-rigged, four-masted Norwegian ship. In 1972 she joined another school-at-sea program, this one on the 120-foot schooner *Westward* for a cruise down the West Coast to the Galapagos Islands, a place which made a deep impression upon her. She remembers the experience today:

"I had always been in love with the ocean and with sailing, but that first trip to the Galapagos changed my life. I had grown up in Chicago very much a city person. The Galapagos took me from the limited world of concrete and culture to the kind of attunement you reach in quiet, beautiful places. For the first time I felt really in touch with the whole world of nature."

Back in San Francisco Crowley became a director of the nonprofit Oceanic Society, which operated a travel program for its members. In 1979 she started Ocean Voyages across the bay in Sausalito and took as her company's motto an ancient Phoenician proverb: "The gods do not deduct from man's allotted span those hours spent in sailing." That first year she represented 14 boats. Today she has a fleet of 500 vessels at her disposal and a reputation as the Aristotle Onassis of recreational sailing. Each year she sends 3,000 clients out on her ships. "My dreams have come pretty far in a pretty short time," she admits.

A major reason for Crowley's success has been the care with which she selects her boats and captains. "My policy is that I or one of my staff visit and spend time to get to know each vessel, staff, and captain," she explains. "We choose very special people who are not only knowledgeable sailors but also sensitive to the passengers' needs and interests. Our skippers come from a wide range of backgrounds. They may be former teachers, scientists, or successful businesspeople. Many are old sailing friends of mine. I look for people I'd like to spend two or three weeks with on a boat."

One of Crowley's favorite projects concerned legendary Pitcairn Island, where the *Bounty* mutineers led by Fletcher Christian settled. Within a few years most of the mutineers were dead. Today some 45 or so of their descendants continue to eke out an existence on their island.

"As someone who loves sea stories, I have always had a fascination for Pitcairn Island because of its associations with the novel and film, *The Mutiny on the Bounty*," Crowley admits. "One day I got a call from England, a man named Glynn Christian, the great-great-great-great-grandson of Fletcher Christian. Glynn was busy at work on a biography of his notorious relative. He had been trying without luck for eight years to get a ship to Pitcairn to finish his research. Then someone gave him my name. I was able to get him a period ship, a square-rigged vessel that had some romance to it, and a crew as well. So he recreated his ancestor's voyage and sailed from Tahiti to Pitcairn."

That trip yielded an award-winning documentary film and a special relationship between Crowley and the residents of the most inaccessible island in the world. Once a year Ocean Voyages sends a ship to Pitcairn with much-needed supplies. "On the 200th anniversary of the island's founding, I was able to organize a terrific celebration with Australian and Italian television crews and journalists from all over the world," Crowley says proudly. "We took to Pitcairn 19 people who were born on the island themselves or whose parents or grandparents were."

Matt Herron, a close friend since her teaching days on the *Staatsraad Lehmkuhl*, suggests some reasons for her success: "Friendship is Mary's medium, the modus operandi of her business. It has been suggested that on the West Coast, and maybe throughout the Pacific, Mary Crowley has some kind of friendship with virtually everyone who is doing anything interesting with boats. She sits at the center of this web of cronies, spinning out her telephone calls and visits to the ocean peripheries of her world, negotiating, cajoling, optimistically weaving together people, vessels, and governments in a mesh of innovative projects. It is a job she does well. She's a good judge of character, and she is by nature an enthusiast, an advocate, even a visionary. Where others see problems, Crowley is inclined to see possibilities."

10

EXPEDITIONARY CRUISING

"Why take a cruise when you can take an expedition?" asks the advertisement for one major operator.

Why, indeed! Adventure cruise ships sail to remote regions such as Antarctica, the outlying islands of Polynesia, and the Arctic, areas that are virtually inaccessible by any other means. Their passengers book into these cruises not for the food and entertainment but for the adventure, wildlife, and exotic cultures. The more remote the destination, the stronger the appeal. And these are expeditionary cruises in the true sense of the word, with risks no ordinary cruise ship would experience. In the late summer of 1988, for example, the passengers on the 236-foot *Explorer* found themselves trapped in pack ice 50 miles northeast of Point Barrow, Alaska, as they attempted to navigate the historic and perilous Northwest Passage. A Coast Guard icebreaker finally freed them. (In 1984 the *Explorer* became the first passenger ship in history to make the journey pioneered by Norwegian explorer Roald Amundsen in 1906.)

Unlike conventional cruise ships, expeditionary ships are smaller, with shallow drafts, allowing them easy access to areas closed to the larger vessels. Some have reinforced hulls and bows to allow them to push through polar ice packs. Each carries a fleet of agile, swift Zodiac inflatable boats to facilitate safe landings in remote wilderness areas. And most carry a staff of naturalists, anthropologists, and historians, who lecture on the regions being visited.

The 21st century will see the expansion of expeditionary cruises below the surface of the world's oceans. The first fleet of tourist submarines already carries thousands of awed passengers as deep as 150 feet to view reefs, shipwrecks, and fish life. And in production is a radically different kind of submarine—a craft with a clear acrylic hull that will make passengers feel as though they have become a part of the undersea environment.

"Whatever you can do or dream you can, begin it. Boldness has genius, power, and magic in it."

GOETHE

AFRICA

SEYCHELLES, ALDABRA, AND COMOROS ISLANDS

Wildlife Cruise in the Indian Ocean

Few Americans have discovered the scenic beauty and abundant wildlife on the legendary Seychelles Islands, located some 1,000 miles off the African coast in the Indian Ocean. Like the Galapagos Islands, they appeal powerfully to lovers of unspoiled places, who thrill at the sight of plant and animal species found nowhere else. But unlike the arid and inhospitable Galapagos, the Seychelles' lovely beaches of white coral sand, waving palm fronds, and turquoise waters are the tropical islands of popular fantasy. Participants on these expeditionary cruises board the vessel *Caledonian Star to* visit both the northern and southern groups of islands. Two days are then spent at Aldabra Atoll Natural Reserve for one of nature's most spectacular congregations of wildlife: 150,000 giant tortoises; the world's second-largest breeding colony of frigate birds; thousands of sacred ibises, flamingos, and red-footed boobies; and magnificent coral reefs. Another two days are passed in the Comoros Islands, rugged landscapes of steep mountains and active volcanoes, where tourism has yet to intrude.

Operator:
Natural Habitat Adventures,
2945 Center Green Court S.,
Boulder, Colo. 80301;
(800) 543-8917 or
(303) 449-3711.
Price: Expensive.
Season: March.
Length: 19 days.
Accommodations: Shipboard cabins. Five percent discount with BBAT coupon.

ANTARCTICA

Cruising the Antarctic Peninsula

Inhospitable as Antarctica may be to humans, its waters support a fantastic concentration of wildlife. In the south polar regions the number of species is severely limited, but each is represented by such an

Operator: Marine Expeditions, 13 Hazleton Ave., Toronto, Ont., Canada M5R 2E1; (800) 263-9147 or (416) 964-9069. *Price:* Expensive. *Season:* November through March. *Length:* 14 days. *Accommodations:* Shipboard cabins. Five percent discount with BBAT coupon.

abundance of numbers that the effect is overwhelming. The Antarctic area is completely free of onshore predators. As a result, birds and mammals have never been conditioned to fear anything on land and human visitors can approach to within a few feet. The accessibility and abundance of wildlife translate into a paradise of opportunity for both the naturalist and photographer. Members of this expedition explore the wonders of the Antarctic Peninsula on the *Marine Discoverer*, a comfortable Russian research vessel. They enjoy frequent shore excursions to explore the sights.

Antarctica offers the visitor spectacular mountain and ice scenery, great concentrations of wildlife, and the opportunity to explore our globe's last major frontier

Marine Expeditions

Wildlife Cruise to South Georgia Island and the Falkland Islands

Located 1,200 miles east of Cape Horn, South Georgia Island is an inhospitable but beautiful world of craggy mountains of alpine proportions. Around its fringes, the pebble beaches and grassy slopes teem with one of the richest concentrations of wildlife in the world. Fur and elephant seals carpet the shores, multitudes of gentoo and king penguins come and go from rookeries, while thousands of seabirds nest among the clumps of hardy tussock grass. For 60 years South Georgia was the center of the Antarctic whaling industry. Visitors to the former administrative center of Grytviken can explore at leisure the elaborate gadgetry of a major whaling station. Everything was left behind; nothing was salvaged. Most visitors make their way to the town's small cemetery to pay homage at the grave of the famous Antarctic explorer, Sir Ernest Shackleton. During the expedition passengers also visit the Falkland Islands, a paradise for birders, and the Antarctic Peninsula.

Operator:
Marine Expeditions,
13 Hazleton Ave., Toronto,
Ont., Canada M5R 2E1;
(800) 263-9147 or
(416) 964-9069.
Price: Expensive.
Season: November and
December.
Length: 24 days.
Accommodations: Shipboard
cabins. Five percent discount with BBAT coupon.

THE ATLANTIC

Islands of the South Atlantic

This lengthy repositioning expeditionary cruise allows travelers the opportunity to visit some of the most remote and legendary of the world's islands. Passengers board in Ushuaia, Argentina, the world's southernmost town. They spend three days exploring the Falkland Islands, home to a rich selection of seabirds and marine mammals, before journeying to frozen South Georgia Island, for 60 years the center of the Antarctic whaling industry. Then the ship heads north for Tristan da Cunha, a volcanic cone that is now home to 300 lobster fishermen and their families; St. Helena Island, where Napoleon was exiled in 1816; Ascension Island, the principal Atlantic breeding ground for marine green turtles; Cape Verde Islands, an archipelago of some ten islands of volcanic origin, where the inhabitants share an African culture; and finally the popular resort island groups of Canary and Madeira. The cruise terminates in London.

Operator:
Marine Expeditions,
13 Hazleton Ave., Toronto,
Ont., Canada M5R 2E1;
(800) 263-9147 or
(416) 964-9069.
Price: Expensive.
Season: March and April.
Length: 50 days.
Accommodations: Shipboard
cabins. Five percent discount with BBAT coupon.

AUSTRALASIA

AUSTRALIA

Cruising the Great Barrier Reef

Operator:
Adventure Center,
1311 63rd St., Suite 200,
Emeryville, Calif. 94608;
(800) 227-8747 or
(510) 654-1879.
Price: Moderate.
Season: Year-round.
Length: 4 days.
Accommodations: Shipboard
cabins. Five percent discount with BBAT coupon

The world's largest living structure, Australia's Great Barrier Reef covers an area the size of England and Scotland combined. Only a tiny portion of the massive reef breaches the ocean's surface in the form of islands and outcroppings. A handful of the hundreds of islands are inhabited or developed for tourists. The others are rarely visited except by occasional fishermen and sailors. The *Coral Princess,* a 115-foot, luxurious, fully air-conditioned catamaran, cruises between Townsville and Cairns each week, exploring the picturesque islands and superb reefs in the heart of the world's largest marine park. Passengers spend no more than half a day at a time actually cruising; the rest of their time is spent ashore exploring the islands or snorkeling over the reefs.

CANADA

Exploring Canada's Maritime Provinces and Coastal Maine

Operator:
American Canadian
Caribbean Line,
P.O. Box 368,
Warren, R.I. 02885;
(800) 556-7450 or
(401) 247-0955.
Price: Moderate.
Season: July.
Length: 15 days.
Accommodations: Shipboard
cabins. Five percent discount with BBAT coupon.

The coasts of eastern Canada and Maine present an incomparable mix of weathered promontories, sheltered coves, historic islands, picturesque fishing villages, and an abundance of whales, seabirds, and seals. The *Caribbean Prince* carries 80 passengers on a cruise from Quebec to Warren, Rhode Island. Highlights along the way include Cape Breton Island, site of Canada's largest historical park; Bonaventure Island, home to 200,000 birds, including a huge gannet colony; delightful Prince Edward Island, home of Anne of Green Gables; Nova Scotia's bustling port of Halifax; Bar Harbor, Maine, a picturesque seaport; Acadia National Park, made

The *Spirit of Discovery* is a shallow-draft vessel built to explore the coastal wilderness areas off Alaska and British Columbia far from the usual cruise ship routes
Alaska Sightseeing Cruise West

famous by Longfellow's poem, "Evangeline"; and Newport, Rhode Island, a popular summer watering hole for the rich and famous.

BRITISH COLUMBIA

Cruising Canada's Inside Passage

In the spring of 1993, Alaska Sightseeing Cruise West pioneered a major new small-ship cruise through Canada's much-heralded but rarely visited Inside Passage. Although these waters are within an overnight cruise from Seattle, they are seldom visited except by private yacht. The larger cruise ships always pass through the area at night on their way to and from Vancouver. The *Spirit of Discovery*, a shallow-draft expeditionary cruise vessel, carries 84 passengers on an exploration of mountainous fjords covered with forest primeval, small port towns, and islands that time forgot. A highlight is the day spent at the head of Princess Louisa Inlet, a spectacular, mountain-walled fjord only 4 miles long, that the readers of *Condé Nast Traveler* magazine in 1992 named one of the "world's ten most beautiful places."

Operator: Alaska Sightseeing Cruise West, 4th & Battery Bldg., Suite 700, Seattle, Wash. 98121; (800) 426-7702 or (206) 441-8687.
Price: Moderate.
Season: April and October.
Length: 8 days.
Accommodations: Shipboard cabins.

THE CARIBBEAN

A Leisurely Cruise of the Caribbean Islands aboard a Freighter

Operator: Windjammer Barefoot Cruises, P.O. Box 120, Miami Beach, Fla. 33119; (800) 327-2601 or (800) 432-3364 in Florida. *Price:* Inexpensive. *Season:* Year-round. *Length:* 19 days. *Accommodations:* Shipboard cabins. Five percent discount with BBAT coupon.

Built in Scotland in 1955, the *Amazing Grace* was once used by the British government to service Scotland's lighthouses. She was also occasionally employed by the British Royal Family when their yacht *Britannia* was unavailable. Today she carries up to 60 passengers, as she ferries supplies to the fleet of tall ships belonging to Windjammer Barefoot Cruises. Each trip begins and ends in Freeport, Bahamas. Along the way she visits the Dominican Republic, British Virgin Islands, St. Maarten, and Antigua. Passengers enjoy considerable time ashore to explore the historic and scenic attractions of each island, shop, swim, and snorkel.

EUROPE

BRITAIN

Exploring the Wild Coasts of Britain and Ireland

Operator: Special Expeditions, 720 Fifth Ave., New York, N.Y. 10019; (800) 762-0003 or (212) 765-7740. *Price:* Expensive. *Season:* May. *Length:* 17 days. *Accommodations:* Shipboard cabins.

Members of this expedition board the MS *Polaris* to visit areas where few other cruise ships venture. A fleet of Zodiac inflatable boats allows the freedom to land on isolated beaches and approach closely the otherwise inaccessible cliffside seabird rookeries. Stops are made at the islands of Scilly, where legend tells us King Arthur once ruled over a lovely land before it vanished beneath the ocean; the Skellig Islands, home to tens of thousands of nesting seabirds, and site of a perfectly preserved eighth-century monastic settlement; the Aran Islands, with their imposing prehistoric monuments; Iona Island, where Shakespeare's Macbeth is reputed to have

Anchored off the coast of remote St. Kilda Island, the *Polaris* circumnavigates Great Britain each spring, visiting numerous islands rich in antiquities and birdlife
James C. Simmons

been buried; the Orkney Islands, rich in antiquities; and the Isle of Noss in the Shetland group, the site of one of Europe's largest seabird colonies.

GREENLAND

Greenland to Baffin Island

Greenland is the world's largest island, three times bigger than Texas. It is a cold, forbidding, inhospitable, inaccessible, and yet beautiful world. A vast ice sheet up to 11,000 feet deep covers most of the country. Slow-moving glaciers coming off this ice sheet spawn monstrous bergs that plague shipping in the North Atlantic sea lanes. These cathedrals of ice make up an endless parade of abstracts riding an ink-blue sea. Passengers on this popular expedition explore the wonders of Greenland by means of the *Marine Discoverer*, a comfortable, one-class expeditionary cruise ship. They visit quaint fishing villages, calving glaciers, ruins of ancient Viking settlements, Eskimo handicraft centers, bird sanctuaries, and Inuit settlements. Then they cruise westward with stops at remote Kekerten Island, Baffin Island, and Walrus Island, ending at Churchill, the polar-bear haven.

Operator:
Marine Expeditions,
13 Hazleton Ave., Toronto,
Ont., Canada M5R 2E1;
(800) 263-9147 or
(416) 964-9069.
Price: Expensive.
Season: July and August.
Length: 12 days.
Accommodations: Shipboard cabins. Five percent discount with BBAT coupon.

NORWAY
Beyond the North Cape

Operator:
Special Expeditions,
720 Fifth Ave.,
New York, N.Y. 10019;
(800) 762-0003 or
(212) 765-7740.
Price: Expensive.
Season: July.
Length: 16 days.
Accommodations: Shipboard
cabins.

Sculpted by the last Ice Age into an extraordinary landscape of deep fjords, plunging mountains, and craggy islands, the Norwegian coast is the most dramatic in Europe. Passengers on this cruise board the MS *Polaris* to explore 1,500 miles of diverse coastal scenery, from the tidy medieval quarters of Bergen's waterfront district to the brooding glaciers of Spitsbergen. The cruise itinerary includes Geiranger Fjord, often thought to be the most beautiful in Norway; the remote Lofoten archipelago, where granite mountains dwarf storybook fishing villages; Tromso, the largest town north of the Arctic Circle and a staging point for numerous early Arctic expeditions; and Bear Island, with its abundant populations of fulmars, kittiwakes, guillemots, and gulls. Three days are spent exploring Spitzbergen, visiting old whaling stations, and searching for polar bears and walruses.

SWEDEN
Exploring the Stockholm Archipelago by Small Ship

Operator:
Special Expeditions,
720 Fifth Ave.,
New York, N.Y. 10019;
(800) 762-0003 or
(212) 765-7740.
Price: Expensive.
Season: June through
August.
Length: Seven days.
Accommodations: Small inns.

Scattered along Sweden's eastern coast lie some 24,000 islands, skerries, and islets. The archipelago is really two environments: the wooded, protected inner part and the barren, wild outer islands, home to seabirds, seals, and a handful of hardy fishermen. Participants travel through this corner of Scandinavia on their private boat, the 128-foot *Swedish Islander*, which carries bicycles and fishing equipment. Stops are made at Mariefred, dominated by the imposing Gripsholms Castle, one of the most famous in Sweden; Roslagen, which has inspired many of Sweden's most beloved artists and writers; and Ängso National Park, Sweden's first protected reserve and a haven for wildflowers and abundant birdlife.

LATIN AMERICA

A small expeditionary cruise ship is a perfect way to explore the wonders of the world's largest barrier reef, off the coast of Belize

James C. Simmons

BELIZE

Cruising Belize's Coral Coast

Belize lays claim to the world's second-longest barrier reef, boasting over 200 islands ranging in size from a few hundred square yards to big Ambergris Cay, some 25 miles long. All but one of the Western Hemisphere's large atolls can be found there. The United Nations has recently proposed this splendid natural resource for designation as a World Heritage Site. However, without a private yacht the reef is virtually inaccessible except by the small cruise vessel *Caribbean Prince,* which carries up to 80 passengers on cruises along the entire length of the reef. Numerous stops are made at deserted islands, with their white, sandy beaches topped by palm trees swaying in the sunshine for some of the finest snorkeling in the Caribbean. Three days are also spent exploring rarely visited northeastern Guatemala, where the ship cruises up the Rio Dulce at the bottom of a jungle-filled gorge to Lake Izabal, the largest in the country.

Operator:
American Canadian Caribbean Line,
P.O. Box 368,
Warren, R.I. 02885;
(800) 556-7450 or
(401) 247-0955.
Price: Moderate.
Season: December through March.
Length: 12 days.
Accommodations: Shipboard cabins. Five percent discount with BBAT coupon.

BRAZIL

Exploring the Amazon Basin above Manaus by Houseboat

Operator:
Journeys International,
4011 Jackson Rd.,
Ann Arbor, Mich. 48103;
(800) 255-8735 or
(313) 665-4407.
Price: Moderate.
Season: Year-round.
Length: 9 days.
Accommodations: Shipboard
cabins. Five percent discount with BBAT coupon.

Like the sinuous veins of an enormous leaf, the tangled tributaries of the Amazon writhe across an area two-thirds the size of the United States. Members of this expedition explore the pristine Amazonian rain forest from their very own motorized houseboat with a local captain, cook, and guide. After a tour of the isolated jungle metropolis of Manaus, participants board the *Amazon Explorer,* specially designed to navigate the shallow waters of the Amazon's tributaries, inland lakes, and island archipelagos beyond the range of the larger ships. They visit Lake Januaca and its tributaries, looking for exotic bird species such as hoatzins and horned screamers. They then cruise up the Rio Cuieiras through a region of lakes and virgin rain forest to explore the Anavilhanas Archipelago, a collection of several hundred forest-covered islands; and visit the region drained by the Rio Negro for short hikes into the forest beyond the riverbanks.

The Adventure Travel Hall of Fame: ROSITA FORBES

The adventurer is by nature a gambler who lets herself go and takes a chance on fate. Nowhere is this willingness to risk it all on the throw of the dice more evident than with those adventurers who brave the uncertainties of desert travel. And of all the great deserts, none is more fearful than the vast Sahara, with an area larger than the continent of Australia.

In 1920 Rosita Forbes, a young Englishwoman who made a career out of dangerous travel, determined she would visit the legendary oasis of Kufra, deep in the Libyan desert. In Benghazi she took instruction in Arabic language and customs, assumed the robe and veil of local Muslim women, and secretly hired five

COSTA RICA

Wildlife Cruise off Costa Rica's Pacific Coast

The Pacific coast of Costa Rica is particularly rich in sea-level rain forests which support a broad range of exotic flora and fauna. Yet many of the best regions are virtually inaccessible by land. The 185-foot *Temptress Explorer* transports 99 passengers and their naturalist guides along the entire length, from the Curu Biological Reserve in the north to Golfito in the far south. Numerous stops are made where passengers explore the rain forest in the company of naturalists/guides. The highlights of this seven-day cruise include Corcovado National Park, one of the country's crown jewels, which supports large populations of exotic birds, chattering monkeys, and lush tropical vegetation; Tortuga, an uninhabited island of resplendent white-sand beaches, studded with palm trees and edged with azure waters; and Manuel Antonio National Park, Costa Rica's most popular, where passengers can expect to see white-face monkeys and tree sloths. Scuba diving, snorkeling, sea kayaking, water skiing, and sport fishing are other options.

Operator: Temptress Voyages, 351 N.W. LeJeune Rd., Penthouse Suite 6, Miami, Fla. 33126; (800) 336-8423 or (305) 871-2663.
Price: Expensive.
Season: Year-round.
Length: 7 days.
Accommodations: Shipboard cabins. Five percent discount with BBAT coupon.

Arabs. Posing as merchants, they purchased camels and supplies and headed into the Sahara toward Kufra, 600 miles to the south. Their way lay through unmapped territory teeming with Muslim fanatics who murdered any outsiders unfortunate enough to fall into their hands. The adventurers' food ran out; twice they fought off bandits. The Arab caravans they met along the way extended the traditional desert hospitality, never suspecting that the woman behind the veil was, in fact, a wealthy English lady.

Six weeks later Forbes' expedition reached the fabled oasis of Kufra, where only one European in history had preceded her. The Arab chieftain there proved suspicious and arrested the entire party. Forbes, as a woman, was allowed limited freedom to explore the oasis. This she did, all the time clutching a revolver in her robes. After a week they were released and made their way out of the Sahara by way of Egypt.

MEXICO

Among the Blue Whales

Operator:
Baja Expeditions,
2625 Garnet Ave.,
San Diego, Calif. 92109;
(800) 843-6967 or
(619) 581-3311.
Price: Expensive.
Season: March and April.
Length: 7 days.
Accommodations: Shipboard
cabins. Five percent discount with BBAT coupon.

The blue whale is in the record books as the largest animal ever to live: one female was measured at 98 feet; another weighed in at 329,000 pounds. These behemoths live almost exclusively on shrimp-like creatures called krill. Blue whales are found throughout the world's oceans, but the opportunity for extended observation of their behavior is rare. An exception occurs each spring in an area south of Isla Carmen in the Sea of Cortez where numbers of blue whales congregate to feed, mate, and nurse their young. The expeditionary cruise vessel *Don Jose* takes 20 passengers on cruises into this special area to allow them an extended opportunity to observe and photograph the big whales' activities from close range. They can also expect to see other whale species, including humpback, sperm, fin, pilot, minke, gray, and killer. Daily land excursions on desert islands or at fishing villages are also included.

Circumnavigating the Baja California Peninsula

Operator:
Special Expeditions,
720 Fifth Ave.,
New York, N.Y. 10019;
(800) 762-0003 or
(212) 765-7740.
Price: Expensive.
Season: January through
March.
Length: 10 days.
Accommodations: Shipboard
cabins.

The Sea of Cortez is the world's largest deep-water gulf, nearly 11,000 feet deep at its mouth. John Steinbeck, Joseph Wood Krutch, and Erle Stanley Gardner are three who spent long periods of time there and found themselves seduced by its breathtaking scenery, remoteness, and wondrous profusion of wildlife. This is a naturalist's paradise. Its many islands, most uninhabited, have plant and animal species found nowhere else, earning them the reputation as a Mexican Galapagos. Of the region's 110 species of cacti, for example, 60 are endemic to the Sonoran Desert. The isolation of populations has speeded the process of evolutionary change, much as it has in the Galapagos. Passengers on this cruise circumnavigate much of the Baja peninsula, putting ashore on such rarely visited islands as Isla Espiritu Santo, Los Islotes, and Isla Santa Catalina.

"It is, of course, absurd to think that one gets away from the world by moving into lonely places. All that happens is that one reaches a simplified world, with few personal attachments of one's own. In its less crowded atmosphere, it is easier to see the proper shape of things, since other shapes impinge much less upon them."

FREYA STARK,
"REMOTE PLACES"

PANAMA

Cruise along the Caribbean and Pacific Coasts

For thousands of years the tiny isthmus of Panama has served as the land bridge between the North and South American continents. The existence of this link has had a profound effect on the distribution of plants, animals, and humans. Barely 50 miles wide at its narrowest point, Panama "funnels" the millions of birds which annually move between the temperate and tropic zones. These popular cruises explore the coastal wilderness areas on both sides of the isthmus. Several days are spent in the San Blas Islands among the Cuna Indians, famous for their colorful textile art form, the mola, which is produced mainly by the women. The ship then passes through the world-famous Panama Canal to the Pacific Ocean, to visit several of the exotic islands in that area. A visit is also made to Darien to meet the Choco Indians, whose small settlements can be reached only by plane or ship. Plenty of time is allowed for beachcombing, swimming, and snorkeling at deserted beaches.

Operator:
American Canadian
Caribbean Line,
P.O. Box 368,
Warren, R.I. 02885;
(800) 556-7450 or
(401) 247-0955.
Price: Expensive.
Season: February and
March.
Length: 12 days.
Accommodations: Shipboard
cabins. Five percent discount with BBAT coupon.

THE PACIFIC

Exploring the Lost Islands of the Pacific

Operator:
Nature Expeditions
International,
P.O. Box 11496,
Eugene, Ore. 97440;
(800) 869-0639 or
(541) 484-6529.
Price: Expensive.
Season: March through May.
Length: 20 days.
Accommodations: Shipboard
cabins. Five percent discount with BBAT coupon.

Because of their remoteness from normal shipping and air lanes, most of the islands of the South Pacific have maintained a tranquility and beauty unspoiled by contact with the major forces of the 20th century. This cruise begins on Easter Island amidst the monuments left behind by the most advanced Polynesian civilization ever to flourish—hundreds of enormous stone heads which bear mute testimony to the energy of this vanished people. From there, aboard the *Explorer,* the cruise visits Pitcairn Island, home to the descendants of the *Bounty* mutineers; Mangareva Island, where in the 19th century a mad priest forced the islanders to construct from coral blocks the largest cathedral in the Pacific; Rapa Island, an important site of prehistoric Polynesian forts, where Thor Heyerdahl undertook excavations; and Raivavae, for a day of traditional dances, snorkeling, and visits to ancient tikis. An anthropologist, naturalist, and marine biologist accompany the group.

The Adventure Travel Hall of Fame:
REINHOLD MESSNER

Reinhold Messner is by all rights the greatest mountain-climber of all time. He is the only man to have climbed all the important classical faces throughout the Alps, the Pyrenees, and the Andes and to have climbed six of the world's highest peaks over 25,000 feet. A climber since the age of 5, Messner has dedicated his life to reducing the distance between humans and mountains. He has sought to replace technical climbing with personal strength, consummate skill, and pure will.

Messner decided that climbing Everest would be his supreme test. He evolved a plan to conquer the mountain by "fair

FRENCH POLYNESIA

By Freighter to the Marquesas Islands

In 1985 the cargo ship *Aranui* began monthly service from Tahiti to all six inhabited Marquesas Islands, among the most isolated and legendary in the Pacific. Up to 100 passengers ride deck-passage; the others travel in comfort in air-conditioned cabins, eat meals prepared by a French chef, and are cared for by an English-speaking hostess. Ample shore time is allowed. Of particular interest are Atuona on Hiva Oa, where French artist Paul Gauguin lived out his final years and is buried; the enormous stone tikis of Puamau, also on Hiva Oa; and Hanavave, a tiny village of 200 tucked away in the spectacular Bay of Virgins on Fatu Hiva. Full-day stops are also made at Takapoto, Ahe, and Rangiroa atolls in the Tuamotu group. This just may be the best adventure going in the Pacific.

Operator:
Compagnie Polynesienne
de Transport Maritime,
2028 El Camino Real S.,
Suite B,
San Mateo, Calif. 94403;
(415) 574-2575.
Price: Moderate to expensive, depending upon the type of accommodation.
Season: Year-round.
Length: 16 days.
Accommodations: Shipboard cabins.

"Certain travellers give the impression that they keep moving because only then do they feel fully alive. Going from place to place gives them the feeling that they are mastering their particular circumstances."

ELLA MAILLART,
"MY PHILOSOPHY OF TRAVEL"

means," without artificial oxygen and with a minimum of technical aids. His goal was not so much getting to the top as it was to prove and discover himself. In May 1978, Messner and his longtime climbing partner Peter Habeler climbed 29,028-foot Mount Everest without using oxygen apparatus or major technical assistance. Three months later Messner scaled 26,650-foot Nanga Parbat alone. Today, after 40 years of climbing, he virtually dominates the world of mountaineering.

"I don't climb mountains simply to vanquish their summits," Messner wrote in his book, Everest: Expedition to the Ultimate. "What would be the point of that? I place myself voluntarily into dangerous situations to learn to face my own fears and doubts, my innermost feelings."

UNITED STATES

ALASKA

Prince William Sound Aboard the Discovery

Operator:
Geographic Expeditions,
2627 Lombard St.,
San Francisco, Calif. 94123;
(415) 922-0448.
Price: Expensive.
Season: May through
September.
Length: 5 and 8 days.
Accommodations: Shipboard
cabins. Five percent dis-
count with BBAT coupon.

Southeastern Alaska is where you go to find a vivid glimpse of what most of the Northern Hemisphere looked like 10,000 years ago when the last ice age was in retreat. Everywhere you look are long ribbons of ice flowing to the sea, resculpting the land in the process. Prince William Sound is also home to a rich selection of wildlife. Seals, bears, otters, beavers, and deer abound, with more than 200 species of birds and fish along the Sound's 3,000 shoreline miles of bays, coves, and deep fjords. Visitors on this cruise explore this wonderland from the deck of the 65-foot vessel *Discovery* with its six snug cabins. Plenty of opportunity is allowed for shore walks and close-up tours on inflatable rafts.

Cruising among the Aleutian Islands

Operator:
Marine Expeditions,
13 Hazleton Ave., Toronto,
Ont., Canada M5R 2E1;
(800) 263-9147 or
(416) 964-9069.
Price: Expensive.
Season: June.
Length: 16 days.
Accommodations: Shipboard
cabins. Five percent dis-
count with BBAT coupon.

Participants on this popular cruise explore the most inaccessible wilderness in the United States, the extreme southwestern coast of Alaska and the chain of Aleutian Islands. The area is notorious for its unpredictable weather and tricky inland passages. Yet the spectacular scenery, the splendid isolation, the vast wilderness, and the great wealth of wildlife make the area a natural for expeditionary cruise ships. This expedition begins in Juneau and then travels to Kenai Fjords National Park, a coastal mountain-fjord system capped by the 300-square-mile Harding Icefield; Kodiak Island, the largest island in Alaska and home to a large population of Kodiak brown bears; Semedi Island and the Shumagin Islands, rarely visited spots that are rich in marine mammal communities and seabird rookeries; Pribilof Islands, the only breeding ground for the northern fur seal, which comes ashore almost 2,000,000 strong each summer along with 180 species of birds; Arakamchechen Island, a famous walrus haulout; and Yttygran Island, which has interesting Eskimo archaeological sites.

Passengers go ashore to explore the coastal wilderness in the Bay of Eternity in the province of Quebec
James C. Simmons

A Wildlife Cruise Along the Inside Passage

Southeastern Alaska has long been popular with tens of thousands of travelers for its dramatic scenery—especially Glacier Bay—and numerous colorful towns, some of great historic interest. Avoiding all the usual ports of call, the *Sea Bird* and the *Sea Lion*, one-class expeditionary cruise vessels, explore the wilder parts of the Inside Passage that are known to only a handful of bush pilots, fishermen, and hunters. Passengers on these cruises visit Le Conte Bay, a narrow fjord with an active tidewater glacier at its end; photograph the humpback whales that congregate off Point Adolphus; "flightsee" over the mountains and massive ice fields of Glacier Bay National Park; and cruise up Tracy Arm, a spectacular 20-mile-long fjord with many waterfalls flowing over its high, glacially carved walls. Naturalists accompany all groups.

Operator: Special Expeditions, 720 Fifth Ave., New York, N.Y. 10019; (800) 762-0003 or (212) 765-7740. *Price:* Expensive. *Season:* June through August. *Length:* 8 days. *Accommodations:* Shipboard cabins.

NEW YORK

Cruising the Erie Canal

Operator:
American Canadian
Caribbean Line,
P.O. Box 368,
Warren, R.I. 02885;
(800) 556-7450 or
(401) 274-0955.
Price: Moderate.
Season: June through
mid-October.
Length: 12 days.
Accommodations: Shipboard
cabins. Five percent dis-
count with BBAT coupon.

This itinerary will delight the sailor, historian, lover of flora and fauna, engineer, and architecturally inclined. The ships carry 80 passengers and have been designed with special shallow drafts and retractable pilot houses to allow them to pass under numerous low bridges. Passengers board in Warren, Rhode Island, then sail along the New England shoreline and up the Hudson River, past the manor homes of Franklin Roosevelt, Martin Van Buren, Washington Irving, and Frederick Vanderbilt. The heart of the cruise is the passage up the historic Erie Canal and through its numerous locks. Next the ships travel along the St. Lawrence Seaway to Montreal and Quebec, then to the scenic Saguenay River, a breeding ground for beluga whales. The cruise ends in Montreal and the passengers return to Providence, Rhode Island, by chartered bus. The last two cruises by both ships feature New England fall foliage.

PROFILE

LUTHER BLOUNT
AMERICAN CANADIAN
CARIBBEAN LINE

"In early February of 1993 I was on my company's ship, the *Mayan Prince*, for a cruise along the coast of Venezuela when I decided to do a little exploring on the Macereo River," Captain Luther Blount remembers. "No tourists had ever gone into that area, and no accurate map exists. All the local officials insisted I could never get my ship up that river. Well, the experts were wrong. I took my ship and passengers on a great two-day cruise through dense jungle. We stopped at Indian villages where the people still wore their native costumes and had never seen a ship before. We learned not to blow our ship's horn because the noise frightened the Indians, who then hid in the jungle. None of these people knew anything about money. The Venezuelan government had had almost no contact with them. Almost every tree had monkeys, parrots, and macaws. We saw crocodiles in the muddy water and caught enormous piranhas off our ship's stern. Later our passengers boarded a small plane for a flight over Angel Falls, the highest in the world. That cruise was one of the best experiences of my life."

Blount is a pioneer in the cruise industry, the man who singlehandedly developed the concept of the small, shallow-draft passenger ship that has made his company, American Canadian Caribbean Line (ACCL), both New England's most successful cruise operation and a major player in Caribbean cruising. His fleet of three small ships spends the winters island-hopping throughout the Caribbean. In recent years he has pioneered major cruises along the eastern coast of Central America.

"I am just an ordinary guy who has been lucky," Blount reflects. "I tried hard and made a lot of mistakes. But I learned from them."

Blount is a remarkable combination of cruise-line CEO, engineer, fisherman, machinist, inventor, businessman, photographer (his pictures illustrate his company's catalog), beekeeper, oyster-farmer, and hunter. Since 1946 he has run the highly successful Blount Marine Corporation, which has launched over 300 vessels. Not only did he develop the concept for the small cruise ship which has revolutionized the industry, but he also constructed all his ships in his own shipyard. He owns 20 patents, including one for a revolutionary marine toilet that is in widespread use on yachts. His efforts on behalf of the cruise industry and ship construction have earned him three honorary doctorates from East Coast universities. But his own formal education stopped after just two years of technical college.

Dressed in his uniform of corduroy pants, flannel shirt, and suspenders, Blount reflected about his early beginnings:

"I was born in 1916 and grew up in Warren on my uncle's oyster boat. After school I would hang out at his oyster shop. About three o'clock the boat would go out to the oyster beds, and I was always on board. My uncle allowed me to keep the scallops and flounders, and I would take those home to my mother. Then on Saturdays I would go out with the boat for the entire day. By late afternoon I came back with so many scallops I could sell the extra and make enough money to go to the movies."

Early on, young Blount felt the pull of the sea that was his family's heritage. In 1933, while still in high school, he and two friends set out on a 36-foot English cutter for Africa. Ten days later a storm washed the small craft ashore in front of the Manhasset Yacht Club on Long Island. Soon afterwards he designed his first boat, a kayak for duck hunters.

After a stint in the Army Quartermaster Corps during the Second World War, Blount returned to Warren and founded the Blount Marine Corporation in 1946. It specializes in the construction of vessels designed to perform specific tasks—cable ferries, tugboats, short-haul freighters, oilers, etc.—that go largely unheralded but play a crucial role on the waterways of the country.

"I got into the cruising business for fun," Blount says. "I am a workaholic. But I could have fun going out on my boats as a way to get away from the construction business. I began carrying family and friends in the late 1950s for free on trips up the coast to Maine and sometimes even farther north, to Nova Scotia or through the Erie Canal up to Montreal. Then my friends suggested they pay for the trips, and that was when it became a business."

Blount sold five of his patents and raised $50,000, which he then used to capitalize his new cruise company. In 1969 he designed and built his most ambitious cruise ship to date, the *Mt. Hope,* which accommodated 44 passengers. He ran her on 12-day cruises between Warren and Montreal. "This was my first money-making boat," he recalls today. And thus was born the company that would soon be known as the American Canadian Caribbean Line and would within a few years revolutionize the cruising industry, allowing passengers to go into remote areas closed to larger ships.

Today ACCL boasts a fleet of three vessels. Blount designed and constructed each one. All his ships have shallow drafts and bow ramps (another one of Blount's innovations) which allow passengers to land at remote places, such as sandy keys, for swimming and snorkeling. He keeps his little fleet

close to home each summer for 12-day cruises between Warren and Quebec City along the Hudson River, the Erie Canal, and the St. Lawrence Seaway. For the rest of the year the ships are stationed in the Caribbean, where each plies a different area: the Grenadines, Virgin Islands, Bahamas, Belize, and the coastal regions of Panama and Venezuela. In 1995 Blount started service in the American heartland, running a ship between New Orleans and Chicago and going head-to-head against the giant Delta Queen Steamboat Company, which has long enjoyed an "exclusive" on overnight cruising on the Mississippi and Ohio Rivers.

Blount's introduction to the Caribbean came in 1975, when he began a series of 12-day cruises in the Bahamas. The popularity of these trips encouraged him to add a circumnavigation of the big island of Jamaica and later cruises to island clusters farther afield. But it was Belize, with the world's second-longest barrier reef, that really tugged at his imagination. Back in 1987, when ACCL put its first cruise ship into the area, much of that country was still largely frontier where few tourists penetrated.

Blount was particularly intrigued by the Rio Dulce, flowing out of Lago de Izabal on the northern frontier of Guatemala. He had first visited the region in the mid-1970s. But all the local officials insisted that the river was too shallow and no cruise ship could possibly navigate its length. He refused to become discouraged. Then, acting true to form, he mounted his own expedition. As he recalls that adventure today:

"I made arrangements with a guy in Belize to hire a dugout canoe at Punta Gorda, and I flew down there with my knapsack and my pith helmet. I got in the dugout and went across the Gulf of Honduras, which is 27 miles wide there. We were out of sight of land for much of the trip. Me and one guy with an outboard. It was a nice day but a little on the splashy side. Meanwhile, we had checked with the Guatemalan authorities, and they said, 'No, you can't get up there; it's too shallow and there's nothing but Indians up there.' As we made our way up the river, I was sounding and finding a lot of mud. At 3, 3½ feet, it started going into mud. I didn't know whether I could get my ship through. Then, after you get through the mud, except for some rocks here and there, it's not bad."

Satisfied that the Rio Dulce could indeed be navigated, Blount ordered the captain of his ship to make an unscheduled detour up the Rio Dulce from its itinerary on the Belize barrier reef. The excursion to Lago de Izabal proved a great success with the passengers, and he then added it to his Belize itinerary as a regular adventure.

"Luther is the chief reason ACCL has been such a success," insists Yvette

Behrendt, a company veteran of 15 years, who has observed him in the field under demanding conditions doing exhaustive research on proposed itineraries. "He really loves the experience of scouting his trips. He has a feel for the unusual. He speaks to people, who turn out to be fountains of information, that the average person would never think to consult. He always finds a way to make these remote areas work for us. This is the magic of the guy."

So popular are the ACCL cruises that many must be booked six months in advance. One reason is that the company prices its cruises at an industry low of $99 per day for its minimum cabins. Many travelers like the fact that the ships carry a maximum of 80 passengers, thus allowing for a more intimate cruise experience. Accommodations are best described as basic—comfortable but with no frills. "We've never claimed to sell elegance," Blount has always advised his clients up front in his trip brochure. "We leave that to the other lines, the big guys intent on surface exposure."

ACCL boasts the greatest percentage of repeaters within the highly competitive cruise industry. "Recently, we concluded a study of our passengers and were surprised to learn that repeaters made up 68 percent of our bookings last year," says Blount's associate Behrendt. "Whenever we introduce a new cruise, our regulars book it up immediately."

The success of ACCL does not appear to surprise Blount: "If you ask me why we're doing so well, all I can say is that I offer something completely different from the other cruise lines. I go to different places. And maybe, too, because we are all at heart explorers and adventurers."

11

DIVE EXPEDITIONS

Since the beginning of time, man has looked at bodies of water and slipped into their depths to investigate. Legend tells us that Alexander the Great, who sighed for new worlds to conquer, ordered a glass diving bell built and visited the lower depths of the ocean.

Today's explorers have the safety and freedom provided by modern scuba equipment. They can swim along a coral reef teeming with an almost limitless variety of sea creatures, enjoying a circus with endless performances. Fish, large and small, dart about, chasing or being chased in the eternal pecking order of the sea.

Or divers may chose to explore one of the thousands of wrecks that litter the bottoms of the world's oceans. The first encounter with a wreck instills a sense of awe in all divers. Many of these ghost ships are hidden beneath encrusting corals or festooned with seaweed. Others are little more than piles of rubble laced with artifacts. Since 1985, the city of Fort Lauderdale has sunk 16 large ships within a mile of shore to create artificial reefs and lure sport divers.

Dive vacations, which can be enjoyed around the world, come in many variations—the choice is sometimes overwhelming. Since 1984, the growing fleet of luxury live-aboard dive boats has worked a quiet revolution, opening up the most remote underwater frontiers. Divers can now explore virgin reefs often hundreds of miles from the nearest inhabited land, reefs that were virtually inaccessible just a few years ago.

Today there are over 2 million Americans who are active sport divers, with perhaps five times as many certified and making recreational dives in exotic locales a couple of times a year. These men and women have taken to heart Jacques-Yves Cousteau's advice: "The best way to observe a fish is to become one."

"Man is a unique living organism. He must choose to live, choose his goals, and choose to achieve them. . . . In other words, life, your life, is as dull or exciting, as happy or painful, as meaningful or meaningless, as you make it. The world is a place of unlimited potential for human greatness, achievement, and happiness. But no one can experience it for you. No one can live for you. You just can't live life secondhand."

JACK WHEELER,
THE ADVENTURER'S GUIDE

Nikonos Underwater Photography Seminars

Operator:
See & Sea Travel Service,
50 Francisco St., Suite 205,
San Francisco, Calif. 94133;
(800) DIV-XPRT or
(415) 434-3400.
Price: Expensive.
Season: Year-round.
Length: 7 days.
Accommodations: Shipboard
cabins. Five percent discount with BBAT coupon.

These popular cruises provide an opportunity for novice photographers to develop their underwater techniques. A top professional underwater photographer leads each of these cruises. The entire focus of the trip is photography. The leader gives slide shows and lectures on a broad range of underwater photographic techniques. Nikon provides camera equipment, including bodies, lenses, and strobes, for passengers' use. Each boat has a photographic laboratory so that pictures can be developed the same day. Individual consultations with the professional allow passengers ample opportunity to get answers to any questions or solve problems that may develop. The cruise areas include Belize, the Cayman Islands, the Philippines, and Fiji.

ASIA

THAILAND

Diving the Andaman Sea

Operator:
Bolder Adventures,
P.O. Box 1279,
Boulder, Colo. 80306;
(800) 642-2742 or
(303) 443-6789.
Price: Expensive.
Season: Year-round.
Length: 5 and 7 days.
Accommodations: Shipboard
cabins. Five percent discount with BBAT coupon.

Thailand is Asia's latest frontier of diving, with new discoveries being reported each year. Divers travel by live-aboard dive yachts to explore virgin locations in the Andaman Sea. The operator offers a choice of boats and locations. The major sites include the Similan Islands, a chain of nine uninhabited islands boasting dramatic walls and coral-encrusted giant boulders swarming with marine life; the Surin Islands along the Burmese border where divers can expect to see many kinds of large pelagic fish (including whale sharks) as well as Sea Gypsies, a shy, primitive people who roam from island to island earning a livelihood from the sea; and the Burmese Banks, offering some of the finest shark-diving in Asia.

AUSTRALASIA

AUSTRALIA

Heron Island

One of only two resort islands located directly on the Great Barrier Reef, Heron enjoys an international reputation among divers. Poised atop the southern end of the reef, the island provides unrivaled ease of access to the marine wonderland beyond. The reefs around Heron are part of a national marine park and support over 1,500 species of fish and 500 species of coral. Boats take divers out for half-day dives. Heron offers other attractions, including the only public-accessible green-turtle rookery on the Great Barrier Reef, and large numbers of exotic nesting birds. Nights are spent in comfortable bungalows.

Operator:
Adventure Center,
1311 63rd St., Suite 200,
Emeryville, Calif. 94608;
(800) 227-8747 or
(510) 654-1879.
Price: Moderate.
Season: Year-round.
Length: 7 days.
Accommodations:
Comfortable bungalows.
Five percent discount with
BBAT coupon.

A diver plays with a cuttlefish in the Coral Sea
Carl Roessler/See & Sea Travel Service

The Southern Coral Sea

Lying between New Caledonia and Australia, the Coral Sea offers some of the world's finest dive sites, all lying well north of the Great Barrier Reef.

Operator:
See & Sea Travel Service,
50 Francisco St., Suite 205,
San Francisco, Calif. 94133;
(800) DIV-XPRT or
(415) 434-3400.
Price: Expensive.
Season: August through
December.
Length: 10 days.
Accommodations: Shipboard
cabins. Five percent dis-
count with BBAT coupon.

Skin Diver magazine calls this "the best dive spot in the world." Divers board the *Elizabeth E II* for ten-day expeditions in the southern Coral Sea to dive Marion Reef, a very large coral atoll encircling a protected lagoon where some 50 coral pinnacles reach 200 feet; and the SS *Yongala*, a 350-foot cargo-passenger ship that vanished in 1911 during a cyclone and usually ends up on most lists of the world's ten finest wreck dives. Sharks, sea snakes, and tuna are common in these waters. Visibility often ranges up to 300 feet.

The Northern Coral Sea

Operator:
See & Sea Travel Service,
50 Francisco St., Suite 205,
San Francisco, Calif. 94133;
(800) DIV-XPRT or
(415) 434-3400.
Price: Expensive.
Season: August through
December.
Length: 10 days.
Accommodations: Shipboard
cabins. Five percent dis-
count with BBAT coupon.

Divers again use the live-aboard dive boat *Elizabeth E II* to visit the fantastic dive sites along the famous Bougainville and Osprey reefs in the northern Coral Sea. Both offer great diving in a remote paradise few divers have experienced. Bougainville Reef has crystal-clear water and 6,000-foot drop-offs loaded with gigantic soft-coral formations, some 6 feet tall. Nearby, in shallow water, lies the wreck of the *Antonio Terrabacchi*, a WWII Liberty boat. Osprey Reef teems with one of the densest concentrations of fish in the Pacific, including giant groupers, moray eels, manta rays, schools of barracuda, and many sharks. A stop is made the final day at the celebrated Cod Hole, home to ten tame giant groupers which approach divers to be petted and hand-fed.

Diving Among the Whale Sharks of Western Australia

The greatest congregation of whale sharks in the world occurs each spring on the Ningaloo Reef off western Australia. These enormous creatures of the deep reach lengths of 50 feet but feed on shrimp and plankton. In late March and early April of each year they appear like clockwork, drawn by the coral spawns which, in turn, attract vast numbers of shrimp. At each daybreak a spotter plane is dispatched to locate the schools of sharks. Up to six whale sharks may be found together at a time. Divers live on board an air-conditioned dive boat.

"Misery is a part-time diet of adventurers. But it is a transient fare; ahead are richer satisfactions."
WHIT BURNETT,
THE SPIRIT OF ADVENTURE

Operator: Outer Edge Expeditions, 45500 Pontiac Trail, Walled Lake, Mich. 48390; (800) 322-5235 or (810) 624-5140.
Price: Expensive.
Season: March and April.
Length: 13 days.
Accommodations: Shipboard cabins. Five percent discount with BBAT coupon.

PAPUA NEW GUINEA

New Guinea Diving

The coral reefs of PNG not only support a huge variety of fish life but the reef structures themselves are also incredibly varied. The area offers great visibility, plunging walls, rich and colorful coral gardens, big-animal encounters, and a rich variety of wrecks dating from the Second World War, including a B-17 *Flying Fortress* bomber sunk in clear water. There are also huge manta rays, whale sharks, and such rare species as the deadly hot-pink stonefish and the red-and-yellow shrimpfish which occur in large schools. These trips utilize live-aboard dive boats for some of the finest diving in the Pacific.

Operator: See & Sea Travel Service, 50 Francisco St., Suite 205, San Francisco, Calif. 94133; (800) DIV-XPRT or (415) 434-3400.
Price: Expensive.
Season: Year-round.
Length: 7 and 10 days.
Accommodations: Shipboard cabins. Five percent discount with BBAT coupon.

CARIBBEAN

Diving Odyssey among the Windward Islands

The live-aboard dive boat *Caribbean Explorer* operates out of St. Maarten and takes divers on cruises to some of the most beautiful islands in the Caribbean—St. Maarten, St. Kitts, and Saba. The

Operator: Explorer Ventures, P.O. Box 310, Mills, Wyo. 82644; (800) 322-3577 or (307) 235-0683. *Price:* Moderate. *Season:* Year-round. *Length:* 8 days. *Accommodations:* Shipboard cabins. Five percent discount with BBAT coupon.

itinerary guarantees at least five dives daily on shoals, reefs, walls, and submerged offshore pinnacles. The highlights include the celebrated Saba Marine Park, a mecca for underwater photographers because of its impressive variety of marine life, abrupt drop-offs, and shallow reefs. Special seminars on such topics as underwater photography, night diving, and diving physiology are offered on specific weeks. Non-diving companions can spend the days ashore exploring some of the prettiest unspoiled islands in the Caribbean.

BAHAMAS

A Sail, Snorkeling, and Scuba Adventure in the Bahamian Islands

Operator: Blackbeard's Cruises, P.O. Box 661091, Miami Springs, Fla. 33266; (800) 327-9600 or (305) 888-1226. *Price:* Moderate. *Season:* Year-round. *Length:* 7 days. *Accommodations:* Shipboard cabins.

Blackbeard's Cruises operates three 65-foot, custom-built sloops on weekly cruises to the remote western Bahamian islands. Typically, they set sail with no predetermined itinerary, leaving the actual course to be decided by the passengers. Normally the expeditions explore the pristine reefs of the Bimini Islands chain, Grand Bahama Island, and numerous deserted cays. The special attractions of this area include Bimini, located just 50 miles off Miami, which offers deep walls and abundant marine life;

The Adventure Travel Hall of Fame: TOM NEALE

On October 7, 1952, Tom Neale, a 50-year-old drifter from New Zealand, stepped ashore on uninhabited Suwarrow Atoll in the Cook Islands. He had taken as his life's motto Thoreau's words of wisdom, "A man is rich in proportion to the

number of things which he can afford to let alone." For the next 25 years he lived a relatively idyllic life—alone, as a modern Robinson Crusoe on his tiny atoll, 200 miles from the nearest inhabited land, surviving sharks, hurricanes, fevers, and a monotonous diet. He became a legend throughout

Ocean Cay, with two excellent wrecks, the tug-boat *Panther* and the barge *Miami;* and Victory Reefs, with huge groupers and lush forests of deep-water gorgonians. Non-divers have the options of snorkeling, shell collecting, and beachcombing. The cabins are air-conditioned.

BRITISH VIRGIN ISLANDS

The Trimaran Cuan Law

The operator of this 105-foot, 20-passenger live-aboard dive boat bills his ship as the world's largest and most luxurious trimaran. She goes out weekly for cruises among the 50 or so islands, islets, cays, and rock outcroppings of the British Virgin Islands. Dive conditions there are unusually inviting: visibility averages 80 to 100 feet, while depths rarely exceed 80 feet. A highlight is always the wreck of the *Rhone* (where the movie *The Deep* was filmed), a British mail ship that crashed against the rocks in 1867 and now lies in shallow water. Another wreck is the *Chikuzen*, a 250-foot Korean refrigerator ship lying in 80 feet of water. Other dive sites include The Chimneys, a series of submarine arches and canyons, and Alice's Wonderland, named for the proliferation of mushroom-shaped coral heads found there.

Operator:
Trimarine Boat Co.,
P.O. Box 4065,
St. Thomas, U.S.V.I. 00803;
(809) 494-2490.
Price: Expensive.
Season: Year-round.
Length: 7 days.
Accommodations: Shipboard cabins. Five percent discount with BBAT coupon.

~~~~~~~~~~~~~~~~~~~~~~~~~~~~~~~~~~

the South Pacific, a man known simply as the Hermit of Suwarrow. Visitors were rare, usually off yachts making a transpacific crossing.

What did Neale miss the most about civilization? Apples! "There's no better fruit than an apple," he told one visitor. "But I tell myself, 'Neale, if you want an apple so badly, you can go where they are.'" His memoirs, An Island to Oneself, are a lyrical and sensitive evocation of his experiences on the atoll.

The idyll's end was augured in 1976 when Neale developed a chronic pain in his stomach. He returned to Rarotonga, where doctors diagnosed his complaint as stomach cancer. On November 30, 1977, the man who once defined himself as "just an ordinary guy who wanted to go it alone" died.

CAYMAN ISLANDS
Live-Aboard Dive Boats

Operator: See & Sea Travel Service, 50 Francisco St., Suite 205, San Francisco, Calif. 94133; (800) DIV-XPRT or (415) 434-3400. *Price:* Expensive. *Season:* Year-round. *Length:* 7 days. *Accommodations:* Shipboard cabins. Five percent discount with BBAT coupon.

Skin Diver magazine calls the Cayman Islands "the highest pinnacle of adventure and pleasure in today's world of vacation diving." Among their many attractions are crystal-clear water with visibility often up to 150 feet; coral reefs with remarkable vertical drop-offs and magnificent profusions of marine life; and Stingray City, a community of a dozen tame stingrays that can be handled and fed. *The Cayman Aggressor II* and *Cayman Aggressor III* permit serious divers an opportunity for a week of more concentrated diving than they could get from a shore-based vacation. These floating dive resorts transport divers between Little and Grand Cayman islands; allow them to make as many as four dives a day; and also let them explore more remote areas, such as the fabulous North Wall, with its incredibly lush marine life.

LATIN AMERICA
BELIZE
Diving the Barrier Reef

The world's second-longest barrier reef lies just 30 miles off Belize and runs for 185 miles along the coast, providing divers with the finest diving in the western Caribbean. Divers spend a week aboard *The Dancers* exploring the wonders of remote Lighthouse Reef, a huge, football-shaped atoll with sheer walls covered with coral, sponges, and schools of fish. Large sea animals abound here, including sharks, barracudas, turtles, rays, and groupers. Of special interest is the Blue Hole, a nearly perfect hole 1,000 feet across in the middle of a shallow reef. In the early 1970s Jacques

Coral reefs welcome divers with some of the world's
lushest marine growths
Carl Roessler/See & Sea Travel Service

Cousteau dove 412 feet in a mini-sub and decided
it was a submerged cave. Divers can swim down a
sheer wall to the 130-foot level to see, under a
ledge, enormous stalactites hanging in the darkness. Hammerhead sharks often congregate in the
area. The small, uninhabited islands support large
rookeries of red-footed boobies. A curious sight on
Lighthouse Reef is the stranded hulks of several
large ships, whose captains carelessly drove them
right atop the coral.

Operator:
See & Sea Travel Service,
50 Francisco St., Suite 205,
San Francisco, Calif. 94133;
(800) DIV-XPRT or
(415) 434-3400.
Price: Expensive.
Season: Year-round.
Length: 7 days.
Accommodations: Shipboard
cabins. Five percent dis-
count with BBAT coupon.

COSTA RICA

Dive Cruise to Cocos Island

Operator:
See & Sea Travel Service,
50 Francisco St., Suite 205,
San Francisco, Calif. 94133;
(800) DIV-XPRT or
(415) 434-3400.
Price: Expensive.
Season: Year-round.
Length: 10 days.
Accommodations: Shipboard
cabins. Five percent discount with BBAT coupon.

In the voluminous accounts of buried treasure, no place on earth can match Cocos Island for the sheer size of the pirate hoards reputed to have been buried there, stories that have inflamed men's imaginations for over a century. Relics from earlier treasure-seeking expeditions abound at Chatham Bay. Lying 300 miles off the Pacific coast of Costa Rica, Cocos Island is now part of that country's national park system. Today's visitors will probably be more interested in exploring the only sea-level tropical rain forest to evolve in complete isolation from the mainland, and in diving among the large schools of whitetip, hammerhead, tiger, and mako sharks. Travel to Cocos is on the *Undersea Hunter,* a luxurious live-aboard dive boat. Divers have the chance each day for three deeper dives for the larger fish plus an optional fourth dive in shallow water for rich, close-up photography.

ECUADOR

Diving the Galapagos Islands

Operator:
Trimarine Boat Co.,
P.O. Box 4065,
St. Thomas, U.S.V.I. 00803;
(809) 494-2490.
Price: Expensive.
Season: Year-round.
Length: From 7 to 14 days.
Accommodations: Shipboard
cabins. Five percent discount with BBAT coupon.

Nowhere else can divers swim with sea lions, fur seals, sea turtles, marine iguanas, flightless cormorants, and penguins. These remote volcanic islands are among the most unusual dive destinations in the world, and have been famous since Charles Darwin visited them and developed his theory on natural selection. Divers, who also explore numerous underwater lava formations from recent volcanic activity, live aboard the luxurious 95-foot trimaran *Lammer Law* for trips that offer plenty of time to enjoy the wonders of the islands. There are also professional naturalist guides on board and ample opportunities for shore excursions. This is cold-water diving, with water temperatures averaging 63 to 69 degrees. Divers can extend their trips to include an excursion into the Amazonian rain forest.

MEXICO

Diving the Sea of Cortez

Born some 15 to 30 million years ago when tremendous earthquakes tore the Baja Peninsula away from the Mexican mainland, the Sea of Cortez is young by geological measures. Underwater volcanic activity threw up a fascinating landscape of sea mounts and cinder cone islands. Divers on these trips use live-aboard dive boats to explore a variety of locations. Highlights include El Bajo seamount, famous for its hundreds of schooling hammerhead sharks and congregations of giant manta rays with 20-foot wingspans; a sea-lion rookery off Los Islotes; the wreck of the *Salvatierra*, which lies in 60 feet of water and is covered with a lush growth of fans and gorgonians; and Isla Las Animas, which offers excellent diving along walls with colorful fan corals and gorgonian fans as well as intriguing underwater caves.

Operator:
Baja Expeditions,
2625 Garnet Ave.,
San Diego, Calif. 92109;
(800) 843-6967 or
(619) 581-3311.
Price: Expensive.
Season: June through November.
Length: 8 days.
Accommodations: Shipboard cabins. Five percent discount with BBAT coupon.

Socorro Islands Expedition

Eons ago, a great molten churning spat out a Pacific archipelago—Islas Revillagigedos—300 miles below the southern tip of Baja California. Together they constitute a smaller Mexican version of the Galapagos Islands and provide a home to an exciting selection of flora and fauna with many endemic forms. Most of the animals show no fear of humans. The waters teem with fish, invertebrates, birds, and large marine animals. The largest of the four Revillagigedos and the only one with freshwater springs, Socorro was until recently merely a reference point on mariners' charts and the subject of botanical, zoological, and geological research expeditions. Members of this expedition

Operator:
Baja Expeditions,
2625 Garnet Ave.,
San Diego, Calif. 92109;
(800) 843-6967 or
(619) 581-3311.
Price: Expensive.
Season: November through May.
Length: 10 days.
Accommodations: Shipboard cabins. Five percent discount with BBAT coupon.

board the live-aboard dive ship *Copper Sky* for an intensive exploration of this extraordinary marine environment. They have an excellent opportunity to observe large sharks, manta rays, giant tunas, and other species. Seawalls, sandy bottoms, and jumbled volcanic rocks all make for excellent diving in a variety of habitats.

MIDDLE EAST

SUDAN

Diving the Red Sea

Operator: See & Sea Travel Service, 50 Francisco St., Suite 205, San Francisco, Calif. 94133; (800) DIV-XPRT or (415) 434-3400. *Price:* Expensive. *Season:* Year-round. *Length:* 10 days. *Accommodations:* Shipboard cabins. Five percent discount with BBAT coupon.

The Red Sea offers some of the finest diving in the world, with an endless variety of undersea life, colors, and shapes: fish, coral, submerged valleys, cliffs, canyons, and caves. These cruises begin and end at Sharm-el-Shiekh, thus avoiding the political problems of Sudan. The cruise covers 700 miles and visits six different reef groups. Divers on these cruises on the live-aboard dive ship *Poseidon's Quest* explore a variety of sights, including several important wrecks.

"Women who travel as I do are dreamers. Our lives seem to be lives of endless possibility. Like readers of romances, we think that anything can happen to us at any time. We forget that this is not our real life—our life of domestic details, work pressures, attempts and failures at human relations. We keep moving. From anecdote to anecdote, from hope to hope. Around the next bend something new will befall us. Nostalgia has no place for the woman traveling alone. Our motion is forward, whether by train or daydream. Our sights are on the horizon, across strange terrain, vast desert, unfordable rivers, impenetrable ice peaks."

MARY MORRIS,
NOTHING TO DECLARE

PACIFIC

FIJI

Dive Adventure on the Nai'ii

In Fiji, many of the finest dive sites are scattered and can be reached only from a live-aboard boat. Divers on these cruises explore the famed Great Astrolabe Reef, which offers excellent water clarity, massive underwater topography, and memorable concentrations of soft corals and tropical fish. On certain trips the *Nai'ii* cruises to the remote Lau Islands, where great walls, brilliant coral gardens, and profuse marine life make for exciting dive adventures.

Operator:
See & Sea Travel Service,
50 Francisco St., Suite 205,
San Francisco, Calif. 94133;
(800) DIV-XPRT or
(415) 434-3400.
Price: Expensive.
Season: April through November.
Length: 7 and 10 days.
Accommodations: Shipboard cabins. Five percent discount with BBAT coupon.

A diver in Truk Lagoon examines a deck gun on a Japanese ship sunk by American bombers during World War II

Carol Roessler/See & Sea Travel Service

MICRONESIA

Diving the Ghost Navy of Truk Lagoon

On February 17 and 18, 1944, 30 waves of U.S. carrier-launched warplanes swooped down on the Japanese fleet stationed at Truk Lagoon, sending more than 60 ships and 250 aircraft to the bottom

Operator:
See & Sea Travel Service,
50 Francisco St., Suite 205,
San Francisco, Calif. 94133;
(800) DIV-XPRT or
(415) 434-3400.
Price: Expensive.
Season: Year-round.
Length: 7 days.
Accommodations: Shipboard cabins. Five percent discount with BBAT coupon.

and putting a quick end to Japanese naval dominance in the Pacific. Today Truk combines drama and echoes of the past with some of the finest reef-diving in the Pacific. Most of these wrecks have blossomed into magnificent coral reefs draped in a living tapestry of soft corals, hard corals, sponges, and a wealth of marine creatures. Divers stay on the live-aboard dive boat *Thorfinn* for a week of concentrated wreck diving. Many of the ships lie in shallow water and are quite accessible. Sites include the 430-foot *Fujikawa Maru,* with a cargo of new Zero fighter planes in its hold; the *Suzuki,* a destroyer with depth charges still racked on her stern; *Gosei Maru,* a 275-foot freighter with a cargo of torpedoes; and a twin-engine *Betty Bomber* that was shot down just after takeoff by a U.S. Marine fighter plane.

"We do not live to eat and make money. We eat and make money in order to be able to enjoy life. This is what life means and what life is for."

MOUNTAINEER GEORGE LEIGH MALLORY,
WHO DIED CLIMBING MOUNT EVEREST

Palau

Operator:
See & Sea Travel Service,
50 Francisco St., Suite 205,
San Francisco, Calif. 94133;
(800) DIV-XPRT or
(415) 434-3400.
Price: Expensive.
Season: Year-round.
Length: 7 and 10 days.
Accommodations: Shipboard cabins. Five percent discount with BBAT coupon.

Remote and isolated, lying almost 500 miles from the nearest land mass, the distinctive reefs and islands of Palau make it a premiere diving location. The giant lagoon holds over 400 small islands, most uninhabited. The Rock Islands look like fuzzy, emerald mushroom caps floating on the blue waters. Palau is home to 700 known species of coral and 1,500 species of fish, including several bizarre life forms found nowhere else, such as the stingless jellyfish. Divers use the live-aboard boat *Ocean Hunter* to dive the top sites, which include the 900-foot sheer Ngemelis Wall; Blue Point, a 60-foot high coral pinnacle that draws an amazing concentration of sharks, turtles, rays, jacks, and other fish; and underwater caverns filled with stalactites.

UNITED STATES

FLORIDA

Diving for Treasure off the Florida Coast

Florida's east coast offers encrusted rocky ledges that run for miles, budding coral-patch reefs, and numerous wrecks sunk both accidentally and intentionally. South Florida has become a mecca for divers with a yearning to track down old Spanish shipwrecks—two major Spanish treasure fleets perished there; ten ships carrying tons of treasure smashed to pieces near Cape Canaveral in a 1715 hurricane; while another 11 treasure ships perished in the Upper Keys in a 1733 hurricane. *Skin Diver* magazine reports that sport divers along this stretch of coast are finding pieces of Spanish treasure more frequently now than ever before. This operator specializes in wreck dives. Divers visit a variety of sites, including the *Enfante, El Capitan,* and *Tres Puentes,* Spanish treasure galleons sunk in 1733 in shallow waters; the 287-foot wreck of the freighter *Eagle* and the U.S. Coast Guard cutters *Duane* and *Bibb,* three of Florida's most spectacular artificial reefs; and the remains of an early 19th-century iron-masted schooner.

Operator:
Lady Cyana Divers,
P.O. Box 1157,
Islamorada, Fla. 33036;
(800) 221-8717 or
(305) 664-8717.
Price: Inexpensive.
Season: Year-round.
Length: 1 day. Five percent discount with BBAT coupon.

MISSOURI

Diving the Bonne Terre Mine

Few people suspect that North America's most unusual dive site lies deep underground in a 19th-century lead mine, the largest man-made cavern in the United States. As miners extracted the lead ore, they left behind enormous pillars, 50 feet in diameter and 200 feet high, to hold up the ceilings. When mining ceased in 1962 and the pumps were turned off, the lower levels filled with clear spring

Operator:
West End Diving,
11215 Natural Bridge Rd.,
Bridgeton, Mo. 63044;
(573) 731-5003.
Price: Moderate.
Season: Year-round.
Length: 1 day.
Five percent discount
with BBAT coupon.

water. Over 15,000 divers a year visit the Billion Gallon Lake Resort with its 17-plus miles of navigable waterways. Guides lead divers along some 25 underwater trails. When the mine was closed, everything was left in place—nothing was salvaged—thus the site is a perfectly preserved time capsule. Divers can examine carts, cranes, equipment sheds, pneumatic jackhammers, and even an occasional lunch pail. The spacious underwater trails are illuminated by over 250,000 watts of dramatic lighting; visibility ranges from 80 feet to more than 150 in some places. Nights can be spent nearby in an early 20th-century mansion which once belonged to the mine president but now has been converted to an antique-filled country inn.

A diver examines an ore cart in Missouri's Bonne Terre Mine, where visibility can exceed 150 feet

West End Diving

PROFILE

CARL ROESSLER
SEE & SEA TRAVEL SERVICE

"There's a friend of mine who swears he's seen God," insists Jim Crockett, an avid scuba diver for many years. "I've seen the Great White Shark. We're about even."

Crockett belongs to diving's most exclusive club. Fewer than 300 people in the world have intentionally gone into the water with a white shark. Remember that scene in *Jaws* when Richard Dreyfuss goes overboard in a steel cage to confront the great white? Well, ten divers a year pay $8,000 each for the privilege of doing just that on Dangerous Reef off the southeastern coast of Australia. Once their boat reaches the dive spot, a mixture of chopped fish is spilled into the current, creating a "highway in the sea" that may stretch for 20 miles. Any white shark crossing the scent will turn and swim toward the dive boat. Then the divers, cameras in hand, climb into steel cages with flotation collars to be lowered into the water for what is billed as "the ultimate dive experience for the sport diver"—their own private confrontation with a great white shark. As many as six sharks may appear together. They average 15 feet in length and weigh up to 1,700 pounds each—and they are hungry. On one expedition they ate all the meat from two horses and 35 giant tuna as well as a ton of scrap tuna meat.

"Always there was the tense feeling of expectancy," recalls Carl Roessler, owner of San Francisco–based See & Sea Travel Service. "At any moment the sharks might appear. When they did, they fulfilled all our dreams of the ultimate photo subject. Enormous, graceful, deliberate, a relentless survivor of eons in the savage sea, they invariably appeared where least expected. Like some great toothed ghost materializing from the empty sea one would suddenly be there—behind you!—no matter how carefully you were scanning the surrounding waters. This uncannily stealthy approach is an important element of the mystique of these legendary creatures."

Roessler, the creator of the white-shark dive expedition, is a former IBM computer salesman who ended up becoming the dive-trip industry's most energetic pioneer and the owner of its largest and most successful agency. He has pioneered such major dive destinations as the Coral Sea off Australia, Truk Lagoon in Micronesia, the Maldives in the Indian Ocean, the Galapagos Islands off Ecuador, and the Philippine Islands. He proved a major force behind the introduction in 1984 of luxurious live-aboard dive boats, which have already effected a major revolution in dive travel. Over the past two

decades he has emerged as the world's premiere underwater photographer. To date, he has accumulated over 350,000 slides. Thousands of his pictures have appeared in encyclopedias, textbooks, and magazines. He has written more than 400 magazine articles and published seven lavishly illustrated books on diving, including two that became Book of the Month Club selections.

Roessler's romance with diving began in the summer of 1950 when he was a "water rat" and lifeguard on a beach in Connecticut. A friend's father introduced him to a strange new scuba device. Soon Roessler and his friends were hooked on diving. "We started all that cold-water wreck diving business," he recalls today, "where you can't see, where ropes get tangled around your legs, where you freeze—things like that." In 1957 he finally enrolled in a scuba course through the New Haven YMCA. His instructor was a young diver named Paul Tzimoulis, who would eventually become the publisher of *Skin Diver* magazine.

After college, Roessler started a job in his father's Connecticut meat-packing plant. Then he stumbled into a position as a computer salesman for IBM, where one of his clients was Yale University. They hired him away from IBM to develop a new information systems department. Soon he was made the director of computation at Yale. He began taking dive vacations with his family in the Caribbean: the Virgin Islands, Puerto Rico, and Bonaire. "You have to remember that in the 1960s the dive business in the Caribbean was virtually undeveloped," he says. "What you had was resorts with a half dozen tanks which were generally rusty. Most of the popular dive areas today were virtually virgin back then. Facilities for divers were almost nonexistent."

Then came 1969, Roessler's year of reckoning. He was toying with the idea of moving to another university or perhaps starting his own high-technology company. But his memories of those vacations in the Caribbean kept haunting him. "I started thinking about what I wanted to do long-term with my life," he says. "And that never came up computers. I realized that what I really wanted to do was to move to the Caribbean and start a dive business. I saw that as the opportunity of the future. In 1969 almost no one was doing dive trips. My gut feeling was that sooner or later this would become a viable business. I felt that if other divers could hear about what I had experienced on my few diving trips in the Caribbean, then they would want to dive those places, too."

Roessler checked around. He finally decided upon the islands of Curaçao and Bonaire, off the Venezuelan coast. Curaçao offered hospitals, schools, and a certain amount of culture, whereas undeveloped Bonaire had excellent div-

ing. He took his entire family to Curaçao where he began organizing and leading dive trips in the area for Dewey Bergman at See & Sea in San Francisco, then the only U.S. operator of dive trips abroad. He never looked back to Yale and his computers. "I've always been a risk-taker, so the change of careers was not hard to do," he says.

Twenty years ago the concept of tropical travel was foreign to most divers. Except for a handful of adventurous individuals, most people dived within 100 miles of their homes. Tropical diving was considered too expensive, too dangerous, and too time-consuming.

Slowly that perception began to change. Roessler's influence was felt in these formative years, not only in the small groups he guided among the reefs and wrecks of the Caribbean waters near Bonaire, but also through the steady stream of articles and pictures he published about his experiences. From 1969 to 1972 he built up a prosperous dive program. In those early years See & Sea was running a total of about 150 clients a year. In 1972 Bergman told Roessler that he wanted to retire in five years and offered to make him a partner. Roessler jumped at the opportunity and invested in the business. He soon took over and in 1977 bought Bergman out.

In the 20 years since Roessler made that critical move to the Caribbean, both See & Sea and the dive industry have gone through profound changes. The 100,000 certified divers in 1969 have grown to over 3 million today, with active divers numbering about 500,000. And warm-water diving is now all the rage. *Skin Diver* magazine estimates that a mass migration of over 1.2 million dive trips to warm water takes place annually. And divers are seeking out more exotic destinations in places like Papua New Guinea, the Maldive Islands, the Sudan, and the Solomon Islands. See & Sea has seen its annual client load climb to over 7,500.

Roessler's success has not been without risks. In 1972 he was almost killed on a dive expedition to the Coral Sea when he was suddenly attacked by 25 gray sharks in a feeding frenzy. And once, off Australia, a great white almost bit him in half. As he stood in his cage waiting to be lowered into the water, he reached up to get his camera. Suddenly, a 15-foot white shark breached. Roessler dropped back into the cage just as the big white landed on top of his cage, its jaws snapping shut on the space where he had been a second before.

For years, divers were hotel-based and often spent up to 90 minutes in bone-jarring speedboats to get to their dive sites. Reefs were damaged by overcrowding. And many of the world's premiere diving sites were beyond the range of day-dive boats. The handful of live-aboard dive boats were generally crude affairs.

Roessler helped change all that. He was a major force in the development of the live-aboard luxury dive boat, which has revolutionized diving since 1984. He worked closely with groups of investors who built boats designed to See & Sea's specifications, with spacious kitchens, huge sundecks, air-conditioned cabins, hot showers, TV and videotape equipment, and modern electronics—in short, all the conveniences and comforts formerly associated with hotels. Boats like the *Thorfinn* in Truk Lagoon and the *Elizabeth E II* in the Coral Sea are floating dive resorts. They boast all the amenities of first-class hotels but can also cruise 200 miles to anchor where the reef diving is the best.

"In the old days men would go off on diving trips, while their wives stayed home," Roessler says. "When the luxury dive boats entered the market, suddenly we had women and families going on live-aboard boats. Business exploded. Since See & Sea shifted over in 1984 to an emphasis upon trips built around live-aboard luxury dive boats, our growth has been phenomenal—about 35 percent a year. Today we represent about one-third of all live-aboard dive boats in the world and handle about 60 percent of the business."

What makes for a great dive destination?

"The greatest dive sites are usually very remote," Roessler avers. "They are seldom dived and retain a precious wildness and purity. What makes them great is the presence of large animals—sharks, turtles, rays, tuna—occurring naturally. The sense of awe and wonder these sites arouse in us is the greatest high in our sport."

As Roessler moves through the sixth decade of his life he continues his work of exciting people about the ocean through his trips, photographs, and writing. He sees this as his mission in life. As he once explained to a reporter for *Skin Diver* magazine: "I want to communicate to people what a fantastic, unbelievable, colorful, complicated world the reef is, a world of never-ending surprises. It's there every day, too. Whether we dive it tomorrow or not, it's still there. I like to think I can help encourage people to go and see it for themselves."

GEOGRAPHICAL INDEX

OPERATOR INDEX

HOW TO USE THE COUPONS

A few points to bear in mind regarding the coupons:

• Each coupon is good for one trip for one person. Couples must purchase two copies of *The Big Book of Adventure Travel* in order to get two coupons for a particular trip. Please do not ask operators to apply one coupon toward two or more people booking a particular trip.

• Many operators have extended these discounts to all the trips listed in their catalogs and not just to those described in *The Big Book of Adventure Travel*. Readers should first check with individual operators to see what restrictions, if any, apply to any particular coupon. The coupons cannot be used in conjunction with other discounts.

• Most of the discounts are for 5 percent; some are for 10 percent. Readers should check the individual trip descriptions to learn the amount of the discount a particular operator offers.

• All coupons expire on December 31, 2000. After that date they are worthless. Some operators may decide to set earlier expiration dates.

• Readers must submit the **original** coupon when booking a trip. Under no circumstances will an operator accept a photocopy or other duplicate. The reader will then receive a credit for the amount of the discount against the final payment for the trip.

ABOVE THE CLOUDS TREKKING

THE BIG BOOK OF ADVENTURE TRAVEL

DISCOUNT COUPON

NAME

Good for One Person on One Trip
Expires December 31, 2000

ACTION WHITEWATER ADVENTURES

THE BIG BOOK OF ADVENTURE TRAVEL

DISCOUNT COUPON

NAME

Good for One Person on One Trip
Expires December 31, 2000

ADIRONDACK RIVER OUTFITTERS

THE BIG BOOK OF ADVENTURE TRAVEL

DISCOUNT COUPON

NAME

Good for One Person on One Trip
Expires December 31, 2000

ADVENTURE CENTER

THE BIG BOOK OF ADVENTURE TRAVEL

DISCOUNT COUPON

NAME

Good for One Person on One Trip
Expires December 31, 2000

ALASKA DISCOVERY

THE BIG BOOK OF ADVENTURE TRAVEL

DISCOUNT COUPON

NAME

Good for One Person on One Trip
Expires December 31, 2000

The
BIG
Book
of
ADVENTURE
TRAVEL

JAMES C. SIMMONS

JOHN MUIR PUBLICATIONS

SANTA FE, NEW MEXICO

The
BIG
Book
of
ADVENTURE
TRAVEL

JAMES C. SIMMONS

JOHN MUIR PUBLICATIONS

SANTA FE, NEW MEXICO

ALASKAN BICYCLE ADVENTURES

THE BIG BOOK OF ADVENTURE TRAVEL
DISCOUNT COUPON

NAME

Good for One Person on One Trip
Expires December 31, 2000

ALLAGASH CANOE TRIPS

THE BIG BOOK OF ADVENTURE TRAVEL
DISCOUNT COUPON

NAME

Good for One Person on One Trip
Expires December 31, 2000

AMERICAN CANADIAN CARIBBEAN LINE

THE BIG BOOK OF ADVENTURE TRAVEL
DISCOUNT COUPON

NAME

Good for One Person on One Trip
Expires December 31, 2000

ANNAPOLIS SAILING SCHOOL

THE BIG BOOK OF ADVENTURE TRAVEL
DISCOUNT COUPON

NAME

Good for One Person on One Trip
Expires December 31, 2000

APPALACHIAN WILDWATERS

THE BIG BOOK OF ADVENTURE TRAVEL
DISCOUNT COUPON

NAME

Good for One Person on One Trip
Expires December 31, 2000

JAMES C. SIMMONS
JOHN MUIR PUBLICATIONS
SANTA FE, NEW MEXICO

JAMES C. SIMMONS
JOHN MUIR PUBLICATIONS
SANTA FE, NEW MEXICO

ARCTIC ODYSSEYS

THE BIG BOOK OF ADVENTURE TRAVEL
DISCOUNT COUPON
NAME
Good for One Person on One Trip
Expires December 31, 2000

ASIAN PACIFIC ADVENTURES

THE BIG BOOK OF ADVENTURE TRAVEL
DISCOUNT COUPON
NAME
Good for One Person on One Trip
Expires December 31, 2000

BACK-COUNTRY

THE BIG BOOK OF ADVENTURE TRAVEL
DISCOUNT COUPON
NAME
Good for One Person on One Trip
Expires December 31, 2000

BACKROADS

THE BIG BOOK OF ADVENTURE TRAVEL
DISCOUNT COUPON
NAME
Good for One Person on One Trip
Expires December 31, 2000

BAJA EXPEDITIONS

THE BIG BOOK OF ADVENTURE TRAVEL
DISCOUNT COUPON
NAME
Good for One Person on One Trip
Expires December 31, 2000

The BIG Book of ADVENTURE TRAVEL

JAMES C. SIMMONS

JOHN MUIR PUBLICATIONS

SANTA FE, NEW MEXICO

The BIG Book of ADVENTURE TRAVEL

JAMES C. SIMMONS

JOHN MUIR PUBLICATIONS

SANTA FE, NEW MEXICO

BAJA'S FRONTIER TOURS

THE BIG BOOK OF ADVENTURE TRAVEL

DISCOUNT COUPON

NAME

Good for One Person on One Trip
Expires December 31, 2000

BATTENKILL CANOE

THE BIG BOOK OF ADVENTURE TRAVEL

DISCOUNT COUPON

NAME

Good for One Person on One Trip
Expires December 31, 2000

BOLDER ADVENTURES

THE BIG BOOK OF ADVENTURE TRAVEL

DISCOUNT COUPON

NAME

Good for One Person on One Trip
Expires December 31, 2000

BOUNDARY COUNTRY TREKKING

THE BIG BOOK OF ADVENTURE TRAVEL

DISCOUNT COUPON

NAME

Good for One Person on One Trip
Expires December 31, 2000

CANYONEERS

THE BIG BOOK OF ADVENTURE TRAVEL

DISCOUNT COUPON

NAME

Good for One Person on One Trip
Expires December 31, 2000

The BIG Book of ADVENTURE TRAVEL

JAMES C. SIMMONS

JOHN MUIR PUBLICATIONS

SANTA FE, NEW MEXICO

The BIG Book of ADVENTURE TRAVEL

JAMES C. SIMMONS

JOHN MUIR PUBLICATIONS

SANTA FE, NEW MEXICO

CICLISMO CLASSICO

THE BIG BOOK OF ADVENTURE TRAVEL
DISCOUNT COUPON

NAME

Good for One Person on One Trip
Expires December 31, 2000

CLASSIC ADVENTURES

THE BIG BOOK OF ADVENTURE TRAVEL
DISCOUNT COUPON

NAME

Good for One Person on One Trip
Expires December 31, 2000

DESERT ADVENTURES

THE BIG BOOK OF ADVENTURE TRAVEL
DISCOUNT COUPON

NAME

Good for One Person on One Trip
Expires December 31, 2000

DINAMATION INTERNATIONAL SOCIETY

THE BIG BOOK OF ADVENTURE TRAVEL
DISCOUNT COUPON

NAME

Good for One Person on One Trip
Expires December 31, 2000

DVORAK'S KAYAK & RAFTING EXPEDITIONS

THE BIG BOOK OF ADVENTURE TRAVEL
DISCOUNT COUPON

NAME

Good for One Person on One Trip
Expires December 31, 2000

The
BIG
Book
of
ADVENTURE
TRAVEL

JAMES C. SIMMONS

JOHN MUIR PUBLICATIONS

SANTA FE, NEW MEXICO

The
BIG
Book
of
ADVENTURE
TRAVEL

JAMES C. SIMMONS

JOHN MUIR PUBLICATIONS

SANTA FE, NEW MEXICO

EARTH RIVER EXPEDITIONS

THE BIG BOOK OF ADVENTURE TRAVEL
DISCOUNT COUPON

NAME

Good for One Person on One Trip
Expires December 31, 2000

EASY RIDER TOURS

THE BIG BOOK OF ADVENTURE TRAVEL
DISCOUNT COUPON

NAME

Good for One Person on One Trip
Expires December 31, 2000

ECOSUMMER EXPEDITIONS

THE BIG BOOK OF ADVENTURE TRAVEL
DISCOUNT COUPON

NAME

Good for One Person on One Trip
Expires December 31, 2000

EURO-BIKE TOURS

THE BIG BOOK OF ADVENTURE TRAVEL
DISCOUNT COUPON

NAME

Good for One Person on One Trip
Expires December 31, 2000

EUROPEDS

THE BIG BOOK OF ADVENTURE TRAVEL
DISCOUNT COUPON

NAME

Good for One Person on One Trip
Expires December 31, 2000

The BIG Book of ADVENTURE TRAVEL

JAMES C. SIMMONS

JOHN MUIR PUBLICATIONS

SANTA FE, NEW MEXICO

The BIG Book of ADVENTURE TRAVEL

JAMES C. SIMMONS

JOHN MUIR PUBLICATIONS

SANTA FE, NEW MEXICO

EXPLORER VENTURES

THE BIG BOOK OF ADVENTURE TRAVEL
DISCOUNT COUPON

NAME

Good for One Person on One Trip
Expires December 31, 2000

FAR FLUNG ADVENTURES

THE BIG BOOK OF ADVENTURE TRAVEL
DISCOUNT COUPON

NAME

Good for One Person on One Trip
Expires December 31, 2000

FAR HORIZONS ARCHAEOLOGICAL & CULTURAL TRIPS

THE BIG BOOK OF ADVENTURE TRAVEL
DISCOUNT COUPON

NAME

Good for One Person on One Trip
Expires December 31, 2000

GEOGRAPHIC EXPEDITIONS

THE BIG BOOK OF ADVENTURE TRAVEL
DISCOUNT COUPON

NAME

Good for One Person on One Trip
Expires December 31, 2000

GLACIER RAFT COMPANY

THE BIG BOOK OF ADVENTURE TRAVEL
DISCOUNT COUPON

NAME

Good for One Person on One Trip
Expires December 31, 2000

The BIG Book of ADVENTURE TRAVEL

JAMES C. SIMMONS

JOHN MUIR PUBLICATIONS

SANTA FE, NEW MEXICO

The BIG Book of ADVENTURE TRAVEL

JAMES C. SIMMONS

JOHN MUIR PUBLICATIONS

SANTA FE, NEW MEXICO

GRAND
CANYON
DORIES

THE BIG BOOK OF ADVENTURE TRAVEL
DISCOUNT COUPON
NAME
Good for One Person on One Trip
Expires December 31, 2000

GREEK
ISLANDS
CRUISE
CENTER

THE BIG BOOK OF ADVENTURE TRAVEL
DISCOUNT COUPON
NAME
Good for One Person on One Trip
Expires December 31, 2000

GUNFLINT
NORTHWOODS
OUTFITTERS

THE BIG BOOK OF ADVENTURE TRAVEL
DISCOUNT COUPON
NAME
Good for One Person on One Trip
Expires December 31, 2000

HIKING
HOLIDAYS

THE BIG BOOK OF ADVENTURE TRAVEL
DISCOUNT COUPON
NAME
Good for One Person on One Trip
Expires December 31, 2000

HIMALAYAN
TRAVEL

THE BIG BOOK OF ADVENTURE TRAVEL
DISCOUNT COUPON
NAME
Good for One Person on One Trip
Expires December 31, 2000

JAMES C. SIMMONS
JOHN MUIR PUBLICATIONS
SANTA FE, NEW MEXICO

JAMES C. SIMMONS
JOHN MUIR PUBLICATIONS
SANTA FE, NEW MEXICO

HUGHES RIVER EXPEDITIONS

THE BIG BOOK OF ADVENTURE TRAVEL

DISCOUNT COUPON

NAME

Good for One Person on One Trip
Expires December 31, 2000

HURRICANE CREEK LLAMA TREKS

THE BIG BOOK OF ADVENTURE TRAVEL

DISCOUNT COUPON

NAME

Good for One Person on One Trip
Expires December 31, 2000

HYAK WILDERNESS ADVENTURES

THE BIG BOOK OF ADVENTURE TRAVEL

DISCOUNT COUPON

NAME

Good for One Person on One Trip
Expires December 31, 2000

JOURNEYS INTERNATIONAL

THE BIG BOOK OF ADVENTURE TRAVEL

DISCOUNT COUPON

NAME

Good for One Person on One Trip
Expires December 31, 2000

JOURNEYS INTO AMERICAN INDIAN TERRITORY

THE BIG BOOK OF ADVENTURE TRAVEL

DISCOUNT COUPON

NAME

Good for One Person on One Trip
Expires December 31, 2000

The
BIG
Book
of
ADVENTURE
TRAVEL

JAMES C. SIMMONS

JOHN MUIR PUBLICATIONS

SANTA FE, NEW MEXICO

The
BIG
Book
of
ADVENTURE
TRAVEL

JAMES C. SIMMONS

JOHN MUIR PUBLICATIONS

SANTA FE, NEW MEXICO

KOLOTOUR HOLIDAYS

THE BIG BOOK OF ADVENTURE TRAVEL
DISCOUNT COUPON

NAME

Good for One Person on One Trip
Expires December 31, 2000

LADY CYANA DIVERS

THE BIG BOOK OF ADVENTURE TRAVEL
DISCOUNT COUPON

NAME

Good for One Person on One Trip
Expires December 31, 2000

LOST WORLD ADVENTURES

THE BIG BOOK OF ADVENTURE TRAVEL
DISCOUNT COUPON

NAME

Good for One Person on One Trip
Expires December 31, 2000

MARINE EXPEDITIONS

THE BIG BOOK OF ADVENTURE TRAVEL
DISCOUNT COUPON

NAME

Good for One Person on One Trip
Expires December 31, 2000

MICHIGAN BICYCLE TOURING

THE BIG BOOK OF ADVENTURE TRAVEL
DISCOUNT COUPON

NAME

Good for One Person on One Trip
Expires December 31, 2000

JAMES C. SIMMONS
JOHN MUIR PUBLICATIONS
SANTA FE, NEW MEXICO

JAMES C. SIMMONS
JOHN MUIR PUBLICATIONS
SANTA FE, NEW MEXICO

MOUNTAIN TRAVEL-SOBEK

THE BIG BOOK OF ADVENTURE TRAVEL

DISCOUNT COUPON

NAME

Good for One Person on One Trip
Expires December 31, 2000

NANTAHALA OUTDOOR CENTER

THE BIG BOOK OF ADVENTURE TRAVEL

DISCOUNT COUPON

NAME

Good for One Person on One Trip
Expires December 31, 2000

NATURAL HABITAT ADVENTURES

THE BIG BOOK OF ADVENTURE TRAVEL

DISCOUNT COUPON

NAME

Good for One Person on One Trip
Expires December 31, 2000

NATURE EXPEDITIONS INTERNATIONAL

THE BIG BOOK OF ADVENTURE TRAVEL

DISCOUNT COUPON

NAME

Good for One Person on One Trip
Expires December 31, 2000

NAUTICAL HERITAGE SOCIETY

THE BIG BOOK OF ADVENTURE TRAVEL

DISCOUNT COUPON

NAME

Good for One Person on One Trip
Expires December 31, 2000

JAMES C. SIMMONS

JOHN MUIR PUBLICATIONS

SANTA FE, NEW MEXICO

JAMES C. SIMMONS

JOHN MUIR PUBLICATIONS

SANTA FE, NEW MEXICO

NEW ENGLAND HIKING HOLIDAYS

THE BIG BOOK OF ADVENTURE TRAVEL
DISCOUNT COUPON

NAME

Good for One Person on One Trip
Expires December 31, 2000

NEW ENGLAND OUTDOOR CENTER

THE BIG BOOK OF ADVENTURE TRAVEL
DISCOUNT COUPON

NAME

Good for One Person on One Trip
Expires December 31, 2000

NEW ZEALAND ADVENTURES

THE BIG BOOK OF ADVENTURE TRAVEL
DISCOUNT COUPON

NAME

Good for One Person on One Trip
Expires December 31, 2000

NORTHERN LIGHTS EXPEDITIONS

THE BIG BOOK OF ADVENTURE TRAVEL
DISCOUNT COUPON

NAME

Good for One Person on One Trip
Expires December 31, 2000

O.A.R.S.

THE BIG BOOK OF ADVENTURE TRAVEL
DISCOUNT COUPON

NAME

Good for One Person on One Trip
Expires December 31, 2000

JAMES C. SIMMONS

JOHN MUIR PUBLICATIONS

SANTA FE, NEW MEXICO

JAMES C. SIMMONS

JOHN MUIR PUBLICATIONS

SANTA FE, NEW MEXICO

OCEAN VOYAGES

THE BIG BOOK OF ADVENTURE TRAVEL
DISCOUNT COUPON
NAME

Good for One Person on One Trip
Expires December 31, 2000

OCEANIC SOCIETY EXPEDITIONS

THE BIG BOOK OF ADVENTURE TRAVEL
DISCOUNT COUPON
NAME

Good for One Person on One Trip
Expires December 31, 2000

ORANGE TORPEDO TRIPS

THE BIG BOOK OF ADVENTURE TRAVEL
DISCOUNT COUPON
NAME

Good for One Person on One Trip
Expires December 31, 2000

OUTER EDGE EXPEDITIONS

THE BIG BOOK OF ADVENTURE TRAVEL
DISCOUNT COUPON
NAME

Good for One Person on One Trip
Expires December 31, 2000

REI ADVENTURES

THE BIG BOOK OF ADVENTURE TRAVEL
DISCOUNT COUPON
NAME

Good for One Person on One Trip
Expires December 31, 2000

The BIG Book of ADVENTURE TRAVEL

JAMES C. SIMMONS

JOHN MUIR PUBLICATIONS

SANTA FE, NEW MEXICO

The BIG Book of ADVENTURE TRAVEL

JAMES C. SIMMONS

JOHN MUIR PUBLICATIONS

SANTA FE, NEW MEXICO

REMARKABLE JOURNEYS

THE BIG BOOK OF ADVENTURE TRAVEL
DISCOUNT COUPON

NAME

Good for One Person on One Trip
Expires December 31, 2000

ROADS LESS TRAVELED ADVENTURES

THE BIG BOOK OF ADVENTURE TRAVEL
DISCOUNT COUPON

NAME

Good for One Person on One Trip
Expires December 31, 2000

ROCKY MOUNTAIN RIVER TOURS

THE BIG BOOK OF ADVENTURE TRAVEL
DISCOUNT COUPON

NAME

Good for One Person on One Trip
Expires December 31, 2000

RYDER-WALKER ALPINE ADVENTURES

THE BIG BOOK OF ADVENTURE TRAVEL
DISCOUNT COUPON

NAME

Good for One Person on One Trip
Expires December 31, 2000

SAIL THE SAN JUANS

THE BIG BOOK OF ADVENTURE TRAVEL
DISCOUNT COUPON

NAME

Good for One Person on One Trip
Expires December 31, 2000

JAMES C. SIMMONS

JOHN MUIR PUBLICATIONS

SANTA FE, NEW MEXICO

JAMES C. SIMMONS

JOHN MUIR PUBLICATIONS

SANTA FE, NEW MEXICO

SCHOONER NATHANIEL BOWDITCH

THE BIG BOOK OF ADVENTURE TRAVEL

DISCOUNT COUPON

NAME

Good for One Person on One Trip
Expires December 31, 2000

SIERRA MAC RIVER TRIPS

THE BIG BOOK OF ADVENTURE TRAVEL

DISCOUNT COUPON

NAME

Good for One Person on One Trip
Expires December 31, 2000

SIERRA MADRE EXPRESS

THE BIG BOOK OF ADVENTURE TRAVEL

DISCOUNT COUPON

NAME

Good for One Person on One Trip
Expires December 31, 2000

SILVER CLOUD EXPEDITIONS

THE BIG BOOK OF ADVENTURE TRAVEL

DISCOUNT COUPON

NAME

Good for One Person on One Trip
Expires December 31, 2000

SLICKROCK KAYAK ADVENTURES

THE BIG BOOK OF ADVENTURE TRAVEL

DISCOUNT COUPON

NAME

Good for One Person on One Trip
Expires December 31, 2000

JAMES C. SIMMONS

JOHN MUIR PUBLICATIONS

SANTA FE, NEW MEXICO

JAMES C. SIMMONS

JOHN MUIR PUBLICATIONS

SANTA FE, NEW MEXICO

SOURDOUGH OUTFITTERS

THE BIG BOOK OF ADVENTURE TRAVEL
DISCOUNT COUPON

NAME

Good for One Person on One Trip
Expires December 31, 2000

SOUTHERN YOSEMITE MOUNTAIN GUIDES

THE BIG BOOK OF ADVENTURE TRAVEL
DISCOUNT COUPON

NAME

Good for One Person on One Trip
Expires December 31, 2000

ST. REGIS CANOE OUTFITTERS

THE BIG BOOK OF ADVENTURE TRAVEL
DISCOUNT COUPON

NAME

Good for One Person on One Trip
Expires December 31, 2000

STAR CLIPPERS

THE BIG BOOK OF ADVENTURE TRAVEL
DISCOUNT COUPON

NAME

Good for One Person on One Trip
Expires December 31, 2000

STEVE CURRY EXPEDITIONS

THE BIG BOOK OF ADVENTURE TRAVEL
DISCOUNT COUPON

NAME

Good for One Person on One Trip
Expires December 31, 2000

The
BIG
Book
of
ADVENTURE
TRAVEL

JAMES C. SIMMONS

JOHN MUIR PUBLICATIONS

SANTA FE, NEW MEXICO

The
BIG
Book
of
ADVENTURE
TRAVEL

JAMES C. SIMMONS

JOHN MUIR PUBLICATIONS

SANTA FE, NEW MEXICO

SUNDANCE EXPEDITIONS

THE BIG BOOK OF ADVENTURE TRAVEL

DISCOUNT COUPON

NAME

Good for One Person on One Trip
Expires December 31, 2000

SUNRISE COUNTY CANOE EXPEDITIONS

THE BIG BOOK OF ADVENTURE TRAVEL

DISCOUNT COUPON

NAME

Good for One Person on One Trip
Expires December 31, 2000

TALL SHIP ADVENTURES

THE BIG BOOK OF ADVENTURE TRAVEL

DISCOUNT COUPON

NAME

Good for One Person on One Trip
Expires December 31, 2000

TIMBERLINE BICYCLE TOURS

THE BIG BOOK OF ADVENTURE TRAVEL

DISCOUNT COUPON

NAME

Good for One Person on One Trip
Expires December 31, 2000

TRAVERSE TALL SHIP COMPANY

THE BIG BOOK OF ADVENTURE TRAVEL

DISCOUNT COUPON

NAME

Good for One Person on One Trip
Expires December 31, 2000

JAMES C. SIMMONS

JOHN MUIR PUBLICATIONS

SANTA FE, NEW MEXICO

JAMES C. SIMMONS

JOHN MUIR PUBLICATIONS

SANTA FE, NEW MEXICO

**TREK &
TRAIL
ADVENTURES**

THE BIG BOOK OF ADVENTURE TRAVEL
DISCOUNT COUPON
NAME
Good for One Person on One Trip
Expires December 31, 2000

**TURTLE
TOURS**

THE BIG BOOK OF ADVENTURE TRAVEL
DISCOUNT COUPON
NAME
Good for One Person on One Trip
Expires December 31, 2000

**USA
RAFT**

THE BIG BOOK OF ADVENTURE TRAVEL
DISCOUNT COUPON
NAME
Good for One Person on One Trip
Expires December 31, 2000

**UYAK
AIR
SERVICE**

THE BIG BOOK OF ADVENTURE TRAVEL
DISCOUNT COUPON
NAME
Good for One Person on One Trip
Expires December 31, 2000

**VERMONT
BICYCLE
TOURING**

THE BIG BOOK OF ADVENTURE TRAVEL
DISCOUNT COUPON
NAME
Good for One Person on One Trip
Expires December 31, 2000

JAMES C. SIMMONS

JOHN MUIR PUBLICATIONS

SANTA FE, NEW MEXICO

JAMES C. SIMMONS

JOHN MUIR PUBLICATIONS

SANTA FE, NEW MEXICO

**WEST
END
DIVING**

THE BIG BOOK OF ADVENTURE TRAVEL
DISCOUNT COUPON

NAME

Good for One Person on One Trip
Expires December 31, 2000

**WILD
HORIZONS
EXPEDITIONS**

THE BIG BOOK OF ADVENTURE TRAVEL
DISCOUNT COUPON

NAME

Good for One Person on One Trip
Expires December 31, 2000

**WILDERNESS
INQUIRY**

THE BIG BOOK OF ADVENTURE TRAVEL
DISCOUNT COUPON

NAME

Good for One Person on One Trip
Expires December 31, 2000

**WILDERNESS
TRAVEL**

THE BIG BOOK OF ADVENTURE TRAVEL
DISCOUNT COUPON

NAME

Good for One Person on One Trip
Expires December 31, 2000

**WINDJAMMER
BAREFOOT
CRUISES**

THE BIG BOOK OF ADVENTURE TRAVEL
DISCOUNT COUPON

NAME

Good for One Person on One Trip
Expires December 31, 2000

The
BIG
Book
of
ADVENTURE
TRAVEL

JAMES C. SIMMONS

JOHN MUIR PUBLICATIONS

SANTA FE, NEW MEXICO

The
BIG
Book
of
ADVENTURE
TRAVEL

JAMES C. SIMMONS

JOHN MUIR PUBLICATIONS

SANTA FE, NEW MEXICO

WORLDWIDE ADVENTURES

THE BIG BOOK OF ADVENTURE TRAVEL

DISCOUNT COUPON

NAME

Good for One Person on One Trip
Expires December 31, 2000

YANKEE SCHOONER CRUISES

THE BIG BOOK OF ADVENTURE TRAVEL

DISCOUNT COUPON

NAME

Good for One Person on One Trip
Expires December 31, 2000

YELLOWSTONE ECOSYSTEM STUDIES

THE BIG BOOK OF ADVENTURE TRAVEL

DISCOUNT COUPON

NAME

Good for One Person on One Trip
Expires December 31, 2000

YELLOWSTONE LLAMAS

THE BIG BOOK OF ADVENTURE TRAVEL

DISCOUNT COUPON

NAME

Good for One Person on One Trip
Expires December 31, 2000

The BIG Book of ADVENTURE TRAVEL

JAMES C. SIMMONS

JOHN MUIR PUBLICATIONS

SANTA FE, NEW MEXICO

The BIG Book of ADVENTURE TRAVEL

JAMES C. SIMMONS

JOHN MUIR PUBLICATIONS

SANTA FE, NEW MEXICO

Cater to Your Interests on Your Next Vacation

**The 100 Best Small Art Towns in America
3rd edition**
Discover Creative Communities, Fresh Air, and
Affordable Living
U.S. $16.95, Canada $24.95

**The Big Book of Adventure Travel
2nd edition**
Profiles more than 400 great escapes to all corners
of the world
U.S. $17.95, Canada $25.50

Cross-Country Ski Vacations
A Guide to the Best Resorts, Lodges, and Groomed
Trails in North America
U.S. $15.95, Canada $22.50

Gene Kilgore's Ranch Vacations, 5th edition
The Complete Guide to Guest Resorts, Fly-Fishing,
and Cross-Country Skiing Ranches
U.S. $22.95, Canada $35.50

Indian America, 4th edition
A traveler's companion to more than 300 Indian
tribes in the United States
U.S. $18.95, Canada $26.75

Saddle Up!
A Guide to Planning the Perfect Horseback
Vacation
U.S. $14.95, Canada $20.95

Watch It Made in the U.S.A., 2nd edition
A Visitor's Guide to the Companies That Make Your
Favorite Products
U.S. $17.95, Canada $25.50

The World Awaits
A Comprehensive Guide to Extended Backpack
Travel
U.S. $16.95, Canada $23.95

**JMP travel guides are available
at your favorite bookstores.
For a FREE catalog or to place a
mail order, call: 800-888-7504.**

John Muir Publications ◆ P.O. Box 613 ◆ Santa Fe, NM 87504